Your Personal
HOROSCOPE
—— 2009 ——

Your Personal
HOROSCOPE
—— 2009 ——

*The only one-volume horoscope
you'll ever need*

Joseph Polansky

The author is grateful to the people
of STAR ★ DATA, who truly fathered
this book and without whom it
could not have been written.

HarperElement
An Imprint of HarperCollins*Publishers*
77–85 Fulham Palace Road,
Hammersmith, London W6 8JB

The website address is www.thorsonselement.com

and *HarperElement* are trademarks of
HarperCollins*Publishers* Ltd

Published by HarperElement 2008

1 3 5 7 9 10 8 6 4 2

© Star ★ Data, Inc. 2008

Star ★ Data assert the moral right to
be identified as the authors of this work

A catalogue record for this book is
available from the British Library

ISBN-13 978-0-00-727128-3
ISBN-10 0-00-727128-X

Printed and bound in China by South
China Printing Co. Ltd

Contents

Your Personal
HOROSCOPE
—— 2009 ——

Introduction

Welcome to the fascinating and intricate world of astrology!

For thousands of years the movements of the planets and other heavenly bodies have intrigued the best minds of every generation. Life holds no greater challenge or joy than this: knowledge of ourselves and the universe we live in. Astrology is one of the keys to this knowledge.

Your Personal Horoscope 2009 gives you the fruits of astrological wisdom. In addition to general guidance on your character and the basic trends of your life, it shows you how to take advantage of planetary influences so you can make the most of the year ahead.

The section on each Sign includes a Personality Profile, a look at general trends for 2009, and in-depth month-by-month forecasts. The Glossary (*page 3*) explains some of the astrological terms you may be unfamiliar with.

One of the many helpful features of this book is the 'Best' and 'Most Stressful' days listed at the beginning of each monthly forecast. Read these sections to learn which days in each month will be good overall, good for money, and good for love. Mark them on your calendar – these will be your best days. Similarly, make a note of the days that will be most stressful for you. It is best to avoid taking important meetings or major decisions on these days, as well as on those days when important planets in your Horoscope are retrograde (moving backwards through the Zodiac).

The Major Trends section for your Sign lists those days when your vitality is strong or weak, or when relationships with your co-workers or loved ones may need a bit more effort on your part. If you are going through a difficult time, take a look at the colour, metal, gem and scent listed in the 'At a Glance' section of your Personality Profile. Wearing a piece of jewellery that contains your metal and/or gem will strengthen your vitality; just as wearing clothes or decorating your room or office in the colour ruled by your Sign, drinking teas made from the herbs ruled by your Sign, or wearing the scents associated with your Sign will sustain you.

Another important virtue of this book is that it will help you to know not only yourself but those around you: your friends, co-workers, partners and/or children. Reading the Personality Profile and forecasts for their Signs will provide you with an insight into their behaviour that you won't get anywhere else. You will know when to be more tolerant of them and when they are liable to be difficult or irritable.

In this edition we have included foot reflexology charts as part of the health section. So many health problems could perhaps be avoided or alleviated if we understood which organs were most vulnerable and what we could do to protect them. Though there are many natural and drug-free ways to strengthen vulnerable organs, these charts show a valid way to proceed. The vulnerable organs for the year ahead are clearly marked in the chart. It's very good to massage the whole foot on a regular basis, as the feet contain reflexes to the entire body. Try to pay special attention to the specific areas marked in the chart. If this is done diligently, health problems can be avoided. And even if they can't be completely avoided, their impact can be softened considerably.

I consider you – the reader – my personal client. By studying your Solar Horoscope I gain an awareness of what is going on in your life – what you are feeling and striving for and the challenges you face. I then do my best to address these concerns. Consider this book the next best thing to having your own personal astrologer!

It is my sincere hope that *Your Personal Horoscope 2009* will enhance the quality of your life, make things easier, illuminate the way forward, banish obscurities and make you more aware of your personal connection to the universe. Understood properly and used wisely, astrology is a great guide to knowing yourself, the people around you and the events in your life – but remember that what you do with these insights – the final result – is up to you.

Glossary of Astrological Terms

Ascendant

We experience day and night because the Earth rotates on its axis once every 24 hours. It is because of this rotation that the Sun, Moon and planets seem to rise and set. The Zodiac is a fixed belt (imaginary, but very real in spiritual terms) around the Earth. As the Earth rotates, the different Signs of the Zodiac seem to the observer to rise on the horizon. During a 24-hour period every Sign of the Zodiac will pass this horizon point at some time or another. The Sign that is at the horizon point at any given time is called the Ascendant, or Rising Sign. The Ascendant is the Sign denoting a person's self-image, body and self-concept – the personal ego, as opposed to the spiritual ego indicated by a person's Sun Sign.

Aspects

Aspects are the angular relationships between planets, the way in which one planet stimulates or influences another. If a planet makes a harmonious aspect (connection) to another, it tends to stimulate that planet in a positive and helpful way. If it makes a stressful aspect to another planet, this disrupts the planet's normal influence.

Astrological Qualities

There are three astrological qualities: *cardinal, fixed* and *mutable*. Each of the 12 Signs of the Zodiac falls into one of these three categories.

Cardinal Signs	Aries, Cancer, Libra and Capricorn The cardinal quality is the active, initiating principle. Those born under these four Signs are good at starting new projects.
Fixed Signs	Taurus, Leo, Scorpio and Aquarius Fixed qualities include stability, persistence, endurance and perfectionism. People born under these four Signs are good at seeing things through.
Mutable Signs	Gemini, Virgo, Sagittarius and Pisces Mutable qualities are adaptability, changeability and balance. Those born under these four Signs are creative, if not always practical.

Direct Motion

When the planets move forward through the Zodiac – as they normally do – they are said to be going 'direct'.

Grand Trine

A Grand Trine differs from a normal Trine (where two planets are 120 degrees apart) in that three or more planets are involved. When you look at this pattern in a chart, it takes the form of a complete triangle – a Grand Trine. Usually (but not always) it occurs in one of the four elements: Fire, Earth, Air or Water. Thus the particular element in which it occurs will be highlighted. A Grand Trine in Water is not the same as a Grand Trine in Air or Fire, etc. This is a very fortunate and happy aspect, and quite rare.

Grand Square

A Grand Square differs from a normal Square (usually two planets separated by 90 degrees) in that four or more planets are involved. When you look at the pattern in a chart you will see a whole and complete square. This, though stressful, usually denotes a new manifestation in the life. There is much work and balancing involved in the manifestation.

Houses

There are 12 Signs of the Zodiac and 12 Houses of experience. The 12 Signs are personality types and ways in which a given planet expresses itself; the 12 Houses show 'where' in your life this expression takes place. Each House has a different area of interest. A House can become potent and important – a House of Power – in different ways: if it contains the Sun, the Moon or the Ruler of your chart, if it contains more than one planet, or if the Ruler of that House is receiving unusual stimulation from other planets.

1st House	Personal Image and Sensual Delights
2nd House	Money/Finance
3rd House	Communication and Intellectual Interests
4th House	Home and Family
5th House	Children, Fun, Games, Creativity, Speculations and Love Affairs
6th House	Health and Work
7th House	Love, Marriage and Social Activities
8th House	Transformation and Regeneration
9th House	Religion, Foreign Travel, Higher Education and Philosophy
10th House	Career
11th House	Friends, Group Activities and Fondest Wishes
12th House	Spirituality

Karma

Karma is the law of cause and effect which governs all phenomena. We are all where we find ourselves because of karma – because of actions we have performed in the past. The universe is such a balanced instrument that any act immediately sets corrective forces into motion – karma.

Long-term Planets

The planets that take a long time to move through a Sign show the long-term trends in a given area of life. They are important for forecasting the prolonged view of things. Because these planets stay in one Sign for so long, there are periods in the year when the faster-moving (short-term) planets will join them, further activating and enhancing the importance of a given House.

Jupiter	stays in a Sign for about 1 year
Saturn	2½ years
Uranus	7 years
Neptune	14 years
Pluto	15 to 30 years

Lunar

Relating to the Moon. See also 'Phases of the Moon', below.

Natal

Literally means 'birth'. In astrology this term is used to distinguish between planetary positions that occurred at the time of a person's birth (natal) and those that are current (transiting). For example, Natal Sun refers to where the Sun was when you were born; transiting Sun refers to where the Sun's position is currently at any given moment – which usually doesn't coincide with your birth, or Natal, Sun.

Out of Bounds

The planets move through the Zodiac at various angles relative to the celestial equator (if you were to draw an imaginary extension of the Earth's equator out into the universe, you would have an illustration of this celestial equator). The Sun – being the most dominant and powerful influence in the Solar system – is the measure astrologers use as a standard. The Sun never goes more than approximately 23 degrees north or south of the celestial equator. At the winter solstice the Sun reaches its maximum southern angle of orbit (declination); at the summer solstice it reaches its maximum northern angle. Any time a planet exceeds this Solar boundary – and occasionally planets do – it is said to be 'out of bounds'. This means that the planet exceeds or trespasses into strange territory – beyond the limits allowed by the Sun, the Ruler of the Solar system. The planet in this condition becomes more emphasized and exceeds its authority, becoming an important influence in the forecast.

Phases of the Moon

After the full Moon, the Moon seems to shrink in size (as perceived from the Earth), gradually growing smaller until it is virtually invisible to the naked eye – at the time of the next new Moon. This is called the waning Moon phase, or the waning Moon.

After the new Moon, the Moon gradually gets bigger in size (as perceived from the Earth) until it reaches its maximum size at the time of the full Moon. This period is called the waxing Moon phase, or waxing Moon.

Retrogrades

The planets move around the Sun at different speeds. Mercury and Venus move much faster than the Earth, while Mars, Jupiter, Saturn, Uranus, Neptune and Pluto move more slowly. Thus there are times when, relative to the Earth, the planets appear to be going backwards. In reality they are always going forward, but relative to our vantage point on Earth they seem to go backwards through the Zodiac for a period of time. This is called 'retrograde' motion and tends to weaken the normal influence of a given planet.

Short-term Planets

The fast-moving planets move so quickly through a Sign that their effects are generally of a short-term nature. They reflect the immediate, day-to-day trends in a Horoscope.

Moon	stays in a Sign for only 2½ days
Mercury	20 to 30 days
Sun	30 days
Venus	approximately 1 month
Mars	approximately 2 months

T-square

A T-square differs from a Grand Square in that it is not a complete square. If you look at the pattern in a chart it appears as 'half a complete square', resembling the T-square tools used by architects and designers. If you cut a complete square in half, diagonally, you have a T-square. Many astrologers consider this more stressful than a Grand Square, as it creates tension that is difficult to resolve. T-squares bring learning experiences.

Transits

This refers to the movements or motions of the planets at any given time. Astrologers use the word 'transit' to make the distinction between a birth or Natal planet (see 'Natal', above) and the planet's current movement in the heavens. For example, if at your birth Saturn was in the Sign of Cancer in your 8th House, but is now moving through your 3rd House, it is said to be 'transiting' your 3rd House. Transits are one of the main tools with which astrologers forecast trends.

Aries

♈

THE RAM
*Birthdays from
21st March to
20th April*

Personality Profile

ARIES AT A GLANCE

Element – Fire

Ruling Planet – Mars
  Career Planet – Saturn
  Love Planet – Venus
  Money Planet – Venus
  *Planet of Fun, Entertainment, Creativity and
    Speculations* – Sun
  Planet of Health and Work – Mercury
  Planet of Home and Family Life – Moon
  Planet of Spirituality – Neptune
  *Planet of Travel, Education, Religion and
    Philosophy* – Jupiter

Colours – carmine, red, scarlet

*Colours that promote love, romance and social
  harmony* – green, jade green

Colour that promotes earning power – green

Gem – amethyst

Metals – iron, steel

Scent – honeysuckle

Quality – cardinal (= activity)

Quality most needed for balance – caution

Strongest virtues – abundant physical energy, courage, honesty, independence, self-reliance

Deepest need – action

Characteristics to avoid – haste, impetuousness, over-aggression, rashness

Signs of greatest overall compatibility – Leo, Sagittarius

Signs of greatest overall incompatibility – Cancer, Libra, Capricorn

Sign most helpful to career – Capricorn

Sign most helpful for emotional support – Cancer

Sign most helpful financially – Taurus

Sign best for marriage and/or partnerships – Libra

Sign most helpful for creative projects – Leo

Best Sign to have fun with – Leo

Signs most helpful in spiritual matters – Sagittarius, Pisces

Best day of the week – Tuesday

Understanding an Aries

Aries is the activist *par excellence* of the Zodiac. The Aries need for action is almost an addiction, and those who do not really understand the Aries personality would probably use this hard word to describe it. In reality 'action' is the essence of the Aries psychology – the more direct, blunt and to-the-point the action, the better. When you think about it, this is the ideal psychological makeup for the warrior, the pioneer, the athlete or the manager.

Aries likes to get things done, and in their passion and zeal often lose sight of the consequences for themselves and others. Yes, they often try to be diplomatic and tactful, but it is hard for them. When they do so they feel that they are being dishonest and phony. It is hard for them even to understand the mindset of the diplomat, the consensus builder, the front office executive. These people are involved in endless meetings, discussions, talks and negotiations – all of which seem a great waste of time when there is so much work to be done, so many real achievements to be gained. An Aries can understand, once it is explained, that talks and negotiations – the social graces – lead ultimately to better, more effective actions. The interesting thing is that an Aries is rarely malicious or spiteful – even when waging war. Aries people fight without hate for their opponents. To them it is all good-natured fun, a grand adventure, a game.

When confronted with a problem many people will say 'Well, let's think about it, let's analyse the situation.' But not an Aries. An Aries will think 'Something must be done. Let's get on with it.' Of course neither response is the total answer. Sometimes action is called for, sometimes cool thought. But an Aries tends to err on the side of action.

Action and thought are radically different principles. Physical activity is the use of brute force. Thinking and deliberating require one not to use force – to be still. It is not good for the athlete to be deliberating the next move; this will only slow down his or her reaction time. The athlete must act instinctively and instantly. This is how Aries people tend to behave in life. They are quick, instinctive decision-makers and their decisions tend to be translated into action almost immediately. When their intuition is sharp and well tuned, their actions are powerful and successful. When their intuition is off, their actions can be disastrous.

Do not think this will scare an Aries. Just as a good warrior knows that in the course of combat he or she might acquire a few wounds, so too does an Aries realize – somewhere deep down – that in the course of being true to yourself you might get embroiled in a disaster or two. It is all part of the game. An Aries feels strong enough to weather any storm.

There are many Aries people who are intellectual. They make powerful and creative thinkers. But even in this realm they tend to be pioneers – outspoken and blunt. These types of Aries tend to elevate (or sublimate) their desire for physical combat in favour of intellectual, mental combat. And they are indeed powerful.

In general, Aries people have a faith in themselves that others could learn from. This basic, rock-bottom faith carries them through the most tumultuous situations of life. Their courage and self-confidence make them natural leaders. Their leadership is more by way of example than by actually controlling others.

Finance

Aries people often excel as builders or estate agents. Money in and of itself is not as important as are other things – action, adventure, sport, etc. They are motivated by the need to support and be well-thought-of by their partners. Money as a way of attaining pleasure is another important motivation. An Aries functions best in their own businesses or as manager of their own departments within a large business or corporation. The fewer orders they have to take from higher up, the better. They also function better out in the field rather than behind a desk.

Aries people are hard workers with a lot of endurance; they can earn large sums of money due to the strength of their sheer physical energy.

Venus is their money planet, which means that Aries need to develop more of the social graces in order to realize their full earning potential. Just getting the job done – which is what an Aries excels at – is not enough to create financial success. The co-operation of others needs to be attained. Customers, clients and co-workers need to be made to feel comfortable; many people need to be treated properly in order for success to happen. When Aries people develop these abilities – or hire someone to do this for them – their financial potential is unlimited.

Career and Public Image

One would think that a pioneering type would want to break with the social and political conventions of society. But this is not so with the Aries-born. They are pioneers within conventional limits, in the sense that they like to start their own businesses within an established industry.

Capricorn is on the 10th House (Career) cusp of Aries' Solar Horoscope. Saturn is the planet that rules their life's work and professional aspirations. This tells us some interesting things about the Aries character. First off, it shows that, in order for Aries people to reach their full career potential, they need to develop some qualities that are a bit alien to their basic nature: They need to become better administrators and organizers; they need to be able to handle details better and to take a long-range view of their projects and their careers in general. No one can beat an Aries when it comes to achieving short-range objectives, but a career is long term, built over time. You cannot take a 'quickie' approach to it.

Some Aries people find it difficult to stick with a project until the end. Since they get bored quickly and are in constant pursuit of new adventures, they prefer to pass an old project or task on to somebody else in order to start something new. Those Aries who learn how to put off the search for something new until the old is completed will achieve great success in their careers and professional lives.

In general, Aries people like society to judge them on their own merits, on their real and actual achievements. A reputation acquired by 'hype' feels false to them.

Love and Relationships

In marriage and partnerships Aries like those who are more passive, gentle, tactful and diplomatic – people who have the social grace and skills they sometimes lack. Our partners always represent a hidden part of ourselves – a self that we cannot express personally.

An Aries tends to go after what he or she likes aggressively. The tendency is to jump into relationships and marriages. This is especially true if Venus is in Aries as well as the Sun. If an Aries likes you, he or she will have a hard time taking no for an answer; many attempts will be made to sweep you off your feet.

Though Aries can be exasperating in relationships – especially if they are not understood by their partners – they are never consciously or wilfully cruel or malicious. It is just that they are so independent and sure of themselves that they find it almost impossible to see somebody else's viewpoint or position. This is why an Aries needs as a partner someone with lots of social grace.

On the plus side, an Aries is honest, someone you can lean on, someone with whom you will always know where you stand. What he or she lacks in diplomacy is made up for in integrity.

Home and Domestic Life

An Aries is of course the ruler at home – the Boss. The male will tend to delegate domestic matters to the female. The female Aries will want to rule the roost. Both tend to be handy round the house. Both like large families and both believe in the sanctity and importance of the family. An Aries is a good family person, although he or she does not especially like being at home a lot, preferring instead to be roaming about.

Considering that they are by nature so combative and wilful, Aries people can be surprisingly soft, gentle and even vulnerable with their children and partners. The Sign of Cancer, ruled by the Moon, is on the cusp of their Solar 4th House (Home and Family). When the Moon is well aspected – under favourable influences – in the birth chart an Aries will be tender towards the family and want a family life that is nurturing and supportive. Aries likes to come home after a hard day on the battlefield of life to the understanding arms of their partner and the unconditional love and support of their family. An Aries feels that there is enough 'war' out in the world – and he or she enjoys participating in that. But when Aries comes home, comfort and nurturing are what's needed.

Horoscope for 2009

Major Trends

Last year was a banner career year for most of you. In many cases, you attained lifetime highs – peak career experiences. Whatever your age or stage in life, you advanced career-wise. There were promotions, raises, honours and recognition. Your career horizons were widened. In many cases (especially among those who are retired), there were no promotions, but just more honour and recognition for who you are and for past achievements. In the cases of younger Aries, important and fortunate career paths opened up – if only in your mind – for the future. This year, the trend will shift. Career goals have been attained and your focus will be more on friendships, group activities and networking. Many of you will manifest your fondest hopes and wishes this year.

Health and health issues were very important last year and the trend continues in the year ahead (especially until October 29). In fact we could say that good health has been (and will continue to be) your mission in life until October 29. (More on your health later.)

Saturn's move into your 7th House of Love and Marriage from October 29 onwards marks a whole new trend in love. In general we can say that relationships – especially relationships of the heart – will get tested. Many will go down in flames. The good relationships (and this includes marriage and business partnerships) will thrive and survive through this testing, but the inherently flawed ones will most probably dissolve. You are in a year (from October 29 onwards) for reducing your social activities. A cosmic re-organization is taking place. The whole area of love is being put into right order; a cosmic order. You will need to focus on quality relationships rather than quantity. While your heart relationships will get tested, your casual relationships – your circle of friends – is being greatly expanded. This is generally a very happy area this year.

This year, 2009, is unique in that we will have six eclipses (two Solar Eclipses and four Lunar ones). Generally we get only four eclipses in a given year. But what is noteworthy for you is that four Lunar eclipses show much change and turmoil in the family situation. There will be dramatic events in the lives of family members and there will be a need to learn calmness amidst the changes and disruptions.

Your most important areas of life this year will be spirituality, friendships and group activities, career, health (until October 29) and love (after October 29).

Your paths of greatest fulfilment in the year ahead are friendships, group activities (all year) and career (after July 27).

Health

(Please note that this is an astrological perspective on health and not a medical one. In days of yore there was no difference, both of these perspectives were identical. But in these times there could be quite a difference. For the medical perspective, please consult your doctor or health professional.)

Health for those born under Aries has been basically reasonable for the past few years, but the dynamics in the cosmos are changing. Last year Pluto began to make a stressful aspect to you, but he was not consistent. Sometimes he was in stressful aspect and sometimes not (he was moving in and out of Capricorn last year). This year he moves into a stressful aspect to you for many years to come.

Saturn was leaving you alone last year. This year, on October 29 he too starts to make a stressful aspect to you (and this will last for two and a half years).

These are not things to panic about, only to understand. Your normal super-abundant vitality will not be up to its usual standards. Sure, you will have plenty of energy to do what you need to do but not for the frivolous things. So you need to be like a businessman with your energy, investing it only in worthwhile things.

My experience has been that when energy levels are normal, people get away with many sins. But when energy gets lowered, they tend to get hit in their vulnerable organs – the organs that were vulnerable by birth. (Those things can only be known by casting a personal Horoscope for your exact time and date of birth and then doing a specialized analysis from a health perspective.) In general, though, the lungs, small intestine, heart, arms and shoulders tend to be most important for Aries and this is a year to pay special attention to those parts (see our chart below).

Simple things will help you get through the next few years. Your arms and shoulders should be regularly massaged. There are hosts of natural, drugless therapies that can strengthen the lungs, heart and the small intestine – foot

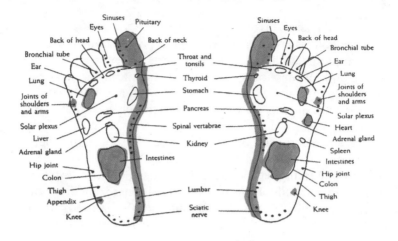

Reflexology

Try to massage the whole foot on a regular basis, but pay extra attention to the points highlighted on the chart. When you massage, be aware of 'sore spots', as these need special attention. It's also a good idea to massage the ankles and top side (as well as the soles) of the feet.

and hand reflexology, acupuncture, acupressure, shiatsu, chi gong, yoga, kinesiology and massage just to name a few. Giving extra attention to these organs this year will prevent many a problem from developing. And, even if a problem develops it will be much milder than if nothing were done. What could have been a devastating knock out blow will be just a minor love tap.

The good news is that until October 29 health and health issues are important for Aries, and you give them the attention they deserve. Also you seem more into healthy lifestyles, disciplined health regimes and diets this year (this has been a trend for some years now). And these good habits will now stand you in good stead in coming years. (The cosmos in its love and mercy tends to give us the answer before the problem develops.)

Still, the most important thing will be to maintain high energy levels. Rest when tired, work with a rhythm and take frequent breaks, plan your activities so that more gets done with less energy, avoid arguments, worry and emotional negativity (easier said than done!) as these can deplete a person more (and faster) than hours on a chain gang.

Your health planet, Mercury, goes Retrograde four times this year (this is also highly unusual; normally he travels backwards only three times in a year). These will be times to review your health, health regime and health attitudes to see where improvements can be made. However, these are not times to make drastic changes to your regime, or to make important health decisions, only to review it. This year, these periods are from January 11 to 31; May 7 to 30; September 7 to 29 and December 26 to 31.

Home and Family

Your 4th House of Home and Family is not a House of Power this year, thus there is not as much interest here as usual. Generally this shows that the cosmos is not pushing you one way or another and you have more freedom and latitude in this department. Generally it denotes a status quo kind of year.

However, this year I'm not so sure about this. There are, as was mentioned, FOUR Lunar eclipses this year, and the Moon is your home and family planet. In addition, there is a Solar Eclipse on July 22 in your 4th House. Perhaps by temperament you would prefer the status quo, but it's not going to happen.

These eclipses show either moves (sudden and disruptive), repairs in the home (unexpected), dramatic events in the lives of family members and parent figures, and major changes in the family and domestic pattern.

Eclipses are never punitive, but they can feel that way, especially if a person is making plans, or is attached to things that are not part of his or her plan in life. Then, the function of the eclipse is to 'blow it to smithereens' and bring the person back to his or her path. If the person is already following the cosmic plan for the life, the eclipse will only reveal hidden flaws and allow corrections to be made.

Are family relationships ties that are holding you back? Are family attachments unhealthy and uncosmic? Is family preventing you from fulfilling your divine destiny (or perhaps the reverse is true)? Are you supposed to be living in another place? The eclipses will expose all this and lead to life changes.

The challenge now (as was mentioned earlier) is to keep the emotions in harmony. This is not easy but it can be done. Those of you who are worldly will probably medicate, although this is a stop-gap solution. A spiritual discipline, an awareness of your feelings without judgement, prayer and meditation will be longer-lasting solutions, solutions that will cure the very root causes of the problems.

Parents or parent figures in your life are undergoing deep and profound transformations. This seems on a very personal level. Some are having surgery (both cosmetic and more serious types). Some are getting involved in serious detox regimes. Some are having near death experiences. Some are getting involved in spiritual disciplines that involve transformation. The process of transformation is seldom pleasant – and you will need patience with your parents – but the end result is beautiful.

The parents or parent figures (in a man's chart what we see refers to the father or father figures; in a woman's chart it refers to the mother or mother figures) are confronting the 'dark angel' in various ways. He is letting them know that he is around, that life is short (compared to Eternity) and fragile and it's time to get down to the essentials of life. The 'dark angel' is only reminding them of what is really important in life.

If you are planning heavy construction work or renovations in the home, June 21 to July 22 and August 25 to October 16 are good times. If you are looking to beautify the home in a cosmetic sort of way (repainting or buying furniture or art objects) August 1 to 26 is a good time.

Finance and Career

Your 2nd House of Finance is not a House of Power this year, thus you seem satisfied with the status quo and have no need to make major financial changes. It is true that you have more freedom in this area – the planetary powers neither push you one way nor another – but there is a lack of interest and this tends to the status quo. (Career is another matter and we'll discuss it later.)

Your financial planet is Venus. She is a very fast moving planet and will move through all the Signs and Houses of your Horoscope in any given year. Thus financial opportunity will come to you in many ways and through many people as the year unfolds. It all depends on where Venus is at any given time and these issues are best discussed in the monthly reports.

Venus serves double duty in your Horoscope. She is BOTH the financial planet AND the love planet. Thus there is a very strong connection between love and money. When love is going well, there tends to be prosperity. When prosperity is strong, love tends to go well. So if you want to improve your bottom line, work on maintaining harmony with your spouse, current love or friends.

Venus rules the beauty industry – cosmetics, fashion, perfumes, jewellery, antiques, art and the like. Thus all these industries are interesting to you, both as investments or as ways to earn a living. People involved in these industries also tend to be important in your financial life.

Professional investors should look at copper (the commodity) and real estate for profit opportunities.

The job situation seems stressful for many of you. You don't seem to be enjoying it as much as you should. The spiritual lesson here is to transcend how you feel and just do the right thing – do a good job – regardless of how you feel. There is a need to develop some discipline in this area.

Those of you who hire others seem to be cutting back on employees and doing a major re-structuring in this area. This doesn't mean failure. Downsizing, especially when done with skill, can actually increase profits. The object here is to eliminate waste and bring a cosmic order into the employee situation.

Last year you worked hard, and you saw the results of that hard work. You gained promotions, honours and raises. Yes, you had luck in your career, but it was your hard work that created the luck. This year you are still working hard and succeeding in this way.

With Pluto now in your 10th House of Career for many years to come, there is a sense that you are re-evaluating your career, purifying it, detoxing it of effete attitudes, motives and emotions. This purification often leads to near-death experiences in the career. Sometimes it leads to actual death and then a resurrection. The good news here is that there is an intense focus – a drive for success – and a single-minded concentration on the career goals. Attainment of these goals is very likely now (and for years to come) but you have to be willing to undergo the transformation – the detox.

We also see a complete transformation of your industry, the leaders of your industry and your corporate hierarchy in coming years. This won't happen overnight, but over many years. A few years from now you will hardly recognize your industry or your corporate hierarchy; the changes will be deep and profound.

With ALL the long-term planets above the horizon of your chart (and Pluto right on the Midheaven) there is great ambition. You need to be careful not to ignore family or to ride rough shod over others in your drive to the top. Your intense interest could be seen as a ruthlessness by others.

Your most prosperous periods this year will be from February 3 to July 5.

Your best career periods will be from January 1 to 20; April 19 to May 20; August 22 to September 22 and December 21 to 31.

Love and Social Life

Your 7th House of Love and Marriage is not a House of
Power for most of the year (until October 29). Thus, until
that time I expect a status quo kind of situation. Marrieds
will tend to stay married and singles will tend to stay single.
Of course singles will date and have fun – they will have a
social life – but there doesn't seem to be anything special on
the horizon.

As Saturn moves into your 7th House on October 29, he
will bring many changes to your love and social life. As we
mentioned earlier, he will test existing marriages and business partnerships in the same sort of way a company road
tests a new vehicle. It gives the vehicle some rough handling
– abnormally rough handling – to see where the flaws are –
to see how the vehicle handles stress – and to see how reliable the vehicle is. This road testing is very valuable to the
maker; improvements can either be made or the vehicle can
be released for production. So it is with your marriage and
business partnerships. They get some rough handling. If you
perform well, you will have an enduring marriage or partnership and will know where and how you can improve
things.

Faulty marriages, like faulty vehicles, will probably get
destroyed by the road testing. The cosmos wants the best for
you, and will send you another partner in due course.

The Horoscope is not only showing us the problems in
love, but also the cure. If the marriage is troubled, there is a
need to make it the priority in your life, to keep your full
focus on the marriage. You sort of have to make it your
'spiritual mission' for the year. Only that kind of priority can
save it (and both parties have to be willing to do this). Also,
it might help to be more helpful in your spouse's or partner's
career; be a staunch advocate and supporter of it.

There is a whole reorganization of social life happening
after October 29. Jupiter in your 11th House is bringing you
all kinds of new friends and acquaintances. Perhaps you are
socializing too much to the detriment of other areas of your

life. So, Saturn will come and test these friendships and force you to focus only on the good ones. Saturn's philosophy is 'better to have a few good friends than to have hordes of mediocre ones'.

After October 29 singles are probably better off staying single. There is a need to review your love attitudes and what your true needs are. Date less, but make the dates you go on more serious and of a higher calibre. You are in a period where the cosmos is showing you that love and marriage is not just a 'good time' but has many serious responsibilities attached to it.

Saturn moving through the 7th House is not considered an especially happy transit for love. Yet it does have some very positive points to it, some of which we mentioned. When he is through with you, your marriage, partnerships and social life will be solid indeed, reliable, of good quality and healthy. Also, it shows that you will be mingling with people of high status – his political or corporate power – in the year ahead. You will have a more practical approach to love.

Saturn, your career planet, in the 7th House often shows the classic office romance: romance with the boss or superior. The danger with these kinds of relationships is that they can become purely material and utilitarian, without any deep feelings of love involved.

Our discussion above relates to those in or working on their first marriage. Those in or working on their second marriage will have a status quo kind of year. Marrieds will tend to stay married and singles will tend to stay single. There are love opportunities with friends, introductions of new friends, and in groups and organizations.

Those working on the third marriage have very wonderful marriage aspects now and a marriage or serious relationship is likely.

Your best love and social periods this year will be from September 23 to October 22 and from October 15 to 29.

Venus will make one of her rare Retrogrades from March 6 to April 17. This tends to introduce glitches in the love life.

Relationships seem to go backwards instead of forwards. But there is a spiritual purpose here: to review your current love situation and see where improvements can be made. Better to make long-term love decisions after April 17. (By the way this Retrograde also applies to finances.)

Self-improvement

Spirituality has been an important focus for some years now and the trend continues in the year ahead. Uranus is in your 12th House. Thus you are (and if not, you should be) exploring the scientific side of spirituality. A good scientific understanding of what you are doing will be a great help in keeping the faith during the tough times. The spiritual side of Astrology also seems interesting.

Uranus moving through your 12th House shows that you have been (and will continue) making dramatic changes in your spiritual regime and practice. It seems to me that these changes have been coming from inner revelation. And you can expect more of this in the year to come. Revelation will hit you with the suddenness of a lightning bolt. You might practise, practise, practise and nothing seems to be happening. Then one day, when you least expect it, boom! You have inner revelation and everything in your life changes.

This is a year for friendship and group activities, but it seems to involve spirituality as well. You are attracting spiritual kinds of friends. You are involved with spiritual groups and organizations.

Your spiritual mission for the year ahead (as it has been for the past two years) is staying healthy, learning more about your health, and incorporating healthy habits into your everyday life. It is also about developing your own personal healing abilities – we all have them. Being of practical service to others will not only help you in your worldly career, but also spiritually as well. Leadership is a form of service to others and you are seeing this more clearly in the year ahead.

After October 29, your spiritual mission will change. It will be about being there for your friends and spouse, supporting them and helping them.

Month-by-month Forecasts

January

    Best Days Overall: 3, 4, 12, 21, 22, 30, 31
    Most Stressful Days Overall: 10, 11, 16, 17, 23, 24
    Best Days for Love: 9, 10, 16, 17, 18, 19, 28, 29
    Best Days for Money: 6, 7, 9, 10, 16, 18, 19, 25, 26, 28, 29
    Best Days for Career: 6, 14, 15, 23, 24

You begin your year with 80 to 90 per cent of the planets above the horizon. Your 10th House of Career is very power-ful: 50 per cent and sometimes 60 per cent of the planets are either there or moving through there this month. You are right in the middle of a yearly career peak. This is the main interest and focus in the coming month. Your 4th House of Home and Family, by contrast, is empty. So you can safely de-emphasize family concerns and focus on your career. No question that this is the best way to serve your family. You are working hard, no question about it, fending off competitors and doing whatever you need to do to reach your goals. What I like here is that you are personally recognized, not just for your career achievements but for who you are. You are honoured and appreciated by the powers that be. You are on top, probably above everyone in your family and above your spouse or current love. You are calling the shots. Last year was a beautiful career year, and the trend continues this month. Pay rises and promotions are still likely. The only fly in the ointment (here on Earth things are seldom perfect) is the Retrograde movement of your career planet, Saturn. This suggests that you need to do more homework on the various career opportunities or promotions that are coming your way – they might not be what they seem.

Last month (December 2008) the planets shifted from the social western sector of the Horoscope to the independent East. This trend is now in full swing for the next 6 months or so. You are very independent by nature and so this trend is comfortable for you. This is a time to have things your way and to create conditions as you desire them to be. You have more freedom of action now. You are not so much in need of the good graces of others to achieve your goals.

But career interest is waning this month and the focus, little by little, will shift to friendships, group activities and organizations. Jupiter will enter your 11th House on the 5th and the Sun on the 19th. So this is a happy and successful area of life now. Moreover, there is a Solar Eclipse on the 26th that occurs in this House. This suggests that now new friends – important ones – are coming into your life. You are re-evaluating existing friendships – friendships are getting tested – and in many cases, existing friendships will dissolve and new ones will come to replace them. This Solar Eclipse brings dramatic changes in the lives of children, dramas (both personal and financial) in the lives of parent figures, and shakeups in religious or educational institutions you are involved in. Many of you (especially students) will be changing your educational plans – changing schools or changing courses. Your college or university might be making important rule changes that affect you. If you are involved in legal issues, there is now a dramatic turn. Since you have basically good aspects this year, I expect legal issues will go in your favour. Avoid speculations during the eclipse period.

Health is good overall, but rest and relax more until the 19th. The ankles, spine, knees, teeth, bones and overall skeletal alignment need special attention.

February

> Best Days Overall: 1, 8, 9, 17, 18, 27, 28
> Most Stressful Days Overall: 6, 7, 12, 13, 19, 20, 21
> Best Days for Love: 8, 9, 12, 13, 17, 18, 27, 28
> Best Days for Money: 2, 3, 4, 5, 8, 9, 12, 13, 17, 18, 22, 23, 27, 28
> Best Days for Career: 2, 3, 10, 11, 19, 20, 21

Mercury your health planet starts to move forward on the 1st. It was Retrograde last month from the 11th to the 31st. So now it is safe to make changes to your health regime or diet. Health is much improved over last month, but you can enhance it even further by giving more attention to the same organs as last month – the spine, knees, teeth, bones and overall skeletal alignment until the 14th and the ankles afterwards. It might be wise to see a chiropractor more often this month and to give more support to the ankles, especially when you exercise. Regular ankle massage is good too. Until the 14th, as your health planet is in an Earth Sign, you will get good results from being in places with a strong earth energy: mountains, old forests, caves, or mineral springs. Crystal therapy will be more powerful as well. After the 14th, as your health planet moves into an Air Sign, fresh air is good for you. Breathing exercises will also be beneficial.

A Lunar Eclipse on the 9th shakes things up with family, family members and perhaps parent figures. Children are also affected. They seem to be making important changes to their image, self-awareness and spiritual changes – changes to their spiritual regime or practice. (You too are making important changes to your spiritual regime, probably because of new revelation and understanding.) You seem involved in certain scandals; it might not be with you personally but with people you are involved with. Certain hidden information now gets disclosed and there is some upheaval about this. Flaws in the home tend to be revealed by every Lunar Eclipse and this one is no different. Be patient with family members now. This eclipse will also test love affairs. Unsound ones can dissolve right now.

But singles need not worry about love. Venus, your love planet, crosses your Ascendant from the 2nd to the 4th. Love is seeking you and will find you. There is nothing much you need to do – just show up! Love pursues you, not the other way around. And this will be the case for the whole month. Venus in your own Sign also shows prosperity – financial windfalls that come to you, and expensive personal items, like clothing or jewellery, as well. Venus in your own Sign from the 3rd onwards enhances your physical appearance and glamorizes it. Your sense of style is enhanced. You radiate (unconsciously, without trying) charm and grace and the opposite sex takes notice. What the cosmos might take away by the eclipse, it will replace with better.

Financial opportunities are seeking you out and will find you. This is a prosperous month. You adopt the image of wealth this month too.

March

Best Days Overall: 7, 8, 16, 17, 18, 26, 27
Most Stressful Days Overall: 3, 4, 12, 13, 19, 20
Best Days for Love: 7, 8, 12, 13, 16, 17, 18, 26, 27
Best Days for Money: 1, 2, 3, 4, 7, 8, 12, 13, 16, 17, 18, 21, 22, 23, 26, 27, 28, 29, 30, 31
Best Days for Career: 1, 2, 10, 19, 20, 28, 29

This month you have three main interests. Like last month, it is a very social month. Friendships, group activities and involvement with organizations are still a dominant interest. But your 12th House of Spirituality is also very strong this month, especially until the 20th. A good period to pursue spiritual and charitable interests, to go on that yoga or spiritual retreat, to take meditation classes or get involved in prayer circles and the like. A good period to review the past year, correct mistakes, re-evaluate and set new goals for the year ahead. You are about to have your personal new year – which begins on your birthday. You want to start this new year – this new cycle – fresh, with a clean slate.

On the 20th, as the Sun enters your own Sign, there is a great interest in the body: the image and the pleasures of the body. You enter one of your yearly personal pleasure periods – a time to pamper yourself and enjoy life.

Health is wonderful all month, but especially after the 20th. The Sun in your own Sign gives you the energy of ten people. (Even older Aries will feel more bouncy now.) If there were health problems in the last month you should experience healings now. Until the 8th you can enhance your health even further by giving more attention to the ankles. Massage them regularly and give them support (you seem more active this month, more into sports and exercise, so this is important). Fresh air – air purity in general – is important until the 8th. Afterwards, enhance the health by giving more attention to the feet: regular foot massage would be wonderful then. After the 8th you will also get good results from spiritual-type healing – meditation, prayer, reiki, the laying on of hands and the manipulation of subtle energies. This will be a wonderful period to advance your knowledge of these things.

The love life is just super. Whether you are looking for fun and games kinds of relationships or something more serious, it is there for you – and these people are seeking you out. You are having your way. Just be yourself and go about your business; these people will find you. Marrieds will find that their spouses are more devoted and attentive. However, Venus starts to Retrograde on the 9th. And this complicates the love life. This is a period for reviewing your relationships and seeing where improvements can be made. And though you have many love opportunities, don't jump into them right away – let them develop slowly (very difficult for you Aries, but it is wise.)

Like last month there is prosperity. Financial opportunities are seeking you out. There is luck in speculations (especially around the Spring Equinox). Your personal appearance plays a huge role in earnings, and since you look good these days this is a positive wealth signal. Prosperity is only going to get stronger in the next few months. Again Venus's Retrograde suggests that you do more homework with all the financial opportunities coming to you. They may not be all they are made out to be.

April

Best Days Overall: 4, 5, 13, 14, 22, 23
Most Stressful Days Overall: 2, 3, 8, 9, 15, 16, 29, 30
Best Days for Love: 4, 8, 9, 20, 21
Best Days for Money: 4, 8, 9, 18, 19, 20, 21, 25, 26, 27, 28
Best Days for Career: 6, 7, 15, 16, 25, 26

Most of the planets are still in the East. Your own Sign, Aries, is very powerful all month. Your 1st House of Self and Self Interest is very powerful, while your 7th House of others is empty (only the Moon will visit there on the 8th and 9th). So this is the most independent period of your year, much more even than the past few months. This is the time to make those changes you want to make – to change the conditions of your life that might be irksome to you or that you feel can be improved. Go forward boldly. Reach for the stars. Have things your way. If others don't go along, go it alone (but it seems to me that others will go along). Create your life now – the cosmos supports you – only create wisely. You will have to live with your creation later on.

Health is just super, even better than last month. The Sun is in your own Sign until the 19th and Mars, your Ruling Planet, will enter on the 22nd. You have all the energy you need to achieve any goal you set for yourself. You are dynamic and attractive. You exude energy, life and magnetism. The only problem here – from a health perspective – can come from too much of a good thing. You might overdo things, become overactive and push the body beyond its limits, so just be more aware of the body. Also haste, impatience and temper can be a problem. You want things done quickly and haste can lead to unneeded adventures. Many of you don't realize your force these days. You have so much energy that a curt or short remark can devastate another person – never mind a temper tantrum. Go out of your way to be gentler with others. Watch your driving too: speeding is the problem.

You excel in sports and exercise regimes this month. Athletes will be performing at their top levels these days, breaking their own personal records. Libido is very powerful now too. Probably a sexually active kind of month.

Your love planet is still Retrograde until the 17th. There is love in your life, no question about it, but it can seem to go backwards instead of forwards. But it seems to me that the lover or love opportunity will come back. Venus will once again cross your Ascendant on the 24th, and love (and financial) opportunities are seeking you out and coming to you.

Finances are wonderful this month. And in spite of Venus's Retrograde you are prospering. Perhaps there are a few glitches or delays, but the basic trend is good. You will really feel your prosperity after the 19th. Venus will go forward on the 17th (bringing back your financial confidence and judgement) and the Sun will enter your money house on the 19th. You are entering a yearly financial peak – enjoy.

May

> Best Days Overall: 1, 2, 10, 11, 20, 21, 28, 29
> Most Stressful Days Overall: 5, 6, 12, 13, 14, 26, 27
> Best Days for Love: 1, 2, 5, 6, 10, 11, 20, 21, 28, 29
> Best Days for Money: 1, 2, 5, 6, 10, 11, 15, 16, 20, 21, 22, 23, 24, 25, 28, 29
> Best Days for Career: 3, 4, 12, 13, 14, 22, 23, 30, 31

Late last month – after the 24th – the planetary power made an important shift from the upper to the lower half of your Horoscope. This represents the 'night time' of your year. The activities of night are highlighted. Night is for regenerating and gathering your forces, for dreaming and planning your next moves, for working towards your goals in a more inner way. Sure, you still have a career, and there are external demands, but now is the time to further your career by internal rather than external means. Visualize what you want to do and where you want to be. Imagine what you would like to achieve. Hold your image steadfast. In due course, your inner seeds will bloom into outer actions and events. Now is a time for cultivating emotional harmony and for preparing the psychological ground for future success. It is during the night, when we seem inert and inactive (outwardly) that the forces are gathered for the success of the day. So, you can focus more on the family now and de-emphasize the career. It is a time for psychological progress.

You are still well into a yearly financial peak this month. There is prosperity. Money is earned in happy ways, perhaps as you indulge in leisure activities. You spend more on these things too. As we have seen in the past few months, financial opportunities are seeking you out; wealth is rushing towards you. You just have to accept it when it comes. There is a short-term financial crisis – perhaps involving taxes or debt – early this month, but you will get past it and the prognosis is bright. You are a financial star. There is luck in speculations (but only do this under intuition). Children also seem prosperous these days.

Love seems happy. There could be a short-term lover's spat – an upheaval due to jealousy – but let the passions die down and your love will resume. You and the beloved are together, on the same page, seeing eye to eye, basically in harmony. A business partnership or joint venture seems in the works. There is definitely opportunity here. Problems in a marriage can be helped by doing adventurous things together as a couple, like mountain climbing, hiking, white-water rafting or by exercising or indulging in sports together. It seems like a sexually active period.

Health is still excellent. You are magnetic and project much sex appeal. You are glamorous and charming as well.

Your sense of style continues to be excellent and it is still a great period for buying clothing or accessories. Your taste is excellent. You can enhance your health even further by paying more attention to the arms, shoulders and lungs; your arms and shoulders should be regularly massaged. After the 14th pay more attention to the neck and throat – neck massage will be very powerful.

June

Best Days Overall: 6, 7, 8, 16, 17, 25
Most Stressful Days Overall: 2, 3, 9, 10, 23, 29, 30
Best Days for Love: 2, 3, 9, 19, 27, 28, 29, 30
Best Days for Money: 2, 3, 9, 11, 12, 13, 18, 19, 21, 22, 27, 28, 29, 30
Best Days for Career: 9, 10, 19, 27, 28

Your yearly financial peak is still going strong. Prosperity is even greater than last month. A business partnership or joint venture is still very likely. Your lover, spouse and friends are very co-operative on a financial level. Social contacts – always important for you – are even more important in the month ahead. What I like here is that you have a strong interest in finance – a strong personal interest – and this focus tends to bring success. You are working hard physically, and this is important, but you also need to market your product or service better.

Health is still very good, but it won't hurt to rest and relax more after the 21st. Enhance your health by giving more attention to the neck and throat (like last month) until the 14th and to the arms, shoulders and lungs afterwards. Regular neck, arm and shoulder massage will do wonders for you. Until the 14th your health planet is in an Earth Sign (Taurus), so you benefit from the healing powers of the Earth. If you feel under the weather get out into the mountains, or old forests or caves. You will feel much better. After the 14th get out into the fresh air and take deep, deep, breaths – this is also rejuvenating when you feel under the weather. Wind bathing is also wonderful; get as naked as practical and let the wind blow all over your body.

Love is still happy this month. Elders – parents or parent figures – might be obstructing, but love still happens. For singles love opportunities come as you pursue your normal financial goals. Often this aspect (the love planet in the money house) shows opportunities with people who are involved with your money: bankers, brokers, financial advisers, etc. Wealth is definitely an allurement. Material gifts turn you on. This is how you show love and this is how you feel loved. If a marriage is having difficulties, material gifts can do much to help. Also try working on your finances as a couple – share the responsibility and the decision making.

Uranus is very close to your Ascendant this month, within orb of a conjunction. This is especially so with those of you born early in the Sign of Aries, from March 20 to 25. This is manifesting a restlessness, a desire for change, a desire for total freedom. Those of you involved with Aries romantically (especially those born early in the Sign) should take note and give them a lot of space.

Aside from finance and love, the major interests in the month ahead are intellectual interests and communication, home and family. Try to avoid power struggles in your career this month – you don't need to fight. Ride out the rough spots. Things will change in coming months.

July

Best Days Overall: 3, 4, 5, 14, 15, 22, 23, 31
Most Stressful Days Overall: 6, 7, 20, 21, 26, 27
Best Days for Love: 9, 18, 19, 26, 27
Best Days for Money: 9, 10, 16, 17, 18, 19, 26, 27
Best Days for Career: 6, 7, 16, 17, 24, 25

Retrograde activity is increasing this month and for you this is a challenge. Yes, you like things done quickly – yesterday – but this is a month for learning patience. Forty per cent of the planets are Retrograde now. Make haste slowly. Be more methodical in everything you do. Since it is summer and you are in a party mood, it is a good period for a vacation. Not much is happening in the world anyway, so you might as well enjoy yourself.

Friendships, group activities and organizations are still a major focus this month, as they have been all year. But now, all the planets involved with these things are Retrograde so you need to be patient with your friends. Friendships – or relations with a group or organization – seem to be going backwards instead of forwards, but there is a review going on; everything will work out well in the end.

Most of the planets are below the horizon of the Horoscope and your 4th House of Home and Family is very strong until the 22nd. So, continue to de-emphasize the career and give more attention to the home and family. If you have a choice between making that extra deal or being there for the kids or parents, be there for the kids and parents. Other deals will come. Now you need your emotional harmony. (Of course you can't avoid your career altogether, but where there are choices, focus on the home.)

Health is not up to its usual standards until the 22nd, but there are no serious issues that we can see here. Just lower vitality. This makes a person more vulnerable. So rest and relax more and enhance your health by giving more atten-tion to the stomach and breasts (from the 3rd to the 17th) and to the heart (after the 17th). Diet is more of an issue health-wise until the 17th, as is emotional health. Work to keep your moods constructive and upbeat. If there are health problems they seem connected to family disharmony (or disharmony with children) or to unresolved traumas from the past. Restore the harmony and chances are the health problem will just fade away. Your normal exuberant good health returns after the 22nd. It's like magic – a shot of adrenalin. The Sun moves into fiery Leo and you are restored.

We mentioned that you are in a party period now, espe-cially after the 22nd. It is another of your yearly personal pleasure peaks. Enjoy. For singles this is a period for love affairs. But communication and intellectual interests are also important to you. And this is a good period to make those calls you need to make and write those letters that you owe to people. It is also good for taking courses in subjects that interest you – and singles might find more than education at these courses or lectures.

Finances are not a big issue this month. I read this as a good sign. You've basically achieved your financial goals and seem satisfied. Like last month though, good communication – good marketing – good use of the media – is very important.

August

Best Days Overall: 1, 10, 11, 19, 27, 28
Most Stressful Days Overall: 2, 3, 4, 16, 17, 23, 24, 30, 31
Best Days for Love: 7, 8, 9, 16, 17, 23, 24, 25, 26
Best Days for Money: 5, 6, 7, 8, 9, 12, 13, 14, 15, 16, 17, 23, 24, 25, 26
Best Days for Career: 2, 3, 4, 12, 13, 21, 30, 31

Retrograde activity is still strong this month so you might as well keep the party going. Have fun. Enjoy yourself. Explore the rapture side of life. After the 22nd you enter a more serious, work-oriented period.

Home and family are still an important focus, more important than your career. For a time (this is only temporary) you seem content to be humble and let others be in charge. You just want to be happy. There could be important renovations or repairs going on in the home after the 24th. A parent or parent figure could be contemplating surgery, although it looks more like a cosmetic type.

The simple pleasures of the home – far from the peaks of power – seem alluring to you. A home-cooked meal; watching the children play catch; sitting in the living room watching TV. There is something very wonderful about these things. Even love, for singles, seems to happen at home or close to home.

Perhaps Mr or Miss Right comes through a family introduction or at a family gathering. Romantic evenings at home, far from places of glitz and glamour, strike exactly the right tone. Giving and receiving emotional support is more important than material gifts. Singles are looking for partners with strong family values now. This changes after the 26th, but this is the way it is for most of the month.

Financial opportunities come at home too. Family seems very supportive financially. There are earnings opportunities in real estate and the family business (either your own or someone else's). Earning opportunities come through family connections. Most probably you are spending more on the home and family as well.

There is a Lunar Eclipse on August 6 in your 11th House. This will test your friendships, and there have been many new ones of late and they need some testing. The good ones will survive while the flawed ones will dissolve for a time. There are some dramas at home and with the children (or those who are like children to you). And, as with every Lunar Eclipse, repairs could be needed in the home. There are shakeups and upheavals in organizations that you belong to, and this perhaps changes your relationship with these organizations. This eclipse is benign to you but it won't hurt to take a reduced schedule anyway. There are probably dramas in the lives of friends.

September

> Best Days Overall: 6, 7, 15, 16, 23, 24, 25
> Most Stressful Days Overall: 13, 14, 19, 20, 26, 27
> Best Days for Love: 6, 7, 15, 16, 19, 20, 26, 27
> Best Days for Money: 1, 2, 6, 7, 8, 9, 11, 12, 15, 16, 19, 20, 26, 27, 28, 29, 30
> Best Days for Career: 8, 9, 17, 18, 26, 27

Retrograde activity is still strong this month, so continue to make haste slowly. Patience, patience, patience is the name of the game now. Pluto will start to move forwards on the

11th after many months of Retrograde motion and this will clarify issues involving debt, estates and taxes. But Mercury will be Retrograde from the 7th to the 27th and there are still 40 per cent of the planets moving Retrograde for most of the month.

Mercury's Retrograde suggests more homework and care with regard to health regimes and dietary changes. These things need to be studied before you implement them. For jobseekers it suggests a need for more study of job offers that come – and by the way they will come. This is an excellent month for jobseekers.

Health is a major interest this month. And health is basically good. After the 22nd you need to rest and relax more. You can enhance your health by giving more attention to the kidneys and hips (until the 18th) and to the intestines afterwards. Drive more defensively early in the month, and be more safety conscious in the home.

This month – after the 22nd – the planetary power will shift to the upper half of the Horoscope (you will feel this more strongly next month, but the shift is beginning now). Also Saturn, your career planet, is receiving much positive stimulation. Your career is becoming more active and important and there should be interesting and happy career opportunities coming your way from the 15th to the 19th – probably as you pursue leisure activities or attend parties.

Home and family is still important this month and you seem focused here; perhaps you are doing repairs or renovations or are involved with parent figures. But very soon, the home and family situation will be where you want it and you can focus on your external career.

Your financial planet is in the speculative Sign of Leo until the 20th. There are some very positive things about this: you earn money in happy ways, speculations tend to be favourable and you have a sense of financial optimism and confidence. You spend freely, and the danger here is overspending. But this will change after the 20th as Venus, the financial planet, moves into Virgo. Then you become more cost conscious and will tend to get value for your money.

Love is happy, but not very serious, until the 22nd. You basically want a good time and will tend to attract people who feel this way as well. But after the 22nd, you enter a yearly social peak and more serious romance is likely for singles.

October

Best Days Overall: 3, 4, 12, 13, 21, 22, 31
Most Stressful Days Overall: 10, 11, 16, 17, 23, 24
Best Days for Love: 6, 7, 15, 16, 17, 26, 27
Best Days for Money: 6, 7, 8, 9, 15, 16, 17, 26, 27
Best Days for Career: 6, 7, 14, 15, 23, 24

The planetary shift that we discussed last month becomes very dramatic this month. By the end of the month, 80 to 90 per cent of the planets will be in the upper half of your chart. Day is dawning in your year. Time to use all the energy you acquired during the night for productive purposes. Career is becoming the main focus now for the rest of the year ahead. Push forward boldly towards your goals. You can safely let family issues slide (especially after the 16th) and focus on your career.

The main headline this month is love and social life. Your 7th House of Love and Marriage is where the planetary action is. But it is a kind of bittersweet experience. Singles are meeting new people; there is much going out; but Saturn's move into the 7th House on the 29th initiates a period where your new relationships will get tested. From the cosmic point of view it is not enough just to meet new friends and love partners: they need to be found worthy. Until the 15th restrain your tendencies to carp, criticize and nit-pick. Sure, you are entitled to perfect love, but criticism – especially of the destructive kind – will not bring it to you. Try to focus on quality relationships rather than on the mediocre ones.

An office romance is developing.

Saturn, your career planet, makes a major move from Virgo into Libra at the end of the month. This shows career changes, and a different attitude to your career. For two and a half years you succeeded the hard way, through hard work and sheer merit. There was nothing wrong with this, but now you need to develop your social skills too. It is not enough that you are good at your job – people need to like you. Those of you who are in managerial positions will advance more on the 'likeability' factor than on the merit factor. This transit also shows that you can advance your career by social means – by attending and hosting the right parties and making the right friends.

Health is more delicate now and you need to pay more attention here for the rest of the year (and for the next two years). Pay special attention until the 23rd. Enhance your health by paying more attention to the intestines (and the diet) until the 10th, and to the kidneys and hips after this date. Disharmonies in love can affect the physical health now, so work to keep the harmony in your marriage and with your friends.

Retrograde activity is lessening dramatically this month. By the 18th, 80 per cent of the planets will be moving forward. The pace of life and change accelerates.

November

> Best Days Overall: 1, 8, 9, 17, 18, 27, 28
> Most Stressful Days Overall: 6, 7, 13, 14, 20, 21
> Best Days for Love: 4, 5, 13, 14, 15, 16, 25, 26
> Best Days for Money: 2, 3, 4, 5, 13, 14, 15, 16, 22, 23, 25, 26, 29, 30
> Best Days for Career: 4, 13, 20, 21, 22

The forward momentum of the planets increases even more this month. When Neptune starts moving forward on the 4th, 90 per cent of the planets will be moving forward. You should see quick progress towards your goals. You also have greater confidence in most areas of your life.

Love is romantic and idealistic until the 8th. But afterwards it is less about romance and more about sexual attraction –

physical chemistry. For those of you of appropriate age this is a sexually active kind of month. (Even older Aries will have more libido than usual.) There is still an office type of romance happening for you. (The opportunity is there for sure.)

In love you seem to be different people all occupying the same body these days. One part of you is romantic and idealistic and wants only 'the feeling of love'. Another part of you only cares about the physical chemistry. And still another part of you seems of a 'practical bent' – the good provider, the person who can advance your career, the power person: this is what allures. If you can find all these qualities in one person, you have the ideal now.

With your 8th House very powerful this month, the period is good for detox regimes, both physical and emotional. It is a time where you have more power to reinvent yourself – to give birth to the person you want to be. It is a very good time now to make an inventory of your possessions and get rid of what you don't need. It is a time to clean house – physically, emotionally and materially.

Your spouse or partner is prospering this month and will be more generous with you. In general (especially after the 8th) this is a time to prosper by prospering other people, by putting their financial interests ahead of your own. As you succeed at this your own prosperity will happen very naturally. This is also a good month to access outside sources of capital, either through borrowing or through attracting investors or backers. The credit line should increase now.

Health improves after the 22nd but still needs watching. Enhance your health by giving more attention to the heart (all month) the colon, bladder and sexual organs (until the 16th) and the liver and thighs (after the 16th). Safe sex (and sexual moderation) is important until the 16th. Regular thigh massage is good after the 16th.

December

The forward momentum of the planets is even stronger than last month. Until the 20th ALL the planets are moving forward (highly unusual); even afterwards, the percentage is still high – 90 per cent moving forward. So the pace of life is quick and progress is rapid. For you the only challenge is deciding on what you really want. The Retrograde of Mars (from the 20th onwards) is stronger on you than on most people – it is the Lord of your Horoscope. You seem directionless on a personal level, but success is still happening. On the 21st the Sun enters your 10th House initiating a yearly career peak. Many other beneficial planets are crossing your Midheaven as well – Mercury on the 5th and Venus on the 25th. There are pay rises and promotions in store. This can be with your present company or with another. You are in demand now.

Push forward boldly towards your career goals – reach for the stars now. Let family and emotional issues go for a while. Career opportunities are coming in many ways now – through friends in right places, through attending the right parties, and through good sales, marketing and promotion. (Of course old-fashioned hard work is also part of the equation, but it's not the total picture.)

Health needs more attention all month, but especially after the 21st. Rest and relax more, this is the main thing. Don't allow yourself to get overtired. Enhance your health by giving more attention to the liver and thighs (until the 5th) and to the spine, knees, teeth, bones and skeletal alignment afterwards. If you feel under the weather a visit to a chiropractor or osteopath might be a good idea. Give the knees more support when exercising.

You are not only advancing career-wise this month, but we also see much spiritual growth. Jupiter and Neptune (two spiritual planets in their own right) will be conjunct most of the month. This shows inner revelation, spiritual and religious breakthroughs, an active dream life and supernatural-type experiences.

Love is happy this month – especially later on in the month. Venus (your love planet) and Saturn (your career planet) are in mutual reception (each is a guest in the other's Sign and House – a very positive aspect). Again this shows an office romance. Your career and love life blend together very well. You tend to socialize with people of high status and prestige – those above you in status. You find love as you pursue career goals, and the reverse is also true. Career opportunities can happen at parties or as you pursue your social goals. For marrieds this shows your spouse's co-operation with your career and also your spouse's career success.

Taurus

♉

THE BULL
*Birthdays from
21st April to
20th May*

Personality Profile

TAURUS AT A GLANCE

Element – Earth

Ruling Planet – Venus
   Career Planet – Uranus
   Love Planet – Pluto
   Money Planet – Mercury
   Planet of Health and Work – Venus
   Planet of Home and Family Life – Sun
   Planet of Spirituality – Mars
   *Planet of Travel, Education, Religion and
      Philosophy* – Saturn

Colours – earth tones, green, orange, yellow

*Colours that promote love, romance and social
   harmony* – red–violet, violet

Colours that promote earning power – yellow,
   yellow–orange

Gems – coral, emerald

Metal – copper

Scents – bitter almond, rose, vanilla, violet

Quality – fixed (= stability)

Quality most needed for balance – flexibility

Strongest virtues – endurance, loyalty, patience, stability, a harmonious disposition

Deepest needs – comfort, material ease, wealth

Characteristics to avoid – rigidity, stubbornness, tendency to be overly possessive and materialistic

Signs of greatest overall compatibility – Virgo, Capricorn

Signs of greatest overall incompatibility – Leo, Scorpio, Aquarius

Sign most helpful to career – Aquarius

Sign most helpful for emotional support – Leo

Sign most helpful financially – Gemini

Sign best for marriage and/or partnerships – Scorpio

Sign most helpful for creative projects – Virgo

Best Sign to have fun with – Virgo

Signs most helpful in spiritual matters – Aries, Capricorn

Best day of the week – Friday

Understanding a Taurus

Taurus is the most earthy of all the Earth Signs. If you understand that Earth is more than just a physical element, that it is a psychological attitude as well, you will get a better understanding of the Taurus personality.

A Taurus has all the power of action that an Aries has. But Taurus is not satisfied with action for its own sake. Their actions must be productive, practical and wealth-producing. If Taurus cannot see a practical value in an action they will not bother taking it.

Taurus' forte lies in their power to make real their own or other people's ideas. They are generally not very inventive but they can take another's invention and perfect it, making it more practical and useful. The same is true for all projects. Taurus is not especially keen on starting new projects, but once they get involved they bring things to completion. Taurus carries everything through. They're finishers and will go the distance so long as no unavoidable calamity intervenes.

Many people find Taurus too stubborn, conservative, fixed and immovable. This is understandable, because Taurus dislikes change – in the environment or in the routine. They even dislike changing their minds! On the other hand, this is their virtue. It is not good for a wheel's axle to waver. The axle must be fixed, stable and unmovable. Taurus is the axle of society and the heavens. Without their stability and so-called stubbornness, the wheels of the world (and especially the wheels of commerce) would not turn.

Taurus loves routine. A routine, if it is good, has many virtues. It is a fixed – and, ideally, perfect – way of taking care of things. Mistakes can happen when spontaneity comes into the equation, and mistakes cause discomfort and uneasiness – something almost unacceptable to a Taurus. Meddling with Taurus' comfort and security is a sure way to irritate and anger them.

While an Aries loves speed, a Taurus likes things slow. They are slow thinkers – but do not make the mistake of assuming they lack intelligence. On the contrary, Taurus people are very intelligent. It is just that they like to chew on ideas, to deliberate and weigh them up. Only after due deliberation is an idea accepted or a decision taken. Taurus is slow to anger – but once aroused, take care!

Finance

Taurus is very money-conscious. Wealth is more important to them than to many other Signs. Wealth to a Taurus means comfort and security. Wealth means stability. Where some Zodiac Signs feel that they are spiritually rich if they have ideas, talents or skills, Taurus only feels wealth when they can see and touch it. Taurus' way of thinking is, 'What good is a talent if it has not been translated into a home, furniture, car and holidays?'

These are all reasons why Taurus excels in estate agency and agricultural industries. Usually a Taurus will end up owning land. They love to feel their connection to the Earth. Material wealth began with agriculture, the tilling of the soil. Owning a piece of land was humanity's earliest form of wealth: Taurus still feels that primeval connection.

It is in the pursuit of wealth that Taurus develops intellectual and communication ability. Also, in this pursuit Taurus is forced to develop some flexibility. It is in the quest for wealth that they learn the practical value of the intellect and come to admire it. If it were not for the search for wealth and material things, Taurus people might not try to reach a higher intellect.

Some Taurus people are 'born lucky' – the type who win any gamble or speculation. This luck is due to other factors in their Horoscope; it is not part of their essential nature. By nature they are not gamblers. They are hard workers and like to earn what they get. Taurus' innate conservatism makes them abhor unnecessary risks in finance and in other areas of their lives.

Career and Public Image

Being essentially down-to-earth people, simple and uncomplicated, Taurus tends to look up to those who are original, unconventional and inventive. Taurus likes their bosses to be creative and original – since they themselves are content to perfect their superiors' brain-waves. They admire people who have a wider social or political consciousness and they feel that someday (when they have all the comfort and security they need) they too would like to be involved in these big issues.

In business affairs Taurus can be very shrewd – and that makes them valuable to their employers. They are never lazy; they enjoy working and getting good results. Taurus does not like taking unnecessary risks and they do well in positions of authority, which makes them good managers and supervisors. Their managerial skills are reinforced by their natural talents for organization and handling details, their patience and thoroughness. As mentioned, through their connection with the earth, Taurus people also do well in farming and agriculture.

In general a Taurus will choose money and earning power over public esteem and prestige. A position that pays more – though it has less prestige – is preferred to a position with a lot of prestige but lower earnings. Many other Signs do not feel this way, but a Taurus does, especially if there is nothing in his or her personal birth chart that modifies this. Taurus will pursue glory and prestige only if it can be shown that these things have a direct and immediate impact on their wallet.

Love and Relationships

In love, the Taurus-born likes to have and to hold. They are the marrying kind. They like commitment and they like the terms of a relationship to be clearly defined. More importantly, Taurus likes to be faithful to one lover, and they expect that lover to reciprocate this fidelity. When this doesn't happen, their whole world comes crashing down. When they are in love Taurus people are loyal, but they are also very possessive. They are capable of great fits of jealousy if they are hurt in love.

Taurus is satisfied with the simple things in a relationship. If you are involved romantically with a Taurus there is no need for lavish entertainments and constant courtship. Give them enough love, food and comfortable shelter and they will be quite content to stay home and enjoy your company. They will be loyal to you for life. Make a Taurus feel comfortable and – above all – secure in the relationship, and you will rarely have a problem.

In love, Taurus can sometimes make the mistake of trying to control their partners, which can cause great pain on both sides. The reasoning behind their actions is basically simple: Taurus people feel a sense of ownership over their partners and will want to make changes that will increase their own general comfort and security. This attitude is OK when it comes to inanimate, material things – but is dangerous when applied to people. Taurus needs to be careful and attentive to this possible trait within themselves.

Home and Domestic Life

Home and family are vitally important to Taurus. They like children. They also like a comfortable and perhaps glamorous home – something they can show off. They tend to buy heavy, ponderous furniture – usually of the best quality. This is because Taurus likes a feeling of substance in their environment. Their house is not only their home but their place of creativity and entertainment. The Taurus home tends to be truly their castle. If they could choose, Taurus people would prefer living in the countryside to being city-dwellers. If they cannot do so during their working lives, many Taurus individuals like to holiday in or even retire to the country, away from the city and closer to the land.

At home a Taurus is like a country squire – lord (or lady) of the manor. They love to entertain lavishly, to make others feel secure in their home and to encourage others to derive the same sense of satisfaction as they do from it. If you are invited for dinner at the home of a Taurus you can expect the best food and best entertainment. Be prepared for a tour of the house and expect to see your Taurus friend exhibit a lot of pride and satisfaction in his or her possessions.

Taurus likes children but they are usually strict with them. The reason for this is they tend to treat their children – as they do most things in life – as their possessions. The positive side to this is that their children will be well cared for and well supervised. They will get every material thing they need to grow up properly. On the down side, Taurus can get too repressive with their children. If a child dares to upset the daily routine – which Taurus loves to follow – he or she will have a problem with a Taurus parent.

Horoscope for 2009

Major Trends

Last year was a party year – a year for exploring the joys of life, for leisure activities and sports. This trend continues for a little while but is basically weakening.

Instead, 2009 is a career year; a lifetime (for many of you) career peak; a year for promotions, raises, honours and public recognition. Career success rarely comes without taking on more responsibility, so you will be working more and playing less. Until October 29 you are trying to do both but from then on it will be work, work, work – work and success.

As with Aries we see (but in a different language) a detox and transformation happening in the career (and also with parents and parent figures). More on this later.

Health was good last year and the trend continues in the year ahead. The main headline in 2009 is Saturn's move into your 6th House of Health. This shows a greater focus on health and a need for steady, disciplined, health regimes.

The love attitudes underwent dramatic change last year as your love planet, Pluto, moved in and out of Capricorn. This year, these changes will be more established. Love will become more practical and down to earth. You will be more conservative in love matters. You will be more cautious and do more homework.

Finances were status quo last year (which I read as a good thing) and the trend continues in 2009.

Your path of greatest fulfilment this year is the career. Keep your focus here and push for the heights.

Your most important areas of interest this year are children, creativity and exploring the joy of life (until October 29); health and work (after October 29); religion, philosophy, metaphysics, higher education and foreign travel (for many years to come); career and the parents; friendships and group activities.

Health

(Please note that this is an astrological perspective on health and not a medical one. In days of yore there was no difference, both of these perspectives were identical. But in these times there could be quite a difference. For the medical perspective, please consult your doctor or health professional.)

As we mentioned, health was good last year and should stay good in the coming year. Most of the long-term planets are kind to you. Vitality and energy seem good.

The main change that is happening is Saturn's move into your 6th House of Health on October 29. This is a major transit. Saturn will stay there for the next two and a half years. His move into your 6th House is basically a good thing. As we mentioned, he will tend to make you more serious about health, tend to make it easier to take on disciplined health regimes, and make you take a long-term perspective on health – you are not looking for a quick fix, but for a long-term cure. In general Saturn tends to make people more conservative when it comes to health. Thus in many cases you will feel more comfortable with orthodox medicine. But even for those of you who don't believe in orthodox medicine, you will seek out the more traditional therapies in the alternative field, therapies that have stood the test of time and that have been well researched. You are not into experimenting with your health for the next few years.

Saturn's move into your House of Health also shows that you can improve your already good health by giving more attention to the spine, knees, teeth, bones, gall bladder and overall skeletal alignment. There are many natural and drugless ways to do this. There are yoga postures that are excellent for the spine. Regular back massage is good. Foot and hand reflexology is wonderful – see our chart later on. Seeing a chiropractor on a regular basis might be a very good idea – it is very important that the vertebrae be kept in alignment. If you are involved in vigorous exercise, give the

Reflexology

Try to massage the whole foot on a regular basis, but pay extra attention to the points highlighted on the chart. When you massage, be aware of 'sore spots', as these need special attention. It's also a good idea to massage the ankles and top side (as well as the soles) of the feet.

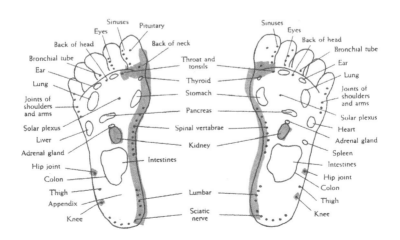

knees more support. The Alexander Technique is an excellent therapy for keeping the posture right, and it helps the spine. There are many other therapies not mentioned here, but which are excellent.

With Venus as your health planet, giving more attention to the kidneys and hips will also enhance your health. Regular massage of the hips is good.

Venus is a fast-moving planet. Every month she will be in a different Sign and House (usually). Thus there are many therapies that are effective for the short term. And these issues are best dealt with in the monthly reports.

Our regular readers already understand that disease might wind up in the physical body but never begins there. Always it has its origins in other areas, other more subtle bodies and realms of the mind. The beauty of the Horoscope is that it shows us where these spiritual root causes of disease tend to be and thus we can address them. In your case (should problems arise) there is a need to examine your love life (Venus), your self-esteem (Venus, the Ruler of your Horoscope) and your use of power and authority (Saturn). If you can bring these areas back into harmony, correcting the mistakes, the chances are that your health problem will dissolve of its own weight. And even if the services of a health professional are needed, the healing will go much faster and quicker.

Your health planet will make one of her rare Retrogrades this year from March 6 to April 17. This is a period for a review of your health and health regimes to see where improvements can be made. It is not a period for making drastic changes in the diet or important health decisions.

Home and Family

Your 4th House of Home and Family is not a House of Power this year, Taurus. Thus you seem satisfied with the status quo and have no need or burning desire to make major changes here. You can if you want to – you have more freedom here than usual – but you don't seem to have the desire.

Your 4th House will become more important later on in the year as Mars spends an unusual amount of time there (from October 16 well into 2010). This augers some major renovations at home – heavy construction work. In some cases it will be just renovation, but in other cases, it shows the actual construction of a home. During this period it would be wise to improve the safety of the home. It is good to have working smoke detectors, burglar alarms and things of that nature. There is a tendency to accidents in the home with this transit, so in general be more careful. If there are young children at home, keep things like matches or other flammable items away from them.

On February 9th there is a Solar Eclipse in your 4th House. Every Solar Eclipse tends to affect the home and family – this is because the Sun is your family planet – but this one will be even stronger as it is occurring in the 4th House as well. Thus the home will get tested. If there are hidden flaws there, they will be revealed so that you can make corrections. The same applies to the family relationship. Hidden flaws, things beneath the surface, are exposed, so that you can correct them. Emotions in the family tend to run high under this aspect. They are more temperamental than usual. So be patient and keep calm. These transits can be likened to being on a drug – people behave differently under the influence of certain drugs; so too under certain transits. When the drug (or transit) passes their behaviour normalizes. Understanding these things is a big help.

A parent or parent figure is prospering this year and next – he or she is now in a cycle of prosperity – thus they can move. Whether or not they actually move, they will be travelling more this year and the effect will be like a move.

When Mars moves into Leo on October 16, the marriage (or business partnerships) of the parents or parent figures will get a severe testing. The problem is a power struggle. If the relationship is fundamentally sound it can survive and actually get better, but not right away.

Siblings (or people who are like siblings to you) are feeling cramped at home (especially after October 29) but a move seems unlikely – many delays and obstructions involved there. They are better off making better use of the space they have, re-organizing the home in a more efficient way.

Business partners are moving this year and otherwise investing and prospering from the home. The spouse or current love would probably like to move, but it takes two to tango, and it is not likely this year.

Children of appropriate age are having a status quo home and family year. They might continually upgrade the home or install high-tech kinds of gadgetry, but an actual move is not likely.

If you plan to make heavy renovations in the home – or to embark on major construction work – after October 16 seems best. If you merely want to beautify the home on a cosmetic level, July 22 to September 20 seems best.

Finance and Career

Your 2nd House of Finance is not a House of Power this year, Taurus, and I read this as a good thing. You seem satisfied with finances and have no need to make major changes. You have more freedom in this department in the year ahead as the cosmos neither pushes you one way nor another.

Of course, there will be periods in the year ahead where finances DO become very important – from April 19 to May 20 and from May 31 to July 12. You will be focusing more on finance in those periods and they will tend to be your yearly financial peaks. But in general, finance doesn't seem a big issue in the year ahead.

This is probably the major financial headline this year – that money *per se* is not that important. For a Taurus this is saying something! (I have seen this tendency for the past few years, and perhaps many of you are scratching your heads about this.) However, if you were prosperous last year, you will be prosperous in the year ahead.

Really, this year is about career, about public recognition, about attaining to status and prestige in your chosen profession and industry. And it is very good. Many of you are in lifetime career peaks this year. Those of you who work for others will have pay rises and promotions. Those of you who are not yet in the workforce are making important and positive career choices and decisions now. Those of you who are retired and no longer in a career will be honoured (in various ways) for your past achievements and perhaps be receiving interesting career opportunities. All of you, whatever your stage, will have happy career opportunities coming to you.

Jupiter moving across the Midheaven of the Horoscope is a classic signal of success. But the success will be proportional to your stage and position in life. The secretary or entry level person is unlikely to become president of the company, but will rise according to his or her level. The Vice-President or high executive is likely to become President or CEO of the company.

Often with this aspect we find people getting involved (appointed or elected to) positions in government, local or national. There is more involvement in public affairs these days.

Taurus people (in general) are not especially status conscious (your personal Horoscope cast just for you could modify what I'm saying here). You tend to be 'bottom line' oriented – show me the cash and you can have the glory. But this year, you are seeing that there is more to life and to a career than just money. Public and professional respect and esteem is very important and you are learning about this now. Also public esteem does eventually increase the bottom line – perhaps not right away, but in due course – and for this reason alone should be given more attention.

Go forward fearlessly towards your career goals this year. Take the leap into the unknown; underneath are the everlasting arms. And, you might discover that you don't need the arms but can soar. Victory, victory, victory is your mantra this year.

Mercury is your financial planet. This year he will be Retrograde four times! (Usually it is only three.) Thus this is a year where you need to do more financial homework and be more patient, especially during those periods when Mercury is Retrograde. We will deal with this more fully in the monthly reports.

Our regular readers know that Mercury rules communication, sales, marketing, teaching, writing and journalism. Whatever your business, communication and good marketing is very important. Professional investors should look at telecommunications, media and transportation for profit ideas.

Love and Social Life

Your 7th House of Love is not a House of Power this year, and I read this as something good – your marriage or partnership and social life is pretty much where you want it to be and you have no need to make drastic changes. It is a status quo kind of year. Marrieds will tend to stay married and singles will tend to stay single.

By the way, status quo for a Taurus is great bliss – they are very conservative types of people. So the love life is happy now.

The real excitement this year (and this has been so for a number of years) is in the area of friendships. New and exciting friends are coming into the picture suddenly and unexpectedly. These people are not 'run of the mill' types, but are highly creative, spiritual and genius-type people. Glamour people as well. The only problem is that your friendships are unstable. They can come suddenly and end suddenly. You don't know who is going to be your friend, when, and so it is difficult to make long-term social plans. For a Taurus this kind of instability is difficult to handle, but this is the spiritual lesson of these past few years. You need to be comfortable and centred regardless of the social change going on all around you. You don't own your friends, and possessiveness will only create pain. Sit loose and enjoy the change.

There are dramatic events in the lives of your friends as well and this adds to the instability. Many of your friends are involved in spirituality, going deeper into it, and this is also

creating much change. (If they are not involved in spirituality then there is probably excessive drug or alcohol use going
on and this too will lead to dramatic events in their lives.)

Your love planet recently made an important and long-
term move. Pluto moved from the Sign of Sagittarius (where
he was for over 15 years) into Capricorn. Last year he was
just flirting with the Sign of Capricorn; this year he is in
there for good. Existing marriages don't seem too much
affected, but singles are certainly becoming more conservative and traditional in love. They will gravitate to older,
more established kinds of people. They will tend to have a
very pragmatic approach to love, seeing it as another career
move – a job – rather than moonlight and fireworks. The
good provider is more alluring than the beefy hunk.

With your love planet now in your 3rd House of
Communication and Intellectual Interests for years to come,
there is another dimension to love than just the physical and
the financial. There needs to be intellectual and mental
compatibility. You need to fall in love with the other
person's thought process as much as with the body and
social position. Good communication is perhaps just as
important as financial support and sexual compatibility. You
are in a period where communication means love: if you
talk to me, you love me. If you don't talk to me you don't
love me.

If there are problems in the current relationship, the
Horoscope is showing us how they can be cleared up: focus
on better communication. Take courses together as a couple.
Read the same books and discuss them. Cultivate the intellectual side of the relationship.

Those working on their second marriage have excellent
prospects this year. Those working on their third are better
off staying single, dating and enjoying their freedom.
Marriage and love opportunities are there, but there is great
instability. Those in or working on the fourth marriage have
a status quo kind of year.

Siblings are having their marriages or current relationships tested. There are near-death experiences in love. The

love life is getting detoxed and it is not pleasant while it is happening. The end result, though, is good.

Parents or parent figures who are single will have very good marriage opportunities this year; it is also a good year for business partnerships. Children of marriageable age are better off staying single for a while. If they are married their marriages are being severely tested (and this has been going on for some years now).

Self-improvement

Saturn has been in your 5th House of Children, Creativity and Fun for the past few years. Thus, one of the lessons was learning how to discipline children in positive and constructive ways, setting firm but fair limits. Not disciplining them, not setting boundaries, will mean that you will pay the price for it later on, in 20 or 30 years' time. This lesson continues in the year ahead; it is difficult but it must be done. There needs to be just the right balance between justice and mercy. And discipline should never be administered in anger.

The other lesson you've been learning is how to enjoy life in positive, constructive ways, without abandoning your lawful and legitimate responsibilities. This lesson is still going on for much of the year ahead.

In October (the 29th) Saturn will move into your 6th House of Health and Work. And the cosmos is going to reorganize this whole area. You will learn how to deal with employees in a better way, to be just and fair with them, have their obedience, and otherwise manage them properly. This is also a period of hard work, as we mentioned. You are being promoted and elevated and hard work, more responsibility, is the price for it.

This is also a period where you change your health attitudes. It is time to abandon the quick fix, the short-term solution, and focus on therapies that actually cure – long term.

Since Saturn is also your religious and philosophical planet, it shows a need to re-organize your whole philosophy of health and healing. This is more important than most people realize, for this will determine what makes us sick and what cures us.

The message here is that you will benefit more from metaphysical types of therapy – prayer and speaking of the word. There is a need for philosophical purity in coming years, as the Horoscope is telling us that philosophical or religious errors are likely to be the root causes of physical health problems. Your health looks good this year, but if there are persistent problems, it will be good to examine this area of life. You should also examine your relationships with co-workers or employees.

Your spiritual mission this year (as it has been for many years) is to be there for your friends and to support and enhance various groups and organizations that you are involved in.

Month-by-month Forecasts

January

> Best Days Overall: 6, 14, 15, 23, 24
> Most Stressful Days Overall: 12, 18, 19, 26, 27
> Best Days for Love: 5, 9, 10, 13, 18, 19, 23, 28, 29
> Best Days for Money: 7, 8, 16, 17, 23, 24, 25, 26
> Best Days for Career: 1, 2, 10, 11, 18, 19, 26, 27, 28, 29

A Solar Eclipse on the 26th is announcing very positive and happy career changes for you. Yes, there are probably disruptions or shocking events (probably at work, your company's hierarchy or in your industry) but for you all these events are merely doors opening. Barriers to your success are being blown to smithereens. Career is really the main headline of the month ahead, and the coming year. On the 5th Jupiter crosses your Midheaven bringing very happy career opportunities – honours, pay rises, promotions, recognition and a general elevation. On the 19th the Sun crosses the Midheaven bringing more of the same, perhaps just elaborating on what Jupiter began earlier. Between 50 and 60 per cent of the planets are either in, or passing through, your 10th House of Career this month. You can't ask for better career aspects right now. Go for gold.

In general you are in the day period of your year: 80 to 90 per cent of the planets are above the horizon. Your 10th House is very powerful all month, while your 4th House of Home and Family is empty (only the Moon visits there on the 12th and 13th). So, you can safely de-emphasize family and emotional issues and focus on your career. Happily even the family seems supportive of career goals now, so your focus shouldn't bring much of a conflict. Family members also seem successful this month. The family as a whole is elevated. You seem to be investing in the home – some expensive types of items or renovating – from the 23rd to the 26th. Family members have financial windfalls then too.

Aside from your career there is a great interest in travel, higher education, religion and philosophy. There are happy travel and educational opportunities, especially until the 19th. College students are successful and happy at their studies.

Love is pretty much status quo this month. There is a happy love opportunity from the 4th to the 6th but it seems short lived. For marrieds or those in relationships this can bring a happy social invitation or social experience.

Health is basically good these days, but after the 19th you probably need to pace yourself better. The demands of your career are very strong and you might need to let lesser things go. You can't be everywhere and do everything. Focus on what is important.

Finances are positive. Elders and bosses – and your generally good professional reputation – are contributing to earnings. Money is always high on your list of priorities but especially this month. Mercury (your financial planet) is Retrograde, which suggests more caution and homework from the 11th to the 31st.

February

Best Days Overall: 2, 3, 10, 11, 19, 20, 21
Most Stressful Days Overall: 8, 9, 15, 16, 22, 23
Best Days for Love: 2, 8, 9, 10, 15, 16, 17, 18, 19, 27, 28
Best Days for Money: 2, 3, 4, 5, 10, 11, 12, 13, 22, 23
Best Days for Career: 6, 7, 15, 16, 22, 23, 24, 25, 26

A Lunar Eclipse on the 9th is one of the major headlines of the coming month. It is strong on you so take a reduced schedule. Do what you must do, but re-schedule elective things. Try to spend more quiet time at home during the eclipse period (a few days before and after). This eclipse occurs in your 4th House and thus impacts on the home and family. Family members can have dramatic experiences in their lives – out of the ordinary. Emotions run high at home. Perhaps your career focus is creating undue stress at home, which you will need to address. Siblings have dramatic kinds of experiences. Cars and communication equipment get tested. (If they survive this eclipse period, they will probably survive further, until their natural life-span is complete.)

You are still right in the midst of both a yearly and life-time career peak. Your 10th House of Career is still strong all month, while your 4th House of Home and Family is empty (only the Moon visits there on the 8th and 9th). So continue with your career focus and let family issues slide (the eclipse won't let you completely ignore this area, but you can keep your major focus on your career.)

Health needs more watching until the 18th. Keep energy levels high. Avoid burning the candle at both ends. Foot massage is very powerful and beneficial until the 3rd (it was especially good last month as well). After the 3rd, scalp and facial massage is powerful. The scalp contains reflexes to the entire body and so you are reviving the whole body when you do this. Cranial sacral therapy is also beneficial this month. This month, you see good health as being 'physically fit' and so vigorous physical exercise will be good too.

Finances are good this month and now that Mercury is moving forwards, your financial judgement is more astute as well. Until the 14th, financial opportunities come from foreigners or foreign kinds of investments. Your financial goals are bigger and so you attain more. After the 14th earnings come from pay rises, parent figures, the government and your good professional reputation. Your good reputation leads to referrals and the like. In general, the authority figures in your life are co-operating with your financial goals and supplying funds directly or supplying opportunities. Professional investors should look at the high-tech field for profit opportunities. There is a nice windfall on the 23rd or 24th. If you are involved in tax, estate or debt issues, this period is fortunate.

There are nice love opportunities from the 18th to the 21st and these can come from family connections or from close to home. Those already in a relationship have a harmonious month. (A short-term spat early in the month is just that – short term. Harmony returns after that.)

March

Best Days Overall: 1, 2, 10, 19, 20, 28, 29
Most Stressful Days Overall: 7, 8, 14, 15, 21, 22, 23
Best Days for Love: 1, 7, 8, 9, 14, 15, 16, 17, 18, 19, 26, 27, 28
Best Days for Money: 3, 4, 12, 13, 14, 15, 21, 22, 23, 25, 26, 30, 31
Best Days for Career: 5, 6, 14, 15, 21, 22, 23, 24, 25

Career is still going great guns. You are working hard, achieving and succeeding. You are very motivated here and this is 90 per cent of success. There is more competition for your position or within your company but you seem up to the task. The disclosure of hidden information is forcing you to work harder (this was so last month as well). There could have been some scandals in your corporate hierarchy too.

Your challenge this month is to somehow balance your busy and dynamic career with a social life – especially friendships – and with your spiritual and charitable interests. Spirituality becomes very important after the 20th. The spirit of altruism which this brings is often at odds with the values of worldly success and this creates conflict. However, you can heal the conflict by getting more involved in charitable and voluntary kinds of activities.

Health is much improved over last month and will get even better after the 15th as Mars moves away from his stressful aspect with you. You can enhance your good health even further by giving more attention (like last month) to the head and face. Keep the head warm if you live in a cold climate. Regular face and scalp massage will do wonders. Maintain your regime of physical exercise.

Love, though not perfect, is basically harmonious in the month ahead. A spat between the beloved and a family member from the 20th to the 23rd complicates things, but it is short term. Marriages seem status quo this month, likewise other kinds of long-term relationships. Serious love opportunities are still in foreign lands or at educational or religious settings. Singles have opportunities for love affairs as they pursue their career goals (until the 8th), through friends and organizations, group activities (from the 8th to the 25th) and in spiritual-type settings (after the 25th).

Your financial planet moves very speedily this month and this shows great financial confidence, quick decisions (and probably good ones) and a sense that you cover a lot of ground financially. You are making quick progress. Until the 8th earnings and financial opportunities still come from your career, good professional reputation, the favour of elders and parent figures and authorities in your life. After the 8th earnings come through friends and through involvement with professional or trade organizations (perhaps charitable organizations as well). Financial intuition is important after the 25th (it is always important, but now more so).

April

Best Days Overall: 6, 7, 15, 16, 25, 26
Most Stressful Days Overall: 4, 5, 10, 11, 18, 19, 25, 26
Best Days for Love: 4, 6, 10, 11, 15, 20, 21, 25
Best Days for Money: 4, 5, 8, 9, 15, 16, 18, 19, 25, 26, 27, 28
Best Days for Career: 2, 3, 10, 11, 18, 19, 20, 21, 29, 30

Saturn has been the handle of a 'bucket-type' chart for some months now and is still so this month. This shows that regardless of your success and many interests, it is your faith, your religion, your positive world view that helps you lift up your life.

Last month Venus, your personal planet, the Ruler of your Horoscope, went Retrograde. And although this didn't stop your career success or social life, it left you with a feeling of being directionless – you were not quite sure what you really wanted. You have tasted career success and are probably asking yourself, 'Is that all there is?' It is good for you to be thinking like this, reviewing your goals – especially your personal ones – re-evaluating and seeing where you can make improvements. The timing for this Retrograde couldn't be better. For by the time Venus starts to move forward on the 17th, you will be clearer on your goals, and when the Sun moves into your sign on the 19th you will be ready to leap into action.

Keep in mind that most of the planets now (and it's been this way for the past few months) are in the Eastern, personal sector of your chart. They are reaching the maximum point very shortly. You have the power to create conditions as you desire them to be with minimum outside interference. If you do your personal homework and review during Venus's Retrograde, your creation will be much better and happier.

Though you still have many interests this month – career, friendships, group activities and organizations – the main headline this month is spirituality. Your 12th House is chock full of planets: 50 per cent of the planets are either there or moving through there in the month ahead. So this is a month for making spiritual progress, for spiritual break-throughs and revelations. Your innate spiritual gifts are very much increased. You will have more supernatural-type experiences (though some of you might regard them as 'coincidence'). Your dream life will be more active and you will be more open to spiritual teachings. This is a great period to go on that spiritual retreat or pilgrimage to a holy place; it is also good for getting involved in charities and altruistic kinds of activities. As you follow the call of your spirit you will find (especially until the 9th) that all your financial needs are taken care of as well. Generally people feel that spirituality is impractical and that they need to focus on practical issues in life. But this month you will discover that this is not so. It is eminently practical and has prepared for all of your needs.

Love is more complicated this month. Both Venus and your love planet, Pluto, are Retrograde (Pluto begins to Retrograde on the 4th). So you are in a period for reviewing your marriage, love relationship or friendships and seeing where you can make improvements. Avoid making any major love decision (one way or another) right now. Gain clarity and perspective now.

May

> Best Days Overall: 3, 4, 12, 13, 14, 22, 23, 30, 31
> Most Stressful Days Overall: 1, 2, 8, 9, 15, 16, 28, 29
> Best Days for Love: 1, 2, 3, 8, 9, 10, 11, 12, 20, 21, 22, 28, 29, 30
> Best Days for Money: 5, 6, 13, 14, 15, 16, 22, 23, 24, 25
> Best Days for Career: 8, 9, 15, 16, 18, 19, 26, 27

Last month, on the 19th, you entered a yearly personal plea-sure peak – a time for taking care of the body, giving it its due, and for enjoying all the pleasures of the body. This personal pleasure peak is still in full swing. On the 20th, you will enter a yearly financial peak too, so you are in a prosperous period as well. Sounds like Taurus heaven – plenty of money and plenty of sensual delights. Enjoy!

The main interests this month are career (which is wonderful all year, but will get even better after the 20th); the body, the image and personal pleasure; finance (especially after the 20th); and spirituality.

Like last month this is still a great time for going on spiritual retreats, meditation seminars, spiritual lectures or religious-type pilgrimages. And it's also good for getting involved in charitable and altruistic kinds of activities. You are successful and prosperous these days and it is good 'to give back' to the source. Spiritual-type exercises are also good, things like yoga or tai chi.

A spat with the beloved early in the month doesn't interfere much with the overall love life. It passes quickly. Your beloved seems into standard religion, while you are more into spirituality and mystical kinds of experience, but you need not fight about this – both approaches are valid.

Health is good this month. You can enhance it further by giving more attention to the head and face (like last month). Scalp and face massage is excellent. So is cranial sacral therapy.

Your travel planet, Saturn, starts to move forward on the 17th and also receives very wonderful aspects, thus there are travel and educational opportunities happening. Students are doing well in school too.

Finances are good, but keep in mind that Mercury is going Retrograde from the 7th to the 31st of this month and this complicates a basically beautiful financial period. Earnings will continue, wealth will be increased, but there are probably little glitches and delays. As always, do more homework in your financial life – in your decision making – during the Retrograde period. There are happy financial opportunities in real estate, from the family and family connections, restaurants, hotels and the food business. Your spouse or current love is prospering after the 20th and seems generous with you.

June

Best Days Overall: 9, 10, 19, 27, 28
Most Stressful Days Overall: 4, 5, 11, 12, 13, 25
Best Days for Love: 4, 5, 9, 18, 19, 26, 27, 28
Best Days for Money: 2, 3, 9, 10, 11, 12, 13, 21, 22, 29, 30
Best Days for Career: 4, 5, 11, 12, 14, 15, 23

Though the Sun has left your 1st House you are still very much in a personal pleasure peak: Mars moves into your 1st House on the 1st and Venus, your ruling planet, moves in on the 6th. You have a lot of energy, personal magnetism – you exude electricity and sex appeal – charm and grace. Your personal sense of style is very sharp right now. You can get your way through charm and grace or by sheer brute force if you choose. You are still very much in an independent frame of mind and should continue to create conditions as you desire them to be. This is a time where the world needs to adapt to you, not vice versa.

On the 6th the planetary power makes an important shift from the upper to the lower half of your chart. For the next four to five months, most of the planets will be below the horizon of the Horoscope, the first time this has happened this year. Career is still important and very successful now, but many goals have been achieved and it is time to take a breather – the pause that refreshes. Shift some energy to the family and to your emotional life. Cultivate your feeling of harmony. Work on career goals by the methods of night – by dreaming, goal setting and visualization – rather than by the methods of day, which are overt action. You are in a period where you are gathering the inner forces for even greater career expansion later on in the year.

Your yearly financial peak is still in full force. In fact, now that Mercury is moving forward, this month's earnings should exceed last month's. Until the 14th there are many financial opportunities – and good ones – that are coming to you, seeking you out. Financial windfalls come to you with little effort on your part. You are spending on yourself, on your image and on fun-type activities; a wonderful month (especially after the 6th) to buy clothing and accessories. After the 14th enhance your earnings through good use of the media and through creative sales and marketing. Professional investors should look at telecommunications, transportation, real estate, hotels, restaurants and media companies.

Singles are attracting the opposite sex – no doubt about it – but marriage? Not an especially good time for this – your love planet is still Retrograde and will be Retrograde for months to come. Let love develop slowly and solidly. Existing relationships are harmonious but under review. You will have opportunities to make good relationships even better.

Health is excellent. You have a lot of energy. Watch out for haste and impatience: this can cause accidents or injury and is the main health danger. Watch the temper. If someone provokes you take a few deep breaths and count to ten before answering. Enhance your health through scalp and face massage (as in the past few months) until the 6th. After that give more attention to the neck and throat – neck massage will be very beneficial. You are more into health regimes and healthy lifestyles this month and there is a vanity component to it – your state of health dramatically affects your personal appearance.

July

Best Days Overall: 6, 7, 16, 17, 24, 25
Most Stressful Days Overall: 1, 2, 9, 10, 22, 23, 28, 29, 30
Best Days for Love: 1, 2, 6, 9, 16, 18, 19, 24, 26, 27, 28, 29, 30
Best Days for Money: 9, 10, 11, 12, 18, 19, 22, 23, 26, 27, 31
Best Days for Career: 1, 2, 9, 10, 11, 12, 20, 21, 28, 29, 30

Last month the planetary power shifted to the lower half of your Horoscope, making career less of a priority. This month we see further evidence of this. First off, 40 per cent of the planets are Retrograde, and this slows down the pace of world events. Second, the planets that are involved in your career are also Retrograde. So, stop pushing so hard in outward ways and work in the inner ways. Build the psychological groundwork for future career success. Also, the next few months are wonderful for reviewing the career and for seeing where improvements and fine tuning can be made. Your 4th House of Home and Family starts to get strong on the 17th, so pay more attention there.

There are two eclipses this month to boot. The first is a Lunar Eclipse on the 7th. It occurs in your 9th House. For students this shows dramatic changes in educational plans. Sometimes it is normal things, like graduation and the like. But often it shows changes in schools or changes of courses. Often there are regulatory changes at the school that affect the educational plans. This eclipse is basically benign to you (though your personal Horoscope, calculated specially for you, could modify this), but it won't hurt to reduce your schedule anyway.

There are dramatic events in the lives of siblings. Siblings are re-defining their image and personalities during these days. Communications equipment and cars get tested. This eclipse sideswipes Mercury, your financial planet, and thus you will make long-term financial changes – things that have needed to be done for a long time but which you put off doing. Now you are forced to make the changes. Avoid foreign travel this period.

The Solar Eclipse of the 22nd also affects siblings, reinforcing what the Lunar Eclipse was producing. This eclipse brings dramas with family members as well and perhaps repairs in the home. Your dream life will be active during both eclipse periods but pay them no mind. Much of what you dream is merely psychic debris brought on by the eclipses and has little spiritual import or significance.

You are still well into a yearly financial peak. July is a prosperous month. Your financial intuition becomes important after the 12th. Bold financial actions need to be taken.

Perhaps they seem risky to the human mind, but if you are following intuition the so-called risk is the safest course. Sales, marketing, communications and right use of the media is still very important financially. Real estate and family connections are still important as well.

Health is good, but rest and relax more after the 22nd. Enhance your health by giving more attention to the neck and throat (until the 5th) and to the arms, shoulders and lungs after that date. Regular arm and shoulder massage will be very beneficial and invigorating. Air purity becomes more important then too. If you feel under the weather get out in the fresh air and take some deep breaths.

August

Best Days Overall: 2, 3, 4, 12, 13, 21, 30, 31
Most Stressful Days Overall: 5, 6, 19, 25, 26
Best Days for Love: 2, 7, 8, 9, 12, 16, 17, 20, 25, 26, 30
Best Days for Money: 1, 2, 5, 6, 12, 13, 14, 15, 21, 22, 23, 24
Best Days for Career: 5, 6, 7, 8, 9, 16, 17, 25, 26

Another Lunar Eclipse on the 6th again tests cars and communications equipment (if they have survived the recent barrage of eclipses you have good quality merchandise!) and brings more dramatic events in the lives of siblings and perhaps neighbours. This eclipse, like the previous two of last month, affects students (but here it affects those at secondary school level). This can bring new rules and regulations – changes in the school administration – and perhaps changes of school. But this eclipse, unlike the previous two, occurs in your 10th House and this suggests career change. I feel this is positive change but it can be disruptive; there can be changes in your corporate hierarchy, shakeups in your overall industry, new job offers and the like. Things might seem stormy here but it is leading to your advancement. Probably there will be some dramas in the lives of parents or parent figures as well. Since your career planets are still

Retrograde this month you might feel the full impact of this later on. Let the dust settle from this eclipse before making important career changes. You need to do a lot of homework here. This eclipse is a bit stronger on you than the other two have been, so take it easy for a few days before and after. Avoid risky activities. Spend more quiet time at home.

Aside from your career, the major interests this month are home and family, intellectual interests, children and fun.

On the 22nd, the Sun enters your 5th House of Fun and Creativity and you enter another yearly personal pleasure peak. Until the 22nd watch your health more – try to rest and relax more and pace yourself. Enhance your health by giving more attention to the stomach and breasts (until the 26th) and to the heart afterwards. Diet is more of an issue for you health-wise until the 26th. If you feel under the weather you might need to make some changes here. With your health planet in a Water Sign (until the 26th), swimming, boating, soaking in a tub or natural spring will be like a tonic. It might be wise to drink more water too. After the 26th the healing powers of fire are beneficial – sunshine, heat-oriented therapies, saunas and steam baths.

Finances look strong. Mercury moves speedily in the month ahead, progressing through three Signs and Houses. You are making rapid financial progress, covering a lot of ground. Confidence is good. Financial judgement is especially astute from the 2nd to the 25th. Though there are a few bumps on the road – from the 19th to the 22nd – they are short lived. Financial opportunities come from family and family connections until the 2nd. From the 2nd to the 25th you seem more speculative – and this is where the bumps on the road can come from, but it might also come from an unexpected expense related to children as well. You are thrown off your game temporarily, but you will recover.

Love is harmonious after the 22nd, but still go slow here and don't rush anything one way or another.

September

> Best Days Overall: 8, 9, 17, 18, 26, 27
> Most Stressful Days Overall: 1, 2, 15, 16, 21, 22, 28, 29, 30
> Best Days for Love: 6, 7, 8, 15, 16, 17, 21, 22, 26, 27
> Best Days for Money: 1, 2, 11, 12, 18, 19, 20, 27, 28, 29, 30
> Best Days for Career: 1, 2, 4, 5, 13, 14, 21, 22, 28, 29, 30

Last month the planetary power shifted from the Eastern to the Western sector of the Horoscope. But that was only the beginning. This month the shift is stronger. It is time to develop your social skills now. You've had your way for quite a few months. Presumably you've created the conditions that you wanted to create. Now it is time to attain your ends through diplomacy and consensus and not so much by personal effort. Others – and their good graces – are becoming increasingly important.

Continue to focus on your inner wellness, on finding your point of emotional harmony and comfort. Career success is going to be there for you all year, but you need to find your emotional centre and be comfortable with your success. Focus on the simple pleasures of the home and the hearth. Be present at important events in the children's lives. Cement family relationships. All your career planets are still retrograde so you are in a period for review of your career and not for overt actions.

Your 5th House is very strong this month and you are still very much into a yearly personal pleasure peak. Taurus-born people like to work, but have fun as you do so. For singles this is a time for love affairs, and there are many opportunities. You look good and the opposite sex takes notice. You seem more relaxed and at ease this month and this too comes across well with the opposite sex. Those already in serious relationships are having more harmony there. On the 11th, your love planet, Pluto, finally starts to move forwards after many months of Retrograde motion. The social confidence is coming back. If you've used the previous months to review your love life, you are ready to implement your improvements. For singles there is an important romantic opportunity from the 19th to the 21st – this has serious possibilities. For those of you who are attached, this period brings happy social opportunities – invitations to parties or meetings with friends.

After the 22nd you are in a more serious work-oriented period. Though health is good, you seem more focused on it, more into healthy diets and lifestyles. You can enhance your health further by giving more attention to the heart (until the 20th) and the small intestine (after this).

Your financial planet goes Retrograde from the 7th to the 29th so be more cautious in your financial dealings, planning and expenditures. This Retrograde phase won't stop earnings, but more care will prevent much lost time and effort. Mistakes in communications and thinking can be costly. Read the fine print in all contracts and don't be afraid to ask questions and resolve all doubts. Try to avoid speculations from the 18th to the 29th – you will be sorely tempted. Money comes the old-fashioned way, through work. But investors should look at the health field for profitable opportunities.

A parent or parent figure has a drama from the 16th to the 18th – perhaps there is a spat with the mate or current love. Family members seem more temperamental during this period as well. Be more patient with them. There are wild mood swings with family members.

October

Best Days Overall: 6, 7, 14, 15, 23, 24
Most Stressful Days Overall: 12, 13, 19, 20, 26, 27
Best Days for Love: 6, 7, 14, 15, 16, 19, 20, 23, 26, 27
Best Days for Money: 8, 9, 10, 16, 17, 26, 27, 28, 29
Best Days for Career: 1, 2, 10, 11, 19, 20, 26, 27, 28, 29

The cosmos never springs surprises on us. It always announces its intentions long before actual events happen. If you feel that you have been taken by surprise, it only means that you weren't attentive to the messages that were sent. This month, there are very positive messages coming career-wise, and the cosmos is announcing that it is time to get focused here again. Dawn is not here yet but it is about to break – get ready. First off you are hard-working and serious, and this is noticed by your superiors. Second, there are job changes brewing, or changes in the conditions of the workplace. Saturn will move into your 6th House of Work on the 29th – this shows work opportunities in foreign lands or with foreign companies in your native land. There will be travel that is related to your job and career. Jupiter in your House of Career the whole past year starts to move forward again (on the 18th) after many months of Retrograde motion. The Sun will move from the lower half to the upper half of your Horoscope. It's almost time to let go of family issues and achieve your other goals.

Your career is very good this month and next month it will get even better.

Retrograde activity has lessened over the past few months. By the 18th, 80 per cent of the planets will be moving forwards. This allows more rapid progress both in the world and your personal goals.

Finances are good this month too. Until the 10th you earn money in happy ways – doing what you like to do – or perhaps even at leisure activities or parties. Speculations are favourable all month. There is a nice payday on the 20th or 21st. Your spouse or partner prospers and is generous with you. Perhaps you get a very attractive mortgage or loan opportunity, or meet people who are willing to invest in you. Something that you thought valueless turns out to be worth a nice amount of money. But mainly you earn through your work and your social connections.

Love seems happy too. It is a sexually active kind of month. You are in the mood for more than just sex, but this is not always up to you – you and your partner need to compromise more. On the 23rd you enter a yearly social peak. And love will improve. There will be more parties, more social invitations and more going out. There seems to be more family gatherings and entertaining from home. Family members are playing cupid after the 23rd.

Your health is good, but rest and relax more after the 23rd. Enhance your health by paying more attention to the small intestine (until the 15th) and the kidneys and hips afterwards. The spine, knees, teeth and overall skeletal alignment become more important for the next few years – see our discussion in the yearly report (*page 55*).

November

Best Days Overall: 2, 3, 10, 11, 20, 21, 22, 29, 30
Most Stressful Days Overall: 8, 9, 15, 16, 22, 23
Best Days for Love: 2, 4, 5, 10, 15, 16, 20, 25, 26, 29
Best Days for Money: 4, 5, 13, 14, 16, 17, 22, 23, 27, 28
Best Days for Career: 6, 7, 15, 16, 22, 23, 25, 26

Last month the planetary power was about to shift from the lower to the upper half of your Horoscope. This month it actually happens. By the 8th, 70 per cent (and sometimes 80 per cent) of the planets are above the horizon. Jupiter started to move forward last month (in your House of Career) and Neptune (also in your House of Career) moves forward on the 4th – also after many months of Retrograde motion. So, let go of family obligations for a while (or keep them to the bare minimum) and focus on your career.

Jobseekers should have had success last month, but there are still good opportunities this month until the 8th. After the 8th social connections, or perhaps your spouse or partner, have opportunities for you. Those of you who hire others might be thinking of cutting back now, and it might be wise.

You are well into a yearly social peak right now and it will last all month. You are reaching out to others, working to create the social life of your dreams, taking the initiative. There is a very happy romantic opportunity coming on the 8th or 9th. This doesn't mean that you have to take it – the planets rarely take away free will – but the opportunity is there. There are three planets in your House of Love and I read this as three suitors or girlfriends who are vying for your affection. For singles this can be confusing, but it is a nice problem to have. Better that than no opportunity.

Last month was sexually active and the trend continues this month as well. From a health perspective the danger is of overdoing a good thing. Safe sex and sexual moderation are important factors in health from the 8th onwards. You need to rest and relax more until the 22nd. Detox regimes are powerful after the 8th. The kidneys and hips are important before the 8th.

There is a partnership or joint venture opportunity happening until the 16th. In general social connections play a huge role in earnings then. Your spouse or partner is prospering – but working very hard – and there are more challenges (short term) for him or her. This is a wonderful period – all month – for refinancing old debt or paying off debts. It is good to deal with tax issues now too. If you are involved with insurance claims, there might be some delays but the outcome is favourable.

This is a great month to get rid of old possessions you no longer need, and make room for the new that wants to come in. It is also wonderful for personal transformation, personal re-invention, losing weight and the like.

December

Best Days Overall: 8, 9, 17, 18, 27, 28
Most Stressful Days Overall: 6, 7, 12, 13, 19, 20, 21
Best Days for Love: 6, 7, 8, 12, 13, 15, 16, 17, 26, 27
Best Days for Money: 2, 8, 9, 10, 11, 17, 18, 19, 20, 21, 27, 28, 29, 30
Best Days for Career: 4, 12, 13, 19, 20, 21, 22, 23, 31

Many of the trends that we wrote of last month are still in effect this month. The 8th House is very powerful until the 21st. This shows the prosperity of the partner (and his or her finances are much, much better than last month, and probably because of your personal efforts) and his or her generosity with you. It shows the ability to access outside money, such as lines of credit or outside investors if you need them. Debts are easily paid (and easily made). December is a great month (just like last month) for refinancing old debt on more favourable terms. Professional investors, or those of you who have investment portfolios, should look at bonds and the bond market for profit opportunities. After the 5th, as your financial planet moves into Capricorn and your 9th House, foreign investments seem interesting. The blue chip conservative stocks are probably best then. The 9th House is considered the most fortunate House of the Horoscope, so the financial planet moving through there shows good fortune – financial increase. While this is not the aspect for a lottery winner (Capricorn is much too conservative for that) it does show luck with calculated risks.

On a spiritual level the 8th House rules the deeper things of life; deeper understanding of life after death, reincarnation, resurrection and ascension. It shows a person's desire to reinvent and transform him or herself (a form of personal resurrection). So these interests become more important in the month ahead. You will increase your understanding of these subjects.

On a more mundane level it shows enhanced libido and greater sexual activity.

After the 21st your focus is more on foreign travel, foreign affairs and foreign people. You are more interested in foreign cultures and languages. There is a greater interest in religion, philosophy and metaphysics. And with so much power in your 9th House (40 to 50 per cent of the planets are either there or move through there), there will be religious revelation and philosophical breakthroughs if you want them. Happy travel and educational opportunities come. For students there is good fortune in your studies.

Love seems very happy this month and singles have wonderful opportunities from the 20th onwards. There is more closeness in existing relationships too. You and the beloved are basically on the same page, seeing eye to eye. You are not clones of each other – you have your own individuality – but you are in harmony, in agreement, and seeing things from a similar perspective.

Health is excellent all month. You can enhance it further by giving more attention to the liver and thighs (until the 25th) and to the spine, knees, teeth, bones and skeletal alignment all month (and for the next two years).

Gemini

♊

THE TWINS

Birthdays from
21st May to
20th June

Personality Profile

GEMINI AT A GLANCE

Element – Air

Ruling Planet – Mercury
   Career Planet – Neptune
   Love Planet – Jupiter
   Money Planet – Moon
   Planet of Health and Work – Pluto
   Planet of Home and Family Life – Mercury

Colours – blue, yellow, yellow–orange

Colour that promotes love, romance and social harmony – sky blue

Colours that promote earning power – grey, silver

Gems – agate, aquamarine

Metal – quicksilver

Scents – lavender, lilac, lily of the valley, storax

Quality – mutable (= flexibility)

Quality most needed for balance – thought that is deep rather than superficial

Strongest virtues – great communication skills, quickness and agility of thought, ability to learn quickly

Deepest need – communication

Characteristics to avoid – gossiping, hurting others with harsh speech, superficiality, using words to mislead or misinform

Signs of greatest overall compatibility – Libra, Aquarius

Signs of greatest overall incompatibility – Virgo, Sagittarius, Pisces

Sign most helpful to career – Pisces

Sign most helpful for emotional support – Virgo

Sign most helpful financially – Cancer

Sign best for marriage and/or partnerships – Sagittarius

Sign most helpful for creative projects – Libra

Best Sign to have fun with – Libra

Signs most helpful in spiritual matters – Taurus, Aquarius

Best day of the week – Wednesday

Understanding a Gemini

Gemini is to society what the nervous system is to the body. It does not introduce any new information but is a vital transmitter of impulses from the senses to the brain and vice versa. The nervous system does not judge or weigh these impulses – it only conveys information. And does so perfectly.

This analogy should give you an indication of a Gemini's role in society. Geminis are the communicators and conveyors of information. To Geminis the truth or falsehood of information is irrelevant, they only transmit what they see, hear or read about. Thus they are capable of spreading the most outrageous rumours as well as conveying truth and light. Geminis sometimes tend to be unscrupulous in their communications and can do great good or great evil with their power. This is why the Sign of Gemini is called the Sign of the Twins: Geminis have a dual nature.

Their ability to convey a message – to communicate with such ease – makes Geminis ideal teachers, writers and media and marketing people. This is helped by the fact that Mercury, the ruling planet of Gemini, also rules these activities.

Geminis have the gift of the gab. And what a gift this is! They can make conversation about anything, anywhere, at any time. There is almost nothing that is more fun to Geminis than a good conversation – especially if they can learn something new as well. They love to learn and they love to teach. To deprive a Gemini of conversation, or of books and magazines, is cruel and unusual punishment.

Geminis are almost always excellent students and take well to education. Their minds are generally stocked with all kinds of information, trivia, anecdotes, stories, news items, rarities, facts and statistics. Thus they can support any intellectual position that they care to take. They are awesome debaters and, if involved in politics, make good orators.

Geminis are so verbally smooth that even if they do not know what they are talking about, they can make you think that they do. They will always dazzle you with their brilliance.

Finance

Geminis tend to be more concerned with the wealth of learning and ideas than with actual material wealth. As mentioned they excel in professions that involve writing, teaching, sales and journalism – and not all of these professions pay very well. But to sacrifice intellectual needs merely for money is unthinkable to a Gemini. Geminis strive to combine the two.

Cancer is on Gemini's Solar 2nd House (of Money) cusp, which indicates that Geminis can earn extra income (in a harmonious and natural way) from investments in residential property, restaurants and hotels. Given their verbal skills, Geminis love to bargain and negotiate in any situation, but especially when it has to do with money.

The Moon rules Gemini's 2nd Solar House. The Moon is not only the fastest-moving planet in the Zodiac but actually moves through every Sign and House every 28 days. No other heavenly body matches the Moon for swiftness or the ability to change quickly. An analysis of the Moon – and lunar phenomena in general – describes Gemini's financial attitudes very well. Geminis are financially versatile and flexible. They can earn money in many different ways. Their financial attitudes and needs seem to change daily. Their feelings about money change also: sometimes they are very enthusiastic about it, at other times they could not care less.

For a Gemini, financial goals and money are often seen only as means of supporting a family; these things have little meaning otherwise.

The Moon, as Gemini's money planet, has another important message for Gemini financially: in order for Geminis to realize their financial potential they need to develop more of an understanding of the emotional side of life. They need to combine their awesome powers of logic with an understanding of human psychology. Feelings have their own logic; Geminis need to learn this and apply it to financial matters.

Career and Public Image

Geminis know that they have been given the gift of communication for a reason, that it is a power that can achieve great good or cause unthinkable distress. They long to put this power at the service of the highest and most transcendental truths. This is their primary goal, to communicate the eternal verities and prove them logically. They look up to people who can transcend the intellect – to poets, artists, musicians and mystics. They may be awed by stories of religious saints and martyrs. A Gemini's highest achievement is to teach the truth, whether it is scientific, inspirational or historical. Those who can transcend the intellect are Gemini's natural superiors – and a Gemini realizes this.

The Sign of Pisces is in Gemini's Solar 10th House of Career. Neptune, the planet of spirituality and altruism, is Gemini's career planet. If Geminis are to realize their highest career potential they need to develop their transcendental – their spiritual and altruistic – side. They need to understand the larger cosmic picture, the vast flow of human evolution – where it came from and where it is heading. Only then can a Gemini's intellectual powers take their true position and he or she can become the 'messenger of the gods'. Geminis need to cultivate a facility for 'inspiration', which is something that does not originate in the intellect but which comes through the intellect. This will further enrich and empower a Gemini's mind.

Love and Relationships

Geminis bring their natural garrulousness and brilliance into their love life and social life as well. A good talk or a verbal joust is an interesting prelude to romance. Their only problem in love is that their intellect is too cool and passionless to incite ardour in others. Emotions sometimes disturb them, and their partners tend to complain about this. If you are in love with a Gemini you must understand why this is so. Geminis avoid deep passions because these would interfere with their ability to think and communicate. If they are cool towards you, understand that this is their nature.

Nevertheless, Geminis must understand that it is one thing to talk about love and another actually to love – to feel it and radiate it. Talking about love glibly will get them nowhere. They need to feel it and act on it. Love is not of the intellect but of the heart. If you want to know how a Gemini feels about love you should not listen to what he or she says but rather observe what he or she does. Geminis can be quite generous to those they love.

Geminis like their partners to be refined, well educated and well travelled. If their partners are more wealthy than they, that is all the better. If you are in love with a Gemini you had better be a good listener as well.

The ideal relationship for the Gemini is a relationship of the mind. They enjoy the physical and emotional aspects, of course, but if the intellectual communion is not there they will suffer.

Home and Domestic Life

At home the Gemini can be uncharacteristically neat and meticulous. They tend to want their children and partner to live up to their idealistic standards. When these standards are not met they moan and criticize. However, Geminis are good family people and like to serve their families in practical and useful ways.

The Gemini home is comfortable and pleasant. They like to invite people over and they make great hosts. Geminis are also good at repairs and improvements around the house – all fuelled by their need to stay active and occupied with something they like to do. Geminis have many hobbies and interests that keep them busy when they are home alone.

Geminis understand and get along well with their children, mainly because they are very youthful people themselves. As great communicators, Geminis know how to explain things to children; in this way they gain their children's love and respect. Geminis also encourage children to be creative and talkative, just like they are.

Horoscope for 2009

Major Trends

For many years now, your challenge has been in coping with dramatic and sudden change – and this trend is continuing in the year ahead, especially for those of you who are born late in the sign of Gemini (June 15 to 21). The cosmos is not punishing you, but liberating you – breaking many negative kinds of attachments – so that you can pursue your true life path. Yes, the changes have been quite dramatic, but in the end you will see that the barriers to your good – to your happiness – have come down. You will enter your personal promised land with ease and grace.

Last year was a highly sexually active kind of year and this year you are toning it down a bit.

It was also about exploring many of the deeper things in life: past lives, death, life after death, reincarnation, resurrection and ascension. Great progress was made here. And with all of this knowledge under your belt, you are ready – in the year ahead – to go deeper into religion and philosophy and understand them better.

This year, 2009, is also a year for foreign travel, and especially for religious-type pilgrimages. There are many wonderful educational opportunities coming too – and what Gemini can pass this up?

Family life could have been better these past few years and the good news is that the difficulties are just about over with; by October 29 things at home will get better.

Last year was not an especially romantic year (it was sexually active but not romantic – there's a difference) and the trend continues in the year ahead.

Health could also have been better these past few years, but rejoice: things are improving on that front after October 29 as well.

Your major areas of interest this year are career (this has been so for many years); religion, philosophy, higher education, foreign travel and ministry; occult studies, death, rebirth, past lives, reincarnation, personal transformation; home and family (until October 29); children, creativity and fun (after October 29).

Your paths of greatest fulfilment in the year ahead are religion, philosophy, higher education, foreign travel and ministry; and occult studies, death, rebirth, past lives, reincarnation and personal transformation (after July 27).

Health

(Please note that this is an astrological perspective on health and not a medical one. In days of yore there was no difference, both of these perspectives were identical. But in these times there could be quite a difference. For the medical perspective, please consult your doctor or health professional.)

Health has been a stressful area for the past few years. Two major long-term planets were stressing you out – Uranus and Saturn – neither of which you want to trifle with. And while you still need to be very careful with your overall energy, there are improvements happening, as we mentioned.

First off, Jupiter is moving into a very harmonious relationship with you. He is giving more help than he was last year. Second, Saturn will move from a stressful aspect to a harmonious aspect after October 29. You are going to see dramatic improvements in overall health this year, but especially after October 29.

The main problem was energy levels. When two long-term planets are stressing you, it is as if you are walking uphill. You need twice the amount of energy to travel the same distance. And because energy was not what it should have been, you could have been hit in your vulnerable organs, which is what tends to happen.

If you have been having health problems you will see miraculous types of healings after October 29. The healer or doctor will get the credit (and perhaps this is as it should be) but the truth of the matter was that your own life energy – now expanded – merely manifested its natural perfection. (If we could just get out of the way of our own life force, our bodies would always be healthy – but this is easier said than done.)

The other problem was that your 6th House of Health was empty (for the most part) for the past few years (and is still basically empty in the year ahead). Thus, at a time when it was important to focus on health, your tendency was to ignore it. And this trend continues in the year ahead. There is a need to force yourself to focus on health, though you don't feel like it. You will have to find the motivation within yourself; it is not being supplied by the cosmos. (The good news though is that Pluto, your health planet, recently changed signs – now he is in the disciplined Sign of Capricorn – which makes it easier for you to muster up the needed discipline, both in diet and daily lifestyle.)

Pluto is your health planet. In the physical body he rules the colon, bladder and sexual organs. Thus these organs always need more attention. Last year was a sexually active year and you could have gone overboard and forgotten moderation; if so you are paying the price for it these days. Not only is sexual moderation important, but so is safe sex. It is important for everyone but especially for you.

Your health planet spent many years in the Sign of Sagittarius, which rules the liver and thighs, and these organs were ultra important until this year. Now with Pluto in Capricorn, the spine, knees, teeth, bones, gall bladder and overall skeletal alignment are very important. Regular back massage will do wonders for you. Seeing a chiropractor or osteopath on a regular basis will be a good idea; it is very important that your vertebrae are in proper alignment. Yoga is very wonderful for the spine and you should spend more

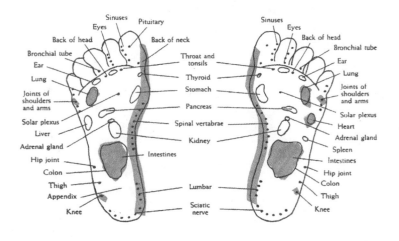

Reflexology
Try to massage the whole foot on a regular basis, but pay extra attention to
the points highlighted on the chart. When you massage, be aware of 'sore
spots', as these need special attention. It's also a good idea to massage the
ankles and top side (as well as the soles) of the feet.

time with the postures that focus on the spine. The
Alexander Technique and Feldenkreis method are other
good therapies for the spine. If you are doing vigorous exercise give the knees more support. Make sure you are getting
enough of the minerals (calcium and Vitamin K) that keep
the bones strong.

Since Pluto will be in Capricorn for many years to come,
the things that we are writing about are long-term health
trends.

Pluto Retrogrades from April 4 to September 11. This is a
period for reviewing your health regime and diet, seeing
where improvements can be made, but not for making drastic decisions about your health. It is best to execute your
health plans either before April 4 or after September 11.

Pluto rules detox and surgery – an interesting fiefdom.
Basically detox does the same thing as surgery (in many
cases), only it takes longer. You especially benefit from detox

regimes, in particular those that involve the colon. Either herbal or mechanical means will be good.

There are many natural, drugless ways to strengthen your vulnerable organs, legions of them, and readers are probably familiar with them. But if not, you can work with the chart on page 92. It is a good beginning.

Home and Family

Home, family and the overall domestic life has been an important focus for some years now, and the trend continues for most of the year ahead.

Saturn has been making a move through your 4th House for some years and will be there until October 29. This shows big, major reorganizations of the home, family relationships and the daily domestic routine. The cosmos is setting out to bring a 'right order' here and it is best to co-operate. There is a need for more order, more efficiency and better management in the domestic life.

Saturn in the 4th House is not an aspect for moving. Many of you would like to as you feel cramped where you are, but it is better to make use of the space that you have, rather than move into a bigger place, and since Saturn rules your 8th House of Detox and Elimination, the message here is that you need to get rid of excess furniture, decorations, or things in the home that are no longer useful. Just as the body benefits when we get rid of surplus material there, so your home life will benefit from getting rid of things that you don't need. Watch how this simple procedure liberates all kinds of space that you didn't know you had. (It's a good idea to go through the basement, cupboards and attics too.)

The message of detox also applies to your domestic routine. Are you doing chores that aren't necessary? Are you keeping house merely the way your parents did it, or the way society ordains it? Now is the time to review these things and eliminate waste.

On a spiritual level, the message of detox refers to your emotional life. There is a need to detox it of all discordant material and patterns – a big job, but this is a good time to do it.

The changes in the family pattern are going very deep. In many cases there has been a literal death in the family – and there is nothing like death to change a pattern, routine or relationship. In other cases there have been near-death experiences of family members. And perhaps a 'near-death' experience of the actual physical home, for we see a need for major renovation here. (This could have already happened in the past two years, but can still happen in the year ahead.) Sometimes the change in the family pattern happens through divorce and things of that nature – the family just breaks up.

None of this should be considered as punitive or 'bad luck'. The cosmos needs to do major repair work to bring your home and domestic life to its pristine ideal, and this is the purpose. But it can feel uncomfortable while the process is going on.

Things will improve in the home after October 29; the cosmic job should be complete by then.

Siblings are having a status quo domestic year. Parents or parent figures are nomadic (and this has been going on for some years as well) – they are exploring their freedom, moving from place to place – and probably their marriages are being tested. Divorces in recent years would not be a surprise.

Children of appropriate age are experiencing much of the same things that you are: there is a detox going on in their home and family situation. The end result will be good.

Finance and Career

Your 2nd House of Finance is not a House of Power this year (and this has been the case for the past few years). It is not a major focus in your life these days and I read this as a good thing. You are basically content with the status quo and have no need to make major changes. Normally this would show a status quo kind of financial year, but this year, I wouldn't read it this way. First off, there are four Lunar Eclipses this year – usually there are two. And since the Moon rules your finances, there is great financial significance to this. Not only that, but there will be two eclipses that occur in your money house: a Solar Eclipse on July 22 and a Lunar Eclipse on December 31.

So you might be satisfied with the status quo and not feel like making changes, but the cosmos is going to force you into it. And if it doesn't succeed the first time, it will repeat another 4 times until you get the message. It is going to purify your financial life – make you rich – in spite of yourself.

There are changes – in investments, in thinking, in strategy, in financial planning – that have long needed to be made. These changes need to go deep, and so you are forced to make them. In certain cases some of you might have wandered into strange byways and got into financial situations or projects that were not part of your destiny. In those cases, the eclipse's job is to blow these things to smithereens and put you back on track.

In your financial life you will need a strong stomach and a stout heart to weather these eclipses, but keep the faith – the end result is good.

We see dramatic changes in the career as well. And for the better. Career has been unstable, changeable and unpredictable for many years now. Sometimes you're at the heights and sometimes at the depths. Employers can be thrilled one moment and the next highly displeased. You are at the top of the world for a while and then in the depths of despair. But this year, there are going to be pay rises, promotions, honours and much success. Jupiter will be travelling with your career planet, Neptune, for a large part of the year, and this is a classic indicator of success.

Perhaps this is the reason why there are so many financial changes. Perhaps you were making plans from a 'beer income' perspective and suddenly you find yourself in a 'champagne income' category – and this necessitates a rethink.

Higher education, taking the courses that you need to take and your willingness to travel, have been big factors in your career success in the past few years, and this trend continues, perhaps even more strongly in the year ahead. But the main catalyst for your success seems to be your social connections and partners. You know the right people in the right places and they are helping you. The other message here is that you should further your career through social means – through hosting or attending the right parties and gatherings.

Your career goals are very high, and have been that way for a long time. This is a year to push forward boldly – fearlessly. You have very powerful cosmic backers.

With the Moon as your financial planet, you have a natural affinity for family kinds of businesses, earning money from the home, real estate (residential), restaurants and lodging companies, also industries that cater to women, families and home owners. But since the Moon moves through every Sign and House of your Horoscope every month (she is the fastest-moving planet) money and financial opportunity often comes to you in a variety of ways and through a variety of means. It all depends where the Moon is on a given day. These things will be discussed in the monthly reports.

In general you will have stronger earning power and more enthusiasm for money matters when the Moon is waxing (getting bigger) than when she is waning. You can schedule your business accordingly.

Also, though you are a logical and level-headed person, when it comes to finances you can be moody. So avoid making important financial decisions when you feel depressed or upset. Sleep on things. Wait for your mood to equalize and then make your decision.

Love and Social Life

Your 7th House of Love and Social Activities is not a House of Power this year and thus I expect we'll see a status-quo kind of year. Marrieds will tend to stay married and singles will tend to stay single.

However, your love planet makes an important move this year. He moves from Capricorn (where he was all last year) into Aquarius. He will be in Aquarius for the entire year ahead (beginning from January 5).

Last year you (but singles especially) were very conservative in love. You almost disbelieved in the notion of romantic love. Love was something practical: a job, a career move, a duty, a responsibility. You felt that if you found the right person, you could 'learn' to love him or her. You gravitated to older, more established people – people above you in status. You were cautious in love, slow to fall in love. Material support and the sexual chemistry were the primal attractions for you. This year we see some changes. We still see you as being status conscious in love – you still see it as a career move – but you want more equality in the relationship. You want a friend as well as a lover. You admire not only a person's position and status, but also their mind and spirit. This year, you seem quicker to fall in love – less afraid.

In some ways, last year's attitudes were easier. This year your love needs are much more complex. You are attracted by wealth, status and power (and are very likely to enter into this kind of romance) but you also need friendship and a good spiritual compatibility. Without the spiritual compatibility – being on the same spiritual wave length, sharing the same spiritual ideals – it is doubtful whether any love relationship could last very long. Your ideal person would be someone creative, poetic or mystical, who was also of high status, perhaps the CEO of a large corporation, and who was also an inventor or innovator. These things are harder to find, but they exist. Astrologers and astronomers – scientists, genius types – are also very alluring.

This year you have the aspects for a classic office romance with a superior, someone above you in the hierarchy. You also have the aspects of the person who falls in love with their guru, mentor or professor.

Love opportunities happen in educational and religious-type settings, at church, mosque or synagogue or at functions sponsored by these kinds of organizations. It can happen in foreign countries and with foreigners. And it can happen as you pursue your career goals. College and university settings are also likely meeting grounds.

If you are single working on your first marriage, the year ahead is a status-quo one. A marriage isn't likely, but you will have romance. If you are working on the second marriage, then marriage IS very likely in the year ahead, with a partner being found in the places mentioned above. Those working on the third or fourth marriage are having status quo kinds of years.

This is a year where you mingle with the high and the mighty – people of power and prestige. These people, as we mentioned, are very helpful career-wise.

A sibling will either marry or enter into a serious love relationship this year. If he or she is already married, there will be more romance within the marriage. The marriage seems happier. Parents or parent figures are having their marriages and business partnerships tested. Children and grandchildren of marriageable age are having status quo kinds of years.

Self-improvement

Saturn has been in your 4th House of Home and Family for some years now and will be there for most of the year ahead. Aside from the practical effects on the home and the family, it is bringing important spiritual lessons. And these lessons are going on in the year ahead.

Basically the cosmos wants you to learn to manage your emotional life better, to neither repress negative feelings (which only brings depression and physical ailments) nor to express them (which only generates negative energy into the universe and brings negative karma on you), but to direct them according to your will – to master them. This requires some understanding of how the emotional-feeling world works and might require some study on your part. But basically emotions will follow attention and focus. If you get control of your attention and keep it on positive and happy things, the overall mood will be better. Prayer and meditation – especially praise and worship – are like vitamins for the emotional life. The Buddhists teach to just observe and experience your emotions without expressing them. This is not repression, because you are experiencing the emotion, but you are not expressing it – dumping it on others. Thus you are not polluting the emotional environment. All the above is good, but I also like writing out negative feelings and then throwing out the paper. Talking them into a tape recorder and then erasing the tape is also effective.

For many years you have been riding a career roller-coaster. Like any roller-coaster ride there are alternating thrills and fears. The purpose here was to teach centredness amidst all the career change and drama. Not to be overly elated by success, nor depressed by failure. Just to keep on keeping on. By now you have learned these lessons and are ready for the career success and opportunity that is happening.

Pluto is moving into your 8th House of Sex permanently this year. Thus you are going deeper into sexuality. It's not just about more sexual activity, but a deeper understanding of what sex is. Unfortunately, the medical and psychological communities seem clueless about it. They see it as a mere neurological release; something physical, mechanical, chemical and emotional. But sex is much, much more than that. And you are in a period for learning more about this. Tantric (for those of you interested in Eastern philosophy) and hermetic science and Kabbalah (for those of you of a more Western bent) have much to teach about these things, and you might want to explore these.

Your spiritual mission in the year ahead (as it has been for many years) is spirituality itself. What we call 'performing the Yoga' – making the union with the Divine within you. This and involvement in ministry, higher education, teaching and publishing (which are really side effects of the above) is your spirit's true calling.

Month-by-month Forecasts

January

> Best Days Overall: 8, 16, 17, 26, 27
> Most Stressful Days Overall: 1, 2, 14, 15, 21, 22, 28, 29
> Best Days for Love: 7, 9, 10, 16, 18, 19, 21, 22, 25, 26, 28, 29
> Best Days for Money: 5, 6, 7, 10, 11, 14, 15, 16, 25, 26, 27
> Best Days for Career: 1, 2, 8, 16, 17, 26, 27, 28, 29

You begin your year with 80 to 90 per cent of the planets above the horizon – a huge, huge percentage. Very soon – next month – you will enter a yearly career peak. You need to get ready for it. So, give more attention and energy to your career – your outer goals – and let family and emotional issues slide for a while. You won't be able to ignore the home and family completely, not with Saturn in your 4th House, but you can shift more energy to your career. Also, the two planets involved with home and family issues are Retrograde this month – so there is not much to be done in that area anyway.

Most of the planets are in the Western social sector as you begin your year. So this is not a time for too much self-assertion or independence. It is a time for cultivating the good graces of others and for getting things done by compromise and consensus. This is a time for developing and honing your social skills. (With your ruling planet Retrograde for most of the month – from the 11th to the 31st – we have another argument against too much self-assertion.)

The main headline this month is the power in your 9th House. Sixty per cent of the planets are either there or moving through there – again, a huge percentage. Moreover, there will be a Solar Eclipse in that House on the 26th. In a way this is Gemini heaven. The month ahead is about education and expanding the mind, and there is nothing more satisfying for a Gemini than this. There will be a lot of Air in the Horoscope too. This sharpens your already sharp mind and enhances your mental and communication abilities even further. Writers, teachers, marketers and PR people will have a banner month (and many of you are in these fields).

It is a very good period for students as well. There is success in your studies. There are some bumps on the road brought on by the eclipse – perhaps changes in your course, or school, or changes in the rules and regulations of your school – but in the end this should all work in your favour.

The Solar Eclipse of the 26th will test your religious and philosophical beliefs. Cherished beliefs will get challenged, and this is a good thing. Whatever can't stand the test of events or truth should go into the rubbish bin. Happy travel opportunities are coming, but try to schedule these around the eclipse period.

Health is good all month. But be careful of too much thinking and too much talking after the 19th, as this can drain energy needlessly and make you vulnerable to problems.

Your love planet makes a major move on the 5th from your 8th House to your 9th House and this shows a major shift in your love attitudes. It is a happy love transit for all of you, but especially for those of you who are working on the second marriage. Love opportunities are now in foreign lands or at religious or educational settings.

February

Best Days Overall: 4, 5, 12, 13, 22, 23
Most Stressful Days Overall: 10, 11, 17, 18, 24, 25, 26
Best Days for Love: 4, 5, 8, 9, 12, 13, 17, 18, 22, 23, 27, 28
Best Days for Money: 4, 5, 6, 7, 12, 13, 22, 23, 24, 25
Best Days for Career: 4, 5, 12, 13, 22, 23, 24, 25, 26

Your 9th House of Religion, Philosophy and Higher Education is still very powerful this month. Like last month, there is a procession of planets moving through there. So, many of the trends that we wrote of last month are still very much in effect. In addition to the happy travel and educational opportunities that come to you – some educational opportunities are in foreign lands or foreign schools – there is religious and philosophical revelation open to you, and those who want this shall receive it. A real religious breakthrough is more powerful than just a psychological breakthrough; it changes your whole world view, your whole perspective on life. It changes the psychology as a matter of course. It is one of the most wonderful things that can happen to a person – and it will happen for many of you now.

Many of you are meeting significant religious teachers or gurus now. It is an excellent time for going on religiously oriented pilgrimages to holy places and the like.

When the 9th House is as strong as it is, people will rather sit around and have an interesting philosophical or theological discussion than go out on the town; it is more pleasurable and exciting.

On the 18th the Sun crosses your Midheaven, initiating a yearly career peak. There is career success and opportunity happening. Sales and marketing, good use of the media and your excellent communication skills are big factors in your success. Siblings are also having a good career month.

On the 9th we have another eclipse – this time Lunar – in your 3rd House. This eclipse will test your cars and communications equipment (and probably bring changes or upgrades). The last eclipse also tested these things. There are dramas in the lives of siblings, but they seem like happy dramas – dramas of success. (They are having very happy love experiences these days as well.) Like last month's eclipse it seems to affect students most strongly. There are changes of school, educational plans, subjects or the rules and regulations of the school. Often these kinds of eclipses bring changes in the administration of the school, shakeups in the hierarchy. Unlike the previous eclipse this one brings career and financial change as well. The timing of the eclipse is fortunate, for the career change is likely to be happy and good.

Health is good this month, but rest and relax more after the 18th. Continue to enhance your health by giving more attention to the colon, bladder, sexual organs, spine, knees, teeth, gall bladder and skeletal alignment – these things are important all year. This month give more attention to the heart as well.

Finances are not a major interest this month, although the eclipse will bring some important changes. Your money house is basically empty. In general, though, you will have greater earning power from the 1st to the 9th and from the 25th onwards than at other times. These periods are when the Moon, your financial planet, waxes.

March

Best Days Overall: 3, 4, 12, 13, 21, 22, 23, 30, 31
Most Stressful Days Overall: 10, 16, 17, 18, 24, 25
Best Days for Love: 3, 4, 7, 8, 12, 13, 16, 17, 18, 21, 22, 23, 26, 27, 30, 31
Best Days for Money: 3, 4, 5, 6, 12, 13, 14, 15, 21, 22, 23, 24, 25, 30, 31
Best Days for Career: 3, 4, 12, 13, 21, 22, 23, 30, 31

You are still very much into a yearly career peak and it is even stronger than last month. Pay rises and promotions are likely. You are on top this month, in power, calling the shots. Very ambitious. Even the family seems supportive of your career goals, and are probably not raising a fuss about neglect. The family as a whole seems elevated this month; family members are succeeding and the family status (as a whole) is elevated.

You are working hard. The demands of career are strong. There are competitors for your position, or in your industry. But you have friends in the right places helping you out.

Personal effort, communication skills, good use of the media and a willingness to travel or get the education you need will carry you through and bring you to your goals.

Continue to watch your health until the 20th. Give attention to the organs mentioned last month and (of course) try to rest and relax more. Your career may be important and demanding, but try to pace yourself better.

On the 20th your 11th House of Friends, Group Activities and Organizations becomes strong. (It was strong last month as well but is now even stronger.) Thus you are making new and important friends. There is joy in group activities or being involved with organizations. Many of you are realizing your fondest hopes and wishes. Your good professional reputation is bringing many new social opportunities.

Love is still very happy. Keep in mind that Venus, the universal planet of love, will make a rare Retrograde movement beginning on the 6th and this could complicate things. For you, it seems to affect love affairs (outside of marriage) rather than your actual marriage. Be more patient with children these days. Your policy towards them might need a review. They in turn need to review their personal goals and see where improvements need to be made. Avoid speculations after the 6th.

The planetary power shifts the month, from the Western social sector to the Eastern sector. By the 15th the East will be dominant. Thus you are becoming more independent and self-confident. You don't need to adapt to situations or toady up to others (though you shouldn't be rude to them). If conditions don't suit you, make changes and create situations the way you desire them to be.

Like last month, finances are not a big deal. I read this as a good sign – you are basically content with your finances. Earning power should be stronger from the 1st to the 11th and from the 26th to the 31st as the Moon is waxing. You can schedule your work accordingly.

April

Best Days Overall: 8, 9, 18, 19, 27, 28
Most Stressful Days Overall: 6, 7, 13, 14, 20, 21
Best Days for Love: 4, 8, 9, 13, 14, 18, 19, 20, 21, 27, 28
Best Days for Money: 2, 3, 4, 5, 8, 9, 13, 14, 18, 19, 25, 26, 27, 28, 29, 30
Best Days for Career: 8, 9, 18, 19, 20, 21, 27, 28

A very interesting love situation is developing with someone above you in status, perhaps a boss or superior in your company. But this is not a smooth ride. There are bumps on the road. This could happen in a foreign country or at a seminar or school-type setting. Students have love interests with their professors too. But Venus is Retrograde so it is wise to go slow here.

Venus will be Retrograde until the 17th so continue to be patient with children and let them work out their issues on their own.

The Retrograde mood of Venus also impacts on your spiritual life (she is your spiritual planet). Thus avoid making important changes to your spiritual practice or regime. Study things more. If you are involved in charities or altruistic causes, this is a time for a review of these things. After the 17th you can act as you see fit.

Career interest is still strong, but becoming weaker than last month. Probably most goals have been achieved (at least, those that were possible to achieve) and you're ready to become more social. Your 11th House of Friends, Group Activities and Organizations is still very strong until the 19th. You have strong networking skills by nature; now they are even stronger.

Spirituality becomes very important this month – especially after the 9th. It is another excellent period for religious or spiritually oriented pilgrimages, spiritual retreats, religious and spiritual breakthroughs. Life will become more 'supernatural' after the 19th. Weird 'synchronistic' experiences will happen that cannot be explained by three-dimensional logic.

This is spirit's way of letting you know that it is around and involved in your life. Your intuition is very sound right now; as you follow it and trust it, it will guide you to love, the right life partner and to the true desires of your heart. How do you know whether an intuition is real? The New Moon of the 25th is going to clarify these issues (and many other spiritual issues).

Health is good this month and you can make it even better by giving attention to the organs mentioned in the yearly report (*see page 91*).

Finances are status quo. You will have more energy and enthusiasm for financial matters from the 1st to the 9th and from the 25th onwards.

May

Best Days Overall: 5, 6, 15, 16, 24, 25
Most Stressful Days Overall: 3, 4, 10, 11, 18, 19, 30, 31
Best Days for Love: 1, 2, 5, 6, 10, 11, 15, 16, 20, 21, 24, 25, 28, 29
Best Days for Money: 3, 4, 5, 6, 12, 13, 14, 15, 16, 24, 25, 26, 27
Best Days for Career: 5, 6, 15, 16, 18, 19, 24, 25

Pluto, your health planet, started to Retrograde on April 4th and will be Retrograde for months to come. This affects your health regimes and practices. This is not a good time to make major changes here but, rather, it is a time for study and review. Overall health is good and getting better, and you have no need to make major changes.

This Retrograde movement of Pluto also affects jobseekers and those who hire others. Though job opportunities are plentiful these days (although last month was a little stronger for this than now) you still need to do more homework. Job descriptions and conditions are probably not what they seem to be. The same is true for prospective employees.

On May 20, as the Sun enters your own Sign, you enter a yearly personal pleasure peak – a time for pampering the body, getting it in shape and for enjoying the pleasures of the senses. You are also entering a period of very great independence (especially after the 20th), but with Mercury going Retrograde from the 7th to the 31st do more homework on the changes you want to make. Yes, you should create conditions as you desire them to be – you should take the bull by the horns and make things happen – but you need to be clear as to exactly what you want. Take some time to think things through and act after the 31st.

Love still seems happy. The office relationship we spoke of last month is still happening and going strong. But this relationship could be with someone involved with your career or just someone of high status compared to you. Love will improve further after the 20th and I wouldn't be surprised if there were wedding bells ringing for singles. Serious love is in the air.

The interest in the spiritual life is still strong until the 20th, so re-read our discussion of this from last month.

Finances are happy but are not an especially strong interest. The Sun in your own Sign after the 20th is always a positive for finances. You have more self-confidence, and thus you have greater earning capacities. The income of your spouse or partner is improving this month, as his or her financial planet starts to move forwards after many months of Retrograde motion. Deals which have stalled start to move on again. Prosperity is stronger for your partner after the 20th than before. After the 20th is also a better time for borrowing money, paying off debt, or attracting outside investors than before this date.

June

Best Days Overall: 2, 3, 11, 12, 13, 21, 29, 30
Most Stressful Days Overall: 6, 7, 8, 14, 15, 27, 28
Best Days for Love: 2, 3, 6, 7, 8, 9, 11, 12, 13, 19, 21, 22, 27, 28, 29, 30
Best Days for Money: 2, 3, 11, 12, 13, 21, 22, 23, 29, 30
Best Days for Career: 2, 3, 11, 12, 13, 14, 15, 21, 29, 30

The Sun in your own Sign and Mercury's forward motion combine to bring you increased energy, self-esteem and self-confidence. Your personal appearance is much improved as well. Your normal mental sharpness is even stronger than usual this month and thus marketers, teachers, writers and journalists should have a banner month.

Health is excellent now, and as we mentioned, you don't have a need to make major changes to your health regime, doctors, or diet right now. Study these things. The time to act will come later on.

You are still in a yearly personal pleasure peak enjoying all the delights of the senses. On the 21st, the Sun enters your money house, initiating a yearly financial peak. This will begin one of the most prosperous periods of your year. It's no surprise that earnings are enhanced through your communication abilities. This is your natural talent – your passbook to riches. Good use of the media is important as well. Trading and retailing also seem interesting. Earnings should be strong from the 1st to the 7th and especially from the 22nd to the 30th, as the Moon waxes.

Your spouse or partner is prospering but working harder for earnings than usual. Things smooth out financially after the 21st.

Spirituality is still very strong this month – 40 per cent of the planets are either in your 12th House or moving through there. Thus it is still a good time for inner growth and for getting involved in charities and the like.

Your career planet, Neptune, went Retrograde late last month (on the 26th) and this month the planetary power is starting to shift to the lower half of the Horoscope. The shift is not yet complete, but it is starting. Your career is slowing down and you need to get ready to shift energy to your home and family and to take more care of your emotional life in general.

Your love planet starts to go Retrograde on the 15th. Thus, although your love aspects – and thus your love life in general – seems very happy, there are more complications. You might feel like getting married, but it is better to delay and wait until Jupiter starts to move forward again in a few months. No need to rush anything. If love is real it will be there in a few months' time as well as now.

July

> Best Days Overall: 9, 10, 18, 19, 26, 27
> Most Stressful Days Overall: 3, 4, 5, 11, 12, 24, 25, 31
> Best Days for Love: 3, 4, 5, 9, 10, 18, 19, 26, 27, 31
> Best Days for Money: 1, 2, 9, 10, 11, 12, 18, 19, 20, 21, 22, 26, 27, 31
> Best Days for Career: 9, 10, 11, 12, 18, 19, 26, 27

Two eclipses right in the midst of a yearly financial peak are showing dramatic financial changes – both for you and your spouse or partner. These changes probably needed to be made for a long time, but now the eclipses force you to do what you should have done before this time. Sometimes a financial near-death experience or scare serves a positive purpose. These are not intended to punish but only to get you on track. Also, you may have been undervaluing yourself – setting too pessimistic a financial strategy – and the eclipse is going to straighten out your thinking. Both eclipses are basically benign to you (though your personal chart, cast especially for you, could modify this). Benign though they are it won't hurt to take a reduced schedule and spend more quiet time at home, a few days before and after the 7th and a few days before and after the 22nd.

The Solar Eclipse of the 22nd will test communications equipment, software and cars. If there are defects you will find out about it then, and be able to make the appropriate corrections. It also brings dramas in the lives of siblings and neighbours.

Venus and Mars are both moving through your 1st House this month; Venus enters on the 5th and Mars on the 12th. Both of these planets do wonders for your personal appearance. (They're much more effective than any cosmetic, although sometimes the cosmetic gets the credit rather than the planet!) You look fabulous. You have mega energy. You exude charisma and sex appeal and the opposite sex is going to notice. Most of you are involved in serious love relationships these days, but these relationships might get tested now as rivals appear on the scene. The opposite sex is seeking you out. It might be helpful to know that these opportunities are not serious ones – just flirtations, fun and games kinds of things. This might help you to avoid temptation.

Venus in your Sign gives a sense of style, so it is a good time to buy clothing or jewellery or have your hair done. Mars in your Sign enhances physical energy – you excel in sports or exercise regimes (even non-athletes will perform better this month).

But Mars in your Sign has a downside. You tend to rush more. And this can lead to accidents or injury. You are more ready to pick a fight, verbally or physically. It can be likened to taking adrenalin pills. You are not your normal self. Arguments are more likely. So you will need to give special attention here. Use the Mars energy for the purposes intended – to enable you to achieve more, work harder and play harder, to develop the body and to overcome fear. Not for gratuitous violence or throwing your weight around. (Self-defence is another story.)

August

Best Days Overall: 5, 6, 14, 15, 23, 24
Most Stressful Days Overall: 1, 7, 8, 9, 21, 27, 28
Best Days for Love: 1, 5, 6, 7, 8, 9, 14, 15, 16, 17, 23, 24, 25, 26, 27, 28
Best Days for Money: 1, 5, 6, 10, 11, 14, 15, 16, 17, 19, 20, 23, 24, 30, 31
Best Days for Career: 5, 6, 7, 8, 9, 14, 15, 23, 24

On the 12th of last month the planetary power shifted from the upper half to the lower half of your Horoscope. Both the planets involved with your career are Retrograde. The message is very clear. Let go of the career for a while.

Do what you need to do of course, but shift more energy to your emotional and family life. Cultivate your feeling of emotional harmony. Work on your career goals in 'inner' ways rather than in outer ways. Set goals, visualize what you want to achieve and where you want to be, dream a little and feel what it would be like with your goal attained. The career is sort of on hold, but it is far from over. It will resume stronger than ever in a few months. (You are successful this year, but next year you will be even more successful.) Many issues with the career need time to resolve; the solutions are not instant. Give them the time.

Finances are still important as both Mars and Venus are in your money house this month. There is luck in speculations this month (until the 26th), but as always only act under intuition. Venus in your money house shows happy money, money earned in happy and enjoyable ways – perhaps as you are out enjoying yourself. It shows financial opportunities through social contacts and through your personal creativity. And since Venus is also your spiritual planet, it shows a time of very good financial intuition – one flash of which is worth many years of hard labour.

Mars enters your money house shortly before Venus leaves (she leaves on the 26th and he enters on the 24th). This gives a whole different philosophy on wealth. It is like being under the influence of Benzedrine or other stimulating drugs. You become more aggressive in financial matters. You want to conquer the world, create wealth where none existed, conquer new markets and take risks. You want your financial life to be an adventure, and there is no adventure without risk. All of this is good, but there are some drawbacks. You can be an impulse spender and investor, and if your intuition is off you will pay the price. You can be impatient in financial matters and this can lead to bad decision making. But no matter, the cosmos wants you to develop more fearlessness in finances and as long as you overcame your fear, you won – regardless of what happened to the bottom line.

Friends are supportive financially and providing money opportunities. Networking – something you're good at – is also important. It is good to be involved with professional and trade organizations too – it is a path to profits.

This is another month of Gemini heaven, especially until the 22nd. Your 3rd House of Communication and Intellectual Interests is very strong. Thus the cosmos is pushing you to do what you always love to do – which can't be bad. Teachers, writers, journalists and PR people should have a great month.

Health is good, but rest and relax more after the 22nd. Enhance your health in the ways discussed in the yearly forecast (*page 90*).

September

    Best Days Overall: 1, 2, 11, 12, 19, 20, 28, 29, 30
    Most Stressful Days Overall: 4, 5, 17, 18, 23, 24, 25
    Best Days for Love: 1, 2, 6, 7, 11, 12, 15, 16, 19, 20, 23,
        24, 25, 26, 27, 28, 29, 30
    Best Days for Money: 1, 2, 8, 9, 11, 12, 13, 14, 17, 18, 19,
        20, 28, 29, 30
    Best Days for Career: 1, 2, 4, 5, 11, 12, 19, 20, 28, 29,
        30

Your health planet starts to move forward on the 11th after many months of Retrograde motion. Thus, it is now safe to make important health decisions or changes in your diet and overall health regime. You need to watch your health this month. Rest and relax more, stay focused on your priorities and let lesser things go. Continue to enhance your health in the ways described in the yearly report. Health and energy should improve after the 22nd.

Pluto's forward motion is also good for jobseekers. There is more clarity in this department and job choices should be good now. Jobseekers in general have good opportunities – especially before the 22nd. Those who hire others have better judgement this period too (after the 11th).

Though Pluto moves forward, there is still a lot of Retrograde activity. The planets involved with your career, home, family and personal goals are all Retrograde. Career, as we mentioned, should be de-emphasized and more attention given to the home and family. Career issues will take time to straighten out and there's not much you can do to rush things.

Your 4th House of Home and Family is the most powerful House and concern in the coming month – 50 per cent of the planets are either there or moving through there this month. So this is a time to be there for the children, for family members, and to get the home in order. Mercury's Retrograde from the 7th to the 29th suggests a need for more caution in how you communicate with family members. Carelessness in communication will lead to all kinds of headaches later on. Spend the extra time to make sure you say what you mean and that you understand what family members are saying. You are probably spending more on the home this month, but it might be better to delay major purchases until after the 29th or to make them before the 7th.

You seem directionless from the 7th to the 29th – and it was intended that way. It is a time to review your personal goals – especially as they relate to your body and image – and see where you can make improvements.

Finances still seem important and, until the 22nd, seem favourable. Like last month friends are financially supportive and providing opportunities for you. You still seem a bit of a risk taker in finance, but sometimes in life bold financial actions are necessary. As long as you calculate your risks you'll be fine.

Love is happy but seems to be going nowhere – without direction. This is OK. Enjoy what you have and let relationships develop as they will, without forcing them. Continue to avoid making important love decisions – one way or another.

October

Best Days Overall: 8, 9, 16, 17, 26, 27
Most Stressful Days Overall: 1, 2, 14, 15, 21, 22, 28, 29
Best Days for Love: 6, 7, 8, 9, 15, 16, 17, 21, 22, 26, 27
Best Days for Money: 8, 9, 10, 11, 16, 17, 18, 26, 27, 28, 29
Best Days for Career: 1, 2, 8, 9, 16, 17, 26, 27, 28, 29

When the Sun entered your 5th House on September 22nd, you entered a yearly personal pleasure peak, which is still very much in effect this month. This is a time for personal creativity (which is unusually strong right now) and for exploring the various joys of life. Overall health is much improved now, and when Saturn moves into Libra on the 29th, it will improve even further.

This is also a period for being more involved with children – either your own or those who are like children to you. You have a good ability to relate to them on their level, a good rapport with them.

There is a lot of Air in the Horoscope this month – and since Air is your native element, you are very comfortable now. Your mind, always sharp, is even sharper and clearer than normal. You inhale knowledge and information with the air that you breathe. It just comes into you naturally. A great month for students, writers, teachers and marketers.

Love is very happy this month. Singles are meeting special someones. Those already in relationships are in harmony. There are both serious and non-serious love opportunities this month. (These non-serious opportunities can test your current relationship, and they might help you clarify your feelings about the beloved.) But still, the Retrograde movement of your love planet (until the 18th) signals caution. This is not a time for important love decisions one way or another. Wait until after the 18th when judgement is better.

Mars is still in your money house until the 16th. You are making bold and aggressive financial moves. Your networking skills are fattening the bottom line. Good use of technology also seems important: perhaps you are getting involved in some high-tech kind of business. It is still good to market to or get involved with professional or trade organizations, from a financial perspective. Bold moves are one thing but haste and rush is something else. It will take much awareness on your part to discern when you are doing what. Your financial power is strongest from the 1st to the 4th and from the 18th onwards – as the Moon waxes.

Jobseekers have good success all month, but especially after the 23rd. In general you are in a more work-oriented mood after the 23rd.

November

Best Days Overall: 4, 5, 13, 14, 22, 23
Most Stressful Days Overall: 10, 11, 17, 18, 25, 26
Best Days for Love: 4, 5, 13, 14, 15, 16, 17, 18, 22, 23, 25, 26
Best Days for Money: 4, 5, 6, 7, 13, 14, 15, 16, 22, 23, 27, 28
Best Days for Career: 4, 5, 13, 14, 22, 23, 24, 25, 26

Many interesting and happy developments are going on now. Your love planet went forward on the 18th of last month after many months of Retrograde motion. Your career planet, Neptune, will start to move forwards on the 4th. By the 16th, the planetary power will shift from the lower half (emotional and family) of the Horoscope to the upper half. So, it is time, as the month progresses, to start focusing on the career again and let family and emotional issues go. Many confusions, snags and blockages in your career are being removed. The road ahead is clearer. You can see your next steps – and you should start to take them.

Also helping your career is your good work ethic this month. Your 6th House is very strong. It's as if you enjoy work now – you are in the mood – and this is noticed by those who count.

Jobseekers have good success for this reason as well; you seem ardent in your search and highly motivated – and this is 90 per cent of success.

Finances are not a big issue this month. Now that Mars has left your money house you probably achieved the goals that you wanted to achieve and can sort of coast financially. No need for major changes or major efforts. In general your earning power – and enthusiasm for finance – will be stronger on the 1st and the 2nd and from the 16th onwards. You can schedule your work accordingly.

Health is wonderful this month (though you should rest and relax more after the 22nd). Saturn's move into Libra last month had powerful health benefits for you, mostly in terms of increased energy, more optimism and the removal of family and emotional burdens and cares. Moreover, this month you are focused on health regimes, healthy lifestyles and diets too. Detox regimes are interesting now too.

Love is basically happy over the long term, but short term there can be some difficulties with the beloved. These are mostly differences of opinion and perspective: the beloved is into travelling, education and fun and you seem more into work and health. But this passes and by the 16th you and the beloved are in synch. Serious love for singles is still in foreign countries, educational or religious settings. But fun kinds of love – love affairs – are at the workplace after the 8th.

On the 22nd you enter a yearly social peak and love will bloom. Existing relationships will get more romantic and new relationships are likely as well. In general you are more socially active these days.

December

Best Days Overall: 2, 10, 11, 19, 20, 21, 29, 30
Most Stressful Days Overall: 8, 9, 15, 16, 22, 23
Best Days for Love: 2, 6, 7, 10, 11, 15, 16, 19, 20, 21, 26, 27
Best Days for Money: 2, 3, 4, 6, 7, 10, 11, 15, 16, 19, 20, 27, 28, 21, 31
Best Days for Career: 2, 10, 11, 19, 20, 21, 22, 23, 29, 30

The planetary momentum is overwhelmingly forward this month – ALL the planets are moving forward until the 20th. After the 20th it is 90 per cent of them, and although it drops after the 26th to 80 per cent, it is still a strong forward momentum. Thus there is progress in your world. You are achieving goals faster and quicker. The events of life move faster too. No more waiting around for things to happen.

You are still very much in a yearly social peak. Romance is very happy now. Marriages (or relationships that are like marriage) can happen. You are mixing with high and important people, and are likely to be romantically involved with these kinds of people too. Love is idyllic – honeymoon-like.

Career too is happy right now. Seventy to 80 per cent of the planets are above the horizon. All your career planets are moving forward and Jupiter makes beautiful aspects to your career planet – this is a classic aspect for promotion, pay rises, honours and general elevation. Enjoy. Your spouse, partner or current love is also succeeding career-wise. An office romance could be re-kindling. You have friends in the right places – or are meeting friends – who can help you in your career. You advance your career through social means, through attending or hosting parties and the like.

This is also a sexually active kind of month – especially after the 5th. Since safe sex and sexual moderation is an issue for your health (more so than for most people), avoid overdoing things. Detox regimes are good this month.

Jobseekers still have success. The jobs are out there if you want them. This is also a month to go deeper into esoteric studies, like past lives, life after death and reincarnation. Philosophy and religion has been an interest all year (and for many years in the past) and these studies fit right in.

Like last month, finances are not a big issue for you. You seem to be where you want to be. You are more interested in power, status and prestige than in mere money. But your spouse, partner or current love seems to be prospering – indeed, having one of his or her strongest financial months of the year – and he or she is more generous with you. This is a good month to pay off debts, deal with tax issues, or borrow money if you need it. Your line of credit should increase this period. If you are involved in tax or insurance issues, the month ahead brings best-case scenarios.

Cancer

THE CRAB

Birthdays from
21st June to
20th July

Personality Profile

CANCER AT A GLANCE

Element – Water

Ruling Planet – Moon
  Career Planet – Mars
  Love Planet – Saturn
  Money Planet – Sun
  Planet of Fun and Games – Pluto
  Planet of Good Fortune – Neptune
  Planet of Health and Work – Jupiter
  Planet of Home and Family Life – Venus
  Planet of Spirituality – Mercury

Colours – blue, puce, silver

Colours that promote love, romance and social
  harmony – black, indigo

Colours that promote earning power – gold,
  orange

Gems – moonstone, pearl

Metal – silver

Scents – jasmine, sandalwood

Quality – cardinal (= activity)

Quality most needed for balance – mood control

Strongest virtues – emotional sensitivity, tenacity, the urge to nurture

Deepest need – a harmonious home and family life

Characteristics to avoid – over-sensitivity, negative moods

Signs of greatest overall compatibility – Scorpio, Pisces

Signs of greatest overall incompatibility – Aries, Libra, Capricorn

Sign most helpful to career – Aries

Sign most helpful for emotional support – Libra

Sign most helpful financially – Leo

Sign best for marriage and/or partnerships – Capricorn

Sign most helpful for creative projects – Scorpio

Best Sign to have fun with – Scorpio

Signs most helpful in spiritual matters – Gemini, Pisces

Best day of the week – Monday

Understanding a Cancer

In the Sign of Cancer the heavens are developing the feeling side of things. This is what a true Cancerian is all about – feelings. Where Aries will tend to err on the side of action, Taurus on the side of inaction and Gemini on the side of thought, Cancer will tend to err on the side of feeling.

Cancerians tend to mistrust logic. Perhaps rightfully so. For them it is not enough for an argument or a project to be logical – it must feel right as well. If it does not feel right a Cancerian will reject it or chafe against it. The phrase 'follow your heart' could have been coined by a Cancerian, because it describes exactly the Cancerian attitude to life.

The power to feel is a more direct – more immediate – method of knowing than thinking is. Thinking is indirect. Thinking about a thing never touches the thing itself. Feeling is a faculty that touches directly the thing or issue in question. We actually experience it. Emotional feeling is almost like another sense which humans possess – a psychic sense. Since the realities that we come in contact with during our lifetime are often painful and even destructive, it is not surprising that the Cancerian chooses to erect barriers – a shell – to protect his or her vulnerable, sensitive nature. To a Cancerian this is only common sense.

If Cancerians are in the presence of people they do not know, or find themselves in a hostile environment, up goes the shell and they feel protected. Other people often complain about this, but one must question these other people's motives. Why does this shell disturb them? Is it perhaps because they would like to sting, and feel frustrated that they cannot? If your intentions are honourable and you are patient, have no fear. The shell will open up and you will be accepted as part of the Cancerian's circle of family and friends.

Thought-processes are generally analytic and dissociating. In order to think clearly we must make distinctions, comparisons and the like. But feeling is unifying and integrative.

To think clearly about something you have to distance yourself from it. To feel something you must get close to it. Once a Cancerian has accepted you as a friend he or she will hang on. You have to be really bad to lose the friendship of a Cancerian. If you are related to Cancerians they will never let you go no matter what you do. They will always try to maintain some kind of connection even in the most extreme circumstances.

Finance

The Cancer-born has a deep sense of what other people feel about things and why they feel as they do. This faculty is a great asset in the workplace and in the business world. Of course it is also indispensable in raising a family and building a home, but it also has its uses in business. Cancerians often attain great wealth in a family type of business. Even if the business is not a family operation, they will treat it as one. If the Cancerian works for somebody else, then the boss is the parental figure and the co-workers are brothers and sisters. If a Cancerian is the boss, then all the workers are his or her children. Cancerians like the feeling of being providers for others. They enjoy knowing that others derive their sustenance because of what they do. It is another form of nurturing.

With Leo on their Solar 2nd House (of Money) cusp, Cancerians are often lucky speculators, especially with residential property or hotels and restaurants. Resort hotels and nightclubs are also profitable for the Cancerian. Waterside properties allure them. Though they are basically conventional people, they sometimes like to earn their livelihood in glamorous ways.

The Sun, Cancer's money planet, represents an important financial message: in financial matters Cancerians need to be less moody, more stable and fixed. They cannot allow their moods – which are here today and gone tomorrow – to get in the way of their business lives. They need to develop their self-esteem and feelings of self-worth if they are to realize their greatest financial potential.

Career and Public Image

Aries rules the 10th Solar House (of Career) cusp of Cancer, which indicates that Cancerians long to start their own business, to be more active publicly and politically and to be more independent. Family responsibilities and a fear of hurting other people's feelings – or getting hurt themselves – often inhibit them from attaining these goals. However, this is what they want and long to do.

Cancerians like their bosses and leaders to act freely and to be a bit self-willed. They can deal with that in a superior. Cancerians expect their leaders to be fierce on their behalf.

When the Cancerian is in the position of boss or superior he or she behaves very much like a 'warlord'. Of course the wars they wage are not egocentric but in defence of those under their care. If they lack some of this fighting instinct – independence and pioneering spirit – Cancerians will have extreme difficulty in attaining their highest career goals. They will be hampered in their attempts to lead others.

Since they are so parental, Cancerians like to work with children and make great educators and teachers.

Love and Relationships

Like Taurus, Cancer likes committed relationships. Cancerians function best when the relationship is clearly defined and everyone knows his or her role. When they marry it is usually for life. They are extremely loyal to their beloved. But there is a deep little secret that most Cancerians will never admit to: commitment or partnership is really a chore and a duty to them. They enter into it because they know of no other way to create the family that they desire. Union is just a way – a means to an end – rather than an end in itself. The family is the ultimate end for them.

If you are in love with a Cancerian you must tread lightly on his or her feelings. It will take you a good deal of time to realize how deep and sensitive Cancerians can be. The smallest negativity upsets them. Your tone of voice, your irritation, a look in your eye or an expression on your face can cause great distress for the Cancerian. Your slightest gesture is registered by them and reacted to. This can be hard to get used to, but stick by your love – Cancerians make great partners once you learn how to deal with them. Your Cancerian lover will react not so much to what you say but to the way you are actually feeling at the moment.

Home and Domestic Life

This is where Cancerians really excel. The home environment and the family are their personal works of art. They strive to make things of beauty that will outlast them. Very often they succeed.

Cancerians feel very close to their family, their relatives and especially their mothers. These bonds last throughout their lives and mature as they grow older. They are very fond of those members of their family who become successful, and they are also quite attached to family heirlooms and mementos. Cancerians also love children and like to provide them with all the things they need and want. With their nurturing, feeling nature, Cancerians make very good parents – especially the Cancerian woman, who is the mother *par excellence* of the Zodiac.

As a parent the Cancerian's attitude is 'my children right or wrong'. Unconditional devotion is the order of the day. No matter what a family member does, the Cancerian will eventually forgive him or her, because 'you are, after all, family'. The preservation of the institution – the tradition – of the family is one of the Cancerian's main reasons for living. They have many lessons to teach others about this.

Being so family-orientated, the Cancerian's home is always clean, orderly and comfortable. They like old-fashioned furnishings but they also like to have all the modern comforts. Cancerians love to have family and friends over, to organize parties and to entertain at home – they make great hosts.

Horoscope for 2009

Major Trends

Last year was a banner social year. Many of you married or got involved in business partnerships. All of you met new and significant friends and socialized more. This year, many of these new relationships will get tested. This seems to be the cosmic pattern with these things. There is an expansion followed by a contraction or testing period. However, sexual activity will be on the increase (for those of you of appropriate age).

Health was good last year and will be good in the year ahead, though you need to watch your energy a bit more. Pluto has now moved into a stressful alignment with you.

Last year was a year for deepening the mental process – the thinking and the speech – and this trend continues in the year ahead.

Though you are always focused on the home and family, in the past few years the focus was lessened. This year – especially towards the end of the year – the focus returns.

The deeper things of life – occult studies, past lives, death and rebirth, religion and philosophy – have been important for many years now, and they become even more important in the year ahead. Many spiritual and religious break-throughs are happening.

There are four – yes four – Lunar Eclipses this year Cancer, and since the Moon is your ruling planet this has an unusual impact on you. First off, you will be redefining your image, your self-concept, who you think you are and this will create many changes in your life. You will change the way you dress and how you appear to others; this usually comes with a redefinition of the self-concept as well. A new you requires a new look and a new wardrobe. In many cases there are detoxes of the physical body as well.

Your most important areas of life in 2009 are communication and intellectual interests (until October 20); home and family (after October 29); love, romance and social activities; sex, death and rebirth, detox, occult studies, personal reinvention and transformation, life after death; religion, philosophy, higher education, ministry and foreign travel.

Your paths of greatest fulfilment in the year ahead are sex, death and rebirth; detox, occult studies, personal reinvention and transformation, life after death; love, romance and social activities (after July 27).

Health

(Please note that this is an astrological perspective on health and not a medical one. In days of yore there was no difference, both of these perspectives were identical. But in these times there could be quite a difference. For the medical perspective, please consult your doctor or health professional.)

Health, as we mentioned, looks good in the year ahead. Perhaps your overall energy is not exactly what it was last year – Pluto is stressing you out – but this is not enough to cause major problems. The fact that your 6th House of Health is empty should be read as a positive health signal: you're not paying attention to health because you have no need to. We don't run to the mechanic when the car is working fine.

But after October 29, as Saturn moves into Libra and joins Pluto in making a stressful aspect to you, you will have to force yourself to pay more attention to health and energy. Both Saturn and Pluto are long-term planets, and so this is good advice for years to come.

There are many ways to prevent problems from developing. The most important way is to keep your energy levels high. Avoid getting over-tired, rest when you are tired, work rhythmically and alternate activities, plan your day so that you achieve more with less energy, and delegate tasks to others whenever possible.

When long-term planets are stressing you out, it might not be pleasant, but there are some very good points to it.

For a start, you are forced to determine what your priorities are in life, and then to focus only on those and let the lesser things go. When energy is high we can be all things to all people and be everywhere. But when energy is low, we must let the trivial things go. Some people will never learn what their real priorities are until they face this kind of situation. So this is good.

You can also enhance your health and prevent problems by giving more attention to your vulnerable organs. These can only be determined fully by casting a personal horoscope just for you, based on your exact time and place of birth, but in general you need to give more attention to the liver and thighs (thighs should be regularly massaged) and to the ankles. (There will be times in the coming year when the feet are also important; regular foot massage – see our chart – will be wonderful.) Ankles should be regularly massaged and given more support when exercising.

Reflexology

Try to massage the whole foot on a regular basis, but pay extra attention to the points highlighted on the chart. When you massage, be aware of 'sore spots', as these need special attention. It's also a good idea to massage the ankles and top side (as well as the soles) of the feet.

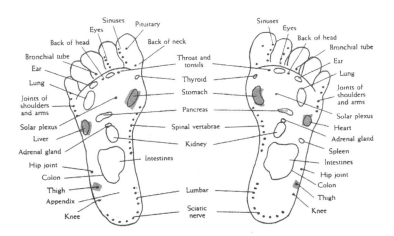

If you can follow these simple procedures you should get through the coming year with flying colours.

Jupiter, your health planet, will be in the Sign of Aquarius this year. Last year he was in Capricorn. Last year you were more conservative and traditional in health matters; this year you are more experimental, more open to alternative healing methods and therapies. This is a year for exploring new and untried therapies.

On a deeper level, this is a year where you learn how you personally function. This is your job in the year ahead. You are a law unto yourself. No one in the universe is wired up the way you are. So, through trial, error, experiment and observation you need to see how you function on certain diets, foods and therapies. This will bring much new health knowledge to you and stand you in good stead in the future.

Home and Family

Things have more or less been static at home and with the family the past few years, and the Horoscope is not showing any major changes. Basically you could put this department of life on 'automatic pilot' and coast through. This is still the case until October 29. But afterwards, more work and attention is needed.

Saturn moves into your 4th House then, and his mission is to reorganize and restructure the home and family life. It is time for a new order to be manifested – a new and better order than you've been following.

How will Saturn do this? No matter, he is a genius at this kind of thing. An older person can come to stay, perhaps a business partner or an ex-spouse, and everything needs to be rearranged. Perhaps you start to feel cramped in the home – merely on an emotional level – and there is a need to create more space or use the current space better. Perhaps your redefinition of your image requires changes in your living arrangements as well.

Saturn also happens to be your love and marriage planet. So his move into your 4th House suggests that you will be entertaining more from home, and this will require a reorganization of the home. Also, your spouse or current love could agitate for this. Singles might find that the current love is moving in with them and this necessitates restructuring. You might want to move to a larger place, but it doesn't seem advisable – better to make better use of the space that you have.

Saturn is very powerful in the Sign of Libra (your 4th House). He is in his most exalted position. Thus the changes you make are likely to be very good. Also the new domestic routine will tend to be beautiful, just and fair.

Your home will be much improved both aesthetically and in terms of lifestyle in the coming years. You are entering a period where you will beautify the home as well. You will be buying art, antiques, objects of beauty – making it a place of beauty as much as a home.

Parents or parent figures probably moved in the past year (or perhaps they bought additional homes), but it seems to me that they are not finished with renovating. Construction seems to be going on.

Siblings are having job changes – good ones – but are not likely to move. Single siblings could marry this year, or enter into a relationship that is like a marriage. Children of appropriate age are moving or buying additional homes – these look happy. They are also prospering from real estate. Grandchildren of appropriate age seem like nomadic figures, wondering and wandering – restless – as if they had no permanent home. They are staying in different places for long periods of time.

Finance and Career

You reorganized your financial life from 2005 to 2007 and it seems to have been effective. Your 2nd House of Finance is not a House of Power this year (nor was it last year) and finances seem pretty much status quo. You have no pressing need to make dramatic changes. (Keep in mind that every year your financial planet, the Sun, is eclipsed twice, and this year is no different. These eclipses bring a testing of your financial strategies and thinking. They bring changes and adjustments that long needed to be made, but since these things happen with regularity I'm reading the year ahead as keeping the status quo.)

However, towards the end of the year, Mars, your career planet, makes an important move into your money house. He will be there from October 16 well into 2010; thus finances (personal wealth) will become important then and it should be a more prosperous period. You will focus on it – and this is 90 per cent of success. Money will come to you as a result of your good professional reputation, from elders, parents, parent figures or the government (or government contracts). The authorities in your life are supporting your financial goals.

The situation at work and with employees also seems pretty much status quo. Jobseekers will have very interesting opportunities in foreign countries or with foreign companies in the year ahead. Those who hire others might want to look abroad as well. However, those who hire others are probably cutting back on staff numbers this year – this is not because of bad business conditions but a desire to get more work with fewer employees, probably due to better technology or automation.

The main financial headline this year is Jupiter's transit through your 8th House. On an overall level, this makes the 8th House the strongest in the Horoscope this year (there will be times when others Houses are stronger, but we're talking overall now). Thus many of you will inherit substantial sums this year. In many cases it will be a literal inheritance, but quite often it shows that someone remembers you in their will, or a trust fund is set up on your behalf. No one needs to actually die. The 8th House also rules royalties and insurance payments – thus if you have insurance claims pending, there are best-case outcomes happening.

When the 8th House is strong, it shows the prosperity of your spouse or business partners and their generosity towards you. Thus spousal support will be better than usual.

The 8th House is all about making money for other people and with other people's money. There is unusually good access to outside money – either from borrowing or outright investment. This is a great year to reduce or refinance debt. The credit line will certainly increase in the year ahead, and there are profits to be made through 'creative financing'. Those of you who have good ideas should have no problem attracting outside investors to your projects. The main point to keep in mind is that you need to put the financial interests of the partners and investors ahead of your own. So long as you prosper them, your own prosperity will certainly happen by the karmic law.

Since the 8th House rules death and rebirth, power in this House – and especially when the planet of abundance, Jupiter, is there – shows that there are financial opportunities to be taken with companies or properties that are troubled (or even bankrupt). This year you have a special ability to see value where others see only death and decay. Thus you can be walking through a junk yard and spot a valuable antique, or see how an old decrepit house can be fixed up and resold, or buy valuable assets at repossession sales. Many a City fortune has been built by buying the bonds of bankrupt companies and cashing in when the company recovered. These kinds of investments are not for the faint of heart, but you have these kinds of abilities these days.

Professional investors should focus on bonds and the bond market this year – especially the bonds of high technology and media companies.

Love and Social Life

As we mentioned earlier, you are coming out of a very powerful year for your love and social life and it is doubtful whether 2009 can match 2008. Many of you married or got involved in serious kinds of relationships, and so this is a year of refining and purifying what you have rather than looking for something new.

Love and social activities are still very important in the year ahead, and for a long time to come. This year Pluto moves permanently into your 7th House and will stay there for many years. (Last year he merely flirted with your 7th House; now he is there for the long haul.)

The honeymoon stage of romance is always the easy part. But now there is a need to perfect the relationship (and the social life in general) by removing the impurities. This detox of the love life is generally not pleasant but if you understand what is going on, it will be wonderful. Yes, it brings near-death, or death and rebirth experiences in the marriage or current relationship, but the end result will be the relationship of your dreams – your ideal relationship – your ideal marriage. The cosmos wants you to have the best; nothing less than perfection will do. The social pains that you feel are merely birth pangs – the birth of something beautiful.

For marrieds, especially those who have been married a long time, Pluto's move into the 7th House will certainly test the relationship. The marriage will certainly die in coming years, but it's up to you whether resurrection happens. It can be with the present spouse or partner or with another. This is true of long-term friendships and business partnerships as well.

The year ahead is an unusually sexually active kind of year. So there is romance in life. Whatever your age or stage in life, the libido will be stronger than usual.

We get a sense of high passion in love. And this is what is enhancing the sexuality. But the high passion has a downside, especially when it turns negative – as it generally does over time. There is a need to keep the passions constructive and not destructive. Jealousy and possessiveness are real dangers in love this year (they are always dangers, but now, and with you, it is very dramatic).

For those of you who are still single we see love affairs; love affairs that are like a marriage – love affairs with people who are 'marriage material' – but will it actually end up that way? The Horoscope is not clear on this.

Your love planet is making a major move this year, towards the end of the year. On October 29, he will move from Virgo into Libra – from your 3rd House to your 4th House. On one level this is a nice transit for love. The love planet in romantic Libra is much better positioned than in Virgo and this should improve things. There will be less analysis, less criticism, less of a mental approach and more of a feeling, romantic approach.

For the past few years intellectual compatibility was very important in love. After October 29, emotional compatibility – the ability to share emotions, feelings and give emotional support – becomes important. You will be attracted by these kinds of people, family-oriented people, people who are emotionally sensitive and supportive.

Until October 29 singles will find love opportunities in educational-type settings – at lectures, seminars and the like. Love is in the neighbourhood and close to home. After October 29, singles find love opportunities through family connections, family gatherings, or through people who are like family to them.

Those working on the second marriage are probably better off enjoying their freedom for a while; the social life is highly unstable. Those in their second marriage have been having their marriages tested (probably there have been divorces here in the past few years). Those in or working on their third marriage have a status-quo kind of year. Marrieds will probably stay married and singles will probably stay single.

Self-improvement

Saturn has been moving through your 3rd House of Communication and Intellectual Interests for the past two years. Thus the cosmos is working on setting your mind, your thinking and your communication skills in right order. It has been working to deepen the thinking. It has forced you to organize your thoughts better and to do your home-work before speaking or forming opinions. This is good, though it hasn't exactly been pleasant. No one likes to be constantly challenged about everything they say or think. Yet, the new depth of thought it brought, the new insights, were worth it.

Now (after October 29) Saturn is moving into your 4th House of the Emotional Life. And, he intends to bring 'right order' there as well. You Canceriens are very moody and emotional people; many of you feel that you can't do anything about it and feel that you are 'victims' of mood, 'victims' of emotion. But you will soon learn that this is not the case. You have full dominion over your emotional life once you learn how it operates. The challenge now is to manage the emotional life 'just so' – neither repressing negative feeling, nor expressing it into the universe. Some, like the Buddhists, suggest that one merely experiences whatever the feeling is without expressing it and without judgement. They have discovered that when this is done, the negative state soon passes. But there are other ways of dealing with these things too. You can write out your negative feelings on paper, holding nothing back, and then throw away the paper. It is a psychological elimination. You've expressed the feelings but in harmless ways, and you will immediately feel better. (Don't reread what you've written – it should be considered as psychic 'waste', and just as you wouldn't re-eat physical waste that you've eliminated, you shouldn't 're-eat' this psychic waste.) You can also speak your feelings into a tape – again not holding anything back – and then erase the tape. Make a statement to the effect that 'just as I am erasing this tape, these thoughts and feelings are also erased', or 'just as I am throwing out these papers, so am I removing all these thoughts, feelings and negativity from my mind; they are now in the cosmic garbage bin', as appropriate.

As we mentioned, 2009 seems like a sexually active year. Neptune, the most spiritual of all the planets, has been in your 8th House of Sex for many years now. The cosmos is working to refine, elevate and spiritualize your sexual attitudes and practice. It's not trying to deprive you of sex, but to make it more sublime and beautiful. Thus you are in a period for learning more about the spiritual dimensions of the sexual act – something that modern medicine and psychology seem oblivious to. There is much more to the sexual act than orgasm or self-fulfilment; it actually creates on all the various levels of being, it creates living forms. So when you study the spiritual side of it, you will learn how to create beautiful and helpful forms, rather than destructive ones. This is a big subject and I've barely scratched the surface – but those who are interested should study the Tantric (Eastern) and hermetic (Western) approaches to it.

Month-by-month Forecasts

January

  Best Days Overall: 1, 2, 10, 11, 18, 19, 28, 29
  Most Stressful Days Overall: 3, 4, 16, 17, 23, 24, 30, 31
  Best Days for Love: 6, 7, 9, 10, 14, 15, 18, 19, 23, 24, 28, 29
  Best Days for Money: 5, 6, 7, 12, 14, 15, 16, 25, 26, 27
  Best Days for Career: 3, 4, 6, 14, 15, 23, 24, 30, 31

Your year begins in the midst of a yearly social peak – a nice way to begin 2009. The social life is active and exciting, and has been this way in 2008 as well. You are enjoying the social whirl, but the interest is starting to wane. Jupiter leaves your 7th House on the 5th and the Sun will leave on the 19th. Your interests will start to shift to the deeper things in life – personal transformation and the renewal of the body. For those of you on the spiritual path, there will be great interest in the ascension and resurrection process, and great progress will be made.

Those not on the spiritual path will have a more active – hyperactive – sex life this month (and for the year ahead). Whatever your age, the libido will be stronger than usual.

What counts is how you use this libido. Used properly it will give you strength to make psychological breakthroughs, develop your mental abilities and enhance your health. Misused, it will just be wasted energy – like having a million dollars and blowing it on a night on the town.

Personal finances don't seem a big issue. Probably you are where you want to be financially and have no need to pay too much attention to this. (However a Solar Eclipse on the 26th is going to force you to pay attention.) The month ahead is more about your spouse's, partner's or current love's finances – and he or she is having a banner month – and a banner year ahead. Right now, from the 5th onwards, he or she is in a yearly financial peak and will be more generous with you.

This is a month where you prosper by prospering others. You seem to be doing this, and are successful. You are very much involved in the financial lives of friends, partners, your spouse or current love. Social contacts – and the good graces of others – are very important financially (and in most other ways too). With 80 and sometimes 90 per cent of the planets in the Western sector of the Horoscope, self-will and personal initiative is not important – and perhaps not even advisable. It is the grace of other people that you need.

If you are involved in tax, estate or insurance issues, this month brings fortunate outcomes. Likewise if you are seeking investors or outside money for your projects.

Many a wedding bell has rung for Canceriens in 2008 and if it hasn't happened yet, it can happen this month. (Probably you are attending more weddings this month too.)

Overall your health is good, but rest and relax more until the 19th. Enhance your health in the ways described in the yearly report (*see page 127*).

February

Best Days Overall: 6, 7, 15, 16, 24, 25, 26
Most Stressful Days Overall: 1, 12, 13, 19, 20, 21, 27, 28
Best Days for Love: 2, 3, 8, 9, 10, 11, 17, 18, 19, 20, 21, 27, 28
Best Days for Money: 4, 5, 8, 9, 12, 13, 22, 23, 24, 25
Best Days for Career: 1, 3, 4, 12, 22, 23, 27, 28

In December 2008, the planetary power shifted from the lower to the upper half of the Horoscope. An important shift. It shows it is the day period of your year. And you need to be focused on your career and outer life. The night is done, the dreams have been dreamt and the images of the future have been forged. Now is the time to make them happen by external activity. Family will always be important to you and you will never ignore them, but you can serve them best by being successful in the world.

The last eclipse – the Solar Eclipse of January 26 – affected your finances and the finances of your spouse, partner or current love. Both of you needed to make important financial changes, and your partner's financial strategy needed rethinking. He or she is probably more prosperous than was thought and so the financial planning needs to change – it was probably too conservative. This month, there is a Lunar Eclipse (on the 9th) in your money house, which affects you more than your partner. Perhaps your spouse's financial changes now force you to make financial changes. A sudden expense or financial disruption will turn out to be a blessing in disguise.

This eclipse also forces you to redefine your personality and image – something that happens twice a year (in general) but this year will happen three more times. A personality – a self-concept – is a lifelong work in progress. It should always be growing and upgrading and expanding, and now you have an opportunity to do this. Often detoxes of the body happen under these aspects. Operate a reduced schedule a few days before and after the eclipse.

The other main headline this month is the power in your 8th House (also strong last month). Sixty per cent of the planets – a huge, huge percentage – are either there or moving through there. So the activities ruled by the 8th House are important now: life and death, life after death, reincarnation, sex, detox, personal transformation and reinvention, debts (making them or paying them), taxes, estates – just to name a few. Please refer to our discussion of these interests in last month's report.

Often when the 8th House is this strong there are near-death experiences, either personal or with people who are close to you. This is not punitive, but only a means by which you deepen your understanding of life and death.

Like last month, you prosper as you prosper others. On a mundane level this need to prosper others is even stronger than last month – it seems almost your spiritual mission. Don't completely ignore your personal financial interests, but try to put the financial interest of your spouse, partner or current love ahead of your own. This is not about financial martyrdom, but about how to focus.

Health is excellent this month. In fact if there have been health problems in the past, there is a likelihood of sudden or miraculous types of healing. Detox is still very good now.

March

> Best Days Overall: 5, 6, 14, 15, 24, 25
> Most Stressful Days Overall: 12, 13, 19, 20, 26, 27
> Best Days for Love: 1, 2, 7, 8, 10, 16, 17, 18, 19, 20, 26, 27, 28, 29
> Best Days for Money: 3, 4, 5, 6, 7, 8, 12, 13, 14, 15, 21, 22, 23, 24, 25, 30, 31
> Best Days for Career: 3, 4, 12, 13, 24, 25, 26, 27

The planetary power is still mostly in the West (though this is soon to change) and it is still advisable to avoid self-will or personal power struggles. Achieve your ends through consensus and compromise. Keep in harmony with others;

you need them. As you keep the harmony and allow things to happen, good will come to you with ease, as if by magic. Your way might not be the best way these days.

On the 18th of last month, your 9th House of Religion, Philosophy, Higher Education and Foreign Travel became powerful, and this is the trend for much of the month ahead. Generally this brings happy travel opportunities (they seem related to finance), educational opportunities and religious or philosophical breakthroughs. Much depends on your personal approach to life. If you are living a standard, mundane kind of life, this will probably manifest as travel or educational opportunities. But those of you on the spiritual path will have religious revelations.

This is an especially good month for students, whether at college or pre-college level. (Last month was also good for them.) The mind is sharp, there is great interest in study, and thus success is more likely to happen.

Until the 15th your mission in life is still about prospering other people; as you do so, you not only personally prosper too, but you further your career as well. After the 15th your mission is about education. It is important that you have the educational background for the career that you want, or for the position that you want. Even if you are already in an established career, it might be a good idea to take seminars or workshops related to your career – or to get that more advanced degree that you need. Your willingness to travel will also play an important role in career advancement.

On the 20th, as the Sun crosses your Midheaven, you enter a yearly career peak. Happy financial and career opportunities open up. Pay rises or promotions are very likely now, although sometimes it shows that elders, bosses and superiors are financially supportive or are giving you opportunities. Your good professional reputation is unusually important right now – and it seems good. Most of the planets are still above the horizon. Your 4th House of Home and Family is basically empty (only the Moon visits there on the 12th and 13th), while your 10th House of Career is powerful. Your family planet, Venus, makes a very rare

Retrograde on the 6th. Therefore let family issues go. Don't try to make important family decisions or moves right now – focus on career.

Health is wonderful until the 20th but afterwards rest and relax more. Enhance your health in the ways described in the yearly report (*page 127*).

There is sudden – unexpected – financial good spell from the 11th to the 14th. There can be important and sudden career changes towards the end of the month, and perhaps a drama with a parent or parent figure. Drive defensively towards the end of the month.

April

Best Days Overall: 2, 3, 10, 11, 20, 21, 29, 30
Most Stressful Days Overall: 8, 9, 15, 16, 22, 23
Best Days for Love: 4, 6, 7, 15, 16, 20, 21, 25, 26
Best Days for Money: 4, 5, 8, 9, 13, 14, 18, 19, 25, 26, 27, 28
Best Days for Career: 2, 3, 10, 11, 21, 22, 23

A very happy job opportunity is coming this month and it might involve a foreign company or work in a foreign land. It's very exciting, but nail down all the details. Those who hire others should perhaps look to foreign countries (or foreigners within your own country).

Continue to drive defensively and avoid risk-taking from the 10th to the 15th. Parents and parent figures should also take it easier. This period is likely to bring sudden career changes too; it seems to me it is positive, but very disruptive. There are probably shakeups in your company or industry during this period as well.

Saturn, your love planet, has been the handle of a bucket-type chart for the past few months. It is this way in the current month too. This shows that your marriage or current love – your social life in general – is the handle – the lever – by which you lift up your life. But this is about to change. By the 22nd (as Mars crosses over to the East) the

Eastern sector of the Horoscope will become stronger than the Western sector. Thus you are entering a period of greater independence. You have more power to act on your own without the permission or approval of others. You don't need to adapt to situations but can actually change them to suit yourself. It is time to have things your way. Be loving and courteous to others, but go your own way. Your way is best for you.

You are still in a yearly career peak and it is only getting stronger. You have to work hard, that's for sure. Success is not being handed to you on a silver platter but you will see the results of your work. Even family members (who still seem without direction this month) are supportive of your career goals. The family as a whole should be more elevated – raised in status – this month. Pay rises and promotions are likely. Elders, bosses, parents and parent figures are more supportive. There are even financial opportunities with the government. After the 19th financial opportunities come through friends, groups, organizations and your ability to network. Real estate and high-tech businesses seem like interesting investments. Before the 19th, it is gold, utilities and energy that promise the most opportunities.

Continue to rest and relax more all month, but especially until the 19th. Spiritual healing has become an important interest and many of you will see miraculous things with this.

Love is very happy after the 19th and those of you who are still single (if there are any of you left) will have many romantic opportunities found through friends, groups, group activities, or in educational settings, like school or lectures. But your love planet is Retrograde – and has been so for the past few months – so let love develop slowly and steadily and don't rush into anything. The natural events of life will show you whether love is true or not.

May

Best Days Overall: 8, 9, 18, 19, 26, 27
Most Stressful Days Overall: 5, 6, 12, 13, 14, 20, 21
Best Days for Love: 1, 2, 3, 4, 10, 11, 12, 13, 14, 20, 21,
    22, 23, 28, 29, 30, 31
Best Days for Money: 1, 2, 3, 4, 5, 6, 12, 13, 14, 15, 16,
    24, 25, 28, 29
Best Days for Career: 1, 2, 10, 11, 20, 21, 28, 29

Keeping your love and financial life balanced seems to be
the main challenge after the 20th. Your financial interests
pull you one way while your love and social interests pull
you in another. There could be some short-term financial
disagreements with the beloved, but this will work itself out
– it is nothing that is enough to damage a good relationship.
The beloved might resent being ignored or because of your
financial interests. Try to keep things in balance. Love is
basically happy aside from this. On the 17th Saturn, your
love planet starts to move forwards after many months of
Retrograde motion, and this will clarify things in existing
relationships. Also it restores your natural clear thinking
about love and social confidence in general.

Career is still important in the month ahead. While it is
not as strong as in the previous two months it is still a focus
– and so it should be. You are working hard and fending off
competitors. You can enhance your status through social
means – networking, attending the right parties and perhaps
hosting them as well – but also through old-fashioned hard
work. This is a time for bold – and perhaps risk-taking –
career moves. If you have thought things through, take that
leap you've been contemplating. You have friends in the
right places who are helping you.

Your friends are also succeeding career-wise this month.
They seem in positions of power and influence.

Your main interests this month (aside from career) are
personal transformation and reinvention, the deeper things
of life (a strong interest all year as well), friendships, group

activities, organizations and spirituality. Friendships and group activities are not only important for your career, but for the bottom line as well – especially until the 20th.

On the 20th, as the Sun moves into your spiritual 12th House, you enter a yearly spiritual peak. This brings spiritual experiences, breakthroughs, and many supernatural-type experiences that can't be explained by logic or science. The dream life tends to be more active and prophetic as well. It is normal during this kind of transit to desire more seclusion and 'personal time'. There is a need to feel your own aura and to connect to the divine in you. This is a wonderful period for going on spiritual kinds of retreats or pilgrimages. Mediation seminars and workshops are also good, likewise charitable types of activities.

Health is good this month. Spiritual healing is still important and powerful. A time to go deeper into this realm.

June

Best Days Overall: 4, 5, 14, 15, 23
Most Stressful Days Overall: 2, 3, 9, 10, 16, 17, 29, 30
Best Days for Love: 9, 10, 19, 27, 28
Best Days for Money: 2, 3, 11, 12, 13, 21, 22, 24, 25, 29, 30
Best Days for Career: 9, 10, 16, 17, 19, 27, 28

Career interests are waning this month. I read this as a good thing. You have probably attained your goals and are ready to spend more time socializing or enhancing your spirituality. Like last month, friendships and networking are important career-wise. Your social connections – having friends in the right places – are furthering your career. Networking and being involved in trade or professional organizations is also helpful.

Finances need more effort this month, especially until the 20th. There are financial disagreements with the beloved or partners that need to be worked out. But with your financial planet in the spiritual 12th House, intuition –

and the guidance of psychics, ministers, spiritual channels and astrologers – will guide you properly. Financial guidance will come to you in dreams and visions too, but you have to be alert here.

With the financial planet in the 12th House the cosmos wants to take you deeper into the spiritual sources of supply. Thus it is good that there are financial conundrums – apparently insoluble conflicts in the external life – so you can be more amenable to the inner guidance.

Avoid speculations from the 20th to the 23rd.

This is still a good period – especially until the 21st – for getting involved in spiritually oriented activities and for making personal spiritual progress. Refer to our discussion of this last month.

Love is mixed this month, bittersweet. Better communication with the beloved will be a big help. Your spiritual mission seems to involve your friends – being there for them – and this (plus financial issues) is complicating your relationship. Serious love opportunities for singles are at educational-type settings, in the neighbourhood or perhaps with neighbours. Romantic opportunities can come through siblings as well.

On the 21st, as the Sun enters your own Sign, you enter a yearly personal pleasure peak. This brings all the delights of the senses – the good life – good food, wine and carnal joys. This is also a wonderful financial period. Financial problems with partners should be resolved by then, and financial windfalls and opportunities are coming to you. You are dressing in a more expensive way – creating an image of wealth. You are investing in yourself and spending on yourself.

Health is excellent all month. The only danger is overdoing the good life. Indulge by all means, but don't over indulge.

July

Best Days Overall: 1, 2, 11, 12, 20, 21, 28, 29, 30
Most Stressful Days Overall: 6, 7, 14, 15, 26, 27
Best Days for Love: 6, 7, 9, 16, 17, 18, 19, 24, 25, 26, 27
Best Days for Money: 1, 2, 9, 10, 11, 12, 18, 19, 22, 23, 26, 27, 31
Best Days for Career: 6, 7, 14, 15, 18, 26, 27

The planets are now in their most Eastern position of your chart. You are in a period of maximum personal independence. You can – and should – have things your way. Push forward to your personal goals. If conditions don't suit you, you have the power to create new ones that do. This is the purpose now. Create your life as you desire it to be. Others will more or less adapt to you.

You are still very much in your yearly personal pleasure peak, enjoying the good life and pampering the flesh. On the 22nd you enter a yearly financial peak as well. Earnings will be very strong (even before that too).

Two eclipses this month seem strong on you. The first, the Lunar Eclipse of the 7th occurs in your 7th House. This is going to test your marriage, current relationships and business partnerships. Be patient as the dirty laundry comes up for resolution. It also brings detoxes of the body and a redefinition of the personality and the image. You will start to change your look – your physical presentation to the world – in coming months.

The 2nd eclipse (a Solar Eclipse on the 22nd) brings much of the same. It is especially strong on those of you born later in your Sign, from July 15 to 23. If you fall into this category be sure to reduce your schedule this period. This eclipse brings important financial changes – changes in outlook, strategy and thinking. I feel the eclipse will bring happy financial surprises to you as you are in a yearly financial peak. Perhaps you have been under-valuing yourself, or making plans based on pessimism. The eclipse will change your thinking.

Spirituality continues to be important this month, as 40 per cent of the planets are either in your 12th House or moving through there. Your spiritual mission this month, especially after the 12th, is just to expand your spiritual understanding and life. For those of you on the spiritual path, just doing your yoga – your spiritual practice – is all that is required of you. Everything else will arise as a result of that. (Just doing your spiritual practice is by itself considered a great service to the world.) For those not on the path, it is still good to focus on charities and altruistic activities. They are not only good in their own right but they will enhance your worldly career in interesting ways. These activities will also bring happy social contacts as well. There is a happy supernatural-type experience on the 2nd or 3rd. A spiritual teacher or guru is coming to you as well.

Health is good, but rest and relax more during the eclipse periods.

August

Best Days Overall: 7, 8, 9, 16, 17, 25, 26
Most Stressful Days Overall: 2, 3, 4, 10, 11, 23, 24, 30, 31
Best Days for Love: 2, 3, 4, 7, 8, 9, 12, 13, 16, 17, 21, 22, 25, 26, 30, 31
Best Days for Money: 1, 5, 6, 10, 11, 14, 15, 18, 19, 20, 23, 24, 30, 31
Best Days for Career: 5, 6, 10, 11, 14, 15, 24

The last eclipse on July 22 affected your personal finances. The Lunar Eclipse of the 6th seems to affect the finances of your spouse, partner or current love. He or she also needs to make dramatic financial changes, things that should have been done long ago but which were being postponed. Now there is no choice. However, your partner or spouse should not just leap into action blindly: there needs to be more than usual study and analysis of these moves. As with the last Lunar Eclipse of July 7th you are again redefining your image and personality – a good thing; whatever wasn't accomplished on the last eclipse will get accomplished now. The changes to your image and personal appearance will be deep. A detox of the body now should not be considered a sickness – just a natural detox. (Often what gets diagnosed as infection and treated with antibiotics is merely a natural detox – the body is getting rid of bad material.)

You are still well into a yearly financial peak and earnings are strong. Assets you own increase in value. There are profit opportunities with gold, utilities, energy and entertainment. Industries that cater to children also seem profitable for those of you with investment accounts. People in these industries can be important on a financial level as well.

Love should be very happy this month. Whether or not you meet Mr or Miss Right is not the issue – you look good, and you are attracting the opposite sex. With Venus in your own Sign until the 26th you dress beautifully and project a beautiful image. A good period for buying clothing and personal accessories (and for sure these are coming to you – the last two eclipses virtually guarantee this). Friends are seeking you out.

On the 24th Mars moves into your Sign. This has many messages. It enhances your physical energy. You excel in sports and exercise regimes (even non athletes will perform better this period). You get things done in a hurry. You are dynamic and exude sex appeal. In your chart, this transit also shows happy career opportunities that are seeking you out. You don't have to run after these things, they come to you. People of high position and power are coming to see you and seem devoted to your interest. (Parents or parent figures are probably also coming to visit.) Avoid rush, hast and anger – this is the main health danger now. These things can lead to accidents or injury. Be dynamic, but not in a rush.

September

Best Days Overall: 4, 5, 13, 14, 21, 22
Most Stressful Days Overall: 6, 7, 19, 20, 26, 27
Best Days for Love: 6, 7, 8, 9, 15, 16, 17, 18, 26, 27
Best Days for Money: 1, 2, 8, 9, 11, 12, 15, 16, 17, 18, 19, 20, 28, 29, 30
Best Days for Career: 4, 5, 6, 7, 13, 14, 21, 22

On August 25, as Mars moved below the horizon of your Horoscope, the planetary power shifted from the upper to the lower half of your Horoscope. The power in the lower half is not overwhelming, but slightly stronger than the upper half. You are entering the night time of your year. Time to de-emphasize the career (you won't be able to ignore it completely, it is still very important) and focus on your first love: the home, the family and your emotional well being – your feeling of emotional wellness. Too often in our drive for worldly success we ignore our feelings. Perhaps we even abuse them – sweep them under the rug and the like, and thus cause problems for ourselves later on. Now is the time to deal with these things. Pursue your career by the methods of night and not the methods of day. Prepare the ground, gather the forces, for future success. Take the pause that refreshes. When day arrives again – in four or five months' time – you will pursue your career with fresh vigour.

Your career planet, Mars, is also below the horizon – another message to pursue your career in emotionally comfortable ways. Blind ambition won't work these days. You need to be in your emotional comfort zone. You need the support of your family and a stable home base.

With Mars in your 1st House all month, career opportunities are seeking you out, like last month. Not much you need to do. These things are pursuing you. You seem in demand. You have choices and you can choose the ones that are most emotionally comfortable.

With Venus in your money house until the 20th, networking and social connections are important on a financial level.

Your friends – the true ones – are like money in the bank. They are supportive and provide opportunities as well. This is a month for manifesting fondest financial hopes and wishes. Your financial planet will be in the 3rd House until the 23rd. This shows that sales, marketing, media activities, teaching or writing are very important financially. You need to get the word out about your product or service (only keep in mind that Mercury, the planet of communication, is Retrograde from the 7th to the 29th and this will complicate marketing and media activities – it might be better perhaps to plan these things in the month ahead and execute them later on).

On the 23rd your financial planet enters your 4th House of Home and Family and this gives many messages. Parents, parent figures and family in general are financially support-ive, more so than usual. Family connections play an impor-tant role in earnings. Opportunities will arise in the family business (your own or someone else's) in the month ahead. You are spending more on the home and family and perhaps in real estate or expensive items for the home.

Health is good, but rest and relax more after the 23rd. Enhance the health in the ways described in the yearly report (*see page 127*).

October

Best Days Overall: 1, 2, 10, 11, 19, 20, 28, 29
Most Stressful Days Overall: 3, 4, 16, 17, 23, 24, 31
Best Days for Love: 6, 7, 14, 15, 16, 23, 24, 26, 27
Best Days for Money: 8, 9, 12, 13, 16, 17, 18, 26, 27, 28, 29
Best Days for Career: 1, 2, 3, 4, 10, 11, 21, 22, 31

Your love planet makes a major, major move at the end of the month, from Virgo, your 3rd House into Libra, your 4th House. Thus you are becoming more romantically oriented. For two years you tended to express your love in very prac-tical ways, unsentimentally. You served the interests of the beloved in practical ways. Perhaps you neglected the

Valentine's Day card, but you made up for it many other ways. Now, the attitude is changed. It is the flowers, the cards, the candies, the love talk and the strolls down moonlit beaches that matter. Love needs to be more than practical – it needs to be beautiful. In many ways, it seems to me, this shift will improve the love life – either the existing relationship or new relationships that arise. There will be less criticism, less demands – and more tolerance and love. This shift could put existing relationships into temporary crisis; the rules have changed and you and the beloved have not yet learned the new rules. For singles there is a very beautiful romantic opportunity from the 7th to the 10th. This happens in the neighbourhood or in an educational setting. This person is either a friend who wants to be more, or comes through the introduction of a friend.

Home and family is still the dominant interest for most of the month ahead. And it should be. Financial goals don't seem to depend on the career these days, more on the good graces of the family and parent figures. Career opportunities, like last month, are seeking you out. Bosses seem devoted to you and to your interest; likewise parents or parent figures.

Communication and intellectual interests are also very strong this month. A very good period to catch up on the letters or phone calls you owe. It's also good for taking courses in subjects that interest you.

For many months now you have been very independent. You were able to have things your way. Your personal initiative was the main ingredient in your success. But by the 29th the planetary power shifts once again to the social West, and these qualities will not be so important. Now your social skills will count. What you are and what you can do is always important, but who you know, and how well liked you are, becomes even more important. Hopefully by now you have created the conditions that you wanted in life (or at least made progress towards them). Now it is time to live in those conditions, to road test them and to see how well you like them. Not so easy to change them now.

Health needs more watching until the 23rd. Try to pace yourself in a comfortable way. Saturn is now moving into a stressful aspect with you and your skill in pacing yourself – working in a rhythm – will be important for the next two years.

November

Best Days Overall: 6, 7, 15, 16, 25, 26
Most Stressful Days Overall: 1, 13, 14, 20, 21, 27, 28
Best Days for Love: 4, 5, 13, 15, 16, 20, 21, 22, 25, 26
Best Days for Money: 4, 5, 6, 7, 8, 9, 13, 14, 15, 16, 22, 23, 27, 28
Best Days for Career: 1, 8, 9, 17, 18, 27, 28

Aside from Saturn's move into Libra, last month brought other very interesting developments. Jupiter, your health planet, started to move forwards after many months of Retrograde motion. This is a positive for the health. Probably there are changes that need to be made to your health regime and now is the time to do it. This is also a positive for jobseekers as it is easier to find work now – and also the judgement is clearer about these things. (Jobseekers will have better success after the 22nd than before; they just need some patience now.) Towards the end of the month there are dream job opportunities, and next month as well.

On October 16th, Mars moved into your money house and will be there for the rest of the year. This shows pay rises and promotions. Parents or parent figures – bosses – and even the government are supportive of financial goals. In career issues you are more concerned with the bottom line than you are with glory, status and prestige. You want the gold; let others have the glory. You measure success in terms of pounds and pence. If you have developed a good professional reputation you will see the results of this – in a bottom-line way – in the month ahead. It leads to referrals and other unexpected surprises. The only problem with Mars in your money house is the tendency to make hasty and rash decisions – perhaps you feel in a rush to attain certain goals – and this is a danger signal. One can make bold moves and even rapid progress from a sense of peace and calm; the feeling of rush can lead to errors in judgement. You are in a more risk-taking mood financially but avoid speculations until after the 22nd. That period will be more prosperous and more fortunate than before the 22nd.

Health is reasonably good this month. Two long-term planets are stressing you, but the other short-term ones are helping you out. You should be OK. You can continue to enhance your health in the ways described in the yearly report (*page 127*).

Last month on the 23rd you entered a yearly personal pleasure peak, and it is still in full swing this month. It's party time in your year. You don't want to miss it. Joy is not only a great healer but it also opens up the creative faculties, and thus you can see solutions that you ordinarily wouldn't see. Happy financial ideas – and perhaps connections – will come to you as you enjoy your life. There will be a tendency to want to speculate, as we mentioned, but better to wait until the 22nd. This is also a period for focusing on children, either your actual children or those who are like children to you.

Love is very delicate all month – there is a crisis.

December

Best Days Overall: 4, 12, 13, 22, 23, 31
Most Stressful Days Overall: 10, 11, 17, 18, 24, 25, 26
Best Days for Love: 1, 2, 6, 7, 10, 15, 16, 17, 18, 19, 20, 26, 27, 29
Best Days for Money: 2, 6, 7, 10, 11, 15, 16, 19, 20, 21, 27, 28
Best Days for Career: 6, 7, 15, 16, 24, 25, 26

Love is still in crisis, but perhaps the worst is over with – at least for a while. In January and February of next year the crisis will be revisited. A good relationship can survive this, but a lukewarm one, or bad one, will not. Your spouse or partner might be opting for surgery – and perhaps you as well – and this is complicating matters. There can be issues of infidelity. Basically, the love life, marriage and social life in general are getting a detox right now. It probably isn't pretty, but the end result (once all the impurities come out) will be good. At least for the holidays there is some hope of harmony. Regardless of the state of your relationship, on the 22nd the Sun will enter your 7th House of Love and Social Activities and this will initiate a yearly social peak (if the aspects were easier, the social peak would be better). This adds more hope of harmony for the holidays. Since you are more interested in social matters, you will pay more attention and seem more willing to overcome all the challenges that you are facing.

For most of the month your focus is on health and work. You are serious and work oriented. Jobseekers continue to have good success: there are interesting opportunities in the health field. Your work ethic attracts the notice of elders and superiors and can lead to a promotion. Your career planet, Mars, makes a rare Retrograde move on the 20th, so take these promotions – or other opportunities that come – with many grains of salt. Analyse them further. Avoid making important career decisions after the 20th.

As we mentioned, some of you might be opting for surgery this month – there are many indications of this. Your health planet is in the 8th House and conjunct to Chiron. Chiron often indicates 'woundedness'. Only keep in mind that detox might be just as effective. Health is reasonable until the 22nd, but after that be more watchful. Definitely rest and relax more, avoid stressful activities, power struggles and the like. Focus only on your priorities and let lesser things go.

Money is earned the normal way this month – through work. But happily, you will see the financial results of your hard work – and not everyone can say this. After the 22nd, it comes from partnerships, social connections and joint ventures. As we mentioned in previous reports, your financial good is dependent on the good graces of others, so again cultivate the social skills and avoid power struggles. You are tempted to speculate from the 22nd to the 25th but avoid it. A calculated, well-hedged risk might pay off, but not a casino-type gamble.

Professional investors, or those of you who have investment portfolios, should look at foreign companies, the health field, travel, airlines and publishers until the 22nd. After that the traditional blue-chip type stocks – the conservative stocks – seem best.

Leo

♌

Personality Profile

LEO AT A GLANCE

Element – Fire

Ruling Planet – Sun
   Career Planet – Venus
   Love Planet – Uranus
   Money Planet – Mercury
   Planet of Health and Work – Saturn
   Planet of Home and Family Life – Pluto

Colours – gold, orange, red

Colours that promote love, romance and social
   harmony – black, indigo, ultramarine blue

Colours that promote earning power – yellow,
   yellow-orange

Gems – amber, chrysolite, yellow diamond

Metal – gold

Scents – bergamot, frankincense, musk, neroli

Quality – fixed (= stability)

Quality most needed for balance – humility

Strongest virtues – leadership ability, self-esteem and confidence, generosity, creativity, love of joy

Deepest needs – fun, elation, the need to shine

Characteristics to avoid – arrogance, vanity, bossiness

Signs of greatest overall compatibility – Aries, Sagittarius

Signs of greatest overall incompatibility – Taurus, Scorpio, Aquarius

Sign most helpful to career – Taurus

Sign most helpful for emotional support – Scorpio

Sign most helpful financially – Virgo

Sign best for marriage and/or partnerships – Aquarius

Sign most helpful for creative projects – Sagittarius

Best Sign to have fun with – Sagittarius

Signs most helpful in spiritual matters – Aries, Cancer

Best day of the week – Sunday

Understanding a Leo

When you think of Leo, think of royalty – then you'll get the idea of what the Leo character is all about and why Leos are the way they are. It is true that, for various reasons, some Leo-born do not always express this quality – but even if not they should like to do so.

A monarch rules not by example (as does Aries) nor by consensus (as do Capricorn and Aquarius) but by personal will. Will is law. Personal taste becomes the style that is imitated by all subjects. A monarch is somehow larger than life. This is how a Leo desires to be.

When you dispute the personal will of a Leo it is serious business. He or she takes it as a personal affront, an insult. Leos will let you know that their will carries authority and that to disobey is demeaning and disrespectful.

A Leo is king (or queen) of his or her personal domain. Subordinates, friends and family are the loyal and trusted subjects. Leos rule with benevolent grace and in the best interests of others. They have a powerful presence; indeed, they are powerful people. They seem to attract attention in any social gathering. They stand out because they are stars in their domain. Leos feel that, like the Sun, they are made to shine and rule. Leos feel that they were born to special privilege and royal prerogatives – and most of them attain this status, at least to some degree.

The Sun is the ruler of this Sign, and when you think of sunshine it is very difficult to feel unhealthy or depressed. Somehow the light of the Sun is the very antithesis of illness and apathy. Leos love life. They also love to have fun; they love drama, music, the theatre and amusements of all sorts. These are the things that give joy to life. If – even in their best interests – you try to deprive Leos of their pleasures, good food, drink and entertainment, you run the serious risk of depriving them of the will to live. To them life without joy is no life at all.

Leos epitomize humanity's will to power. But power in and of itself – regardless of what some people say – is neither good nor evil. Only when power is abused does it become evil. Without power even good things cannot come to pass. Leos realize this and are uniquely qualified to wield power. Of all the Signs, they do it most naturally. Capricorn, the other power Sign of the Zodiac, is a better manager and administrator than Leo – much better. But Leo outshines Capricorn in personal grace and presence. Leo loves power, where Capricorn assumes power out of a sense of duty.

Finance

Leos are great leaders but not necessarily good managers. They are better at handling the overall picture than the nitty-gritty details of business. If they have good managers working for them they can become exceptional executives. They have vision and a lot of creativity.

Leos love wealth for the pleasures it can bring. They love an opulent lifestyle, pomp and glamour. Even when they are not wealthy they live as if they are. This is why many fall into debt, from which it is sometimes difficult to emerge.

Leos, like Pisceans, are generous to a fault. Very often they want to acquire wealth solely so that they can help others economically. Wealth to Leo buys services and managerial ability. It creates jobs for others and improves the general well-being of those around them. Therefore – to a Leo – wealth is good. Wealth is to be enjoyed to the fullest. Money is not to be left to gather dust in a mouldy bank vault but to be enjoyed, spread around, used. So Leos can be quite reckless in their spending.

With the Sign of Virgo on Leo's 2nd House (of Money) cusp, Leo needs to develop some of Virgo's traits of analysis, discrimination and purity when it comes to money matters. They must learn to be more careful with the details of finance (or to hire people to do this for them). They have to be more cost-conscious in their spending habits. Generally, they need to manage their money better. Leos tend to chafe under financial constraints, yet these constraints can help Leos to reach their highest financial potential.

Leos like it when their friends and family know that they can depend on them for financial support. They do not mind – even enjoy – lending money, but they are careful that they are not taken advantage of. From their 'regal throne' Leos like to bestow gifts upon their family and friends and then enjoy the good feelings these gifts bring to everybody. Leos love financial speculations and – when the celestial influences are right – are often lucky.

Career and Public Image

Leos like to be perceived as wealthy, for in today's world wealth often equals power. When they attain wealth they love having a large house with lots of land and animals.

At their jobs Leos excel in positions of authority and power. They are good at making decisions – on a grand level – but they prefer to leave the details to others. Leos are well respected by their colleagues and subordinates, mainly because they have a knack for understanding and relating to those around them. Leos usually strive for the top positions even if they have to start at the bottom and work hard to get there. As might be expected of such a charismatic Sign, Leos are always trying to improve their work situation. They do so in order to have a better chance of advancing to the top.

On the other hand, Leos do not like to be bossed around or told what to do. Perhaps this is why they aspire so for the top – where they can be the decision-makers and need not take orders from others.

Leos never doubt their success and focus all their attention and efforts on achieving it. Another great Leo characteristic is that – just like good monarchs – they do not attempt to abuse the power or success they achieve. If they do so this is not wilful or intentional. Usually they like to share their wealth and try to make everyone around them join in their success.

Leos are – and like to be perceived as – hard-working, well-established individuals. It is definitely true that they are capable of hard work and often manage great things. But do not forget that, deep down inside, Leos really are fun-lovers.

Love and Relationships

Generally, Leos are not the marrying kind. To them relationships are good while they are pleasurable. When the relationship ceases to be pleasurable a true Leo will want out. They always want to have the freedom to leave. That is why Leos excel at love affairs rather than commitment. Once married, however, Leo is faithful – even if some Leos have a tendency to marry more than once in their lifetime. If you are in love with a Leo, just show him or her a good time. Travel, go to casinos and clubs, the theatre and discos. Wine and dine your Leo love – it is expensive but worth it and you will have fun.

Leos generally have an active love life and are demonstrative in their affections. They love to be with other optimistic and fun-loving types like themselves, but wind up settling with someone more serious, intellectual and unconventional. The partner of a Leo tends to be more political and socially conscious than he or she is, and more libertarian. When you marry a Leo, mastering the freedom-loving tendencies of your partner will definitely become a life-long challenge – and be careful that Leo does not master you.

Aquarius sits on Leo's 7th House (of Love) cusp. Thus if Leos want to realize their highest love and social potential they need to develop a more egalitarian, Aquarian perspective on others. This is not easy for Leo, for 'the king' finds his equals only among other 'kings'. But perhaps this is the solution to Leo's social challenge – to be 'a king among kings'. It is all right to be royal, but recognize the nobility in others.

Home and Domestic Life

Although Leos are great entertainers and love having people over, sometimes this is all show. Only very few close friends will get to see the real side of a Leo's day-to-day life. To a Leo the home is a place of comfort, recreation and transformation; a secret, private retreat – a castle. Leos like to spend money, show off a bit, entertain and have fun. They enjoy the latest furnishings, clothes and gadgets – all things fit for kings.

Leos are fiercely loyal to their family and of course expect the same from them. They love their children almost to a fault; they have to be careful not to spoil them too much. They also must try to avoid attempting to make individual family members over in their own image. Leos should keep in mind that others also have the need to be their own people. That is why Leos have to be extra careful about being over-bossy or over-domineering in the home.

Horoscope for 2009

Major Trends

For the past few years you've been reorganizing your financial life in healthier ways. And though most of the job is done, you're not finished until October 29.

Last year was an important work year – many of you landed dream kinds of jobs – and the focus on work is still strong in the year ahead.

However, the main headline of the coming year is love and romance. Jupiter will make a move into your 7th House of Love on January 5 and stays there throughout the year. You are into a lifetime (for many of you) romantic peak. Many a wedding bell will ring. In general the social life will expand – new and important friends are coming into the picture. Business partnerships – lucrative ones – are also likely. More on this later.

The past few years have been more sexually active (for those of you of appropriate age). But it has also been highly experimental; some might call it kinky. What is kinky to one is normal to another and the Horoscope doesn't make value judgements. But these experimental trends are continuing in the year ahead. (As long as you keep it legal and non-destructive, it's probably a good thing.)

Health was important last year and the trend continues this year and for many years to come. Pluto has just entered your 6th House of Health for the long term. He will camp out in this House for years. Again, more on this later.

Your most important interests in the year ahead will be finance (until October 29th); communication and intellectual interests (after October 29); health and work; love and romance; sex, death and rebirth; past lives, occult studies, personal transformation, the prosperity of other people, debt and the repayment of debt.

Your paths of greatest fulfilment this year are love, romance and social activities; health and work (after July 27).

Health

(Please note that this is an astrological perspective on health and not a medical one. In days of yore there was no difference, both of these perspectives were identical. But in these times there could be quite a difference. For the medical perspective, please consult your doctor or health professional.)

Most of the long-term planets are leaving you alone. The two that stress you are not known for causing health problems. Health should be good in the year ahead. Also, your 6th House of Health continues to be strong this year (just as it was last year) and you seem on the case, you are paying attention. You are not letting small things develop into major problems. You are more inclined to be involved in healthy lifestyles, regimes and diets.

Good though your health is, you can improve it even further. Do this by giving more attention to the following organs: the spine, knees, teeth, bones and overall skeletal alignment; the small intestine (until October 29); the kidneys and hips (after October 29); and the colon, bladder and sexual organs (this year and for years to come).

Knees should be given more support when exercising. Regular back massage (and massage of the hips) will be powerful. The spinal vertebrae need to be kept in right alignment and there are many ways to do this – yoga (especially the postures that strengthen the spine), The Alexander Technique, Pilates, Feldenkreis Method and Rolfing are all wonderful for spinal health.

Safe sex and sexual moderation are more important than normal this year (and in the years to come). Leos are known for their libido, so what is moderate for a Leo is probably excessive for most other Signs (except for Scorpio). But if you listen to your body and not your mind, you will know

Reflexology

Try to massage the whole foot on a regular basis, but pay extra attention to the points highlighted on the chart. When you massage, be aware of 'sore spots', as these need special attention. It's also a good idea to massage the ankles and top side (as well as the soles) of the feet.

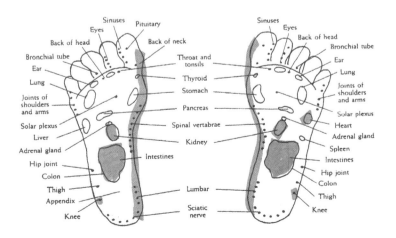

when you've had enough. The mind will never be sated, but the body knows.

There are many therapies that can strengthen all the above organs and I'm sure readers know about them. But if not they can work with the chart above.

With Pluto now in your 6th House of Health for years to come, detox becomes an important therapy. Pluto also rules surgery and many of you will opt for this as a kind of quick fix for a problem. But in general, detoxing – even fasting – will have a better effect. Though it might take longer, it is certainly less painful than surgery, and will get to the root cause of the problem. Detox of the colon and kidneys seems especially powerful.

Your health planet spends most of the year in the money house and this suggests that you are spending more on health this year. (But it also shows that you can earn from this field as well.) Also, it shows that financial challenges – financial disharmonies – can have an undue effect on health this year. Don't allow this to happen. You are more than your bank account – infinitely more. Money is only money, but health is more important. Decouple these two areas in your mind. If health problems arise the Horoscope is saying that you need to see how you've been handling money, as this could be a root cause for the health problem. Have you been using it the way it was intended, or manipulatively or harmfully?

After October 29 your health planet will be in Libra and your 3rd House of Communication and Intellectual Interests. The message here is that mental health becomes very important to your overall health. The mind must be pure and free of error. The mental body needs to be given its due. It needs right nutrition (right ideas), right exercise (the study of different subjects that interest you) and right elimination (right expression). Blockages in communication can impact on your health. If you have friends with whom you can discuss your intellectual ideas and insights all well and good, but if not, keep a diary and express yourself that way.

Overall emotional health is also important this year (and for years to come). If health problems arise examine your relationship with family members and bring them back into harmony.

Home and Family

Your 4th House of Home and Family is not a House of Power this year Leo, thus it is not a major focus in the year ahead. The cosmos neither pushes you one way nor another – you have more freedom in this area. However, since you lack the interest, you will probably have a status-quo kind of year.

The one change that we see here is the major move of your family planet from Sagittarius into Capricorn. Last year the family planet (Pluto) was flirting with Capricorn, now he is there for many years to come.

This move shows many things. First, you are more concerned about the health of family members and seem more personally involved here. As we mentioned earlier, disharmony with family members can affect your own health too. Second, we see that you are concerned with making the home a healthier place. For many years you were transforming the home into a kind of playground – an amusement park – a place of entertainment. Now you are transforming it into a kind of health spa. You will be installing exercise equipment, hot tubs, perhaps a gym. You will be filling it with health gadgets and the like.

There will be a greater focus on the family diet and on right nutrition.

It might be a good idea to check your water supply and septic tank for health issues. Those into metaphysics know that houses often have geo-pathological fields, negative energy zones and the like. And there are professionals who know how to clear these things – this is another area to explore. There are many recorded cases of sicknesses healed (and marriages as well) by merely clearing the home of negative energy fields.

Pluto in Capricorn shows that you are moving to a more traditional kind of family life and domestic routine. Everything is going to be organized and on schedule. Everyone will have their chores and their role. The home is run like a corporation. Very efficient. Only, in your drive for efficiency (and there are many virtues to this) don't make the home so cold that there is no warmth or feeling there. There is a reason why the 4th House (the Home) and the 10th House (the Career) are opposite each other. Each has different needs.

A parent or parent figure is moving in the year ahead, but this could also show that he or she is merely purchasing an additional home or additional property. This seems happy. There is profit from real estate and from industries dealing with the home. Siblings most probably moved last year, but there is still construction and renovation going on in the home. They are taking on more responsibility in the year ahead – especially later in the year – and seem cold or depressed. They need to force themselves to show warmth to others. Their egos are getting 'reality checked' and this is not always pleasant. Children of appropriate age are nomadic and can have multiple moves in the coming year; perhaps they just live in different places for long periods of time. Children are successful in school this year. Older ones are getting new cars or communications equipment. Grandchildren of appropriate age are having a status quo year at home. The social life seems happy and they will benefit from group activities.

If you are planning to beautify the home – or buy art objects for the home – October 23 to December 1 seems like the best time.

Finance and Career

As we mentioned earlier, you have been going through a two-year process of financial reorganization and consolidation. It probably hasn't been pleasant, as you've been forced to modify many of your Leo ways.

In general you are a big earner and a big spender. You are one of the great speculators and risk takers of the Zodiac (though Aries and Sagittarius could give you a run for your money). You rarely think about the cost when you spend and rarely give any thought to investing or saving for the future. But for the past two years this has changed – and the trend continues for most of the year ahead.

There has been a need to modify the risk taking, to be more conservative in your financial decision making. Risks were (and probably still are) necessary in the year ahead, but these risks should be calculated, well hedged, well thought out. Casino-type speculations will not pay off (though in the past you have undoubtedly done well with these things), but calculated risks will succeed.

If you have been responsible in your financial life and dealings, this Saturn transit in your money house is nothing to fear. In fact, when it's over (after October 29) you should find yourself richer (and with a more secure kind of wealth) than ever before. But if you have been irresponsible in financial matters, this transit can be quite traumatic: the bills for past misdemeanours become due, and Saturn will make sure they are collected. Bankruptcies often happen under this aspect.

It is important to understand that this is not punishment. The cosmic work crews want to set your financial life in a right order – in a healthy order – and sometimes they need to destroy before they can rebuild. What is the point of pouring in cosmic affluence into a leaky vessel? The vessel needs to be either repaired or replaced. You can rest assured that the whole process will be done with cosmic justice in mind.

I have found that with Saturn transits one must understand what the spiritual lesson and message is. Until this happens there tends to be pain and suffering. But once the lesson is understood, the pain and suffering leave at that instant. Yes, it is instant. Suffering is never prolonged a moment longer than necessary.

So this is a period (and this has been the case for the past two years) for reviewing your financial life, your financial

behaviour and attitudes and making the appropriate corrections. If you do this sincerely, the transit will be a breeze.

Saturn is your work planet. His presence in your House of
Money has various meanings. The most obvious one is that
you earn the hard way this year, through work and practical
service to others, not through speculation or smoke and
mirrors. It is a year for strengthening the work ethic. The
other message is that there are profit opportunities in the
health field; professional investors should look at these kinds
of companies – there are hosts of them publicly traded. Both
the bonds and the shares look interesting. The blue-chip
type stocks in general – the traditional types of companies –
also look most interesting this year.

This is a period for getting involved in disciplined, regular,
systematic savings and investment programmes; for taking a
long-term perspective with your finances. No matter what
your age it is good to plan financially for your retirement
(the earlier you start the better). This is very difficult for a
Leo, but it is what's called for these days. This is also a period
for gaining more control over finances through budgeting
and keeping the spending proportional to income. Another
hard lesson for a Leo. Once you learn it though you will
have something valuable for the rest of your life.

After October 29, as Saturn moves out of the money
house these lessons will have been learned and earnings will
come easier.

Up till now we have been discussing the overall financial
picture. But with speedy Mercury as your financial planet
there are many short-term trends that happen month to
month, depending on where Mercury is at any given time.
These are best discussed in the monthly reports.

This year your financial planet will go Retrograde on four
occasions! Usually it only happens three times. So this is a
year for more financial review, more caution, more homework, less rush and less risk taking. It reinforces the symbolism of Saturn in the money house.

Jobseekers (if there are still any out there after last year)
should look to family and family connections for leads.

Love and Social Life

It is wonderful how the cosmos compensates us. If it gives trials and tests in one area of life (finances in your case), it gives bountifully in other areas. This year it is in your love and social life.

The love and social life have been important for many years now and this year even more so. Benevolent Jupiter is moving into this House on January 5 and will be there for the rest of the year ahead.

As we mentioned earlier, this is a banner social year – you are in many cases in a lifetime social peak. Many will marry or get involved in relationships that are like a marriage. Those of you already married will have more romance within the marriage, and this is a great year to go on a second honeymoon and renew your vows.

It is a year of social bliss. There are more parties, more gatherings, and more new and important friends in your life. You are attracting a 'glamour crowd' socially: you are more involved with these kinds of people and this is Leo heaven.

For years now you have been attracting spiritual and creative types of people into your social circle, and this year even more so. This year you are perhaps mingling with celebrities, entertainers, musicians and dancers. The main turn on in love these days is fun – you want a person you can have fun with. The other things (money, status, intellect) don't seem that important. But spiritual compatibility continues to be important.

No one loves a party more than Leo – and this is a year for it.

Though the love life has been unstable for many years, this year, marriage is likely. Love seems like a gigantic honeymoon – a long party. Totally fun and with little responsibility.

Love opportunities happen in the usual places this year, at parties, resorts and places of entertainment. But with your love planet in the 8th House it could also happen at funerals, wakes, or as you comfort a bereaved person.

Those working on the second or third marriages will have a happy social life, but marriage for singles isn't likely. It is a status quo year for them. Those working on the fourth marriage are likely to marry now.

The entire year is going to be socially active, but the most active period seems to be right at the beginning of the year – from January 5 to March 15.

For singles the main problem seems to be too much of a good thing. There are so many opportunities – so many choices – that it can be confusing. Still, this is a nice problem to have – much better than the reverse.

Self-improvement

Learning the science or art of money management is still the major spiritual lesson of the year ahead, as we discussed. Good money management – budgets, proportionality in spending – is not about lack and limitation as many suppose. It is about being in control of your money rather than money controlling you. It is about financial mastery. A good budget should include enough for every happy thing – in right proportion. You should budget in what you think you will need for fun and leisure activities as much as you budget for the daily necessities. Also, it is about beauty. Beauty is always 'right proportion', and our finances should be a thing of beauty as much as our home or wardrobe. The long-term perspective on finances is about preventing lack in the future. You take steps in the NOW that prevent problems in the future.

Your spiritual mission in life tends to involve your spouse, friends, the arts and creativity, though this can be modified by your personal Horoscope cast for your exact date and time of birth. Since Venus moves very quickly, your mission will tend to change (at least in a tactical way) month by month, depending on where Venus happens to be at any given time. We will discuss this in the monthly reports.

Sexuality is always important to you and this year more than most. Since abuse of the sexual force is one of the main root causes of many sexual diseases and dysfunction, it might be a good idea to learn more about the spiritual perspective on sex. If you gravitate to the Eastern religions, Tantra would be an interesting study. If you gravitate to the Western teachings, hermetic science and Kabbalah would be interesting. Both systems have much wisdom about sexual practice.

On October 29, Saturn is going to move into your 3rd House of Communication and Intellectual Interests. You are entering a period where the cosmos is going to set your mind, your thinking and your speech into a right order. The thought process will be deepened and become more organized (not random and haphazard). You will probably talk less, but when you do it will be more effective. It will be a good period to learn as much as you can about the science of communication.

Month-by-month Forecasts

January

> Best Days Overall: 3, 4, 12, 21, 22, 30, 31
> Most Stressful Days Overall: 6, 12, 18, 19, 26, 27
> Best Days for Love: 1, 2, 9, 10, 11, 18, 19, 26, 27, 28, 29
> Best Days for Money: 7, 8, 14, 15, 16, 17, 23, 24, 25, 26
> Best Days for Career: 5, 6, 9, 10, 18, 19, 28, 29

Health is an important priority this month and happily you are on the case. Not only is your 6th House very strong (60 per cent of the planets are either there or moving through there) but Saturn, your health planet, is the handle of a bucket-type chart. This shows that it is through having good health – through your physical wellness – that you will lift up your entire life. It makes health even more important than the chart itself will show. So, you are into right diet, healthy lifestyles and daily disciplined health regimes. This will stand you in good stead after the 19th when overall energy is not what it should be. Your focus will prevent many problems from developing.

Work too is an important priority now, and what we mentioned above can be applied to work. Through your hard work and good work ethic, you will lift up your entire life. Jobseekers have had good success in 2008, and continue to have good success now in the month ahead. Those who hire others continue to expand the workforce. With the wonderful work ethic that you have now, prosperity is good. Only keep in mind that your financial planet goes Retrograde from the 11th to the 31st, so financial decisions need a lot more homework. Your financial judgement is better after the 22nd as the financial planet moves into practical Capricorn, but really it won't be completely up to par until Mercury starts to move forward at the end of the month. In the meantime use this period to review your finances and see where improvements can be made. This is the purpose of the Retrograde.

Your year begins with 80 and sometimes 90 per cent of the planets in the Western sector. So you are not as independent as you normally are. You are in a social period where social skills need development (no matter how good they are there is always room for improvement). This is not a time to try to change conditions. That time will come later on in the year. Now is a time to adapt to conditions and situations as best you can. Discomforts can be traced to your previous periods of independence where you yourself created the conditions that now irk you. Be patient now.

On the 19th (but you will feel this even earlier) you enter a yearly social peak. As we mentioned in the yearly report, this is going to be a banner social year in general – but now you are in a social peak of a great year. Enjoy. Singles have many, many romantic opportunities – at least six. The problem seems one of too much, not too little. You can feel confused as to whom to choose. It's as if the cosmos presents you with a menu of different types of romances: there are athletes, musicians, educated people, playboys or playgirls, intellectuals, writers, teachers, marketing people, money people, philosophers, poets and mystics. Wow! Perhaps you will try one of each.

A Solar Eclipse on the 26th will help you decide. It will test both current and new relationships, marriages and love affairs. The good relationships will survive, but the unfit ones will go down the tubes. Normally such an eclipse can be traumatic, but with the social life so good now it seems a necessary thing – a shakeout.

February

Best Days Overall: 1, 8, 9, 17, 18, 27, 28
Most Stressful Days Overall: 2, 3, 15, 16, 22, 23
Best Days for Love: 6, 7, 8, 9, 15, 16, 17, 18, 22, 23, 24, 25, 26, 27, 28
Best Days for Money: 2, 3, 4, 5, 10, 11, 12, 13, 22, 23
Best Days for Career: 2, 3, 8, 9, 17, 18, 27, 28

The last eclipse (January 26) not only tested relationships but it also brought physical detoxes and a need to redefine your image and personality. And we see the same kind of phenomena happening on the Lunar Eclipse of the 9th. It occurs in your own Sign and forces you to make image and personality changes. You need to define who you are for yourself or others will do it for you – and they will not be so charitable. This eclipse also brings dramas and upheavals in charitable or spiritual organizations that you are involved with. Also you will be making important changes to your spiritual regime and practice – good changes – necessary ones. Your spouse, partner or current love is forced to make dramatic financial changes – not only in physical finance, but in the way he or she thinks about them. Take a reduced schedule for both eclipses.

Your yearly social peak is very much in effect this month too. Sexual activity is on the increase. The danger here is excess rather than too little, and this can affect health. For singles, the romantic menu is still extensive. Love is honeymoon-like and fun now. An admirer wants to take you on a romantic trip to a foreign country from the 14th to the 19th – it doesn't mean that you have to accept, but the opportunity is there. This is a good time for a second honeymoon for those of you in existing relationships.

There is an interesting and happy encounter with a guru or teacher on the 11th and 12th. The dream life is strong those days too. It is likely that you will have supernatural types of experience.

This month the planets make an important shift from the lower to the upper half of your Horoscope. By the 14th, 70 per cent (and sometimes even 80 per cent) of the planets will be in the upper half of your Horoscope. Dawn is breaking in your year. The Sun is shining. Time to get up and get a handle on your outer life – your worldly career goals. Time to focus here. Let go of family and emotional issues and focus on the career. Over the next few months there will be much progress. Your efforts will produce greater results because you have the momentum of the cosmos behind you.

Health still needs watching until the 18th. Detox is good all month.

Your financial planet is now moving forwards and your financial judgement is very sharp – especially until the 14th. You are careful in money matters, have a long-term perspective, and are getting good value for your money. Until the 14th your money comes from your work (and perhaps this is why you are so careful). But after the 14th it comes from your spouse, partner or through social connections. Partnership or joint-venture opportunities come to you. The good graces of others are not only important in general, but in finances as well.

March

Best Days Overall: 7, 8, 16, 17, 18, 26, 27
Most Stressful Days Overall: 1, 2, 14, 15, 21, 22, 23, 28, 29
Best Days for Love: 5, 6, 7, 8, 14, 15, 16, 17, 18, 21, 22, 23, 24, 25, 26, 27
Best Days for Money: 3, 4, 10, 12, 13, 14, 15, 21, 22, 23, 25, 26, 30, 31
Best Days for Career: 1, 2, 7, 8, 16, 17, 18, 26, 27, 28, 29

Like last month you are still very much in a yearly social peak. You need to be careful not to be so carried away with social and romantic bliss that you ignore your work; this is a challenge now, and it will be tempting. Like last month (and perhaps even more than last month) sexual activity is increased. As long as you listen to your body (and not your mind) all will be well. But excess can affect health.

Your 8th House is very strong this month and this has many messages. For those on the spiritual path it shows much progress in personal transformation and reinvention. You will go deeper into your understanding of resurrection and ascension. You will make major psychological break-throughs and be able to transform many deep-seated emotional patterns – addictions and the like. On mundane level, this shows the prosperity of your spouse or partner and his or her generosity with you. It shows an increased ability to tap into outside sources of capital – credit or investors. A wealthy industrialist once said that the main difference between a rich person and a poor person is that the rich person has a greater capacity to borrow – and so, by that definition, you are richer this month.

Mercury, your financial planet, moves very speedily this month – he goes through three Signs and Houses of your Horoscope. This too shows prosperity. You make quick financial progress. You achieve goals quickly. You have confidence. You cover a lot of territory. You earn in various kinds of ways and through various kinds of people and situations. Keeping the financial interests of others in mind – friends, partners, the spouse or current love – is very important until the 25th. This doesn't mean that you ignore your own interests, but that you give priority to the other person (and try to see things from his or her perspective). As you prosper others, your own prosperity will just naturally happen by the spiritual law.

Most of the planets are above the horizon and career is very important. But on the 6th Venus, your career planet, starts to go Retrograde. This will not stop your career, but suggests a more cautious approach. Career opportunities that are presented to you might not be all that they promise. Career moves need more homework and analysis. Avoid major career decisions until next month. Clarity is more important than blind actions now.

Health is much improved over last month and by the 14th will get even better. You have all the energy you need to achieve your goals. You can enhance your good health even further in the ways mentioned in the yearly report (*see page 162*).

April

> Best Days Overall: 4, 5, 13, 14, 22, 23
> Most Stressful Days Overall: 10, 11, 18, 19, 25, 26
> Best Days for Love: 2, 3, 4, 10, 11, 18, 19, 20, 21, 29, 30
> Best Days for Money: 4, 5, 6, 7, 8, 9, 15, 16, 18, 19, 25, 26, 27, 28
> Best Days for Career: 4, 20, 21, 25, 26

A very rare* Jupiter/Neptune conjunction is happening towards the end of the month (and will be in effect next month as well). This has many messages. First off – for those of you on the spiritual path – it brings great religious and spiritual revelation. Children are meeting spiritual gurus or mentors. On a mundane level it brings happy romantic

* This only happens once every 12–15 years.

experience with creative kinds of people – poets, musicians, actors, film people or spiritual types. Personal creativity (and Leos are VERY creative) is going to be super, and you will have very powerful inspiration. It also brings happy sexual encounters.

Your career planet, Venus, is still Retrograde until the 17th, so continue to research career moves carefully. Try to be free of all doubt before deciding anything. If you use this Retrograde period the way it should be used, you will be ready to enter your yearly career peak (on the 19th) with clarity of mind and a firm purpose. Your progress will be great. When the Sun crosses your Midheaven from the 18th to the 20th, you are personally very elevated. Perhaps you get a promotion at work. You are honoured and appreciated for who you are and not just for your career achievements. You are where you always feel that you belong – at the top, in charge, ruling over all you survey. You can safely let go of home and family issues and continue to focus on your career.

Aside from love and romance (which is an important interest all year), you are focused on foreign lands, foreign travel, religion, philosophy and metaphysics this month. Your 9th House is very powerful – half of the planets are either there or moving through there this month. For students this brings success in their studies, acceptances to universities, and a zest for learning. Even non students will have a yen for learning this month. You should take the educational opportunities that are coming. For those on the spiritual path, this brings religious and philosophical break-throughs. These things, though little understood, have the power to change every department of life – and the life direction as well.

Health is wonderful until the 19th. You have the energy of ten people. You are optimistic and happy. And perhaps – and this is the danger – you might be overactive (until the 19th) and burn the candle at both ends. Burnout is the main danger. After the 19th you need to rest and relax more; you can't continue the pace that you were maintaining early in the month. Take the pause that refreshes. Focus on

important things (like your career and love life) and let
lesser concerns go. You can enhance your health in the ways
described in the yearly report (*page 162*).

May

Best Days Overall: 1, 2, 10, 11, 20, 21, 28, 29
Most Stressful Days Overall: 8, 9, 15, 16, 22, 23
Best Days for Love: 1, 2, 8, 9, 10, 11, 15, 16, 18, 19, 20,
    21, 26, 27, 28, 29
Best Days for Money: 3, 4, 5, 6, 13, 14, 15, 16, 22, 23, 24,
    25, 30, 31
Best Days for Career: 1, 2, 10, 11, 20, 21, 22, 23, 28, 29

Last month brought dramas with parents, parent figures or
bosses and this month brings more of the same. Some of you
are experiencing 'near-death' career experiences – short-
term job insecurities – but remember that after death come
resurrection and renewal. This is the law, and career in
general looks bright this month. You are still in your yearly
career peak. You are still very elevated – high on the totem
pole – above everyone in your family. You are working hard,
and it seems you are travelling in relation to your work.
Parents or parent figures might be having surgery, or
contemplating it.

Finances are a bit of a struggle this month. This in spite of
the fact that pay rises probably came last month and could
happen this month too. Perhaps you are overspending. Your
financial planet goes Retrograde from the 7th to the 31st and
this is affecting your financial judgement and creating insecurities. As always when this happens, use the Retrograde
period to upgrade and fine tune your financial life. Use it for
planning and gaining clarity, not for action. When the
Retrograde is over, your decision making will be better.

Health needs more watching until the 20th. After that
your normal abundant energy returns.

Your 9th House is still very strong, and it seems to be your
spiritual mission to educate yourself further in your career –

to take whatever courses are necessary to enhance your career. For those of you who already have this education, your mission seems to be to teach others what you know. On a spiritual level, power in the 9th House shows that you will make more and more religious and spiritual breakthroughs – you have had a few in the past year, and more are coming.

On the 20th your 11th House of Friends, Groups and Organizations becomes strong, and so the focus will shift from the career to social interests. It will be a strong period both romantically and from a friendship perspective.

Love becomes more volatile and exciting after the 20th – like a soap opera – but this is how you like things. You are trying to juggle a job, health interests, a love relationship and personal desires – and it's a tall order. Something has to give and this is creating some of the drama.

June

Best Days Overall: 6, 7, 8, 16, 17, 25
Most Stressful Days Overall: 4, 5, 11, 12, 13, 19
Best Days for Love: 4, 5, 9, 11, 12, 13, 14, 15, 19, 23, 27, 28
Best Days for Money: 2, 3, 9, 10, 11, 12, 13, 21, 22, 27, 28, 29, 30
Best Days for Career: 9, 19, 27, 28

This month the planets shift from the Western, social sector to the Eastern, personal sector. By the 6th over 50 per cent of the planets will be in the East. So, personal independence is growing stronger day by day. There is more personal freedom. You are not at the maximum yet, but you are getting closer. If conditions don't suit you, you have the power to change them or create new ones according to your liking. No need to adapt yourself, or seek consensus in your decision making (this doesn't mean that you will run roughshod over others, but that you will make your own decisions). Your happiness is in your own hands now; it doesn't depend on other people as much as it did in the previous six months.

Career is still very powerful and successful. Bosses and superiors look on you with favour. Your willingness to travel and educate yourself is a big plus. Pay rises (if they haven't already happened) are still likely.

Your spiritual mission this month is to be successful, but not merely for yourself. In a position of power you are a better instrument to help others.

Health is good this month, but you seem overly experimental with your body, wanting to test its limits (most powerfully from the 14th to the 20th). Hopefully you can find a constructive and safe way to do this, perhaps by getting involved in Yoga or Tai Chi or some martial art. If not, you might be likely to try stunts like bungee jumping, jumping out of aeroplanes or other daredevil exploits. Try to drive more defensively during this period. If you must take risks, take them in a mindful and conscious way.

Love seems more delicate now; you seem rebellious, wanting personal freedom. Those involved with Leos romantically should make note and be more patient with them – the mood will pass. There are some short-term problems with family members (looks like a parent or parent figure) from the 19th to the 23rd as well. This too contributes to your mood of risk taking. But all these things will pass – they are short term – and relations with the beloved and the parent will get back on an even keel later in the month.

These adventures have an upside. They lead you deeper into your spiritual life, into a need for spiritual understanding. And this and this alone, will bring long-term solutions. After the 21st, with your 12th House of Spirituality powerful, it is good to attend spiritual lectures, meditation seminars, or go on spiritual retreats. Your personal planet, the Sun, will start making very nice aspects to Neptune towards the end of the month (besides being in the 12th House) and this is going to bring you all kinds of supernormal experiences. The invisible world is letting you know that it exists – and is sending you these messages.

July

Best Days Overall: 3, 4, 5, 14, 15, 22, 23, 31
Most Stressful Days Overall: 1, 2, 9, 10, 16, 17, 28, 29, 30
Best Days for Love: 1, 2, 9, 10, 11, 12, 18, 19, 20, 21, 26, 27, 29, 30
Best Days for Money: 9, 10, 11, 12, 18, 19, 22, 23, 24, 25, 26, 27, 31
Best Days for Career: 9, 16, 17, 18, 19, 26, 27

Your 12th House of Spirituality is still strong and your Sun is still making nice aspects to Neptune (the most spiritual of all the planets) until the 22nd. So spirituality – and charitable, altruistic kinds of activities – is still important and enjoyable. Refer to our discussion of this last month.

You are getting ready for your personal new year – your birthday. Some of you will have it this month and some next. So it is a good time now to review your past year, make atonement for past mistakes – omissions or commissions – see where you can improve things for the future, and set personal goals for the year ahead. It's very important to start your new year with a clean, fresh slate. Your birthday is a very powerful day. It is in reality a 'celestial event'. Prayers, visualizations and meditations done on that day will have many times the force and potency than at other times, so it is good to do these kinds of things on your birthday. The heavens are open to you and showering you with blessings. Your actions now affect the tone and quality of the entire year ahead.

Career is starting to wind down this month. It has been busy and hectic for the past few months. But by the 12th you have probably achieved your most important goals (or at least made some significant progress towards them) and you can focus on other things – friendships, groups, the love life and spiritual interests.

Being involved with friends, groups and organizations is not only fun in its own right, but it enhances the career. You make important connections at these kinds of activities.

Moreover, your friends are your spiritual mission in the month ahead – to be there for them.

We have two eclipses this month. There is a Lunar Eclipse on the 7th that occurs in your 6th House of Work and shows job changes and changes in your health regime and practice. If you employ others there is probably some employee turnover then. Because you have been focused on spiritual issues this month, the eclipse will also bring new revelation that leads to changes and upgrades of your practice. There are probably shakeups and upheavals in a spiritual organization or charity that you are involved with. Don't take your dreams too seriously during this period.

The Solar Eclipse of the 22nd also brings spiritual changes – changes of your practice and your attitudes. But this eclipse is stronger on you, so be sure to take a reduced schedule. (For those of you born on the 22nd or 23rd, this is a most powerful eclipse showing dramatic changes in your career, image and many other departments of life in the next six months. If you fall into this category take an even more reduced schedule.) For all of you, it brings image changes and a need to redefine the personality. Since we are always growing and changing it is good to redefine the personality periodically. But we seldom do it and unless we are forced to, and the eclipse provides the motivation.

August

Best Days Overall: 1, 10, 11, 19, 27, 28
Most Stressful Days Overall: 5, 6, 12, 13, 25, 26
Best Days for Love: 5, 6, 7, 8, 9, 16, 17, 25, 26
Best Days for Money: 1, 2, 5; 6, 12, 13, 14, 15, 21, 22, 23, 24
Best Days for Career: 7, 8, 9, 12, 13, 16, 17, 25, 26

You've just gone through two eclipses and there is no let up this month – there is another one on the 6th. (The cosmos is relentless when it wants something done and will use all the force necessary to achieve its ends.) This eclipse, like the past two, affects your spiritual life, your spiritual attitudes and practice. If you haven't made the appropriate changes last month, you will have to make them now. But this eclipse, unlike the other two, occurs in your 7th House of Love. With your love life so powerful this year, it can signal a marriage in many cases, especially for singles. Those in existing relationships will have their relationships tested and purified. Friendships and business partnerships also get tested. A romance can have a near-death kind of experience.

Last month, on the 23rd, you entered into a yearly personal pleasure peak, which is still in full swing this month. There is no one who likes personal pleasure more than you Leo, so enjoy. This a period for pampering the body and enjoying the pleasures of the body. Financial opportunities were seeking you out last month and this is the case early this month as well. Finances are good now. On the 22nd you enter a yearly financial peak. You are personally involved in finance rather than delegating it to others. And since your interest is great – you have a passion for wealth now – success is more likely. Jobseekers have good success. You seem to be spending more on health and health issues this month, but you can also earn from this field as well. People in the health professions can be important financially – perhaps as clients or in other ways.

The other message that we get here is that you are working on your financial health; it is not just about 'getting rich', it's about adjusting spending to earnings, reducing waste and getting maximum value. It is about clearing the impurities that clog the financial body.

There is some financial disagreement with your spouse, partner or beloved after the 22nd: compromise is the key. You don't see eye to eye on many things, but this is temporary.

Since last month, you are in your period of maximum personal independence. You are having things your way – and you should. Your way is the best way right now – at least for you. If others don't agree with you, strike out on your own and create your own happiness. Eventually they will change their position.

Health is good this month and you are paying attention. Love will improve next month. Volatile periods always make the new harmonies even more harmonious.

September

Best Days Overall: 6, 7, 15, 16, 23, 24, 25
Most Stressful Days Overall: 1, 2, 8, 9, 21, 22, 28, 29, 30
Best Days for Love: 1, 2, 4, 5, 6, 7, 13, 14, 15, 16, 21, 22, 26, 27, 28, 29, 30
Best Days for Money: 1, 2, 11, 12, 17, 18, 19, 20, 27, 28, 29, 30
Best Days for Career: 6, 7, 8, 9, 15, 16, 26, 27

Last month the planetary power made an important shift from the upper day side of your Horoscope to the lower night side. It is the evening of your year. The night is not evil and has its important functions. Night is a time for rest, for gathering the forces for the coming day, for inner activities, dreaming, visualizing, and getting into emotional harmony. You have been very career oriented for many months and have made much progress. Now it is time to rest. Inner activities are more important than outer activities. Sure you will still have your career, but pursue it by the means of the night rather than by the means of day – through visualizing, setting goals, living inwardly in your realized dream regardless of what the conditions are in the outer world. It is a time to focus on emotional harmony – finding and functioning from your emotional comfort zone; time to get the home and the family situation in order; time to create the psychological and emotional framework – the foundation – for future career success. Shift some energy from the career to the home and family now.

You are still in a yearly financial peak, so your earnings are going to be strong. Money comes to you in various ways: through personal effort, through the favour of elders, parents and parent figures, through your good professional reputation, through media activities, sales and marketing, and through friends and networking. Jobseekers seem very successful this month (the 15th to the 18th seems especially good). Those who employ others also have success – a good employee starts between the 15th and 18th.

The only problem is that your financial planet goes Retrograde from the 7th to the 29th. This is not going to stop your earnings, but it could introduce some delays. Credit card and bank statements need more scrutiny. That great deal might not be such a great deal after all – especially when you read the small print. Friends might mean well but could be uninformed in a given financial situation. Homework, homework, homework – that's the name of the game. In finances, avoid shortcuts and advance in slow, methodical ways.

Love is bumpy from the 16th to the 18th, but the worst should be over by then. You are focused on finance and so is your beloved. You both seem only concerned with your own financial interest and have trouble seeing the other person's perspective. Compromise and patience will help you weather this.

Health is good and you still seem very focused here. You can enhance your already good health even further by following the methods outlined in the yearly report (*page 162*).

October

Best Days Overall: 3, 4, 12, 13, 21, 22, 31
Most Stressful Days Overall: 6, 7, 19, 20, 26, 27
Best Days for Love: 1, 2, 6, 7, 10, 11, 15, 16, 19, 20, 26, 27, 28, 29
Best Days for Money: 8, 9, 10, 14, 15, 16, 17, 26, 27, 28, 29
Best Days for Career: 6, 7, 15, 16, 26, 27

Very happy financial developments are taking place this month. For a start, your financial planet is moving forward again, and this restores your confidence. You have greater clarity in money matters now. But, more importantly, Saturn is leaving your money house on the 29th (after two and a half years there) and this is going to take a lot of pressure off you. By now you have become financially healthier – more savvy – and there is no spiritual purpose in loading you up with burdens. Elders, parents, parent figures (and even the government) are supporting your financial goals in various ways. It can be directly or through their connections or advice. Good sales and marketing – good communication skills – are important always but especially in the month ahead. Trading, buying and selling seems like a path to profits.

There are important changes happening for jobseekers too. Saturn's move shows that job opportunities are in the neighbourhood and perhaps with siblings or the connections of siblings. Good use of the media – placing the right ads in the right places – becomes important job-wise.

Saturn's move also has health implications. For the next two and a half years it is important to give the kidneys and hips more attention. Regular hip massage will be helpful. Health is generally good now, but rest and relax more after the 23rd.

Career is less important now. Basically you seem unconcerned with status and prestige and more concerned with money. You measure your career success in terms of money. Your spiritual mission – especially until the 15th – is to get rich. Yes, the cosmos wants you to be rich – to be comfortable and to use your wealth for personal happiness and to help others. But after the 15th, things change. Your mission seems to involve siblings and neighbours, being there for them. Teaching others what you know is also important. You have something very special to communicate to the world (your world) and you need to be doing that.

Mars, your planet of foreign travel and religion is in your 12th House of Spirituality until the 16th (it was there last month as well). This suggests various things. You are exploring the mystical traditions of your native religion. You are taking religious pilgrimages to sacred sites or going on spiritual retreats to foreign countries. It also suggests a more action-oriented approach to the spiritual ideals. You have a need to act on them, put them into practice, and serve the spirit with your body as well as with your mind.

November

> Best Days Overall: 1, 8, 9, 17, 18, 27, 28
> Most Stressful Days Overall: 2, 3, 15, 16, 22, 23, 29, 30
> Best Days for Love: 4, 5, 6, 7, 15, 16, 22, 23, 25, 26
> Best Days for Money: 4, 5, 10, 11, 13, 14, 15, 16, 22, 23, 27, 28
> Best Days for Career: 2, 3, 4, 5, 15, 16, 25, 26, 29, 30

Your 10th House of Career is empty, while your 4th House of Home and Family is powerful. Between 60 and 70 per cent of the planets are below the horizon. It's a no brainer – let career go and focus on the family and emotional life. It is the 'midnight period' of your year. Not a time for overt actions but for the activities of night. With your career planet moving into your 4th House on the 8th, your family IS your career now.

There are other interpretations to Venus in your 4th House. It can show that you are working more from home, setting up – or expanding – a home office. And, in general, working to make your career more emotionally comfortable (a good thing to be doing). Spiritually it shows that your spiritual mission is your family this period.

Mars is now in your own Sign and will be there for the rest of the year ahead. Since Mars is your travel planet, this suggests that you are travelling abroad now. You are more involved with foreigners. Educational and travel opportunities are seeking you out. This is also a very positive aspect for athletes and exercise buffs: it shows more physical energy and an ability to excel in these things. It is a good health signal too. But still, with many planets stressing you out until the 22nd rest and relax more and pace yourself.

Enhance your health by giving more attention to the spine, knees, teeth, bones, skeletal alignment, kidneys and hips. Conserve energy by talking and thinking less. Health is going to improve dramatically after the 22nd. You are full of your native fire. Magnetic and charismatic. You get things done in a fraction of the normal time. You are bold and courageous. Your natural leadership abilities come out. The only danger is haste and temper. Normally when you lose your temper it is merely unpleasant; this month it will be devastating to others. You have 100 more times force behind it (and perhaps you're not aware of it).

On the 22nd, as the Sun moves into your 5th House you enter another one of your yearly personal pleasure peaks. Leo heaven. It is a time for parties, travel, amusements, theatre and all the various leisure pursuits that make life interesting. You are always the life of the party, but now more so than ever. For singles this shows many love affairs – non-serious romances – dalliances and flirtations (or the opportunities for these things). Speculations become favourable in this period too. And, if intuition dictates, this might be a good period to take that trip to Las Vegas, Atlantic City or Monte Carlo.

Love is happy this month. You and the beloved are in harmony. Past differences seem resolved. But with your love planet still Retrograde let love develop as it will and don't try to force things. Avoid making major love decisions one way or another.

December

Best Days Overall: 6, 7, 15, 16, 24, 25, 26
Most Stressful Days Overall: 12, 13, 19, 20, 21, 27, 28
Best Days for Love: 4, 5, 6, 7, 13, 14, 15, 16, 19, 20, 21, 22, 23, 26, 27, 31
Best Days for Money: 2, 8, 9, 10, 11, 17, 18, 19, 20, 21, 27, 28
Best Days for Career: 6, 7, 15, 16, 26, 27, 28

Mars will make a rare (once in two years) Retrograde turn beginning on the 20th. You are in the mood for travel and are probably doing it, but try to schedule these things before the 20th rather than afterwards. Also keep in mind Mercury will start to Retrograde on the 26th. This means that the two planets that rule travel (Mercury on a generic level and Mars in your Horoscope), will be Retrograde at the same time – another hint to avoid travel that period. If you must travel after the 26th, take more precautions than usual. Insure your ticket so that you can make changes without penalties. Allow more time for getting to and from your destination (clearing security, etc.) and try not to schedule connecting flights too closely.

You are still well into your yearly personal pleasure peak, and the partying is very intense. Speculations are still favourable. Money comes to you in happy ways until the 5th. But you don't need to worry too much about money. When the cosmos throws a party it supplies everything needful for it – and enough to spare.

After the 5th, money comes the old-fashioned way through work and productive service to others. Jobseekers have good success this month too, especially after the 21st. (Before that you don't seem too interested in work – you just want to have a good time.)

Professional investors, or those of you who have investment accounts, should look at the traditional blue-chip kinds of stocks, the health-care field, commercial real estate, and companies that supply the medical profession.

Health is good all month but especially until the 21st. Though energy is lessened after the 21st, you seem focused on health, giving it much attention, and this is a good sign. This will maximize your energy.

Love is very happy this month. Singles can opt for serious or non-serious relationships. Both are on the menu. There is more sexual activity this month as well. Now that your love planet finally goes forward – after many months of Retrograde motion – you are more clear-headed about love and can make better decisions. Wedding bells would not be a surprise.

Jupiter makes another rare conjunction with Neptune this month (it made the first one a few months back). This brings happy sexual opportunities, luck in speculations, and good fortune with insurance, tax and estate issues. Your spouse, partner or current love has a financial windfall – a substantial one. On a spiritual level it brings spiritual revelation and insight.

Virgo

ɱ

THE VIRGIN
Birthdays from
22nd August to
22nd September

Personality Profile

VIRGO AT A GLANCE

Element – Earth

Ruling Planet – Mercury
  Career Planet – Mercury
  Love Planet – Neptune
  Money Planet – Venus
  Planet of Home and Family Life – Jupiter
  Planet of Health and Work – Uranus
  Planet of Pleasure – Saturn
  Planet of Sexuality – Mars

Colours – earth tones, ochre, orange, yellow

Colour that promotes love, romance and social harmony – aqua blue

Colour that promotes earning power – jade green

Gems – agate, hyacinth

Metal – quicksilver

Scents – lavender, lilac, lily of the valley, storax

Quality – mutable (= flexibility)

Quality most needed for balance – a broader perspective

Strongest virtues – mental agility, analytical skills, ability to pay attention to detail, healing powers

Deepest needs – to be useful and productive

Characteristic to avoid – destructive criticism

Signs of greatest overall compatibility – Taurus, Capricorn

Signs of greatest overall incompatibility – Gemini, Sagittarius, Pisces

Sign most helpful to career – Gemini

Sign most helpful for emotional support – Sagittarius

Sign most helpful financially – Libra

Sign best for marriage and/or partnerships – Pisces

Sign most helpful for creative projects – Capricorn

Best Sign to have fun with – Capricorn

Signs most helpful in spiritual matters – Taurus, Leo

Best day of the week – Wednesday

Understanding a Virgo

The virgin is a particularly fitting symbol for those born under the Sign of Virgo. If you meditate on the image of the virgin you will get a good understanding of the essence of the Virgo type. The virgin is, of course, a symbol of purity and innocence – not naïve, but pure. A virginal object has not been touched. A virgin field is land that is true to itself, the way it has always been. The same is true of virgin forest: it is pristine, unaltered.

Apply the idea of purity to the thought processes, emotional life, physical body, and activities and projects of the everyday world, and you can see how Virgos approach life. Virgos desire the pure expression of the ideal in their mind, body and affairs. If they find impurities they will attempt to clear them away.

Impurities are the beginning of disorder, unhappiness and uneasiness. The job of the Virgo is to eject all impurities and keep only that which the body and mind can use and assimilate.

The secrets of good health are here revealed: 90 per cent of the art of staying well is maintaining a pure mind, a pure body and pure emotions. When you introduce more impurities than your mind and body can deal with, you will have what is known as 'dis-ease'. It is no wonder that Virgos make great doctors, nurses, healers and dieticians. They have an innate understanding of good health and they realize that good health is more than just physical. In all aspects of life, if you want a project to be successful it must be kept as pure as possible. It must be protected against the adverse elements that will try to undermine it. This is the secret behind Virgo's awesome technical proficiency.

One could talk about Virgo's analytical powers – which are formidable. One could talk about their perfectionism and their almost superhuman attention to detail. But this would be to miss the point. All of these virtues are manifestations of a Virgo's desire for purity and perfection – a world without Virgos would have ruined itself long ago.

A vice is nothing more than a virtue turned inside out, misapplied or used in the wrong context. Virgos' apparent vices come from their inherent virtue. Their analytical powers, which should be used for healing, helping or perfecting a project in the world, sometimes get misapplied and turned against people. Their critical faculties, which should be used constructively to perfect a strategy or proposal, can sometimes be used destructively to harm or wound. Their urge to perfection can turn into worry and lack of confidence; their natural humility can become self-denial and self-abasement. When Virgos turn negative they are apt to turn their devastating criticism on themselves, sowing the seeds of self-destruction.

Finance

Virgos have all the attitudes that create wealth. They are hard-working, industrious, efficient, organized, thrifty, productive and eager to serve. A developed Virgo is every employer's dream. But until Virgos master some of the social graces of Libra they will not even come close to fulfilling their financial potential. Purity and perfectionism, if not handled correctly or gracefully, can be very trying to others. Friction in human relationships can be devastating not only to your pet projects but – indirectly – to your wallet as well.

Virgos are quite interested in their financial security. Being hard-working, they know the true value of money. They do not like to take risks with their money, preferring to save for their retirement or for a rainy day. Virgos usually make prudent, calculated investments that involve a minimum of risk. These investments and savings usually work out well, helping Virgos to achieve the financial security they seek. The rich or even not-so-rich Virgo also likes to help his or her friends in need.

Career and Public Image

Virgos reach their full potential when they can communicate their knowledge in such a way that others can understand it. In order to get their ideas across better, Virgos need to develop greater verbal skills and fewer judgemental ways of expressing themselves. Virgos look up to teachers and communicators; they like their bosses to be good communicators. Virgos will probably not respect a superior who is not their intellectual equal – no matter how much money or power that superior has. Virgos themselves like to be perceived by others as being educated and intellectual.

The natural humility of Virgos often inhibits them from fulfilling their great ambitions, from acquiring name and fame. Virgos should indulge in a little more self-promotion if they are going to reach their career goals. They need to push themselves with the same ardour that they would use to foster others.

At work Virgos like to stay active. They are willing to learn any type of job as long as it serves their ultimate goal of financial security. Virgos may change occupations several times during their professional lives, until they find the one they really enjoy. Virgos work well with other people, are not afraid to work hard and always fulfil their responsibilities.

Love and Relationships

If you are an analyst or a critic you must, out of necessity, narrow your scope. You have to focus on a part and not the whole; this can create a temporary narrow-mindedness. Virgos do not like this kind of person. They like their partners to be broad-minded, with depth and vision. Virgos seek to get this broad-minded quality from their partners, since they sometimes lack it themselves.

Virgos are perfectionists in love just as they are in other areas of life. They need partners who are tolerant, open-minded and easy-going. If you are in love with a Virgo do not waste time on impractical romantic gestures. Do practical and useful things for him or her – this is what will be appreciated and what will be done for you.

Virgos express their love through pragmatic and useful gestures, so do not be put off because your Virgo partner does not say 'I love you' day-in and day-out. Virgos are not that type. If they love you, they will demonstrate it in practical ways. They will always be there for you; they will show an interest in your health and finances; they will fix your sink or repair your video recorder. Virgos deem these actions to be superior to sending flowers, chocolates or Valentine cards.

In love affairs Virgos are not particularly passionate or spontaneous. If you are in love with a Virgo, do not take this personally. It does not mean that you are not alluring enough or that your Virgo partner does not love or like you. It is just the way Virgos are. What they lack in passion they make up for in dedication and loyalty.

Home and Domestic Life

It goes without saying that the home of a Virgo will be spotless, sanitized and orderly. Everything will be in its proper place – and don't you dare move anything about! For Virgos to find domestic bliss they need to ease up a bit in the home, to allow their partner and kids more freedom and to be more generous and open-minded. Family members are not to be analysed under a microscope, they are individuals with their own virtues to express.

With these small difficulties resolved, Virgos like to stay in and entertain at home. They make good hosts and they like to keep their friends and families happy and entertained at family and social gatherings. Virgos love children, but they are strict with them – at times – since they want to make sure their children are brought up with the correct sense of family and values.

Horoscope for 2009

Major Trends

For years now, you have been learning to cope with dramatic and often sudden – surprising – changes. By now you are probably in very different conditions and circumstances than you were a few years ago. Careers have changed. There have been many divorces and breakups. Business partnerships were blown to smithereens, and your sense of who you are has been rapidly evolving. These changes are far from over, especially if you are born later in the sign of Virgo – September 12 to 22.

In addition to all this instability, Saturn has been moving through your own Sign. You have been forced to take on extra burdens and responsibilities (and it seems to involve children). Your overall energy was not what it should have been. The ego and self-esteem got serious reality checks. You have been going through a character-building kind of period. Generally we don't know the stuff we're made of until the tough times come and we are tested to the full. If you got through the past few years with health and sanity intact, you deserve much credit; you are very strong, you are successful. And when Saturn leaves your Sign towards the end of the year, you will start to soar.

But the cosmos in its wisdom is always compensating us. When there is difficulty in one area, there is bliss in another. In spite of the difficulties of the past year, you did manage to have fun – to find it where it offered. You also managed to be very creative. This year, the party is over and you are more serious and work oriented, even more than normal. Dream job opportunities are coming to you and because you built up your mental and spiritual muscles – by taking on extra responsibilities and building your character – you are well qualified for these new work assignments.

Serious love has been unstable for many years, and the trend continues in the year ahead. Love is still very exciting.

Health was difficult these past few years, but come October 29 you should see great improvement.

Your most important areas of interest this year are love and romance; health and work; children, creativity and fun; the body, image and self concept (until October 29); finance (after October 29).

Your paths of greatest fulfilment this year are health and work; children creativity and fun (after July 27).

Health

(Please note that this is an astrological perspective on health and not a medical one. In days of yore there was no difference, both of these perspectives were identical. But in these times there could be quite a difference. For the medical perspective, please consult your doctor or health professional.)

As we mentioned, health has been difficult these past few years and is still delicate for most of the year ahead. Two very powerful planets – Saturn and Uranus – have been stressing you out continually, and when these were joined by some of the short-term, fast-moving planets, you became very vulnerable to problems.

But there is much good news here too. When the health aspects are difficult the main danger is in ignoring your health and not giving it the attention it deserves. But with your 6th House very strong for many years (and it gets even stronger this year), and with the fact that you are Virgo and health is like a religion to you, this danger wasn't present. You were paying attention and doing what needed to be done. Thus you probably avoided the major health difficulties. Keep up the good work this year.

You can do much – in natural and drugless ways – to enhance your health and prevent problems from developing. For a start (and this is most important), maintain high energy levels. Rest when tired. Try to do more with less energy. Learn the art of relaxation and practise it. Watch how you hold the phone or the pen – do you need to squeeze them that tightly? Little things make a big difference. Avoid arguments and power struggles wherever possible. Talk less and listen more. Think less and look more. Be more aware, in the moment. Your energy can be likened to your financial supply. You want to invest it profitably. Discern sharply between legitimate and illegitimate responsibilities. You have the energy for legitimate ones, but not for the false ones.

Aside from the above, it is good to give more attention to the following organs: the ankles and feet (regular ankle and foot massage is very beneficial now – see our chart below – also give the ankles more support when exercising); the liver and thighs (thighs should be regularly massaged); and the heart.

As always, wear shoes that fit right and don't knock you off balance. Where possible sacrifice fashion for comfort – if you can have both, all the better. Keep the feet warm in the

Reflexology

Try to massage the whole foot on a regular basis, but pay extra attention to the points highlighted on the chart. When you massage, be aware of 'sore spots', as these need special attention. It's also a good idea to massage the ankles and top side (as well as the soles) of the feet.

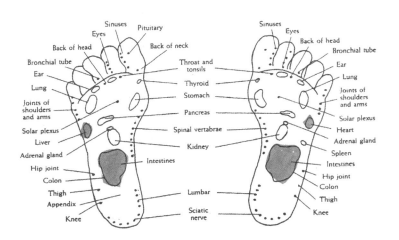

winter. I have seen new machines that detox the body through the feet and you might want to explore this in the year ahead.

The spiritual dimension of healing has been important in your life for many years, as Neptune has been in your 6th House of Health. This trend not only continues in 2009 but actually becomes stronger, as Jupiter (the planet of religion and metaphysics) moves into your 6th House. So continue to explore the power of prayer, meditation, the laying on of hands, reiki and things of that nature. Within you is a Master Physician, the creator of your body. This creator knows the body inside and out and is your sure way out of any health difficulty. In fact, health difficulties could actually be coming from not being in alignment with this life power within you. Like last year, make sure you are in a state of grace and connection.

With Jupiter in your 6th House, the message is to strive for philosophical purity (you are already very much into physical purity, now extend this to your belief systems and philosophy). Errors here will not only cause havoc in your outer life and emotions, but if maintained will actually manifest in the physical body as some form of pathology.

Since Jupiter rules your 4th House of the emotional life – the home and family – the Horoscope is giving us another message. Good health also means a healthy emotional life and harmony with the family. Keep the moods constructive (it will be difficult but worth the work). If health problems arise check your relationship with family members, your spouse or lover and your philosophical beliefs. Restore these to harmony and chances are that the health problem will fall away on its own. And even if you need a health professional, the healing will go much faster and easier.

If you follow these simple guidelines you should sail through the year ahead with flying colours.

Home and Family

Your 4th House of Home and Family is not a House of Power this year Virgo, thus things will be more or less standing still. The cosmos is granting you much freedom to shape this area as you will, but your interest is not there.

The main headline here is Jupiter's move out of Capricorn and into Aquarius – out of your 5th House and into your 6th House.

Last year, with Jupiter in your 5th House, you were making the home a place of entertainment. You probably invested in home theatres, music systems, flat screen TVs and all kinds of toys, both for children and adults. This year (as we saw with Leo) you are making the home a healthier place. Most likely you will be examining the structure of the house for asbestos or lead paint, or other toxic substances. You will probably invest in water and air purifiers. Many will install gyms or exercise equipment. There is even a greater health consciousness with food too.

The home will become more like a health spa than a home.

Also we see more investment in high-tech types of gadgetry. Some of this will be health related, but not all.

There is more involvement with the health of family members and their health or lack of it impacts on your personal health as well.

It looks to me like there is heavy construction or repairs going on from February 4 to March 15. This is a time to take extra safety measures in the home as well. (Keep matches, knives or sharp implements away from children.)

Virgos of childbearing age have been more fertile in recent years, and many have become pregnant. This trend continues in the year ahead. Those not of childbearing age might have adopted children in recent years, and this could still happen in the year ahead.

Relations with children have been bittersweet. On the one hand you want them, but they seem rebellious and difficult to handle. Much patience is needed here.

One of the parents or parent figures in your life has been restless and nomadic for many years. This person could have moved multiple times, and can still move again in the coming year. The problem here is not the residence but the inner state of restlessness. A million moves will not cure this. This person is looking to explore personal freedom and doesn't want any obligations. This type of person is more difficult to handle and should be given a lot of space.

Children of appropriate age are having a status quo domestic year. But they seem very devoted to you. Grown-up children can be coming to stay in your home for prolonged periods.

Siblings are probably moving or buying additional homes or properties – they profit from real estate. There is the happy purchase or sale of a home. Their family circle (perhaps from the in-laws) is expanding through birth or marriage.

Finance and Career

Your 2nd House of Money is not a House of Power for most of the year, thus the status quo will probably prevail. But on October 29, Saturn will move into your money house and inaugurate a two-and-a-half year reorganization. You will go through this much more easily than Leo has (they've been going through it for the past two years) because you innately have the qualities that Saturn is trying to instil: frugality, getting value for money, systematic saving and investing, a long-term perspective on wealth, and getting rich in evolutionary rather than revolutionary ways. (For most Leos these things are alien and need to be consciously learned.)

Yet, because Saturn is the ruler of your 5th House, your speculative urges are stronger than usual. This should be kept in check. If necessary (and if you are in that stage of life where you have an investment portfolio), set up two portfolios – one, a long-term conservative one, with the bulk of your assets and the other a short-term trading, speculation portfolio with no more than 10 per cent of your assets. This way you can indulge your urge without doing too much damage.

Since Saturn rules your 5th House of Fun and Creativity, your challenge now is to get rich and enjoy the process as well. This is easier said than done, but you can do it. You are looking for happy money, not just money. Financial opportunities will start to come to you as you pursue leisure activities – at the golf course, parties, the theatre or sports ground.

Your children – out of the mouths of babes! – can come up with interesting financial ideas or inspire you financially. It is written in the holy texts that every child is born with its own financial supply, and though it might come through the parents it is the child (through its angels) that guides the parents. And it could be that your desire to provide for your children is motivating all the financial changes that are going on.

Professional investors should look at the traditional blue-chip types of stocks, the music and entertainment industry, the gaming industry and industries that cater to children – makers of toys and games and the like. There are interesting profit opportunities here.

For others, these aspects could show work in entertainment, music or gaming. This can be on the business or the performing side. The Horoscope doesn't differentiate between the two.

This is not an especially strong career year. There will be periods in the year where you are more ambitious than usual, but in general the year is about attaining emotional harmony and comfort – feeling good. Most of the long-term planets are below the horizon of the Horoscope. However, there is nothing against a career, and once emotional harmony is attained you can easily succeed in a career from that place.

As we mentioned, jobseekers are having an outstanding year. Dream jobs are out there and you will find them. These things come from family or social connections and not so much from the want ads or media. Those of you who hire others are expanding the workforce this year – a sign of success. Failing businesses are not usually hiring people.

Your most prosperous period this year will be from September 22 to November 8. This is your yearly financial peak.

Love and Social Life

Last year was a banner year for love affairs, but now you seem tired of that – fun-and-games types of relationship – and want something more. In fact marriage was not even advisable last year, but this year it is different.

No question that during the past six years your social life – marriages, friendships and business partnerships – have changed dramatically. It is safe to say that you are in radically different marital and social conditions than you were six years ago, and the changes are still going on.

None of this was punitive, though these changes could have been painful (and could have felt punitive). The object was to liberate you into your true, divinely destined love and social life – the social life of your dreams. But this couldn't happen unless old attachments were broken. You were not being punished, you were being set free.

This year you will see the reason for this. Jupiter will be travelling with Neptune, your love planet, many times during the year, and this is bringing serious love into your life. Marriages and serious relationships are definitely happening. And now you might be ready for it.

For the past years your social life was very experimental. It was exciting. Love came to you in sudden and unexpected ways. You were involved with unique and very interesting people. Genius types. It was a glamorous kind of social life, but highly unstable. There were serial love affairs (and this too was in the stars). In this experimental process – being with different people and experimenting with different kinds of relationships – you gained valuable knowledge. Most likely you learned what 'love was not' and what you didn't want in love. Now, you seem ready for what you truly want – and it is coming.

It was useless for the cosmos to bring you this Mr or Miss Right a few years ago; you probably would have rejected that person. So the timing is cosmically exquisite.

This person will be highly educated, refined, and perhaps a health professional of some sort. He or she will have strong family values and will be very spiritual and idealistic. He or she seems wealthy or at least comfortable. You are likely to meet this person at work or as you pursue your health goals – at the gym, yoga studio, doctors or health seminar. This could also be someone you work with. You have had the aspects for the classic office romance for many years now, and this relationship could also be that type of thing. But this person is definitely marriage material. You're tired of being a nomad in love, you want to settle down.

Other venues for love are foreign countries, family gatherings, religious or educational-type settings.

All of this relates to those who are working on their first marriage. Those working on the second or third (or in their second or third marriage) will have love but perhaps not a marriage. The situation is status quo. Marrieds will tend to stay married and singles will tend to stay single.

The social life will be active all year, but especially from January 19 to March 20 – your yearly social peak.

Siblings, parents or parent figures and children of marriageable age are having a status quo social year. Again, marrieds will most likely stay married and singles will most likely stay single.

Self-improvement

Saturn will still be in your 1st House for most of the year, so the major priority is getting the body and image into shape. You will do this easier than most people as this is one of your natural interests. What will be more difficult to deal with (and you've been going through this for the past two years) is dealing with ego and self-esteem issues. The ego –

the personality – is getting a reality check. The cosmos is working to keep your ego in line with reality. If the ego is overly inflated, it will knock it down. If the ego is too low – unrealistically low – the cosmos will raise it up. And sometimes this means shock therapy. When this transit is over you should have a balanced sense of who you are, your abilities, talents and deficiencies. And this will help you make better judgements for the future.

The spiritual side of healing has been important for many years now, and we discussed it earlier. But this is such a huge subject that six or seven years of involvement are not considered a lot. There are depths upon depths upon depths. The main essential to keep in mind is that there is ONE and ONLY ONE healer. The Divine Power within. This is the power that heals. All the things that happen in a healing process – the doctors, the herbs, the pills, surgery, etc. – are only the side effects of the work of this ONE healer. If health problems arise, don't run to the medicine chest, health food store or health professional. First seek your healing from the ONE healer. If it grants you relief, every pill, potion or therapy will work, but if it doesn't grant this, nothing will work – not for very long anyway. The moment-by-moment intuition is also very important. The intuition, if you listen to it, knows the exact requirements of the hour. Therapies that never worked for you before might do so now. Therapies that always worked before might not work in the present hour. In fact, the cosmos is using health and love to train your intuition.

This is also a great period (and this has been true for many years) to get involved in healing ministries, or prayer circles, that focus on other people. Your own personal health (and healing abilities) will be greatly expanded.

Saturn moving through your money house from October 29 onwards is bringing a cosmic order – a right and correct order – to your financial life. If you co-operate, things will go easier. The object here is to enrich you for the long term, to bring you enduring wealth, and so the thinking has to change. You will be given a long-term perspective on wealth. The important thing now is developing a sense or proportion in spending and investing. Keep business dealings rigorously fair, as Saturn is very strict about these things. This is also a period to get creative with money. In many cases, it shows that your personal creativity – works of art, music, writing, design, etc. – is very marketable. But also it shows that you need to apply some creativity to the way you manage your money. Try to make the process fun. Make a game out of it, and things will go much better.

Month-by-month Forecasts

January

Best Days Overall: 6, 14, 15, 23, 24
Most Stressful Days Overall: 1, 2, 8, 21, 22, 28, 29
Best Days for Love: 1, 2, 8, 9, 10, 16, 17, 18, 19, 26, 27, 28, 29
Best Days for Money: 7, 9, 10, 16, 17, 18, 19, 25, 26, 28, 29
Best Days for Career: 7, 8, 16, 17, 23, 24

You begin your year with most of the planets – 80, sometimes 90 per cent – in the Western, social sector of your chart. Thus you are not as independent as you would like to be and have a need for the good graces of others. Success now comes from your social skills, your ability to enlist the co-operation of others, and not so much from your personal abilities or personal initiative. Since you don't have your normal freedom of action, try to adapt to situations rather than change them. The sages say that this configuration is about 'paying karma'. You are experiencing the consequences of past choices and past creations – past periods of personal independence – and you have to wait for a propitious time to make the corrections. In the meantime you can cultivate your social skills.

Most of the planets are below the horizon of the Horoscope this month. So this is not a period of ambition. It is about cultivating a feeling of emotional harmony, of more inner activity rather than outer activity. It is a time for giving more attention to the family and the home and for preparing the psychological ground for future career actions.

You begin your year right in the midst of personal pleasure peak. You are in party mode. Yes, work is important (and will become even more important later in the month) but right now you want to enjoy life. You work hard but you are also playing hard.

Very happy things are going on work-wise. Jupiter will move into your 6th House of Work on the 5th. The 6th House is chock full of planets, and most of them are benevolent. Also there is a Solar Eclipse on the 26th that occurs in your 6th House. All of this is showing job changes. Happy ones. Dramatic ones. Jobseekers have great success. And those already in a job have new offers and opportunities. This eclipse affects the home and family – perhaps parents or parent figures – bringing dramas into their lives. Perhaps there is a move in store related to the job change. Perhaps there are repairs in the home that need to be made. There are important spiritual changes as well, changes to your practice, regime and attitudes.

Health is always an important interest for you and this month, especially after the 19th, even more so. The Solar Eclipse of the 26th is likely to bring changes in your health regime too. All these things seem positive in the long run, but in the short term they dominate your time and energy. You can't ignore these things.

Love is excellent all month. Serious romance is brewing for singles. You might be backing away from it – stepping back for a while – but the opportunity will happen again next month.

February

Best Days Overall: 2, 3, 10, 11, 19, 20, 21
Most Stressful Days Overall: 4, 5, 17, 18, 24, 25, 26
Best Days for Love: 4, 5, 8, 9, 12, 13, 17, 18, 22, 23, 24, 25, 26, 27, 28
Best Days for Money: 4, 5, 8, 9, 12, 13, 17, 18, 22, 23, 27, 28
Best Days for Career: 2, 3, 4, 5, 10, 11, 22, 23

Though you run and run, you can't escape the love that is happening in your life. Yes, you are afraid. There is much to fear. Real love is like a death – it consumes all that is unlike itself. It is understandable that our psychological selves fear it. But it is life itself – and life will always win any battle. There is a significant meeting with a spiritual kind of person (it can be someone very creative as well) from the 8th to the 14th. Perhaps he or she (it looks more likely to be male) is a guru or spiritual teacher, but this plays a big role in love. Perhaps this person merely sheds new light on your love life or love situation, and that changes things in a positive way. On the 18th as the Sun enters your 7th House, you enter a yearly social peak. So this is a very romantic time for singles.

As we have seen for many years now, the scene of romance is either the workplace or the yoga studio, gym, health spa or doctor's office. Health professionals or co-workers are the most alluring. A romantic date for Virgo can be a jog in the park or a hike in the mountains – something that relates to health.

There is another eclipse this month – a Lunar Eclipse on the 9th. Like the last one it has a profound impact on your spiritual life, on your attitudes to altruistic causes that you have been involved with and in your relations with a charitable organization. Most likely, you are receiving new knowledge, insight or revelation and this changes your spiritual practice. This is quite normal. Our spiritual practice should change as we achieve certain stages. It is like athletics. When you master one set of skills, you set about to master a new set – or take these skills in a new direction.

This Lunar Eclipse will also test friendships and the current love relationship. For singles it can show a marriage; a need to change the marital state. With love opportunities so strong in your Horoscope there is no need to fear a testing of love.

Health is good, but rest and relax more after the 18th. With your 6th House of Health so strong this month, you are not likely to ignore health issues and this is a good sign. You will do whatever is necessary to maintain optimum health.

Continue to focus more on your inner life – your feeling of emotional harmony and wellness and your family situation and family relationships this month. Career doesn't seem a big issue at the moment. Your spiritual mission this month is children (your own or those who are like children to you) and your health and work.

March

Best Days Overall: 1, 2, 10, 19, 20, 28, 29
Most Stressful Days Overall: 3, 4, 16, 17, 18, 24, 25, 30, 31
Best Days for Love: 3, 4, 7, 8, 12, 13, 16, 17, 18, 21, 22, 23, 24, 25, 26, 27
Best Days for Money: 3, 4, 7, 8, 12, 13, 16, 17, 18, 21, 22, 23, 26, 27, 30, 31
Best Days for Career: 3, 4, 14, 15, 25, 26, 30, 31

Saturn has been the handle of a bucket-type chart since the beginning of the year (and it is so this month and next). This shows a need to enjoy life. Work, work, work – which is something that can dominate you – is good up to a point. But have fun too. Also this shows the importance of children and creativity in your life. Through your children, through your personal creativity, through your ability to enjoy your life, you will be able to lift up all your conditions and circumstances.

Your yearly social peak continues, perhaps even more strongly than last month. With Mercury, your ruling planet, moving through your 7th House of Love, you are popular and going out of your way for others and for the beloved. You put the interests of others ahead of your own and this tends to create success. Also you are more aggressive in love. You take the initiative. If you like someone, or are involved with someone, you don't wait for the phone to ring. You let them know of your interest. You are mixing with high people too, and perhaps getting romantically involved with bosses – you have had aspects for the office romance for many years.

Your spiritual mission is other people this month, especially from the 8th onwards. You are supposed to be there for your friends, spouse or current love.

Singles have a huge menu of romantic options: intellectual types, healers and doctors, sexy athletic types, military types and unconventional genius types. But Mars moving into the 7th House on the 15th is going to clear the decks and narrow the choices. He will do a housecleaning, purge the dross from the real, and this will, in the end, promote better love.

Health needs more watching this month. But you are watching. Enhance your health in the ways discussed in the yearly report (*see page 199*). But mainly watch your energy and don't allow yourself to get overtired.

Venus goes Retrograde on the 6th – a rare occurrence. In your chart she rules finances and foreign travel. So this is a time to review your financial life and affairs and see where improvements can be made. Not such a good time for acting on these things – it's more about gaining mental clarity. Foreign trips are better off being rescheduled if you can. If you must travel allow more time for getting to your destination.

Venus Retrograde also shows that a review of your philosophical and religious beliefs is in order. These things are very important and false or only partially true beliefs can be deadly. It will be worth your while to correct these things now.

April

> Best Days Overall: 6, 7, 15, 16, 25, 26
> Most Stressful Days Overall: 13, 14, 20, 21, 27, 28
> Best Days for Love: 4, 8, 9, 18, 19, 20, 21, 27, 28
> Best Days for Money: 4, 8, 9, 18, 19, 20, 21, 27, 28
> Best Days for Career: 4, 5, 15, 16, 25, 26, 27, 28

A parent or parent figure is involved in a romance or business partnership this month. It looks very happy. You seem to be decorating the home, buying art objects or other objects of beauty for the home. For singles, the current love might move in (or you move to his or her place). Major and serious love is happening in your life. This could even lead to marriage or something that is like a marriage.

Last month on the 15th the planets shifted from the lower half to the upper half of your chart. Though both halves are more or less in balance, this is the period of your year where the upper half is most strong. It never really overpowers the lower half (this is just the kind of year it is), but you are in the daytime of your year. Home and family is very important, and keeping the emotional harmony likewise, but now start to shift some energy to your outer goals. Day is for objective doing, not for dreaming or planning. The next four to five months will be about balancing a happy home life with a successful career – about pursuing outer career goals from a place of inner harmony – never going too far in one direction or the other.

With romance going so well it is not surprising that the month ahead is sexually active. (Even older Virgos will be feeling more libidinous than usual.) But the power in the 8th House also shows that your efforts at personal transformation and reinvention are moving forward quickly. You have deeper insight into these things. Your spouse or partner is prospering greatly and is more generous with you. Your line of credit will increase. It will be easier to pay off debts – or make new debts – this month. Those of you who are looking for outside investors should have good success now.

This is a good month for detox regimes of all kinds and on all levels – mental, emotional, spiritual and financial. A detox is also going on in your religious beliefs and you should co-operate with that. For those on a spiritual path there will be new insights into reincarnation, life after death, resurrection and ascension – all 8th House interests.

Some of you will have encounters with the angel of death in various ways. He is not out to get you, but only letting you know that he is around and that life, here on Earth, is short and fragile, and one must be grateful for every moment of it. Sometimes this manifests as near-death experiences on a personal level or with the people around you. Sometimes it can manifest as actual death – but these things can't be predicted in a book like this.

It is a good time to get rid of old possessions, old furniture and the like, to make room for the new. And a good period to cut expenses and eliminate financial waste.

Venus will move forward on the 17th and this is good financially, as it restores clear thinking to this area.

May

Best Days Overall: 3, 4, 12, 13, 14, 22, 23, 30, 31
Most Stressful Days Overall: 10, 11, 18, 19, 24, 25
Best Days for Love: 1, 2, 5, 6, 10, 11, 15, 16, 18, 19, 20, 21, 24, 25, 28, 29
Best Days for Money: 1, 2, 5, 6, 10, 11, 15, 16, 20, 21, 24, 25, 28, 29
Best Days for Career: 5, 13, 14, 22, 23, 24, 25

Retrograde activity increases this month so the pace of events is slowing down, both personally and in the world. In your Horoscope the Retrogrades are affecting key areas of life – the body, image, personal desires, the career, and the love life (your love planet goes Retrograde on the 26th). This doesn't stop good things from happening but it introduces delays and glitches. Patience and good humour is the main spiritual lesson now. When unexpected glitches arise –

especially in an area that is important to us – the tendency is to flare up in irritation. (Have you ever noticed how you feel when another driver cuts you up?) It's an involuntary, instinctual response. But if you can transform this to a smile (because of the knowledge you have from reading this report) you will not lose the harmony of your feeling body and things should go smoother. (Disharmony in the feeling body is perhaps the number one cause of why prayer is not answered or is delayed.)

Love has been torrid of late. Sexual activity is strong. Wedding bells can ring this year. But on the 26th when your love planet goes Retrograde, it might be time for a pause that refreshes – a time to step back and review your love life and current relationship more objectively. Until now you have been under the influence of powerful love aspects. This can be likened to being on narcotics. Reason and good sense are nullified. Now the cosmos will arrange a review. Those who are sure of their feelings can schedule a marriage before the 26th. But those still unsure should wait a few months until Neptune starts to move forward again (towards the end of the year).

There is a brief financial crisis – perhaps an unexpected expense or debt, perhaps a conflict or expense related to a sibling or of an educational nature – but it will pass. Your financial planet is in your 8th House all month. Not only that but it is travelling with the ruler of the 8th House – Mars. This has some good points and some difficult ones. Debt can be a problem. Taxes can bite more than usual. You need to cut expenses and financial waste and the process can be painful (short term). There is a cosmic detox going on in your financial life; the impurities are being removed. When it's over you will be financially healthier. The good points are that there is good spousal support, partners are prospering and generous with you, and you have good access to outside capital or can attract outside investors.

Career is important but complicated now. On the 20th, as the Sun crosses your Midheaven, you enter a yearly career peak. There are happy opportunities coming. You make good career progress. But at the same time Mercury, your career planet, is Retrograde (from the 7th to the 31st) and this suggests that these opportunities – and even your apparent progress – is not what it seems. Focus on your career, but be more methodical and careful. Avoid the short cuts. Take more time and care in the way you communicate to superiors and bosses. Make sure you understand them and that they understand you. Don't take it for granted that your message (or their message) got across. Confirm, confirm, confirm.

June

Best Days Overall: 9, 10, 19, 27, 28
Most Stressful Days Overall: 6, 7, 8, 14, 15, 21
Best Days for Love: 2, 3, 9, 11, 12, 13, 14, 15, 19, 21, 22, 27, 28, 29, 30
Best Days for Money: 2, 3, 9, 11, 12, 13, 19, 21, 22, 27, 28, 29, 30
Best Days for Career: 9, 10, 21, 29, 30

You are still well into your yearly career peak, but this month things will go better and easier. Your career planet is now moving forward. Your judgement is more sound; the career course – the next moves – are clearer. You can enhance your career by personal effort, by good communication, sales and marketing and by getting more involved in charities and altruistic causes. This might seem silly to some of you, but your Horoscope shows that it is important. It will enhance your public image, impress superiors and lead you to important contacts.

Health needed more watching from May 20 onwards, and still needs watching until the 22nd of this month. Probably it is the demands of your career that are causing the stress. Perhaps there are job changes as well. If you have employees under you, they seem rebellious and more difficult to handle. These issues will pass – they are only short-term problems – but in the meantime enhance your health in the ways described in the yearly report (*page 199*).

Love seems happy but progressing at a slower pace. The pace of sexual activity is also slowing down. This is natural. No one can maintain such a torrid pace for too long. Let love develop according to its own pace without trying to force or rush things. Continue with your internal review.

Your 9th House of Religion, Foreign Travel, Higher Education and Metaphysics has been strong for a few months and gets even stronger this month. So there are happy travel and educational opportunities happening. With Jupiter going Retrograde on the 15th, study these things more carefully. Also allow more time for getting to your destination.

This is a month for religious and philosophical break-throughs, especially for those on the spiritual path. What is a breakthrough like? It's like being in a small room and suddenly the walls are shattered and you can see outside: you are no longer trapped in that room. It's what a bird feels like when it pips the shell that enclosed it and now flies free. You no longer have any concern about the walls or the shell – they are history. A very glorious feeling. When it happens many other areas of your life will change, and for the better.

Finances are good this month. Last month was about prospering other people, especially your spouse or partner. You were very involved in his or her earnings. This is still the case until the 6th, but afterwards your financial planet moves into the prosperous and lucky 9th House and good fortune is with you. You not only catch the lucky breaks but you have very sound, down-to-earth financial judgement. Real estate, foreign investments and perhaps foreigners are important financially. You are thinking big this period – and your returns will be big.

July

> Best Days Overall: 6, 7, 16, 17, 24, 25
> Most Stressful Days Overall: 3, 4, 5, 11, 12, 18, 19, 31
> Best Days for Love: 9, 10, 11, 12, 18, 19, 26, 27
> Best Days for Money: 9, 10, 18, 19, 26, 27
> Best Days for Career: 11, 12, 18, 19, 22, 23, 31

Career is still important and your yearly career peak is not over. But other interests are also important. Friendships, group activities, organizations, science, astronomy and astrology are highlighted now. All these activities are happy. You are naturally good at science and technology and this month your understanding increases further.

There are two eclipses this month. Both seem benign to you but they shake things up in the world. The Lunar Eclipse of the 7th occurs in your 5th House of Children, Love Affairs and Creativity. This will test a current love affair and bring important changes in the lives of children (your actual children or those who are like children to you). Some of these changes are normal and natural, but that doesn't make them less disruptive or time consuming. Those of you who are involved in the creative arts make important changes in your creativity. Every Lunar Eclipse tests your friendships and this one is no different. But this month the testing seems more severe. Also there are shakeups in professional or trade organizations that you are involved with, and perhaps spiritual organizations as well.

The Solar Eclipse of the 22nd occurs right on the cusp of the 11th and 12th Houses and will impact on the affairs of both. Again, friendships get tested. There are changes in your spiritual regime and practice – perhaps you change teachers or change paths. There can be scandals or new revelations in a charity or spiritual organization that will take time to digest. Dramatic events are happening in the lives of friends. You might attain a fond hope and wish suddenly and dramatically this month, and sometimes this too creates major disruption in our lives. Eclipses often bring good and happy things but we are forced to make major changes because of them.

Health still needs watching this month. Try to rest and relax more and pace yourself.

There seem to be power struggles going on where you work or in your industry. Heads are rolling. You seem OK personally but you have to work much harder. A parent or parent figure seems in crisis – perhaps there is surgery happening. But it could be another type of crisis as well.

Money comes from pay rises or the support of elders, bosses or parent figures, but there are many strings attached. You are earning every penny. Avoid speculations after the 5th.

August

Best Days Overall: 2, 3, 4, 12, 13, 21, 30, 31
Most Stressful Days Overall: 1, 7, 8, 9, 14, 15, 27, 28
Best Days for Love: 5, 6, 7, 8, 9, 14, 15, 16, 17, 23, 24, 25, 26
Best Days for Money: 5, 6, 7, 8, 9, 14, 15, 16, 17, 23, 24, 25, 26
Best Days for Career: 1, 2, 12, 13, 14, 15, 21, 22

Another Lunar Eclipse on the 6th once again tests friendships (there seems to be no let up here – the cosmos is relentless – friendships will either be pure and good or they are going down the tubes). Like the previous two eclipses of last month, there are changes in your spiritual interests, practices and regimes. This eclipse occurs in your 6th House of Health and Work. So it is also announcing major changes in your health regime (perhaps because of some health scare), diet and means of therapy. Since your health planet is Retrograde don't be so quick to make these changes. Study and analyse your options. Job changes are likely too. This can be within the same company or with another one. The conditions at the workplace are changing – the rules, etc. Those who employ others will probably have some staff turnover now. This eclipse will bring dramatic events in the lives of parents, parent figures, uncles or aunts, and co-workers. Family members are likely to be more temperamental this period so be patient with them.

Spirituality became an important issue on the 22nd of last month and is still important now. This is an excellent period to review the past year, acknowledge and correct mistakes and set goals for the year ahead. You are on the brink of a personal new year, which happens on your birthday: you want to start the new year with a clean slate. It is normal when the 12th House is powerful to want more seclusion. There is nothing wrong with you and you are not being anti-social. But there is no other way to hear the voice of the spirit except in seclusion. And this need is the cause of it.

This is also a good period for going on spiritual retreats, attending spiritual lectures and seminars and increasing your prayer and meditation time. Good for the study of scripture or other kinds of spiritual material.

The planets are now very much in the Eastern personal sector of the Horoscope. This month they are in the maximum Eastern position. So this is a time for taking your destiny in your own hands. If conditions don't suit you, change them. If others don't agree with you, go your own way. You are supposed to create your world as you desire it to be. You have the power to do this now.

On the 22nd the Sun enters your 1st House, initiating another yearly personal pleasure peak. This is a time to pamper the body, get into shape and to enjoy the pleasures of the senses. Since the Sun is also your spiritual planet, a guru or spiritual personality is coming to you – seeking you out, rather than vice versa. You will also receive much insight into spiritual ways to transform the physical body and image.

Finances are good, but trust your intuition. The spiritual aspects of finance are important this month, especially after the 26th. You have much inner help and guidance here. Also it is your mission to achieve financial goals now. The cosmos desires you to be rich, but wants things its way and not yours.

September

> Best Days Overall: 8, 9, 17, 18, 26, 27
> Most Stressful Days Overall: 4, 5, 11, 12, 23, 24, 25
> Best Days for Love: 1, 2, 4, 5, 6, 7, 11, 12, 15, 16, 19, 20, 26, 27, 28, 29, 30
> Best Days for Money: 1, 2, 6, 7, 11, 12, 15, 16, 19, 20, 26, 27, 28, 29, 30
> Best Days for Career: 1, 11, 12, 18, 27

Last month the planetary powers shifted from the upper half to the lower half of the Horoscope. This month the shift is even stronger as Venus moves from the upper to the lower half on the 20th. It is the night time of your year once again. Career and outer activities will become less and less important in the coming months. Sure, you will still have a job and career, but you are shifting more attention to your inner life – to your emotions, family and home. You are getting the home base – both on a physical and psychological level – in order.

Your personal pleasure peak is still in full swing. So enjoy your life and have things your own way. There is a time to be ascetic and spiritual and there is a time to enjoy the pleasures of the earth; now is the time for the latter.

Health is good these days. There is more physical energy than usual. You look good. On the 20th, as Venus enters your Sign, you become even more glamorous. It marks a good time to buy clothing and personal accessories (only keep in mind that Mercury will be Retrograde, so make sure the store has a good returns policy). Financial health is also good, as Venus will bring nice windfalls and financial opportunities. Money is seeking you – running after you – and it will catch up with you; you can't escape your wealth if you tried. You will be dressing more expensively too. Many of you are creating an image of wealth for yourselves, which is a good thing to do now as it will put you in the vibrations of wealth and bring wealth opportunities to you. On the 22nd, you enter a yearly financial peak. Intuition and inner spiritual guidance again becomes important financially. The cosmos wants you to be rich, that's for sure, so follow the inner guidance.

It seems that you are travelling this month, or have the opportunity. But if you won't go to foreign lands, foreign friends might come to you.

Love is still happy, but still complicated, as your love planet, Neptune, remains Retrograde. You feel confused about it. Your lover or partner also seems confused. Avoid important decisions one way or another. Regardless of what is going on in a specific relationship, you are attracting the opposite sex and this gives confidence and self-esteem.

October

Best Days Overall: 6, 7, 14, 15, 23, 24
Most Stressful Days Overall: 1, 2, 8, 9, 21, 22, 28, 29
Best Days for Love: 1, 2, 6, 7, 15, 16, 26, 27, 28, 29
Best Days for Money: 6, 7, 8, 9, 15, 16, 17, 26, 27
Best Days for Career: 8, 9, 10, 16, 28, 29

Personal pleasure and money are the main interests in the month ahead and both areas seem successful.

Venus, your financial planet, is still in your own Sign until the 15th – still bringing you windfalls and opportunities. Personal appearance is more of an issue in finances these days (and this was true last month as well), thus it is good that you are working on your appearance and dressing for success. The major headline financially is Saturn's move into your money house on the 29th. We discussed this at length in the yearly report (see page 199), but you need to get more involved in financial management. You are beginning to reorganize your finances in a healthier way.

Saturn's move into your money house is a very wonderful transit for those of you in the creative arts or entertainment field. It shows that your personal creativity brings you earnings – your work is marketable.

It is very important now on that you enjoy the way that you earn your money. The joy of the work, of the act of making a living, of handling financial affairs is just as important as the actual wages you earn. Yes, you will work, but it shouldn't feel like work – it should feel like fun.

Virgos are not usually speculators, but at this stage of your life you might become more so. Speculations are favourable for the rest of the year ahead. The speculations that I like best for you are the calculated, well thought out ones, not the lottery type. Saturn, your planet of speculation, will reward the calculated risk, but not the casino-type gamble.

Those of you who have grown-up children will find them more financially supportive in the next few years. Those of you who have younger children will probably be spending more on them.

When Saturn leaves your Sign, health and energy improve dramatically – enjoy. It is as if lead weights were taken off your shoulders. You feel light and energetic.

On the 22nd your 3rd House of Communication becomes strong. So this is a time to catch up on all those letters, e-mails and phone calls you owe. It's also good for initiating sales and marketing campaigns and for taking course in subjects that interest you.

Friendships are still getting tested, and there are still dramatic experiences in the lives of friends.

Love gets tested by a flirtation from the 13th to the 15th. If love is true you will pass it by.

November

Best Days Overall: 2, 3, 10, 11, 20, 21, 29, 30
Most Stressful Days Overall: 4, 5, 17, 18, 25, 26
Best Days for Love: 4, 5, 15, 16, 25, 26
Best Days for Money: 4, 5, 13, 14, 15, 16, 22, 23, 25, 26
Best Days for Career: 4, 5, 16, 17, 27, 28

Your love planet starts moving forward on the 4th bringing more social confidence, better judgement and more clarity in your present relationship and in social matters in general. You and the beloved might not be in synch early in the month – perhaps even be in conflict – but the conflict helps to clarify things. When the conflict passes – and it will, by the 16th – love becomes harmonious again. Weddings are still very likely this month, and I prefer after the 16th than before.

Family is a major focus after the 16th. Now with Jupiter, your family planet, moving forward (it began this forward movement on the 13th of last month) there is more clarity in the home and decisions that need to be made will be better. Family is your spiritual mission these days, especially after the 16th. You are here for them. On a mundane level it shows that you are working more from home – taking work home with you, etc. Family members seem more open to spiritual growth and spiritual subjects. This is a good period to hold spiritual meetings – prayer meetings, meditation sessions, lectures, Bible or scripture studies – at home.

Finances become less important after the 8th. By then you will have achieved your most important short-term goals and can focus on other things. The need for good financial management and reorganization is still important and continues for a few years. After the 3rd good communication – good marketing – is important for profits. It's also good to get rid of excess possessions that you no longer need. Make room for the new that wants to come in. Professional investors, or those of you who have investment accounts, should look at bonds, telecommunications, transport and media companies for profit ideas. Creative financing will enhance profits too.

Jobseekers have had good success all year, and I like their prospects this month too. Only, with Uranus still Retrograde, they need to do more analysis on the job opportunities that come to them. Things are not the way they seem.

Health on the long-term level is much improved. But, for the short term, rest and relax more after the 22nd. Continue to avoid making major health decisions, major changes in the diet or regime or therapies until next month when Uranus starts to move forward again.

December

> Best Days Overall: 8, 9, 17, 18, 27, 28
> Most Stressful Days Overall: 2, 15, 16, 22, 23, 29, 30
> Best Days for Love: 2, 6, 7, 10, 11, 15, 16, 19, 20, 21, 22, 23, 26, 27
> Best Days for Money: 2, 6, 7, 10, 11, 15, 16, 19, 20, 21, 26, 27
> Best Days for Career: 2, 8, 9, 17, 18, 27, 28, 29, 30

Uranus has been in your 7th House of Love for many years now. By now you have learned to live with romantic insecurity and change. You are ready for something more serious now and it looks like its happening. Not only is your personal love life wonderful, but there is love in the family circle – family members, parents or parent figures – as well. Singles could again be moving in with their beloveds. Love passions are high right now, so beware of jealousy or possessiveness. These are not love, but impurities in love and they can spoil something really beautiful.

Perhaps in past holiday periods you attended family gatherings but didn't host them. Now it seems that you are the host, and you are enjoying this. Expensive art objects are coming for the home.

Uranus moves forward on the 1st and thus it is now safe to make those changes in the health regime that you've been contemplating. Health still needs watching until the 21st, but after that it improves dramatically. Until the 21st keep the energy levels as high as possible.

Uranus's forward motion is good for jobseekers as well. There is new clarity in their thinking. There are happy job opportunities through social connections or through your spouse or current love.

Home and family are the major interest until the 21st. After that you enter a yearly personal pleasure period. It's party time for the rest of the year. Aside from the normal pleasure pursuits, this is a good time for exploring your creativity and getting more involved with children (your own or those who are like children to you). Personal creativity is very strong now and it would be a shame to waste it.

You might feel like speculation after the 21st but it is best to avoid it. Before the 21st seems better than after. Financial opportunity comes from the family, the family business (your own or someone else's) or family connections. Parents or parent figures are supportive. Probably you are spending on the home and family as well – overspending most likely.

Family is still your spiritual mission until the 5th. After that it is the children and your personal creativity – pushing it further. Career can safely be downplayed.

Libra

⎓

THE SCALES
Birthdays from
23rd September to
22nd October

Personality Profile

LIBRA AT A GLANCE

Element – Air

Ruling Planet – Venus
    Career Planet – Moon
    Love Planet – Mars
    Money Planet – Pluto
    Planet of Communications – Jupiter
    Planet of Health and Work – Neptune
    Planet of Home and Family Life – Saturn
    Planet of Spirituality and Good Fortune –
        Mercury

Colours – blue, jade green

Colours that promote love, romance and social
    harmony – carmine, red, scarlet

Colours that promote earning power –
    burgundy, red-violet, violet

Gems – carnelian, chrysolite, coral, emerald, jade, opal, quartz, white marble

Metal – copper

Scents – almond, rose, vanilla, violet

Quality – cardinal (= activity)

Qualities most needed for balance – a sense of self, self-reliance, independence

Strongest virtues – social grace, charm, tact, diplomacy

Deepest needs – love, romance, social harmony

Characteristic to avoid – violating what is right in order to be socially accepted

Signs of greatest overall compatibility – Gemini, Aquarius

Signs of greatest overall incompatibility – Aries, Cancer, Capricorn

Sign most helpful to career – Cancer

Sign most helpful for emotional support – Capricorn

Sign most helpful financially – Scorpio

Sign best for marriage and/or partnerships – Aries

Sign most helpful for creative projects – Aquarius

Best Sign to have fun with – Aquarius

Signs most helpful in spiritual matters – Gemini, Virgo

Best day of the week – Friday

Understanding a Libra

In the Sign of Libra the universal mind – the soul – expresses its genius for relationships, that is, its power to harmonize diverse elements in a unified, organic way. Libra is the soul's power to express beauty in all of its forms. And where is beauty if not within relationships? Beauty does not exist in isolation. Beauty arises out of comparison – out of the just relationship between different parts. Without a fair and harmonious relationship there is no beauty, whether it be in art, manners, ideas or the social or political forum.

There are two faculties humans have that exalt them above the animal kingdom: their rational faculty (expressed in the Signs of Gemini and Aquarius) and their aesthetic faculty, exemplified by Libra. Without an aesthetic sense we would be little more than intelligent barbarians. Libra is the civilizing instinct or urge of the soul.

Beauty is the essence of what Librans are all about. They are here to beautify the world. One could discuss Librans' social grace, their sense of balance and fair play, their ability to see and love another person's point of view – but this would be to miss their central asset: their desire for beauty.

No one – no matter how alone he or she seems to be – exists in isolation. The universe is one vast collaboration of beings. Librans, more than most, understand this and understand the spiritual laws that make relationships bearable and enjoyable.

A Libra is always the unconscious (and in some cases conscious) civilizer, harmonizer and artist. This is a Libra's deepest urge and greatest genius. Librans love instinctively to bring people together, and they are uniquely qualified to do so. They have a knack for seeing what unites people – the things that attract and bind rather than separate individuals.

Finance

In financial matters Librans can seem frivolous and illogical to others. This is because Librans appear to be more concerned with earning money for others than for themselves. But there is a logic to this financial attitude. Librans know that everything and everyone is connected and that it is impossible to help another to prosper without also prospering yourself. Since enhancing their partner's income and position tends to strengthen their relationship, Librans choose to do so. What could be more fun than building a relationship? You will rarely find a Libra enriching him- or herself at someone else's expense.

Scorpio is the ruler of Libra's Solar 2nd House of Money, giving Libra unusual insight into financial matters – and the power to focus on these matters in a way that disguises a seeming indifference. In fact, many other Signs come to Librans for financial advice and guidance.

Given their social grace, Librans often spend great sums of money on entertaining and organizing social events. They also like to help others when they are in need. Librans would go out of their way to help a friend in dire straits, even if they have to borrow from others to do so. However, Librans are also very careful to pay back any debts they owe, and like to make sure they never have to be reminded to do so.

Career and Public Image

Publicly, Librans like to appear as nurturers. Their friends and acquaintances are their family and they wield political power in parental ways. They also like bosses who are paternal or maternal.

The Sign of Cancer is on Libra's 10th House (of Career) cusp; the Moon is Libra's career planet. The Moon is by far the speediest, most changeable planet in the Horoscope. It alone among all the planets travels through the entire Zodiac – all 12 Signs and Houses – every month. This is an important key to the way in which Librans approach their careers, and also to what they need to do to maximize their career potential. The Moon is the planet of moods and feelings – Librans need a career in which their emotions can have free expression. This is why so many Librans are involved in the creative arts. Libra's ambitions wax and wane with the Moon. They tend to wield power according to their mood.

The Moon 'rules' the masses – and that is why Libra's highest goal is to achieve a mass kind of acclaim and popularity. Librans who achieve fame cultivate the public as other people cultivate a lover or friend. Librans can be very flexible – and often fickle – in their career and ambitions. On the other hand, they can achieve their ends in a great variety of ways. They are not stuck in one attitude or with one way of doing things.

Love and Relationships

Librans express their true genius in love. In love you could not find a partner more romantic, more seductive or more fair. If there is one thing that is sure to destroy a relationship – sure to block your love from flowing – it is injustice or imbalance between lover and beloved. If one party is giving too much or taking too much, resentment is sure to surface at some time or other. Librans are careful about this. If anything, Librans might err on the side of giving more, but never giving less.

If you are in love with a Libra, make sure you keep the aura of romance alive. Do all the little things – candle-lit dinners, travel to exotic locales, flowers and small gifts. Give things that are beautiful, not necessarily expensive. Send cards. Ring regularly even if you have nothing in particular to say. The niceties are very important to a Libra. Your relationship is a work of art: make it beautiful and your Libra lover will appreciate it. If you are creative about it, he or she will appreciate it even more; for this is how your Libra will behave towards you.

Librans like their partners to be aggressive and even a bit self-willed. They know that these are qualities they sometimes lack and so they like their partners to have them. In relationships, however, Librans can be very aggressive – but always in a subtle and charming way! Librans are determined in their efforts to charm the object of their desire – and this determination can be very pleasant if you are on the receiving end.

Home and Domestic Life

Since Librans are such social creatures, they do not particularly like mundane domestic duties. They like a well-organized home – clean and neat with everything needful present – but housework is a chore and a burden, one of the unpleasant tasks in life that must be done, the quicker the better. If a Libra has enough money – and sometimes even if not – he or she will prefer to pay someone else to take care of the daily household chores. However, Librans like gardening; they love to have flowers and plants in the home.

A Libra's home is modern, and furnished in excellent taste. You will find many paintings and sculptures there. Since Librans like to be with friends and family, they enjoy entertaining at home and they make great hosts.

Capricorn is on the cusp of Libra's 4th Solar House of Home and Family. Saturn, the planet of law, order, limits and discipline, rules Libra's domestic affairs. If Librans want their home life to be supportive and happy they need to develop some of the virtues of Saturn – order, organization and discipline. Librans, being so creative and so intensely in need of harmony, can tend to be too lax in the home and too permissive with their children. Too much of this is not always good; children need freedom but they also need limits.

Horoscope for 2009

Major Trends

Your financial planet made a huge move towards the end of 2008, moving from Sagittarius into Capricorn. This brings a whole change in your financial thinking and strategy – not only this year but for many years to come. We will discuss this more fully later on.

Many of you moved in 2008. Your families expanded either through birth or marriage, or through meeting people who were like family. This year the focus is on children and creativity. The year ahead seems mostly a party kind of year. But on October 29, Saturn moves into your Sign and you become more serious.

Health and work were important for many years and the trend is continuing in the year ahead. The job situation has been highly unstable, but nice new opportunities are coming in the year ahead. Jobseekers will change jobs, but the changes will be happy. Health is much improved most of the year, but after October 29 it becomes more delicate. More on this later.

Last year was a highly spiritual type year as well. There was a need to develop a disciplined and difficult spiritual regime and practice. You needed a scientific and structured approach to spirituality and this trend will continue for most of the year ahead.

Your career planet, the Moon, gets eclipsed four times in the year ahead. In addition there will be a Solar Eclipse in your 10th House (on July 22). No question that this bringing major career change in the year ahead. Again, more on this later.

Your most important areas of interest this year are home and family; children, creativity and fun; health and work; spirituality (until October 29); the body, image and self-concept (after October 29).

Your paths of greatest fulfilment in the year ahead are children, creativity and fun; home and family (after July 27).

Health

(Please note that this is an astrological perspective on health
and not a medical one. In days of yore there was no difference, both of these perspectives were identical. But in these
times there could be quite a difference. For the medical
perspective, please consult your doctor or health professional.)

As we mentioned, your health is improved for most of the
year. Two long-term planets are making nice aspects to you
and only one is stressing you. But later on, after October 29,
Saturn moves into a stressful aspect, and you will have to
start watching your energy more and paying more attention
to your health.

Happily, your 6th House of Health is very strong and you
are willing to give health the attention it needs. This is a
positive health signal. It's when you ignore things that problems can develop.

You can enhance your health by giving more attention to
the feet and ankles. Foot and ankle massage will be wonderful in the year ahead. Give the ankles more support when
exercising. Wear sensible shoes that don't knock you off
balance. Keep the feet warm in the winter. Foot baths and
foot whirlpools are also wonderful. There are new machines
that detox the body through the feet and these should be
examined as well.

Your health planet, Neptune, is in the 5th House of
Children, Fun and Creativity. There are many messages
here. Blocked creative urges can impact on the health. Libras
are very creative and artistic people, so a creative hobby will
not only be fun but therapeutic as well. You seem very
involved in the health of children (both your own or other
people's). Problems with children, either with regard to their
health or in your relationship with them, also seem to
impact on health. If health problems arise you will need to
explore this area and bring it into harmony. But the main
message here is to stay happy – joy itself is a great healing
power. Avoid depression like the plague – in fact it should be

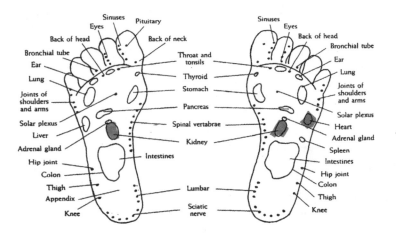

Reflexology

Try to massage the whole foot on a regular basis, but pay extra attention to the points highlighted on the chart. When you massage, be aware of 'sore spots', as these need special attention. It's also a good idea to massage the ankles and top side (as well as the soles) of the feet.

considered the first symptom of a health problem. A night out on the town will, in many cases, do you as much good as a visit to the doctors.

Your health planet rules your health from an Air Sign. Thus, you have a special connection to the healing powers of the Air element. (This is especially so, since you yourself are an Air person.) So, if you feel under the weather get out into the fresh air, into the windy places. Air bathing will be wonderful (you get as naked as practical and let the wind blow all over your body). Breathing exercises are also good. Air purity in general is important and many of you might want to invest in an air purifier this year.

Uranus in your House of Health (for many years now) is also giving us several messages. First, you are more experimental in health matters. Orthodox medicine is probably not for you. You gravitate to the new, the alternative and the technological cutting edge of therapeutics. Also, and more importantly, you are taking the steps that every person eventually needs to do – learn how you function on a personal level. No one is wired up like you. You are unique, a law unto yourself. The rules and principles of health might have value, but some might apply to you and some not. You need (and are probably doing this) to see how you are affected by different diets, regimes, therapies and medication. Throw out all the rule books and study yourself – let your body teach you.

Your health planet Neptune will be Retrograde for many months in the coming year (May 30 to November 4). This is a time for reviewing your health, your therapies and regimes and seeing where you can make improvements. This is not a time to make important health decisions (elective surgery, drastic changes in the diet, etc.) but for study. Important decisions should be made either before May 30 or after November 4.

Home and Family

This was an important area of life last year and continues to be important in the year ahead. Last year Jupiter moved through your 4th House and this was a happy home and domestic period. It brought moves, home improvements, happy and expensive items for the home, the fortunate purchase or sale of a home. Also it expanded the family circle through births, marriages or meeting people who are like family to you. There was good family support last year too.

But now Jupiter leaves the 4th House (on January 5) and Pluto moves in. He will stay there for many years to come (well into 2023). This is showing many, many things, some of a long-term nature. First off, there will be major construction and repairs in the home. Not cosmetic kinds of things but deep things – tearing down walls, ripping out old wiring or plumbing – a reconfiguring of the home. It seems that you are investing in the home in a big way – in the physical house and on family members. But on a deeper level, there is a major detox going on in the home and family pattern. It will die and get born again, like the phoenix. Gut level, family attachments – things that come from the instincts – will get broken, and you will relate to the family on a higher and better level.

It is as if you die to the family as you once knew them, and reconnect from a different place.

In many cases, Pluto's move through the 4th House shows actual, literal deaths in the family. Sometimes it shows near-death experiences in the lives of family members. But equally often, the death is symbolic. Perhaps there is a divorce and that breaks up the home (and it doesn't necessarily have to involve you, but members of the family). Sometimes the family breaks up because of arguments or spats – not necessarily divorce.

The cosmos is detoxing the family life and family situation in the coming years (it will be a long-term process), and in the end you will have the home and family situation of your dreams – the ideal.

The cosmos detoxes in various ways. Usually it applies undue pressure and stress and under the stress the flaws are revealed. This seems to happen after October 29. You need to take on more family responsibility. Perhaps a parent or parent figure is coming to live with you. Perhaps you are involved in more care-taking of family members, or more financial responsibility.

Parents or parent figures are very devoted to you, but you seem uncomfortable with this devotion – is there some element of control at work behind the scenes? Family is a cosmic and important thing. No question about it. It is a survival mechanism for the species. Yet, you feel overly controlled by the family – in bondage – burdened. Perhaps this is the price you pay for the survival mechanism, but perhaps this bondage is a bit unjustified. Only you can discern the situation.

Along with all this we see a focus on children. Libras of childbearing age are unusually fertile and pregnancies are very likely now. Libras beyond childbearing age are probably thinking of adopting or being more involved with children in other ways. New mouths to feed could also account for the symbolism of family burdens and responsibilities. And they could – in the year ahead – show why you are renovating the home.

There are major dramas in the lives of both parents and parent figures in the year ahead. Image changes, changes of the self-concept and perhaps cosmetic types of surgery. They are redefining their personalities this year (and in the case of one of them, it will go on for many years to come).

Finance and Career

Your 2nd House of Finance is not a House of Power this year, Libra, and usually this will show a status-quo kind of year. Things tend to continue as they have been in the past. But late last year, as we mentioned earlier, your financial planet made a very important move from Sagittarius into Capricorn, from your 3rd House into your 4th House. This has huge financial implications, as Pluto will stay in Capricorn well into 2023.

While Pluto was in Sagittarius (from 1995 until 2008) you were more risk taking in your finances. You tended to be an impulse spender. You wanted huge wealth, and quickly to boot. No doubt you prospered during this period as your financial goals were very high – larger than life. Sure, your speculative urges could have hurt you a few times – sure, there were times you regretted your over-spending – but all in all there was a great financial optimism and a tendency to wealth. You picked yourself up from your failures and jumped right back into the arena. Now, with your financial planet in Capricorn you are becoming much more conservative. Quick money is not interesting. Now your whole philosophy of wealth is different. You believe that wealth is accumulated over time in evolutionary ways. It's as if you are becoming the opposite of what you used to be. Quick money is almost abhorrent to you now. Risk-taking likewise. Now you are getting involved in money management – getting good value, eliminating waste, budgeting and systematic saving and investing. These are all Capricorn values.

There is always a degree of risk in any investment or financial strategy. Even the so-called safest investments have some degree of risk (the bank could fail; the government could default on its bonds and obligations etc.). And sometimes the risk in seemingly safe investments is opportunity cost – the same money could have earned larger returns elsewhere. So, Pluto in Capricorn is not going to eliminate risk, but your risks will be calculated, thought out and well hedged – a very different kind of risk-taking from swash-buckling Pluto in Sagittarius.

You will also be developing a long-term perspective on wealth. You will develop a sense (something you always had, but perhaps rarely used) for what an investment will be worth many years from now. You will be planning for the long haul, for many years in the future. Your financial life will probably not be as exciting as when Pluto was in Sagittarius, but dull is often nice in finances. Steady, reliable yearly returns are dull, but they do add up over time.

The other change that we see comes from the change of Houses. While your financial planet was in your 3rd House, the tendency was to earn from sales, marketing, communication, teaching, advertising and PR – earning through your communication skills. Now, it will come from real estate (either residential or commercial), home building, family businesses or industries that cater to the home and family. As we mentioned earlier, you seem to be spending more on the family as well – investing in the home and family. The field of psychology also seems very interesting now.

Pluto, your financial planet, rules bonds and the bond market. So this is an area to look at in the year ahead, especially for professional investors. Also the blue chip, traditional kinds of stocks.

In many cases – much depends on your age and stage in life – the financial planet in the 4th House is showing the prosperity of the family, especially parent and parent figures.

It shows excellent family support on a financial level. Money comes to you either directly through the family or through family connections.

When Pluto was in Sagittarius the main financial danger was over-confidence and over-ebullience. Nothing could ever go wrong with any of your plans and your investments were always foolproof. Now the danger is the reverse – a pessimism about finances and a tendency to always look at the dark side of things. Neither perspective is good. Always we need to look at the good and the bad. Realism in finance (which is what you are developing now) is a wonderful thing, but if it leads to fear, it is not healthy. And this is the danger now.

Jobseekers are very fortunate in the year ahead. There are dream job opportunities coming – jobs that are lucrative and that you will thoroughly enjoy.

Your 10th House of Career is not a House of Power this year. Generally this shows status quo, but as we mentioned earlier, there are four eclipses of your career planet this year (usually there are only two) and these will definitely bring major changes – no question it will be for the better. The problem this year is that you don't seem especially ambitious. You are more focused on family and emotional harmony.

Love and Social Life

Your 7th House of Love, Marriage and Social Activities is not a House of Power this year, thus the year ahead seems a status-quo one. Marrieds will tend to stay married and singles will tend to stay single.

Being a Libra the social life is always important to you, but this year less so than usual. You seem content with the way things are and have no need to make major changes.

Your 5th House of Love Affairs (outside marriage) is very strong and very happy. This is where the action will be in the coming year. There is dating, there are love affairs, but not serious commitment.

In addition, the love planets in your Horoscope, Venus and Mars, will both make rare Retrogrades in the coming year. Venus will be Retrograde from March 6 to April 17. Mars (the actual love planet) will go Retrograde on December 20 (and will continue well into 2010). So, this will be a year, especially during these Retrogrades, for reviewing your marriage and overall relationships and seeing where improvements can be made. Not a time for making important love decisions, one way or another.

Singles don't seem interested in marriage. They are having a big party on the love front. There is an abundance of opportunity. Looks to me like there are two important love affairs this year (there can be more, but we're talking about the important ones). One seems to be with a neighbour and the other someone who is either in the health field, or involved with your health or a co-worker. Both seem very spiritual and idealistic. They are smart, educated and refined. Both just want to have fun, and this seems to fit in with your plans too. They are fun to be with and that's what counts. (There can be some interesting scenarios when these two meet each other, and it's very likely that they will.)

Your most active social period in the year ahead will be from February 3 to June 6 – and especially from March 21 to April 20.

Siblings and children of marriageable age are having status quo social years; marrieds will tend to stay married and singles will tend to stay single.

The parents or parent figures are having their marriages (or serious relationships) tested. Fundamentally sound relationships will survive, but flawed ones will probably end.

Self-improvement

Saturn is still in your 12th House of Spirituality for most of the year ahead. He has been there for the past two years. Thus there is a reorganization happening in your spiritual life, in your attitudes and practice. As we mentioned there is a need to take a more structured, scientific and disciplined approach to it, if you want to succeed and achieve the results that you desire. Too often, people take a lackadaisical attitude to these things; they practise only when they feel like it and other things in life take precedence. Perhaps they have been taught that because spirit is beyond space and time, they don't need to take these things into account. These days you are learning otherwise. It takes as much discipline, commitment and rigour to achieve in the spiritual worlds as to achieve in the mundane world. Many of the same qualities are needed: patience, a stick-to-it attitude, a long-term perspective, a willingness to make progress slowly, step by step. Enlightenment seems to happen suddenly – it bursts into bloom like a flower in spring. But like the flower there are many secret processes that precede the blooming, mostly on an invisible level.

Often when people don't see immediate results in their spiritual practice they want to abandon it, or begin to doubt and disbelieve. This would be a terrible attitude to have right now. You will snatch failure out of the jaws of success. Keep on keeping on; trust, believe, and the results and signs will follow. The signs follow – they don't precede results.

Saturn in the 12th House often denotes deep underground fears, generally emanating from past embodiments, which are holding the person back not only on a spiritual level, but in life in general. Only a disciplined spiritual practice will dissolve these things. (In your case the fears seem to revolve around the parents and the family.)

There has been a lot of insecurity in the job situation for many years. Probably there have been multiple job changes. The spiritual lesson was to learn to be centred, serene and calm amidst all these changes – you will see the payoff in the year ahead. Job changes will be shown to be for the better.

Saturn will move into your 1st House on October 29. This will be a great period – and for the next two years – to lose weight (if you need to) and to get the body in shape. It is true that the body has unlimited capacity. But this is on a theoretical level. At any given time it has certain limits.

True, in the future these limits can be expanded, but at the moment there are certain limits and you will feel those limits keenly. Saturn is also going to adjust your ego – keep it on a realistic level so that you don't make unrealistic or rash decisions. The cosmos (and you will learn this in the year ahead) is not at war with your ego; your ego has a definite place and purpose in the scheme of things. However, the ego needs to be kept in its right place – it is not in charge of policy but only the means where policy (which comes from a higher level) gets carried out.

Your spiritual mission in life tends to revolve around the family and this year is no different. (However, your personal Horoscope cast for your exact time and date of birth could modify this.)

Month-by-month Forecasts

January

Best Days Overall: 8, 16, 17, 26, 27
Most Stressful Days Overall: 3, 4, 10, 11, 23, 24, 30, 31
Best Days for Love: 3, 4, 6, 9, 10, 14, 15, 18, 19, 23, 24, 28, 29, 30, 31
Best Days for Money: 5, 7, 13, 16, 18, 19, 23, 25, 26
Best Days for Career: 5, 6, 10, 11, 14, 15, 25, 26, 27

Your year begins with 80 (and sometimes 90) per cent of the planets below the horizon of the Horoscope. Your 10th House of Career is empty (only the Moon visits there on the 10th and 11th), while your 4th House of Home and Family is ultra-powerful – 60 per cent of the planets are either there or moving through there this month. This is a very clear message. You are in the night-time of your year – midnight actually – and this is a time for the activities of night rather than the activities of day. It is a time to get into emotional harmony, get into feeling right, into right emotional state. As you do this, you will be building the psychological infra-structure for future career success. In our Western culture we too often downplay the importance of the night, but it is vital. A sleep-deprived person is not going to be very successful. So, this is a time for gathering your inner forces for expression later on. You're not wasting time by getting the family and home in order. Subtle and very beautiful processes are taking place.

Aside from the home and family, children also seem a major focus all month, and especially after the 19th. Since this initiates a yearly personal pleasure peak, the child in you is given more play and this child knows how to deal with children.

The party period begins even before the 19th – you will feel it beginning from the 5th – but from the 19th onwards it is strongest. Many of you are in creative types of fields and this will be an unusually creative period. Those of you not into any creativity might want to start a creative hobby now.

Most of the planets are in the social West this month as well. Since this is your favourite sector this is another indi-cator of happiness and success. You get a chance to exercise your social genius and win the co-operation of others. You don't need to assert yourself now. Just allow good to come to you as it wills. Let other people have their way, so long as it isn't destructive, and your good will come to you naturally and beautifully.

For singles love is close to home this month. Perhaps it comes through family connections or through people who are like family to you. This is a month where emotional support and nurturing is important in love – this is how you give it and this is what makes you feel loved. Yes, sexual chemistry is important but there needs to be emotional compatibility and emotional sharing too. Family-oriented people attract you this month. Your beloved needs to have strong family values; it would also be helpful if he or she gets on with your family too. (It seems that they do.)

A Solar Eclipse on the 26th is basically benign to you, but it won't hurt to take a reduced schedule anyway. This eclipse will test friendships and the high-tech gadgets that you own. If there are flaws in these things you will find out about it now. It also impacts on children (your own or those who are like children to you). Be more patient with them during this period. Probably there are dramas in their lives. A love affair (something outside marriage) is getting tested as well. Creative people are making important changes in their creativity.

February

Best Days Overall: 4, 5, 12, 13, 22, 23
Most Stressful Days Overall: 1, 6, 7, 19, 20, 21, 27, 28
Best Days for Love: 1, 3, 4, 8, 9, 12, 17, 18, 22, 23, 27, 28
Best Days for Money: 2, 4, 5, 10, 12, 13, 15, 16, 19, 22, 23
Best Days for Career: 4, 5, 6, 7, 12, 13, 24, 25

A Lunar Eclipse on the 9th will once again test friendships and your electronic gadgetry. Flaws in these things will be revealed so that you can make corrections. This Lunar Eclipse affects the career as well, bringing changes there. It also brings dramatic events in the lives of bosses, parents or parent figures. In spite of this you are still better off focusing on your inner, psychological life – your home and family – than on the career. Work on the career by inner methods – dreaming, visualizing and goal setting – rather than in overt ways.

The party is still very much in effect this month (the whole year will be a party year, but this is one of the strongest months in the year). A happy go lucky time. Your personal happiness inspires your mind – it is very sharp these days – and makes you more attractive to the opposite sex. Work is important, but so is play. You are doing both.

Your love planet changes signs this month, on the 4th. It moves from Capricorn to Aquarius – from your 4th House to your 5th House. This creates a whole new attitude shift in love. Last month you were more conservative, attracted to conservative types, and family-oriented people. This month, you are experimental and fun loving. You want a partner you can play with, someone you can have a good time with, someone who loves a night out on the town, or the theatre, concerts, resorts and hot spots. Also you want something out of the ordinary. Plain vanilla is not for you. You want exotic flavours. You like the rebel, the genius, the unconventional type – someone who is exciting and different. Wealth and status were more of an issue last month. Now, you want experiments. (As long as you keep it legal and non-destructive there's nothing wrong with this.) For marrieds or those involved in serious relationships, this would be a good time for a second honeymoon, for doing fun-type things together as a couple. If there are problems in the marriage a little more fun will fix things.

Personally you seem very popular. You are reaching out to others. Putting others ahead of yourself (as you should these days) and winning the good graces of other people (as you should).

Neither money nor career is much of an issue this month. Finances are status quo, though you seem more prosperous after the 18th than before.

Your 6th House of Health and Work has been strong since the beginning of the year and is even stronger in the month ahead. This is good news for jobseekers and those who employ others. You are into fun, but your work ethic is also strong. Jobseekers can find work while they're having fun – perhaps at a party or on the football field. But it can also come through social connections and networking.

Health is much improved over last month. The fact that you are focused on health, giving it importance, is also a help.

March

> Best Days Overall: 3, 4, 12, 13, 21, 22, 23, 30, 31
> Most Stressful Days Overall: 5, 6, 19, 20, 26, 27
> Best Days for Love: 3, 4, 7, 8, 14, 15, 16, 17, 18, 24, 25, 26, 27
> Best Days for Money: 1, 3, 4, 9, 12, 13, 14, 15, 19, 21, 22, 23, 28, 30, 31
> Best Days for Career: 5, 6, 14, 15, 24, 25

Most of the planets are still in the West: a huge, whopping 80 to 90 per cent are there. So you are in a strong social cycle. Adding to this is that on the 20th you enter a yearly social peak, where your 7th House of Love becomes very powerful and active. This is Libra heaven for sure. Last month was Libra heaven too, but this month more so.

Health is still good and happily you are still focused on health, giving it attention, living a healthy lifestyle and watching your diet. But after the 20th try to rest and relax more. If you feel under the weather it's not because of your health regime or that you need some dietary change – it's most likely about energy. A little rest will do you as much good (in most cases) as a visit to the doctor or that new herb or supplement.

Prosperity is above average, but still not a big issue this month. After the 20th you have some short-term challenges, but nothing too serious. Jobseekers and those who employ others are still successful.

On the 20th, dawn starts to break in your year. It is not daylight yet, but it is the beginning of daylight. Like the dawn, it is still dark outside, but it is the announcement of the new day being born. Career will start to become important but not yet. You're getting ready.

Love is happy now. Any problems in love have to do with you. Venus, your ruling planet, starts to go Retrograde on the 6th and will stay that way until April 17. Singles have abundant love opportunities but seem confused and directionless. The problem is not love, but not being clear as to what you want. There are many people on the menu this month: co-workers, medical people or health professionals, creative types, musicians, poets and techie-type people – whom should you choose? There is also some sexual confusion too: should I sleep with this one or that one? Can I do both? Will it destroy both? Can I pull it off? These are the kinds of issues that singles are dealing with. There is also a need to review your personal goals now, goals related to your image and appearance. See where improvements can be made, and when Venus starts moving forward, you'll be in a good position to implement them.

Your spouse or partner needs to be more careful in financial affairs now. For him or her, this is a period (from the 6th onwards) for a financial review but not for important – major – financial decisions.

April

Best Days Overall: 8, 9, 18, 19, 27, 28
Most Stressful Days Overall: 2, 3, 15, 16, 22, 23, 29, 30
Best Days for Love: 2, 3, 4, 10, 11, 20, 21, 22, 23
Best Days for Money: 6, 8, 9, 10, 11, 15, 18, 19, 25, 27, 28
Best Days for Career: 2, 3, 4, 5, 13, 14, 25, 26, 29, 30

Last month was the dawn of your year. This month there is daylight. The planetary power shifts from the lower half to the upper half – from the night side to the day side – of the Horoscope. Time to wake up and start getting active in the pursuit of your outer goals. Now, you are in the kind of year where career issues will never completely dominate your family interest – the lower half of the Horoscope will always contain a goodly percentage of planets (a minimum of 40 per cent) – but it is now time to shift more energy towards your career. Success in the outer world is a good way to serve your family now.

You will have more enthusiasm and energy for career matters from the 1st to the 9th and from the 25th onwards.

Thus you can schedule yourself accordingly. You are more likely to be successful when the Moon is waxing than when she is waning. (The days when the Moon will be in your 10th House of Career – the 2nd, 3rd, 29th and 30th – are all waxing Moon days, and so there is more success than usual this month.)

Your yearly social peak is still very much underway, and until the 17th (while Venus is Retrograde) there are the same complications that existed last month. After the 17th the love life clarifies. You are clear as to what you want and can make good choices. In spite of Venus's Retrograde this is still a period for parties (attending them or hosting them), gatherings and get-togethers. Until the 22nd you are attracted to creative types of people – mystics, healers, spiritual channels, psychics, musicians and poets. There are also opportunities for office romances, as the workplace is a major scene for romance. After the 22nd you are attracted to athletic and military types. The physical body – the physical chemistry – is the attraction. Love is happy all month, but happier after the 22nd. You and the beloved are in synch, with similar perspectives on things. Existing relationships should become more romantic this period too.

Libras in existing relationship are attending more social events this month too.

Your financial planet, Pluto, starts to Retrograde on the 4th. He will spend many months in Retrograde motion. This isn't going to stop earnings, but it suggests a need for more caution in your financial dealings and decision making. This is a good time to make a serious review of your financial situation – your investments, spending, etc. – and see where you can make improvements. If you produce products or give a service this is a good time to review those things as well.

Rest and relax more this month. Refer to last month's discussion of health.

May

> Best Days Overall: 5, 6, 15, 16, 24, 25
> Most Stressful Days Overall: 12, 13, 14, 20, 21, 26, 27
> Best Days for Love: 1, 2, 10, 11, 20, 21, 28, 29
> Best Days for Money: 3, 5, 6, 8, 9, 12, 15, 16, 22, 24, 25,
>   30
> Best Days for Career: 3, 4, 12, 13, 14, 24, 25, 26, 27

With your 9th House very strong this month (especially after the 20th), travel is on your mind. But keep in mind that your travel planet, Mercury, goes Retrograde from the 7th to the 31st. Thus you should be more cautious here. It might be better to plan your travel this month – research the air fares, prices, hotels and other information – and do the actual travelling next month. If you must travel during this Retrograde period, allow more time for getting to your destination.

A financial challenge – though severe – is short term. It will pass and finances will soon be back to normal. Don't use it as an excuse to make dramatic financial changes; this is still not the time, as Pluto is still Retrograde.

Love seems to remain very happy. You and the beloved are still in harmony. The mood is romantic and marriage – or some kind of permanence – is on both your minds. Your beloved (and friends in general) appreciate your devotion and self-sacrifice on his or her behalf. We see happiness in love in other ways, as sexual activity is on the increase this month. Sexual satisfaction and performance is also better. Libido is stronger, and even older Libras will have more libido than usual.

Singles have been risk takers in love for the past few months, but even more so now. You jump into relationships very quickly. Love tends to happen at first sight. Even though you are aware that you are taking risks, you feel that your social genius, your grace and charm, will bail you out – and perhaps you are right.

With the 8th House strong your spouse, partner or current love is in a yearly financial peak. He or she earns money rather easily and there is luck in speculations. He or she is more generous with you as well.

Friends are having dramatic kinds of experiences – encounters with death or near-death experiences, or perhaps surgery and the like.

Jobseekers have better success after the 20th than before. However, with Neptune starting to Retrograde on the 26th, all these opportunities need more analysis and study.

Health is much improved this month.

Career continues to be more important this month and you are getting ready for your yearly career peak, which will begin next month. In the meantime get as much education as possible – take the seminars or courses that you need for your next steps. Your career should be more successful from the 1st to the 9th and from the 24th onwards, as the Moon is waxing.

June

Best Days Overall: 2, 3, 11, 12, 13, 21, 29, 30
Most Stressful Days Overall: 9, 10, 16, 17, 23
Best Days for Love: 9, 10, 16, 17, 19, 21, 27, 28, 29, 30
Best Days for Money: 2, 3, 4, 5, 9, 11, 12, 13, 18, 21, 22, 26, 29, 30
Best Days for Career: 2, 3, 11, 12, 13, 21, 22, 23, 29, 30

Like last month, your 8th House is strong all through June. Romance is very physical. The physical chemistry seems the most important thing. Libido is stronger than usual. A good sexual chemistry will cover up many sins in a troubled relationship.

But the power in the 8th House has other meanings too. Your spouse, partner or current love is prospering and very focused on finance. You seem personally involved with your spouse's or partner's earnings. Perhaps you are working for him or her. Personal finances are much better now than last month too. This is a good month to pay off debts or deal with tax issues. It's also good if you need a mortgage or bank loan.

The fact that both you and your spouse share a common interest – his or her finances – is a positive for romance.

On a personal level, this is a good period to lose weight and detox the body, and very good for interests such as personal transformation and reinvention. Many of you are thinking of cosmetic surgery these days.

On a more spiritual level you are going deeper into past lives, life after death and an understanding of death. Resurrection and ascension are also strong interests and those of you on the spiritual path will make progress in these areas. With the 9th House also strong all month, there are religious and philosophical breakthroughs happening, and when this happens the whole life changes for these things change the whole perspective on life. One minute you are shut in a dark room and the next you have wings and are soaring through the heavens. These are life-changing experiences.

On the 21st, as the Sun crosses your Midheaven, you enter a yearly career peak. If you have been preparing, there are happy opportunities now. You find favour with elders and bosses. You have friends in the right places. Friends are also succeeding career-wise and this is a help to you – they sort of clear the way.

Health is good this month, but rest and relax more after the 21st. The demands of career are more intense now than they've been all year, and you need to focus on priorities and let lesser things go. Keep the energy levels as high as possible.

Now that your travel planet is moving forward it is safer to make those foreign trips.

July

> Best Days Overall: 9, 10, 18, 19, 26, 27
> Most Stressful Days Overall: 6, 7, 14, 15, 20, 21
> Best Days for Love: 6, 7, 9, 14, 15, 18, 19, 26, 27
> Best Days for Money: 1, 2, 6, 9, 10, 16, 18, 19, 24, 26, 27, 28, 29, 30
> Best Days for Career: 1, 2, 11, 12, 20, 21, 22, 31

You are well into your yearly career peak. Though things are slowing down in the world at large – and many people are on vacation – for you things are moving forward. Perhaps this slowdown is actually helping you in some way. Perhaps it creates an opening where there was none. Advance your career through networking, social contacts and being involved in groups and organizations. Good communication and marketing will be a help too. Charitable activities also seem favourable as you make contacts and cement your public image. Your willingness to travel and to educate yourself (and the fact that you are intelligent enough to handle an education) is another big plus career-wise. This month (and the next) pay rises and promotions are likely.

Money is not an issue this month: prestige and elevation are more important. You might even take less money just to have a more prestigious position (or to be with a more prestigious company).

Love still seems happy, whether you are single or married. You and the spouse or partner are still 'travelling together' – still in synch. Your interests seem aligned.

For singles, Mars's move out of Taurus and into Gemini – your 9th House – on the 12th signals another shift in love attitudes. For the past few months, sexual chemistry and performance seemed the most important thing (wealth didn't hurt either). But now the mental dimension has become important. Good communication on an intellectual level is important. You need to fall in love with the person's mind as well as the body, with the thought process. Education and erudition are important. There is a need for philosophical and religious compatibility as well. You have the aspects now of someone who falls in love with their professor or minister. Love opportunities happen in foreign lands, with foreigners, at college or church/religious-type settings.

On a more spiritual level, singles might be shocked to learn that the Divine expects to be called on for love needs as much as for any other need. And that prayer can bring love faster (and less painfully) than the bars, clubs or cabarets. The Divine is the best matchmaker there is.

On the 22nd your 11th House of Friends becomes powerful, and so there is more involvement with friends – and not just from a career perspective either, but from a fun perspective.

Continue to watch your health until the 22nd. Rest, relax and pace yourself. You have plenty of energy to handle your true needs and responsibilities, but let lesser things go.

August

Best Days Overall: 5, 6, 14, 15, 23, 24
Most Stressful Days Overall: 2, 3, 4, 10, 11, 16, 17, 30, 31
Best Days for Love: 5, 6, 7, 8, 9, 10, 11, 14, 15, 16, 17, 24, 25, 26
Best Days for Money: 2, 5, 6, 12, 14, 15, 20, 23, 24, 25, 26, 30
Best Days for Career: 1, 10, 11, 16, 17, 19, 20, 30, 31

Pay rises and promotions can happen this month as well. Your yearly career peak seems to be extended. Though the Sun has long ago left your 10th House, Venus will be there until the 26th and Mars will enter on the 24th. You are personally elevated these days. You are on top. You have more authority, power and prestige. You are honoured and appreciated for who you are, and not so much for your career achievements. You seem above everyone in your family including your spouse. (This will change later on in the month.) You and your spouse seem to be vying for the top spot.

Advance the career through personal effort, through a good appearance (dress for success and try to look the part for the position you want or are taking) and through your social skills. Likeability (something you understand very well) plays a huge role in your advancement. Your ability to handle other people gracefully, to gain their co-operation, to have them think favourably of you is a very important management skill. Perhaps there are more skilled managers out there than you are, but not too many who have the people skills that you have. Attending and hosting the right parties also seems important.

As Mars enters the 10th House on the 24th your love needs shift again. For singles this shows romantic opportunity at the office, with bosses or superiors – the traditional office romance. It also shows that now you are attracted by power – the ultimate aphrodisiac. Perhaps you are a bit too pragmatic in love. You see it as another job or career move and not just as love. The good provider, the person of high status and prestige, allures you now. Of course he or she should have good family values too. Singles will find love opportunities as they pursue their career goals and perhaps with people who are involved in their career. Married Libras are mixing with high and powerful people this month. Both you and your spouse are being elevated and promoted. Both of you are enjoying career success. Yours happens earlier, the spouse's after the 24th.

Spirituality becomes important after the 22nd. It has been important all year but is now even more so. This creates some interesting challenges. You are ambitious in a worldly sense, and yet have very intense spiritual urges. How do you reconcile these two things? The values of spirit are very different from the values of the world. If you can manage to integrate these two things – and everyone does this in their own way – you will have found an important key to happiness and success.

Though you are busy with your career, perhaps you can arrange for weekend spiritual retreats, or lectures. Perhaps you can wake up a bit earlier and give more time to meditation.

These are just a few suggestions; there are many other ways to handle this too.

September

  Best Days Overall: 1, 2, 11, 12, 19, 20, 28, 29, 30
  Most Stressful Days Overall: 6, 7, 13, 14, 26, 27
  Best Days for Love: 4, 5, 6, 7, 13, 14, 15, 16, 21, 22, 26, 27
  Best Days for Money: 1, 2, 8, 11, 12, 17, 19, 20, 21, 22, 26, 28, 29, 30
  Best Days for Career: 8, 9, 13, 14, 17, 18, 28, 29

The two planets that rule foreign travel in your Horoscope – Jupiter and Mercury – are Retrograde at the same time this month. Mercury will be Retrograde from the 7th to the 29th. If possible, avoid foreign trips (even domestic trips are not advisable this period). Better to travel before the 7th or after the 29th. But if you must travel, protect yourself. Allow more time for getting to and from your destination. Avoid scheduling connecting flights too tightly. It might be wise to insure your ticket so that you don't pay penalties if you make changes. Above all, be patient and philosophical. Maintain your harmony during this rough stretch of cosmic weather.

Career and spirituality are still vying for your love and attention. The outer world is calling to you, but so is the spiritual world. The glitter of the world competes with the peace of the chamber of the heart. Like last month, your challenge is to integrate and harmonize these two urges. Every person is his or her own solution to this problem. Some pursue the mundane career but spend much time involved with charities and causes. Others opt for a spiritual-type career. Some opt for two careers: a spiritual and a mundane one – the right way will open up for you.

Your love planet is still in the 10th House this month. And, like last month, this shows the success of the partner, spouse or current love. He or she is at the top right now –

lording it over you and everyone else. Like last month it shows that you are mixing with high and mighty people, people above you in status. There are still strong tendency for the office romance for singles – romantic opportunities with bosses or those involved with the career. Singles are still attracted by people of power and position. The love attitudes are pragmatic. Love is just another career move. One can learn to love the good provider as well as anyone else, so why not have the good provider?

Love opportunities are still happening as you pursue your career goals. Family connections or family introductions also play a role. A parent, parent figure or boss is playing cupid.

Finances are good this month, but not a big issue. There is a beautiful windfall or financial opportunity around the 20th (it can happen a day before or a day after too). Your financial planet, Pluto, starts to move forward on the 11th after many months of Retrograde motion, and this will clarify your financial thinking and judgement. Many long-stalled projects and plans will start to move forward now.

On the 22nd, the Sun enters your own Sign and initiates a yearly personal pleasure peak – a time to give the body and its desires its due. So many of us take our bodies for granted. We don't realize its heroic efforts to keep working, to serve us, in spite of the many loads we place upon it. It labours incessantly to serve us. Take time to give it thanks and praise and it will respond to you.

October

Best Days Overall: 8, 9, 16, 17, 26, 27
Most Stressful Days Overall: 3, 4, 10, 11, 23, 24, 31
Best Days for Love: 1, 2, 3, 4, 6, 7, 10, 11, 15, 16, 21, 22, 26, 27, 31
Best Days for Money: 6, 8, 9, 14, 16, 17, 19, 20, 23, 26, 27
Best Days for Career: 8, 9, 10, 11, 16, 17, 18, 28, 29

Many important developments are taking place this month. Most of the planets are in the Eastern sector of self. Not your favourite sector, but still favourable. It enables you to be more independent and to have things your way. You have the power now to change undesirable conditions and to create new ones if necessary. Though you are unlikely to 'go it alone', you can if you need to. The world will adapt to you now, not vice versa.

This month the planets make an important shift from the upper to the lower half of the Horoscope. Career and outer activities have been important for the past few months, but now become much less so. It is nightfall in your year, and time to regroup your inner energy, to gather your forces for the future day that will happen next year. It is time to find, and function from, your point of emotional harmony; to spend more time on the family, home and domestic life. This is an important psychological shift.

On the 29th of the month, Saturn (your family planet) will also move into your own Sign, after two and a half years in Virgo. This further underscores the need to focus on the family. You love your family, family is important to you, but there is a downside – it brings responsibilities with it.

Health is good this month, but Saturn moving into your own Sign is a signal that from here on in, for the next two and a half years, you will need to give more attention here. In the meantime, you are magnetic, charismatic and energetic. Your appearance shines. You glow. Your personal sense of style is always good – not too many people can match it – but now it gets even better, especially after the 15th. Your body and image is truly your personal work of art. It's good to buy the clothing and accessories you need and to work on your image now.

Travelling is getting much easier this month, both foreign and local. Mercury will be moving forward all month and Jupiter will start moving forward after the 18th. You seem in a travel mood after the 10th.

Finances are excellent this month. With more personal energy now you can do more, and this always helps. In addition, on the 23rd you enter a yearly financial peak. Your financial planet is moving forward and all systems are go.

Love attitudes change again after the 16th. Mars leaves your 10th House and moves into the 11th. Power is not as alluring as it was. Yes, powerful people can help you career-wise and in the world, but there is a tendency to lord it over you. Now you want a relationship of equals (which creates other problems, as no two people are equal!). You want friendship with the beloved. Also, you want fun. On the positive side, the love planet in the 11th House will often manifest 'fondest hopes and wishes' regarding love. Love seems happy this month. Singles still find love opportunities at work or as they pursue career goals until the 16th, and afterwards at group activities or organizations.

November

Best Days Overall: 4, 5, 13, 14, 22, 23
Most Stressful Days Overall: 1, 6, 7, 20, 21, 27, 28
Best Days for Love: 2, 3, 4, 5, 10, 11, 15, 16, 20, 21, 25, 26, 29, 30
Best Days for Money: 2, 4, 5, 10, 13, 14, 15, 16, 20, 22, 23, 29
Best Days for Career: 6, 7, 15, 16, 27, 28

Family burdens and obligations weigh heavily on you, but now is not the time to shirk the burden. Carry it as best you can. Other, lesser interests will be sacrificed. Health is good this month but watch your energy levels. You are in a great two-year period for getting the body in shape – for losing weight, dieting and sculpting the body according to your desires.

Though you are spending more on family, finances are excellent this month. Whatever the expenses are, there is plenty of income to cover them. You are well into a yearly financial peak, and it will grow stronger next month. Personal effort and personal interest, personal appearance, intuition and friends in the right places are boosting the earnings.

Jobseekers have good prospects this month too – they seem better after the 22nd than before this date. Neptune, the work planet, will start moving forward (after many months of Retrograde motion) on the 4th. This will further clarify the job situation and your thinking about it. Judgement will be better in this area.

Love seems stormy after the 8th. You and the beloved are not in synch, but this is temporary. The problem will pass next month. Love affairs (outside marriage) are also stormy and are probably getting tested until the 22nd. Part of the problem is your focus on earnings and your personal financial interest. This takes attention from the current love, and perhaps (at least according to him or her) makes you less able to meet his or her needs. True love will weather these problems.

Serious love opportunities for singles come through friends, the introduction of friends, groups, group activities and organizations. You also have the kind of aspects for online dating – online matchmaking.

Children seem more temperamental this month. Just be more patient and keep your personal harmony.

Your 3rd House of Communication and Intellectual Interests becomes strong after the 22nd – a good period to take courses in subjects that interest you, attend lectures, and catch up on your mail and phone calls. It's also good for launching sales and marketing campaigns, for getting your message out to the public.

December

Best Days Overall: 2, 10, 11, 19, 20, 21, 29, 30
Most Stressful Days Overall: 10, 11, 17, 18, 24, 25, 26
Best Days for Love: 6, 7, 15, 16, 24, 25, 26, 27
Best Days for Money: 2, 8, 10, 11, 12, 13, 17, 19, 20, 21, 27
Best Days for Career: 4, 6, 7, 15, 16, 27, 28, 31

Though technically your yearly financial peak is over, you have some very nice paydays coming from the 5th onwards. (Probably you are spending more those periods as well.) This being holiday time, these nice paydays and expenditure are not a surprise, but keep in mind that the Horoscope need not surprise us. It only shows us what is – and that is its beauty.

This is a time of year when many of you will be travelling. Keep in mind that Mercury, your travel planet, will go Retrograde on the 26th. Try if you can to schedule your trip before that. (Happily, Jupiter will be moving forward and travel will not be as complicated as in previous months.) If you must travel during that period, keep in mind our previous advice: allow more time for getting to your destination, don't schedule connecting flights too closely, and buy tickets that allow for changes. (The good news is that Mercury's Retrograde happens after most holiday preparation is already done.)

Home and family is still the dominant interest this month, even more so than in previous months. You are in the midnight of your year. At midnight you are inwardly a million miles away from your outer life. On a Soul level, you are working on the outer life by inner means. The soul is always working, setting the groundwork for the next day's activities. And this is what is happening now. Build future career success through meditation, visualization and 'controlled day dreaming'. This is a time for make psychological progress, and when you have these psychological – emotional – breakthroughs, the outer career will also benefit. This is a time for analysing the psychological issues that affect your career and outer life – and for making the corrections.

Health needs much more attention after the 21st. Half the planets will be in stressful aspect to you and this is not something to take lightly. Rest whenever you feel tired. Organize your day so that more gets done with less effort. Delegate tasks wherever possible. Work on your health by spiritual means; this is a month where you will make more progress here.

Jobseekers have wonderful – dream job – opportunities now. Perhaps even in foreign countries or with foreign companies. Employers are expanding their workforce – and in a quality way.

Your love planet goes backwards on the 20th. Serious love is on hold for a while. Avoid making major love decisions, one way or another, for the next few months. Fun and games kinds of love are plentiful.

Scorpio

ⵊ

THE SCORPION
Birthdays from
23rd October to
22nd November

Personality Profile

SCORPIO AT A GLANCE

Element – Water

Ruling Planet – Pluto
   Co-ruling Planet – Mars
   Career Planet – Sun
   Love Planet – Venus
   Money Planet – Jupiter
   Planet of Health and Work – Mars
   Planet of Home and Family Life – Uranus

Colour – red-violet

Colour that promotes love, romance and social
   harmony – green

Colour that promotes earning power – blue

Gems – bloodstone, malachite, topaz

Metals – iron, radium, steel

Scents – cherry blossom, coconut, sandalwood, watermelon

Quality – fixed (= stability)

Quality most needed for balance – a wider view of things

Strongest virtues – loyalty, concentration, determination, courage, depth

Deepest needs – to penetrate and transform

Characteristics to avoid – jealousy, vindictiveness, fanaticism

Signs of greatest overall compatibility – Cancer, Pisces

Signs of greatest overall incompatibility – Taurus, Leo, Aquarius

Sign most helpful to career – Leo

Sign most helpful for emotional support – Aquarius

Sign most helpful financially – Sagittarius

Sign best for marriage and/or partnerships – Taurus

Sign most helpful for creative projects – Pisces

Best Sign to have fun with – Pisces

Signs most helpful in spiritual matters – Cancer, Libra

Best day of the week – Tuesday

Understanding a Scorpio

One symbol of the Sign of Scorpio is the phoenix. If you meditate upon the legend of the phoenix you will begin to understand the Scorpio character – his or her powers and abilities, interests and deepest urges.

The phoenix of mythology was a bird that could recreate and reproduce itself. It did so in a most intriguing way: it would seek a fire – usually in a religious temple – fly into it, consume itself in the flames and then emerge a new bird. If this is not the ultimate, most profound transformation, then what is?

Transformation is what Scorpios are all about – in their minds, bodies, affairs and relationships (Scorpios are also society's transformers). To change something in a natural, not an artificial way, involves a transformation from within. This type of change is a radical change as opposed to a mere cosmetic make-over. Some people think that change means altering just their appearance, but this is not the kind of thing that interests a Scorpio. Scorpios seek deep, fundamental change. Since real change always proceeds from within, a Scorpio is very interested in – and usually accustomed to – the inner, intimate and philosophical side of life.

Scorpios are people of depth and intellect. If you want to interest them you must present them with more than just a superficial image. You and your interests, projects or business deals must have real substance to them in order to stimulate a Scorpio. If they haven't, he or she will find you out – and that will be the end of the story.

If we observe life – the processes of growth and decay – we see the transformational powers of Scorpio at work all the time. The caterpillar changes itself into a butterfly, the infant grows into a child and then an adult. To Scorpios this definite and perpetual transformation is not something to be feared. They see it as a normal part of life. This acceptance of transformation gives Scorpios the key to understanding the true meaning of life.

Scorpios' understanding of life (including life's weaknesses) makes them powerful warriors – in all senses of the word. Add to this their depth, patience and endurance and you have a powerful personality. Scorpios have good, long memories and can at times be quite vindictive – they can wait years to get their revenge. As a friend, though, there is no one more loyal and true than a Scorpio. Few are willing to make the sacrifices that a Scorpio will make for a true friend.

The results of a transformation are quite obvious, although the process of transformation is invisible and secret. This is why Scorpios are considered secretive in nature. A seed will not grow properly if you keep digging it up and exposing it to the light of day. It must stay buried – invisible – until it starts to grow. In the same manner, Scorpios fear revealing too much about themselves or their hopes to other people. However, they will be more than happy to let you see the finished product – but only when it is completely wrapped up. On the other hand, Scorpios like knowing everyone else's secrets as much as they dislike anyone knowing theirs.

Finance

Love, birth, life as well as death are Nature's most potent transformations; Scorpios are interested in all of these. In our society, money is a transforming power, too, and a Scorpio is interested in money for that reason. To a Scorpio money is power, money causes change, money controls. It is the power of money that fascinates them. But Scorpios can be too materialistic if they are not careful. They can be overly awed by the power of money, to a point where they think that money rules the world.

Even the term plutocrat comes from Pluto, the ruler of the Sign of Scorpio. Scorpios will – in one way or another – achieve the financial status they strive for. When they do so they are careful in the way they handle their wealth. Part of this financial carefulness is really a kind of honesty, for

Scorpios are usually involved with other people's money – as accountants, lawyers, stockbrokers or corporate managers – and when you handle other people's money you have to be more cautious than when you handle your own.

In order to fulfil their financial goals, Scorpios have important lessons to learn. They need to develop qualities that do not come naturally to them, such as breadth of vision, optimism, faith, trust and, above all, generosity. They need to see the wealth in Nature and in life, as well as in its more obvious forms of money and power. When they develop generosity their financial potential reaches great heights, for Jupiter, the Lord of Opulence and Good Fortune, is Scorpio's money planet.

Career and Public Image

Scorpio's greatest aspiration in life is to be considered by society as a source of light and life. They want to be leaders, to be stars. But they follow a very different road than do Leos, the other stars of the Zodiac. A Scorpio arrives at the goal secretly, without ostentation; a Leo pursues it openly. Scorpios seek the glamour and fun of the rich and famous in a restrained, discreet way.

Scorpios are by nature introverted and tend to avoid the limelight. But if they want to attain their highest career goals they need to open up a bit and to express themselves more. They need to stop hiding their light under a bushel and let it shine. Above all, they need to let go of any vindictiveness and small-mindedness. All their gifts and insights were given to them for one important reason – to serve life and to increase the joy of living for others.

Love and Relationships

Scorpio is another Zodiac Sign that likes committed, clearly defined, structured relationships. They are cautious about marriage, but when they do commit to a relationship they tend to be faithful – and heaven help the mate caught or even suspected of infidelity! The jealousy of the Scorpio is legendary. They can be so intense in their jealousy that even the thought or intention of infidelity will be detected and is likely to cause as much of a storm as if the deed had actually been done.

Scorpios tend to settle down with those who are wealthier than they are. They usually have enough intensity for two, so in their partners they seek someone pleasant, hardworking, amiable, stable and easy-going. They want someone they can lean on, someone loyal behind them as they fight the battles of life. To a Scorpio a partner, be it a lover or a friend, is a real partner – not an adversary. Most of all a Scorpio is looking for an ally, not a competitor.

If you are in love with a Scorpio you will need a lot of patience. It takes a long time to get to know Scorpios, because they do not reveal themselves readily. But if you persist and your motives are honourable, you will gradually be allowed into a Scorpio's inner chambers of the mind and heart.

Home and Domestic Life

Uranus is ruler of Scorpio's 4th Solar House of Home and Family. Uranus is the planet of science, technology, changes and democracy. This tells us a lot about a Scorpio's conduct in the home and what he or she needs in order to have a happy, harmonious home life.

Scorpios can sometimes bring their passion, intensity and wilfulness into the home and family, which is not always the place for these qualities. These traits are good for the warrior and the transformer, but not so good for the nurturer and family member. Because of this (and also because of their need for change and transformation) the Scorpio may be prone to sudden changes of residence. If not carefully constrained, the sometimes inflexible Scorpio can produce turmoil and sudden upheavals within the family.

Scorpios need to develop some of the virtues of Aquarius in order to cope better with domestic matters. There is a need to build a team spirit at home, to treat family activities as truly group activities – family members should all have a say in what does and does not get done. For at times a Scorpio can be most dictatorial. When a Scorpio gets dictatorial it is much worse than if a Leo or Capricorn (the two other power Signs in the Zodiac) does. For the dictatorship of a Scorpio is applied with more zeal, passion, intensity and concentration than is true of either a Leo or Capricorn. Obviously this can be unbearable to family members – especially if they are sensitive types.

In order for a Scorpio to get the full benefit of the emotional support that a family can give, he or she needs to let go of conservatism and be a bit more experimental, to explore new techniques in child-rearing, be more democratic with family members and to try to manage things by consensus rather than by autocratic edict.

Horoscope for 2009

Major Trends

Last year you experienced the beginning of an important shift in your life. And, this is a long-term trend. Pluto, your ruling planet, made an important move (towards the end of 2008) into Capricorn, from Sagittarius; from your 2nd House into your 3rd. For many years you have been very focused on finance, and now you are starting to be more interested in communication and intellectual interests. You are into developing your mind and communication skills – more into teaching and learning. And what is money for, if not to buy us the freedom to develop our other faculties?

Home and family have been an important focus for many years and this trend will only get stronger in the year ahead, as Jupiter moves into your 4th House and stays there for the rest of the year. More on this later.

Love and marriage have not been a major focus for several years and this trend continues in the year ahead as well. Other things in your life are more important. However, singles are having many happy love affairs. Again, more on this later.

For many years money has been more important than career. This year they are both about equal. You are at the place you want to be in your career and have no need to make major changes. (Keep in mind though, that there are two Solar Eclipses in the year ahead, and these will bring change whether you want it or not.)

Saturn has been in your 11th House of Friends for about two years and will be there for most of the year ahead. This shows the testing of friendships, a weeding out of the true from the untrue, the good from the lukewarm.

Spirituality has not been that important in recent years and perhaps you have neglected it. But come October 29, as Saturn moves into your 12th House, you will be forced to give more attention here. More details later on.

Your travel planet gets eclipsed four times in the year ahead, which is highly unusual. Thus more care should be exercised about foreign trips than normal, especially around the periods of the eclipses. We will discuss this further in the monthly reports.

For students, especially at university level, these eclipses are bringing disruption and change to educational plans, to courses, and perhaps even to the institutions.

Your most important areas of interest this year are communication and intellectual interests (like last year); home, family and the emotional life (like last year); children, creativity and fun (like last year); friendships, group activities and organizations (until October 29); and spirituality (after October 29).

Your paths of greatest fulfilment in the year ahead will be home and family; communication and intellectual interests (after July 27).

Health

(Please note that this is an astrological perspective on health and not a medical one. In days of yore there was no difference, both of these perspectives were identical. But in these times there could be quite a difference. For the medical perspective, please consult your doctor or health professional.)

Health seems basically good this year. Yes, two long-term planets are stressing you out, but two other ones are helping you. The forces are cancelled out. This is the kind of year where the short-term transits will play an unusually large role in health. When they are kind, health and energy will tend to be good. When they are stressful, there are more challenges. However, these are not trends for the year and this should be understood. Problems are only temporary.

Your 6th House of Health is not a House of Power this

Reflexology

Try to massage the whole foot on a regular basis, but pay extra attention to the points highlighted on the chart. When you massage, be aware of 'sore spots', as these need special attention. It's also a good idea to massage the ankles and top side (as well as the soles) of the feet.

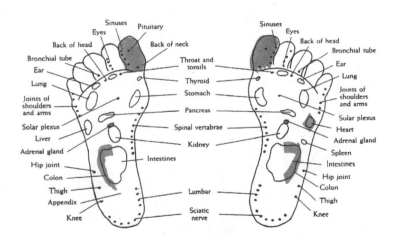

year and I read it as a good thing. You have no need to give this area too much focus as there is nothing wrong. 'If it ain't broke,' the saying goes, 'don't fix it.'

You can enhance your health by giving more attention to the head, face, adrenal gland, colon, bladder and sexual organs – all the organs ruled by Mars, your health planet.

Sexual activity should be kept in moderation (you should be sated without overdoing things), and safe sex is unusually important. As always, regular scalp and facial massage is good. The scalp (and even the face) has reflexes connected to the entire body, so when you massage it you are strengthening the whole body, not just the scalp.

Vigorous physical exercise is always good for you and this is true in the year ahead as well. For you, health is as much about physical fitness as it is about 'no symptoms'.

Mars, your health planet, is a relatively fast-moving planet – he stays in a House and Sign for about 45 days – and these short-term trends are better off discussed in the monthly reports. However, this year Mars will spend a lot of time in Leo (from October 16 well into March 2010). Leo rules the heart, so during this period it might be good to give more attention to this organ. There are natural ways to do this and medical ways. Check your blood pressure regularly (if you are of appropriate age) and watch your cholesterol levels. If you are into alternative therapies you can work with the chart above.

Spiritual healers testify that the spiritual root cause of heart problems is worry. So, this period will be a good time to take a more relaxed view of life. If there is something positive you can do, of course you should do it. If there is nothing to be done, enjoy your day. What will worrying do for you? It will only make matters worse and take a toll on your health.

The health of parents or parent figures can be enhanced by giving more attention to the spine, knees, teeth, bones, overall skeletal alignment, stomach and breasts. Until October 29 they should also focus on the small intestine; after October 29, the kidneys and hips.

Your spouse or partner benefits from attention to the kidneys and hips as well.

The health of children will be enhanced by more focus on the heart, especially from October 16 onwards.

Home and Family

This, as we mentioned, has been an important area of life for many years and the trend gets even stronger in 2009. No question that home and family takes priority over career and the urges for outer success.

Scorpios have been very fertile for many years. There is a great focus on children – having them, raising them and getting on with them. Even Scorpios past childbearing age are still thinking about children – perhaps relating more with their own, perhaps adopting them, or perhaps relating more with other people's children.

This is a year where more babies are coming into the picture. Other family members are having babies as well (perhaps adopting them too). The whole family circle is greatly expanded in the year ahead, through births or marriage or meeting people who are like family to you.

With Jupiter moving through your 4th House, many of you are moving to larger and better quarters. The move seems happy. In some cases you are buying an additional home or additional properties. Sometimes the home is renovated to such a degree that it is like a new home. But it seems to me that you have outgrown your present quarters and the cosmos is going to help you find better ones.

There is also wonderful family support this year. Parents or parent figures are prospering and very generous with you. You are spending on the home and family – investing in these things. Real estate seems profitable, and perhaps you are speculating in this area.

Looks to me like many of you will be earning money from the home; from a home office or home-based business, or perhaps you are taking work home.

Career success has its joys, no question about it. But there is something to be said about family bliss – the simple pleasures of the home, hearth and children. And this is something you are experiencing in the year ahead.

Often with these aspects people seek and find their 'spiritual families'. The biological and the spiritual family are two different things. The biological family tends to be from 'karmic relationships' of the past – there is a need to rebalance the karma and so family members are brought together for this purpose. But the spiritual family is the ideal family; sometimes these spiritual family members are incarnate – in embodiment – but not always. Sometimes a few of them are incarnate and a few discarnate. It is a case-by-case situation. But the spiritual family is the true family. They always behave as family should and are always concerned with your best interest. They love and support you unconditionally. So finding them – either on a spiritual or material level – is great good fortune and will happen for many of you in the coming year.

Finance and Career

As we mentioned, finance has been an ultra-important interest since 1995. Your major focus was on that and by now you have succeeded, have more or less attained your financial goals and can move on to other things. Basically, this is a status-quo kind of year.

Jupiter, your financial planet, makes a major move early in the year from Capricorn into Aquarius – from your 3rd House into your 4th. This denotes some important changes both in financial thinking and strategy.

Last year, you were basically conservative in finances. You wanted value for money, you avoided risk taking, and you had a long-term perspective on wealth. You were into systematic savings and investment programmes. You learned much about money management. But now, your financial planet in Aquarius, while not quite risk taking, is far from conservative. It's as if you are being opposite to what you were last year.

Capricorn loves the tried and true; Aquarius loves the new and the experimental. So, this has many messages for us. You are ready to experiment in financial matters; ready to throw out the rule books and to see what works for you. You are ready to learn about wealth through trial, error and experiment. Last year, if a company or a methodology was new and untried, you shunned it like the plague. This year, the new and untried is actually a financial turn on.

Professional investors (or merely those of you who have investment accounts) will now start to gravitate away from the traditional, blue-chip companies to the new, sexy start ups. When they succeed, they succeed big and the profits are enormous. High technology start ups or companies that are involved with new gadgets and new inventions are also very interesting to you.

Whether or not you are an investor, technology is important in your financial life. For many it means being up-to-date with the latest technology. For others, technology is an actual business. Online activities – websites, e-mail, online businesses – all seem interesting in the year ahead. (People involved in these things could also play an important role in your finances.)

The financial planet in the 4th House of Home and Family for almost all of 2009 has a more obvious meaning too. You are spending on the family and the home. You are investing in expensive items for the home. There is the fortunate purchase or sale of a home. Real estate (especially residential real estate) is also an interesting business or investment. But the symbolism of the chart also indicates the food business, restaurants, lodgings and industries that cater to the home. These are all interesting as businesses, jobs or investments. Those of you who have your own business might want to target these industries.

Family support will be good in the year ahead. Parents or parent figures are prospering and are generous with you. They are supportive of financial goals. There are profit opportunities in the family business, either your own or someone else's family business.

Your financial planet will be travelling with Neptune for most of the year (in different degrees of closeness – the closer the conjunction, the stronger the effect). This gives us many messages. Your financial intuition will be very good this year. Where last year you were very conservative, this year you are ready to speculate – and you seem successful at this (only do this under intuition). You are learning the secrets of spiritual wealth. You are generous and philanthropic – more so than usual. Your financial life will be guided by dreams, astrologers, psychics and spiritual channels.

All of this is good, but there is a downside. There is a need to do more homework in financial dealings; when Neptune is involved in finances, there is a need to get full disclosure from others. Often there are secret, under the table deals that are hidden from you, so do your homework.

Your 10th House of Career is not strong this year and most of the long-term planets are below the horizon of the Horoscope. Thus this is a year for attaining inner, emotional harmony – for feeling good, for taking care of things at home and with the family – rather than for outer success. Your 4th House of Home and Family is much stronger than your 10th House of Career and also seems much more fulfilling. However, there will be two Solar Eclipses in the year ahead, which bring career changes and upheavals. Also, Mars will move into your 10th House from October 16 (and stay there until well into 2010). This shows a need to be more aggressive in the career, to work hard, to defend your position and turf, to fend off competition. There is much activity going on.

Love and Social Life

Your 7th House of Love, Marriage and Social Activities is not a House of Power in 2009. This suggests a status-quo kind of year. Marrieds will tend to stay married and singles will tend to stay single. You seem basically content with the status quo and have no need to make major changes.

For marrieds the year ahead is, as we mentioned, all about setting up the home, creating and sustaining the family, and children – either making them or raising them.

For singles, the year ahead is about love affairs – non-committed kinds of relationships. This is (and has been) a very exciting area for many years. One can understand why you wouldn't want to tie yourself down. Love strikes you anywhere, in the oddest of times and places. Love is always new and unique – never stale, never old hat. The cosmos is making sure that this area is lively.

Many people are experimental in love. But in your case, you are experimental in your love affairs, not in your marriage attitudes. It's as if you are learning about your tastes in love through trial and error and experiment but without having to commit to your experiments. If the experiment fails (and many have) or blows up (and many have) you will try again elsewhere without having to worry about courts, children and alimony. You also seem to gravitate to people who are not really marriage material.

The sense I get from studying your chart is that these experiments are leading you inexorably towards knowledge of what you really want in love. Once this knowledge is attained, singles will be ready for marriage.

Those of you working on or in your first marriage will have a status-quo kind of a year – as we mentioned. But those in their second marriages are having severe tests in the relationship. Four Lunar Eclipses are seeing to that. This doesn't mean that the marriage has to break up, only that the flaws will be revealed – reality will be seen. If the love still exists after that, the marriage will probably survive anything. But hold on to your hat during the rollercoaster ride. This is also true (but to a lesser extent) for those in their third marriages. The honeymoon is over, and now it's about duty and obligation. You never know if you're really in love during the good times. It's the tough times that show you. And this is what is happening.

Those working on the fourth marriage are having a status-quo year. There are, however, many opportunities for love affairs.

Singles will find opportunities for love affairs (but not marriage) close to home, at family gatherings, or perhaps through the introduction of family members or family connections.

Singles should keep in mind that they are unusually fertile these days and that love affairs have consequences.

Friendships have been tested for the past two years and the trend continues for most of the year ahead. Some friendships have dissolved. You are reorganizing this area of life in a healthier way. The cosmos is pruning your friendships the way a farmer prunes the vine. It gets rid of the weak and the unhealthy so that the real friendships you have can grow stronger.

Your most active social period will be from April 20 to May 21.

Self-improvement

We mentioned that friendships were getting tested this year. In many cases, they are being road tested – given some rough treatment – so that the flaws can be revealed and corrected. But there is also a deeper agenda here. You will see just how much 'stress' a friendship can take and still be a friendship. In other words, you are finding out who your real friends are. This can be painful, but rather than focus on the pain, understand that you are gaining revelation – and revelation is beautiful.

You are learning (and many of you have already learned this in the past two years) that in friendship, as in most other areas of life, quality is more important than quantity. Better to have fewer friends but good ones than to have hordes of lukewarm or fair-weather friends.

When friendships end, it is always a two-way street. Seldom are we always blameless. So, these events are times for introspection, times to see where we have failed as friends, times to improve our own ability to be a friend.

From a spiritual perspective it is a time to learn forgiveness and to move on. We should not allow secret grudges (and Scorpio is known for this) to fester and poison the mind. Understand the behaviour, forgive the other person, and forgive yourself. When you forgive the other person, you don't whitewash the behaviour – the behaviour is wrong – but because you understand the stresses and pressures that they are under, you can forgive them as people.

By the end of the year, the friends that have survived all the tests will tend to be friends for life and this is comforting.

As we mentioned, Pluto made a major move into your 3rd House of Communication in 2008, so you are now in a study phase of life – a time to develop the mind and the intellectual interests, to take courses in subjects that interest you and to teach on subjects where you have expertise. Scorpios are not known for their communication skills – individual Scorpios have them of course, and this is revealed by their own personal Horoscope cast personally for them – but this is a time to improve these skills.

Month-by-month Forecasts

January

Best Days Overall: 1, 2, 10, 11, 18, 19, 28, 29
Most Stressful Days Overall: 6, 12, 26, 27
Best Days for Love: 6, 7, 9, 10, 18, 19, 28, 29
Best Days for Money: 7, 16, 21, 22, 25, 26
Best Days for Career: 6, 9, 10, 18, 19, 28, 29

This is a very important month, Scorpio, with many meaningful developments. First off, your financial planet makes a major move from Capricorn into Aquarius, on the 5th. This shows important financial shifts both in thinking and strategy. Second, the planetary power will shift to the Western social sector of your chart (from the East, where it's been for the past few months). This shift will be complete by the 19th. Thus, your personal independence is not as strong as it has been. It is now more difficult for you to change conditions or create new conditions. The favour and grace of other people becomes more important in the attainment of your goals. Personal initiative, which has been strong in recent months, doesn't count as much anymore. Likeability, charm and social skills are starting to play more of a role now. Avoid power struggles and adapt to conditions as best you can. The time will come when you will be able to change them to your liking but not right now. Let others have their way so long as it isn't destructive. Your way might not be the best way these days – consider the perspectives of other people.

You begin the year at the midnight time of your personal year. Your 4th House of Home and Family is chock full of planets. Your 10th House of Career, by contrast is empty (only the Moon will visit there on the 12th and 13th). Eighty per cent (and at times up to 90 per cent) of the planets are below the horizon of your Horoscope. Your mind is a million miles away from the outer world. Nothing wrong with this – it is like being asleep. Without a good night's sleep people will not function right during the day. But sleep is not inactivity; it has its own activities – secret and beautiful. The forces that you need for the coming day (and it will arrive in four months or so) are being gathered now. So co-operate with this beautiful process. Work to maintain emotional harmony and to set family relationships in order. The home base needs to be worked on.

With Jupiter moving into your 4th House of Home and Family and with a Solar Eclipse happening there on the 26th we get a sense that a move or major renovation is going on this month. Though it is disruptive – these things always are – the end result will be good. You are spending on the home and family now. You are buying or planning the purchase of expensive items for the home. A move can happen at any time in the coming year but this month is a likely period. Whether you physically move or just renovate or make improvements, it will be 'as if' you moved. You will have different conditions at home – and better ones.

This eclipse is stressful on you so take a reduced schedule, a few days before and after. Health, in general, needs more watching after the 19th. Your overall health is good, but this is a temporary situation.

Family is financially supportive to you and you to them.

February

Best Days Overall: 6, 7, 15, 16, 24, 25, 26
Most Stressful Days Overall: 2, 3, 8, 9, 22, 23
Best Days for Love: 2, 3, 8, 9, 17, 18, 27, 28
Best Days for Money: 4, 5, 12, 13, 17, 18, 22, 23
Best Days for Career: 4, 5, 8, 9, 12, 13, 24, 25

The Solar Eclipse of January 26 impacted on your career and initiated major changes there. This month's Lunar Eclipse of the 9th also affects your career. So whatever changes were not made last month are getting made now. This eclipse, like the last one, is stressful on you, so take a reduced schedule for a few days before and after. These eclipses are bringing shakeups in your company or industry and dramas in the lives of parents or parent figures. Children seem affected by this eclipse as well, so be patient with them. There are major changes and dramas in their lives – and much of it can be good – but it disrupts the normal routine.

These career changes and upheavals are providing opportunity for you to adjust things at work to make them more emotionally comfortable, more family friendly. For family is still the major focus of the coming month.

Last month (and in all of 2008) there was a powerful interest in education, communication and intellectual pursuits. This area is still strong in the year ahead, but is weakening this month – everything in life is relative. The driving forces are less.

On the 18th, as the Sun enters your 5th House, you begin a yearly personal pleasure peak. Life is not all about work, work, work. Nor is it all about family, important though these things are. It is also about joy. Life itself – if there were no human thinking to mess it up – would be naturally joyful. This is its nature. Where there is sadness and depression, there is always some disconnect from life and from the flow of life force. So, this is a period where you reconnect to the joys of living. There is a great focus on children and a better ability to get on with them. Your inner child awakens this period and this child knows very well – better than you do – how to relate to children. Those of you in the creative fields should have a banner month.

Even the career should be more joyous this month. You will probably be enabled to have more fun in the job, but if not you have to find creative ways to enjoy your career. Children of appropriate age are more ambitious. Children in general are motivating you for success. But still the time is not yet ripe to leap into career activities – keep the status quo and focus on the family.

Finances will be very good this month. Jobseekers have good success after the 4th. You are still spending on the family – or getting good family support. Jobseekers find opportunities through the family or family connections.

Health still needs watching. Rest and relax more until the 18th. Enhance your health by giving more attention to the back, spine, knees, teeth and skeletal alignment until the 4th and to the ankles after the 4th. Emotional health (and the health of family members) is more important this month.

March

Best Days Overall: 5, 6, 14, 15, 24, 25
Most Stressful Days Overall: 1, 2, 7, 8, 21, 22, 23, 28, 29
Best Days for Love: 1, 2, 7, 8, 16, 17, 18, 26, 27, 28, 29
Best Days for Money: 3, 4, 12, 13, 16, 17, 18, 21, 22, 23, 30, 31
Best Days for Career: 5, 6, 7, 8, 14, 15, 24, 25

Love has not been a big issue this year. It seems more or less maintaining its status quo. But this month there are developments going on. Venus, your love planet, makes one of her rare Retrogrades, beginning on the 6th. This can complicate existing relationships. They seem like they are going backwards instead of forwards. Social confidence is not what it should be. With your love planet in hot and fiery Aries your tendency would be to leap into relationships with little thought. Love tends to happen at first sight. You are in the mood for risk taking in love. But Venus's Retrograde motion suggests a more cautious approach – to let love develop slowly, as it will, in natural and unforced ways. You are in a period where you should be reviewing your love life, your current relationship and friendships in general. See where you are satisfied and where not and then look at ways that things can be improved.

Venus's Retrograde is not going to stop the social life. It will only slow it down a bit – and perhaps it needs some slowing down. With Venus in your 6th House all month love opportunities happen at work or with those you work with. It can also happen as you pursue your health goals or with people involved in your health. The love planet in the 6th House shows a concern for a 'healthy' love life and relationship. So perhaps this Retrograde is good – it allows you space to analyse your relationships more.

Love is shown by doing for the beloved; in practical service to the needs of the beloved. This is how you show love and this is how you feel loved. Romantic niceties are not so important now – practical things matter.

Health is improved this month. With your 6th House of Health powerful you are paying attention here and this is good. You can enhance your already good health by giving more attention to the heart (after the 20th), the ankles (until the 15th), the feet (after the 15th), and the arms, shoulders, lungs and small intestine (after the 25th).

Jobseekers have good success this month. The important issue is that you find work that you like. The social dimension of the workplace seems just as important as the pay and benefits. Jobseekers will find job opportunities through family and family connections (until the 15th) and as they pursue their leisure activities afterwards – yes, someone can offer you a job at a party, theatre or club.

April

Best Days Overall: 2, 3, 10, 11, 20, 21, 29, 30
Most Stressful Days Overall: 4, 5, 18, 19, 25, 26
Best Days for Love: 4, 20, 21, 25, 26
Best Days for Money: 8, 9, 13, 14, 18, 19, 27, 28
Best Days for Career: 4, 5, 13, 14, 25, 26

Your ruling planet, Pluto, starts to Retrograde on the 4th. This often produces personal insecurities and a feeling of 'lacking direction'. Personal self-confidence is not what it should be. On the other hand there is a strong positive to this. With between 70 and 80 per cent of the planets in the social Western sector, and with your 7th House of Love becoming powerful after the 19th, perhaps it is good that you are a bit directionless. Direction is coming from others. Personal confidence is not important now. Your social and people skills are what matter. If a little lack of confidence helps you tone down personal will, then it is a good thing. 'My strength is made perfect in your weakness.'

It is good now – and for the next five months – to review your personal goals, body and image, and see where improvements can be made. No need to act on these things – just take stock. Later on, as Pluto starts to move forward, you'll be able to make the changes.

This is still an excellent month for jobseekers. You are, in general, in a more serious, work-oriented mood and this motivates you. You partied out last month and now its time to get serious. Those who employ others should also have good success.

The main financial headline this month is Jupiter's conjunction with Neptune. This brings very beautiful financial intuition – there is luck in speculations. The invisible, spiritual world takes a hand in your financial affairs and thinking. Financial guidance can come to you in strange and mysterious ways – in dreams and visions, through psychics, astrologers, spiritual channels and the like. Those of you involved in the creative arts will make the fortunate sale of one of your works. Children are also prospering this month. (Perhaps you are also spending more on them too.) There is going to be deep revelation about the spiritual sources of wealth and how the spiritual dynamics of it work.

On the 19th you enter a yearly social peak. And the timing is good too. Two days before, Venus, your love planet starts to move forward. You are in a position to both enjoy and capitalize on this social peak. Social confidence is back and you have more clarity about what you want in love. You are mixing with very high status kinds of people this month (after the 19th) and this can lead to interesting career opportunities later on down the road. Though you should still keep your focus on the family and your inner life, you can enhance your career through social means – attending or hosting the right parties and the like. Bosses, parents and parent figures enjoy playing cupid this month, and in certain cases the boss expresses romantic interest.

Try to rest and relax more after the 19th.

May

Best Days Overall: 8, 9, 18, 19, 26, 27
Most Stressful Days Overall: 1, 2, 15, 16, 22, 23, 28, 29
Best Days for Love: 1, 2, 10, 11, 20, 21, 22, 23, 28, 29
Best Days for Money: 5, 6, 10, 11, 15, 16, 24, 25
Best Days for Career: 1, 2, 3, 4, 12, 13, 14, 24, 25, 28, 29

The overwhelming majority of planets are still in forward motion this month. Pluto, your ruling planet is however still Retrograde, and thus you are in a period for reviewing personal goals and issues involving the body, image and personal appearance. (It's not a time to make radical changes to your look – study these things more.) Mercury's Retrograde movement from the 7th to the 31st impacts on your spouse's, partner's or current love's earnings. He or she needs to be more careful about big financial decisions or changes. Earnings will come to him or her, but there are delays and unforeseen bumps on the road. Be more careful in the way you communicate to friends; take more time to ensure that they have understood what you said and vice versa. Avoid major borrowing during this Mercury Retrograde period as well. If you must sign for that mortgage or bank loan, read the fine print very carefully – and perhaps it might be wise to hire legal advice. If you are involved in insurance claims, you need more patience now.

But aside from these minor inconveniences, life is moving forward. The pace of events in your world is fast. And you are making rapid progress towards your goals.

Your yearly social peak is very much in effect. Love is still at the workplace or with co-workers or superiors. Health professionals or those involved with your health are also alluring. There is a saying that 'service is love in action', and this certainly applies to you. You want to show love in practical ways, through service. And, like last month, this is how you feel loved. Flowers and romantic sentiments are nice and you appreciate them, but they are ephemeral. Service endures.

Last month there was a slight shift of the planets from the lower half to the upper half of the Horoscope. And this is the case this month. The major planetary power is still in the lower half, but the cosmos is giving you an announcement that change is happening and that it's getting time to give more attention to the career and outer affairs of your life. By now, you should have found your point of emotional harmony (hopefully), and soon you will be able to pursue your outer goals from that place. You can move your career forward through social means until the 20th. After that your ability to manage other people's money, access credit or attract investors is a positive factor career-wise. These skills seem important now. And your natural ability to see value in dead and decaying properties, companies (or even people) boosts your career.

On the 20th, as the Sun enters your 8th House, you are in Scorpio heaven. All your natural interests are intensified.

Your interest in occult studies, life and death, transformation and personal reinvention are all highlighted.

Health is also much improved after the 20th.

June

>   Best Days Overall: 4, 5, 14, 15, 23
>   Most Stressful Days Overall: 11, 12, 13, 19, 25
>   Best Days for Love: 9, 19, 27, 28
>   Best Days for Money: 2, 3, 6, 7, 8, 11, 12, 13, 21, 22, 29, 30
>   Best Days for Career: 2, 3, 11, 12, 13, 21, 25, 29, 30

This month the planetary power shifts in a decisive way to the upper half of the Horoscope. It is daytime in your year – not yet noon but bright daylight all the same. Thus you can shift some of your energy from the home and family and start to push your career forward. Since the lower half of the Horoscope is still very strong (at least 40 per cent of the planets will be there) you are not going to ignore the home and family, but your challenge will be to balance a happy home life with a successful career. Not an easy job, but you will make progress here.

The love life is still active and happy. Most of the planets remain in the Western, social sector of the chart and your 7th House of Love is probably the strongest in the Horoscope. Other people are still very important to you. You are in a mood for romance. Your intense social interests – your drive – will enable you to overcome whatever barriers exist. You still need to cultivate your social skills and down-play personal will. Put other people first and watch your popularity soar.

We can see your success in love in other ways too. With your 8th House powerful, there is more sexual activity than usual going on.

Many of the love trends that we wrote of last month are still in effect now.

You still have a very strong financial intuition, and are still getting help from the invisible world. But now Neptune and Jupiter are going Retrograde (Neptune started to Retrograde last month and Jupiter will start on the 15th). Thus intuition and dreams – especially those related to finance – need more verification. Perhaps you are getting the right vision or right message, but not interpreting it right. Have your intuition verified with a good psychic, intuitive or astrologer.

Try to make important financial decisions – investments or large purchases – before the 15th. Afterwards you are in a period of financial review, which is basically a healthy thing. Review your products, services and investments and see where improvements can be made. Later on in the year, when Jupiter goes forward, it will be easy to implement any changes.

This month it is good to focus on the prosperity of others. This will not only ensure your personal financial prosperity (although perhaps not right away) but will be very powerful career-wise. A corporate manager is basically a manager of other people's money and assets. His or her job is to prosper the shareholders – to make other people rich. Many lose sight of this basic truth. But if you keep your eye on this, people in power will notice.

July

Best Days Overall: 1, 2, 11, 12, 20, 21, 28, 29, 30
Most Stressful Days Overall: 9, 10, 16, 17, 22, 23
Best Days for Love: 9, 16, 17, 18, 19, 26, 27
Best Days for Money: 3, 4, 5, 9, 10, 18, 19, 26, 27, 31
Best Days for Career: 1, 2, 11, 12, 22, 23, 31

Retrograde activity increases this month. The pace of events in your world – and in the world at large – is slowing down. Home and family decisions need more study and analysis as Uranus, your family planet, starts to go Retrograde this month. And since there are no quick fixes in the home and family situation – only time will resolve certain things – you may as well focus more on your career.

Finance too (like last month) needs more study and review. Earnings are still good this month (but better before the 22nd than afterwards), but delays and annoyances shouldn't upset you. It goes with the territory. This is a period where you need to study your credit card and bank statements more closely. Are there any strange and funny charges there? Has someone been trying to use your credit card in a fraudulent way? Did you get double billed at the supermarket? Did you get hit with a mysterious service charge for transferring money from one account to another? And what does the fine print on that seductive credit card offer really say? Hope you see what I'm driving at here.

Love attitudes are shifting again this month. There are still opportunities at work, or at the gym or yoga studio, but now it is the physical chemistry – the sexual performance – that seems to matter most. Love is physical now. In general you are intense and passionate about things (and this is why you tend to get what you want) but you are even more so this month. You like a good mind and good communication with the beloved, but it is the sexual magnetism that is paramount now. Good sexual chemistry will cover many sins in a marriage these days.

Your 8th House is still powerful this month, so though your personal finances and earnings are slowing down a bit (don't worry; the year ahead is still a prosperous one), your spouse is picking up the slack and is generous with you. Your spouse, partner or current love seems more focused on finance than you are.

Two eclipses this month are shaking up your world a bit. The first is a Lunar Eclipse on the 7th that occurs in your 3rd House. This will test your communications and computer equipment, and probably your car. It brings dramatic events in the lives of siblings and neighbours. There are dramatic changes in your neighbourhood – perhaps a new building development. Students will change their educational plans. The Solar Eclipse of the 22nd is the more powerful one, especially if you were born early in the sign of Scorpio (from October 23 to 26). This eclipse occurs very near the

Midheaven and thus brings career changes, shakeups and dramatic events in your company or industry. And since this eclipse coincides with a yearly career peak, this shakeup is opening doors for you. Just wait for the dust to settle and you'll see what is to be done.

August

Best Days Overall: 7, 8, 9, 16, 17, 25, 26
Most Stressful Days Overall: 5, 6, 12, 13, 19
Best Days for Love: 7, 8, 9, 12, 13, 16, 17, 25, 26
Best Days for Money: 1, 5, 6, 14, 15, 23, 24, 27, 28
Best Days for Career: 1, 10, 11, 19, 20, 30, 31

A Lunar Eclipse on the 6th occurs in your 4th House of Home and Family and is strong on you. Be sure to take a reduced schedule a few days before and after. You should be taking it easy since the 23rd of last month anyway. Many of you have already moved this year, but if not, this is another likely time. With your family planet Retrograde it will be more complicated, but sometimes there is no choice in these matters. Those of you who have already moved might discover flaws in the present home that need correcting. Students are again making important changes in their educational plans. There are dramas with parents or parent figures. Emotions at home will be turbulent. And here is where the challenge is now – you are in a yearly career peak and need to be focused there, but events at home are a huge distraction. It will be tough but you can handle it – you'll sort of have to shuttle back and forth between career and family focus.

Your career is going well and so is your spouse's or partner's. He or she seems very successful this month – perhaps more than you.

Love has many twists and turns this month. Last month it was about sex and physical chemistry. This month it's more about philosophical and religious compatibility. You have learned that even the hottest sexual chemistry won't work if there are strong philosophical differences and world views. You have the kind of chart of a person who falls in love with the professor, mentor or minister. Education and refinement are important. Foreigners are alluring as well. Love opportunities can happen in foreign lands or in religious settings.

Then, the love attitudes shift again.

For singles, Venus's crossing the Midheaven on the 26th shows attraction for people of power and prestige – the high and the mighty. This often brings romantic opportunity with bosses and superiors, or with people involved with your career. Love is pragmatic. Romance is not the issue – it's the person who can help you career-wise, provide for you, offer you status in society that allures you. Of course, it helps if he or she can show you a good time too.

Health improves after the 22nd.

September

    Best Days Overall: 4, 5, 13, 14, 21, 22
    Most Stressful Days Overall: 1, 2, 8, 9, 15, 16, 28, 29, 30
    Best Days for Love: 6, 7, 8, 9, 15, 16, 26, 27
    Best Days for Money: 1, 2, 11, 12, 19, 20, 23, 24, 25, 28, 29, 30
    Best Days for Career: 8, 9, 15, 16, 17, 18, 28, 29

Last month the planetary power shifted from the Western social sector to the Eastern sector of the self. An important shift. You are becoming more independent. You have more freedom of personal action. You can take the bull by the horns and exercise personal initiative. You don't need to adapt to situations that much but have the power to change them if you like. Your happiness and success lie more and more in your own hands. Further, now that your ruling planet Pluto is starting to move forward, from the 11th – the timing of this is just beautiful – you are clear-minded as to what you want and can use your creative power wisely.

The major interest in the month ahead is friends, groups, group activities and organizations. These things are pleasurable in their own right, but will also further your career. Later on in the month these activities become the scene of romance or romantic opportunity. As we saw last month, there is more socializing with people of power and prestige.

Spirituality will become important after the 22nd. And since your career planet will be moving through your spiritual 12th House, it shows that your career can be enhanced by 12th House activities – charities, meditation, prayer, being involved in altruistic causes and the like. Also it shows that your spiritual mission for the period is spirituality itself – a need to get more connected with the Higher Power in you. (Until the 22nd, your spiritual mission involves your friends: being there for them.)

Many of the love trends that we wrote of last month are still very much in effect. But after the 20th your love needs shift again. You want more equality in a relationship, more of a friendship of peers than something practical or pragmatic. You don't want someone lording it over you, but a more peer-oriented relationship. Similarity of interests is important in love – it's not just about sex or power, but being able to do things as friends that you both like to do.

With your love planet in Virgo after the 20th, you need to be careful of being too much of a perfectionist and too exacting in love. This transit gives the desire for perfection in love, and there's nothing wrong with that. But if you start getting critical in a destructive kind of way – and especially over little things – you will kill whatever romantic opportunity you have. Keep the criticism constructive or keep quiet.

Health is good this month and you can enhance it further by giving more attention to the stomach and breasts. Diet will be more of an issue this month.

October

Best Days Overall: 1, 2, 10, 11, 19, 20, 28, 29
Most Stressful Days Overall: 6, 7, 12, 13, 26, 27
Best Days for Love: 6, 7, 15, 16, 26, 27
Best Days for Money: 8, 9, 16, 17, 21, 22, 26, 27
Best Days for Career: 8, 9, 12, 13, 16, 17, 18, 28, 29

Mars's crossing from the Western sector to the East is increasing your personal independence even further than last month. Pluto moving forwards and the Sun entering your Sign on the 23rd are messages to take the initiative and make those changes that need to be made. Don't settle and don't compromise now. Have things your way. This doesn't mean being nasty or dictatorial to others, only that you are responsible for your own happiness. It's up to you. You have the power, the energy, the clarity and the knowledge – and a lot of cosmic support from the planets.

Mars crosses your Midheaven on the 16th and this shows many things. Your career is still important and demanding. You need to work harder and be more aggressive for success. You succeed this month in the old-fashioned way – you just work harder than anyone else. This hard work and drive is being noticed by superiors and other authority figures and will bring very happy career opportunities to you. They will come knocking on your door.

A parent or parent figure is more athletic and into exercise this period. He or she needs to watch the temper and drive more defensively.

Your 12th House of Spirituality is even more powerful than last month. It is the strongest House in the entire Horoscope this month – 50 per cent of the planets will either be there or move through there. So this is a month for supernatural-type experiences. Strange coincidences happen that you can't explain logically. You have an active dream life, enhanced ESP powers, healing ability, and a prophetic gift. For those on the spiritual path it is a month for spiritual breakthroughs – liberation into new dimensions of functioning – encounters with gurus, masters, angels and archangels. The cosmos wants you to develop your spiritual powers this month and to get more connected with the Divine in you.

This is a great period – like last month – for taking that spiritual retreat or meditation seminar, or for spending time in the presence of spiritual people.

All these activities are not only good in their own right but will enhance the career, as there is important career guidance being given in this way.

Even love – especially after the 15th – happens in spiritual environments. Singles looking for love at bars, clubs or parties are wasting their time. The yoga studio or spiritual retreat would be a better milieu.

November

Best Days Overall: 6, 7, 15, 16, 25, 26
Most Stressful Days Overall: 2, 3, 8, 9, 22, 23, 29, 30
Best Days for Love: 2, 3, 4, 5, 15, 16, 25, 26, 29, 30
Best Days for Money: 4, 5, 13, 14, 17, 18, 22, 23
Best Days for Career: 6, 7, 8, 9, 15, 16, 27, 28

Your hard work and your good work ethic attract the attention of the powers that be and very happy career opportunities are coming to you. You seem ambitious on the outside this period, but inside not really. The planets have shifted to the lower half of your Horoscope – it is nightfall in your year – and you have a yearning, a hankering, to 'just feel good' – to just feel in harmony. Name and fame and outer success all pale in comparison to feeling good inside. This is a fortunate position to be in. For you are not likely to just jump at the first happy opportunity. You will be more discerning in your choices. Even the most lucrative career opportunity will not seem attractive if it violates your emotional comfort level or interferes with your family life.

This is a happy month Scorpio. Enjoy. With many planets in your own Sign this month, you are energetic, self-confident and even more charismatic than usual. You are right in the midst of a personal pleasure peak as well. You are independent and having things your own way in life – which you should at this time. Personal power, personal initiative, personal confidence is at a maximum this month. Use all this wisely and you will create paradise for yourself. Abuse it and you will create hell. The conundrum of the entire human condition is your personal conundrum. You can't escape your creative power – it is your birthright – and the only issue is what you create: angels that will bless you or demons that will hound you.

Your personal independence and the changes that you are making in your conditions of life are creating some short-term financial stress. Perhaps you are overspending; perhaps you are not giving finance the attention it deserves – your mind is on personal fulfilment and not money. But this stress is short term. After the 22nd earnings rebound dramatically. You enter into a yearly financial peak (and there are beautiful aspects to your financial planet, Jupiter).

Love is still in spiritual-type settings this month. Love opportunities can happen as you attend charitable functions or get involved in altruistic causes. Those on a spiritual path will have a greater understanding that the Divine is the source of all love and look to that to supply every need in love. After the 8th, as Venus moves into your own Sign, love needs and attitudes shift again. For a start, love will be pursuing you. You don't have to do anything. You have your own way in love as you do in most things. Love is also more physical and sensual these days. Last month, love was spiritual and idealistic, now it is physical. Personal appearance is a huge factor. There needs to be a compatibility of the physical image these days.

December

Best Days Overall: 4, 12, 13, 22, 23, 31
Most Stressful Days Overall: 6, 7, 19, 20, 21, 27, 28
Best Days for Love: 6, 7, 15, 16, 26, 27, 28
Best Days for Money: 2, 10, 11, 15, 16, 19, 20, 21
Best Days for Career: 6, 7, 15, 16, 27, 28

You are well into a yearly financial peak. Your money house is very strong. Elders, bosses, parents, or parent figures are either supporting you directly or providing earning opportunities. Even your spouse, partner or current love is financially supportive. This is a month where pay rises are likely. Sometimes it is your good professional reputation – your good public image – that creates increased earnings, through referrals and the like. But there is much more happening financially. Jupiter once again conjuncts Neptune, which enhances your financial intuition – it's as if the invisible, spiritual world is directly involved in your earnings and showering you with its gifts. There is luck in speculations this month. Children, or those who are like children to you, have very interesting and profitable ideas and suggestions, and by studying them – their likes and dislikes – you can discern profitable trends. Family support in general is very good now.

Children of all ages are prospering this month, big time.

You too are earning big time now – and probably spending big time as well. Perhaps impulsively. But no matter, you can't outspend the spirit. You are spending a lot on the children and family (this has been the case all year, but this month even more so) and probably on entertainment equipment – home theatres, music systems, musical instruments – all expensive items. Truly, the home is becoming an entertainment centre.

The love life and love needs shift yet again this month. Last month it was physical appearance that counted. Now it is wealth. The good provider, the dispenser of material gifts, is the most alluring for singles. Status and position is not much of a factor in love these days, but personal generosity and financial support are. You show love in material ways, through gifts and financial support, and this is how you feel loved. Problems in a marriage can be eased through material gift-giving this month – and by the cultivation of financial harmony. There are business partnerships or joint venture opportunities happening this month as well.

Singles can find love opportunities as they pursue their normal financial goals, and perhaps with people who are involved in their finances.

Health is good and you can enhance it further by giving more attention to the heart. (This was true last month as well.) Your health planet will go Retrograde on the 20th so avoid making major changes to your health regime or diet then (if possible do these things before the 20th). Also avoid making major health decisions after the 20th.

Sagittarius

♐

THE ARCHER

Birthdays from
23rd November to
20th December

Personality Profile

SAGITTARIUS AT A GLANCE

Element – Fire

Ruling Planet – Jupiter
   Career Planet – Mercury
   Love Planet – Mercury
   Money Planet – Saturn
   Planet of Health and Work – Venus
   Planet of Home and Family Life – Neptune
   Planet of Spirituality – Pluto

Colours – blue, dark blue

Colours that promote love, romance and social
   harmony – yellow, yellow-orange

Colours that promote earning power – black,
   indigo

Gems – carbuncle, turquoise

Metal – tin

Scents – carnation, jasmine, myrrh

Quality – mutable (= flexibility)

Qualities most needed for balance – attention to detail, administrative and organizational skills

Strongest virtues – generosity, honesty, broad-mindedness, tremendous vision

Deepest need – to expand mentally

Characteristics to avoid – over-optimism, exaggeration, being too generous with other people's money

Signs of greatest overall compatibility – Aries, Leo

Signs of greatest overall incompatibility – Gemini, Virgo, Pisces

Sign most helpful to career – Virgo

Sign most helpful for emotional support – Pisces

Sign most helpful financially – Capricorn

Sign best for marriage and/or partnerships – Gemini

Sign most helpful for creative projects – Aries

Best Sign to have fun with – Aries

Signs most helpful in spiritual matters – Leo, Scorpio

Best day of the week – Thursday

Understanding a Sagittarius

If you look at the symbol of the archer you will gain a good, intuitive understanding of a person born under this astrological Sign. The development of archery was humanity's first refinement of the power to hunt and wage war. The ability to shoot an arrow far beyond the ordinary range of a spear extended humanity's horizons, wealth, personal will and power.

Today, instead of using bows and arrows we project our power with fuels and mighty engines, but the essential reason for using these new powers remains the same. These powers represent our ability to extend our personal sphere of influence – and this is what Sagittarius is all about. Sagittarians are always seeking to expand their horizons, to cover more territory and increase their range and scope. This applies to all aspects of their lives: economic, social and intellectual.

Sagittarians are noted for the development of the mind – the higher intellect – which understands philosophical, metaphysical and spiritual concepts. This mind represents the higher part of the psychic nature and is motivated not by self-centred considerations but by the light and grace of a Higher Power. Thus, Sagittarians love higher education of all kinds. They might be bored with formal schooling but they love to study on their own and in their own way. A love of foreign travel and interest in places far away from home are also noteworthy characteristics of the Sagittarian type.

If you give some thought to all these Sagittarian attributes you will see that they spring from the inner Sagittarian desire to develop. To travel more is to know more, to know more is to be more, to cultivate the higher mind is to grow and to reach more. All these traits tend to broaden the intellectual – and indirectly, the economic and material – horizons of the Sagittarian.

The generosity of the Sagittarian is legendary. There are many reasons for this. One is that Sagittarians seem to have an inborn consciousness of wealth. They feel that they are rich, that they are lucky, that they can attain any financial goal – and so they feel that they can afford to be generous. Sagittarians do not carry the burdens of want and limitation – which stop most other people from giving generously. Another reason for their generosity is their religious and philosophical idealism, derived from the higher mind. This higher mind is by nature generous because it is unaffected by material circumstances. Still another reason is that the act of giving tends to enhance their emotional nature. Every act of giving seems to be enriching, and this is reward enough for the Sagittarian.

Finance

Sagittarians generally entice wealth. They either attract it or create it. They have the ideas, energy and talent to make their vision of paradise on Earth a reality. However, mere wealth is not enough. Sagittarians want luxury – earning a comfortable living seems small and insignificant to them.

In order for Sagittarians to attain their true earning potential they must develop better managerial and organizational skills. They must learn to set limits, to arrive at their goals through a series of attainable sub-goals or objectives. It is very rare that a person goes from rags to riches overnight. But a long, drawn-out process is difficult for Sagittarians. Like Leos, they want to achieve wealth and success quickly and impressively. They must be aware, however, that this over-optimism can lead to unrealistic financial ventures and disappointing losses. Of course, no Zodiac Sign can bounce back as quickly as Sagittarius, but only needless heartache will be caused by this attitude. Sagittarians need to maintain their vision – never letting it go – but they must also work towards it in practical and efficient ways.

Career and Public Image

Sagittarians are big thinkers. They want it all: money, fame, glamour, prestige, public acclaim and a place in history. They often go after all these goals. Some attain them, some do not – much depends on each individual's personal horoscope. But if Sagittarians want to attain public and professional status they must understand that these things are not conferred to enhance one's ego but as rewards for the amount of service that one does for the whole of humanity. If and when they figure out ways to serve more, Sagittarians can rise to the top.

The ego of the Sagittarian is gigantic – and perhaps rightly so. They have much to be proud of. If they want public acclaim, however, they will have to learn to tone down the ego a bit, to become more humble and self-effacing, without falling into the trap of self-denial and self-abasement. They must also learn to master the details of life, which can sometimes elude them.

At their jobs Sagittarians are hard workers who like to please their bosses and co-workers. They are dependable, trustworthy and enjoy a challenge. Sagittarians are friendly to work with and helpful to their colleagues. They usually contribute intelligent ideas or new methods that improve the work environment for everyone. Sagittarians always look for challenging positions and careers that develop their intellect, even if they have to work very hard in order to succeed. They also work well under the supervision of others, although by nature they would rather be the supervisors and increase their sphere of influence. Sagittarians excel at professions that allow them to be in contact with many different people and to travel to new and exciting locations.

Love and Relationships

Sagittarians love freedom for themselves and will readily grant it to their partners. They like their relationships to be fluid and ever-changing. Sagittarians tend to be fickle in love and to change their minds about their partners quite frequently.

Sagittarians feel threatened by a clearly defined, well-structured relationship, as they feel this limits their freedom. The Sagittarian tends to marry more than once in life.

Sagittarians in love are passionate, generous, open, benevolent and very active. They demonstrate their affections very openly. However, just like an Aries they tend to be egocentric in the way they relate to their partners. Sagittarians should develop the ability to see others' points of view, not just their own. They need to develop some objectivity and cool intellectual clarity in their relationships so that they can develop better two-way communication with their partners. Sagittarians tend to be overly idealistic about their partners and about love in general. A cool and rational attitude will help them to perceive reality more clearly and enable them to avoid disappointment.

Home and Domestic Life

Sagittarians tend to grant a lot of freedom to their family. They like big homes and many children and are one of the most fertile Signs of the Zodiac. However, when it comes to their children Sagittarians generally err on the side of allowing them too much freedom. Sometimes their children get the idea that there are no limits. However, allowing freedom in the home is basically a positive thing – so long as some measure of balance is maintained – for it enables all family members to develop as they should.

Horoscope for 2009

Major Trends

Pluto's move out of your own Sign late last year was something very major. He was in your sign since 1995. This brought all kinds of dramatic events in your life – a need to re-invent and transform the body, many detoxes of the body, near-death experiences, and perhaps some surgery. Your self-image was detoxed by the cosmos and by now it is totally different and much healthier. Now, Pluto has moved into your money house and will start a similar (and very thorough) process there. This is a long-term trend that will go on well into 2023.

Your health still needs watching in the year ahead, but there is steady improvement going on. Pluto's move out of your Sign helped a lot. And, later on in the year (October 29) Saturn will move out of his stressful aspect with you as well. Health is steadily getting better. More on this later.

Last year was not a particularly important romantic year and the trend continues in 2009.

The main headline for the year ahead is the power in your 3rd House of Communication and Intellectual Interests. This has been important for some years now, but this year even more so. Jupiter, your ruling planet, moves in there on January 5 and stays for the rest of the year. So this is a year for expanding and developing the mind, for gaining knowledge and for teaching the knowledge that you already have; a year for taking courses, seminars and attending lectures in subjects that interest you. This is a year for experiencing the joys of the mind – the joys of learning.

The home and family situation has been very volatile for some years now, and families could have actually broken up in the past few years. This volatility is continuing in the year ahead. More details later on.

Career has been important for the past two years and the trend continues in 2009. It's all about succeeding through

earned effort – through merit – these days. And this is difficult. Again, there's more on this below.

Your most important areas of interest in the year ahead
will be finance (and for many years to come); communication and intellectual interests; home, family and the
emotional life; career (until October 29); friends, group
activities and organizations (after October 29).

Your paths of greatest fulfilment this year are communication and intellectual interests (the joys of the mind, of
learning and teaching); and finance (after July 27).

Health

(Please note that this is an astrological perspective on health
and not a medical one. In days of yore there was no difference, both of these perspectives were identical. But in these
times there could be quite a difference. For the medical
perspective, please consult your doctor or health professional.)

If you got through 2007 and 2008 with your health and
sanity intact, you should consider yourself successful. Just
getting through was a wonderful achievement and you
deserve a pat on the back.

As we mentioned, health and energy are vastly improved
over last year, and by the end of the year will get even
better. Still, with two powerful long-term planets stressing
you out (Saturn and Uranus), health still needs watching.
The danger now, with your 6th House of Health not strong,
is that you will ignore things, not pay attention, and then
you will become vulnerable. You will have to force yourself
– motivate yourself – to focus here.

The most important thing is to watch your energy levels.
This is the key to good health. When energy is high we can
get away with many sins, but when it falls below normal, we
can't – the bill comes due.

Always, regardless of aspects, we are given all the energy
we need to handle our true mission and true responsibilities.
But when you have aspects like yours in the coming year,

there is not enough for frivolities or false responsibilities. You are forced now to make very tough choices; you have to be like a surgeon and cut away the false from the true. Never allow yourself to get over tired. No matter what you do, if the tank is empty the car won't run – get it refilled. Rest and relax. When you work when overtired, you are under the illusion that you are accomplishing things, but you discover later that you made mental mistakes that force you to re-do everything you did. Think less and be more aware. Talk less and listen more. Avoid power struggles or vain arguments. Organize your day better so that you do more with less effort; Work rhythmically; alternate activities. All these things will do much to maximize energy.

Give more attention to the heart, kidneys and hips. Hips should be regularly massaged. There are hosts of natural therapies that will strengthen the heart and the kidneys – reflexology (see our chart below), kinesiology, acupuncture,

Reflexology

Try to massage the whole foot on a regular basis, but pay extra attention to the points highlighted on the chart. When you massage, be aware of 'sore spots', as these need special attention. It's also a good idea to massage the ankles and top side (as well as the soles) of the feet.

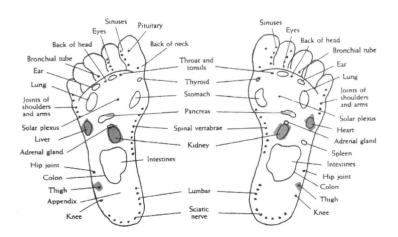

acupressure, yoga, massage and diet. And there are many others too, besides these.

But the point is, whatever mode of therapy you choose, is that you can prevent many problems from developing by focusing on these organs. For these are the vulnerable ones (you could have others, but this can only be known by casting a personal chart just for you, for your birth date, time and place).

Venus is your health planet. In the physical body she rules the kidneys and the hips – hence their importance in your overall health. Venus is a fast-moving planet and will move through all the Signs and Houses of your chart in a given year. Thus there are many therapies that will work some times and not at other times – it all depends where Venus is at any given time. We will discuss these short-term trends in the monthly reports.

Venus will make one of her rare Retrogrades this year, from March 6 to April 17. This will be a time to review your health, your diet and your health regime and see where you can make improvements. This is not a time to make important health decisions, though, such as surgery or major diet change.

With Venus as the health planet there is a spiritual message about health. There is a love and social dimension to it. When love is going well, health tends to be good. When love suffers, health tends to suffer. In fact disharmonies in love will tend to have a dramatic impact on the physical health, and this should be explored if health problems arise. Restore the harmony in love and chances are the health problem will resolve itself; even if you need to consult a health professional, his or her job will be much easier if you do that.

Home and Family

As we mentioned, this has been a wild and turbulent area for many years. There have been family breakups, many moves, many renovations and emotional instability of family members. Perhaps the most difficult thing to handle was the wild and sudden mood swings of family members (and perhaps on a personal level too). There was and is an important need to develop emotional equilibrium.

It is easy to talk about maintaining emotional equilibrium, but it is very difficult to do it. When you succeed here, you will have achieved something great.

In the year ahead moves are still likely. The home is like a work in progress that never ends. The moment you think you have found your ideal, something more ideal comes to view and you want to move there. The minute you think you have the home fixed up the way you want it, a new idea comes to you and you want to redo it again.

The cure for this is not more moves and more renovations. There is a need to cure the emotional restlessness which is at the root of these things. This cure only comes through an inner life – through prayer and meditation.

Also we see (and this too has been going on for many years) you installing all kinds of high-tech equipment and gadgets in the home – satellite TV and radio, broadband, GPS systems, video systems, internet hook-ups for your appliances – and perhaps other kinds of technology not mentioned, especially in the communications field. The home is becoming high tech.

A parent or parent figure is also very restless, and wants to explore his or her personal freedom. They perhaps feel blocked or repressed in this desire, especially over the past two years. This person seems very difficult to handle – very volatile – and you never know what will set him or her off. Give this person a lot of space.

Maintaining high safety standards in the home has been a priority for many years now and the trend continues in the year ahead. Matches, lighters and sharp objects should be kept away from children. Perhaps it is wise to install smoke detectors or burglar alarms. Be especially careful from March 15 to April 23, as fiery Mars moves through your 4th House.

This period is good for doing heavy construction work or renovation in the home, if you choose to do it. You don't have to do it, but if you choose, this is a good period.

If you want to beautify the home or buy artistic objects for its decoration, January 3 to February 3 and April 11 to April 25 are good times.

Finance and Career

Your 2nd House of Finance was very strong last year and continues to be strong in the year ahead. This is a major long-term focus in your life.

You are coming off a banner financial year; 2008 was for many of you a lifetime peak (one of them anyway). You were personally involved in your finances; you didn't delegate to others; you invested in yourself, in your wardrobe, body and appearance in general. And it paid off.

After every financial expansion it is good to consolidate. While the expansion is happening we have a tendency to ignore details, to overspend, to take on extra expenses. The busy-ness of the financial expansion forces us to look at the big picture – the earnings – and ignore the rest. So, this is a year for getting financially healthier. For prospering by cutting back, by removing things in the financial life – waste, unnecessary expenses, unnecessary possessions that have outlived their usefulness – and thus allowing for the new and the better to come in. A detox is going on in your financial life, and it is a healthy thing. If you have been responsible in your financial life, the detox will go easily. But if you have been irresponsible – borrowed unwisely or unnecessarily – the detox can be traumatic. The bills fall due and you must pay them.

However, with Pluto now in your money house, you have some very powerful energy in your favour. You have good access to outside capital; the credit markets are wide open to you (but if you abuse this, it will be harmful). You also have access to outside investors if you have good ideas.

Pluto is a very fanatical kind of planet – he rules fanatics in every field. This is because he gives a single-minded focus – a laser-like intensity – to anything he does. Pluto energy never does anything half way and thus tends to lead to success (but with many dramas and near-death kinds of experiences on the way). If Pluto energy is directed positively, it is unstoppable; great wealth will accrue to you, Sagittarius. But if this intensity is directed negatively there can be many a financial 'death' in store.

Pluto also happens to be the Ruler of your spiritual 12th House. And this is giving us many messages. Intuition is very important in finances. You will prosper by inner spiritual guidance and through the help of astrologers, psychics, spiritual channels and mystical types of people. Spirit is vitally interested in your prosperity, but (and this is what gets many people into trouble) it wants its way, not your way. You have to be willing to give it priority. Alas, this is the bane of modern man: spirit is constantly pouring out its affluence on him, but his plotting, scheming human mind gets in the way.

The deeper message here is that you are in a period for going deeper into the spiritual laws of affluence, as opposed to the material, natural laws. On the surface they are diametrically opposed. In the world, the things and objects – the money, cars, portfolios and homes – are worshiped. The spiritual perspective on wealth is to worship the 'cause' – the power and intelligence – which manifests all those physical things.

You Sagittarians already have an innate understanding of the spiritual laws of wealth, but now you are going deeper into it.

You are already very generous, but now you might want to be more systematic and proportional in your giving. Tithing would be an excellent practice now (and for the long term). Your challenge now is to open the supernatural doors of wealth, not the natural ones. Miracle money is much more interesting to you than natural money.

Professional investors (and those of you who have investment portfolios) will have a good intuition with bonds, the bond market, the blue-chip traditional kinds of stocks, the nuclear power industry, and companies that supply the intelligence services of your country.

Some of you will gravitate to depth psychology or spiritual types of counselling. Others will gravitate to managing
other people's money.

Career is very important now and, as we have mentioned,
challenging. Saturn in your 10th House is very just – very
fair – but demands performance. Thus you are succeeding
the hard way, through merit. In many cases, you will actually get promotions (and more responsibility) through this
attitude.

Money will also come through superiors, bosses, parents
and parent figure. They all seem supportive of your goals.

If you have your own business, government contracts
should be pursued.

Love and Social Life

This is not an especially strong social year, Sagittarius. None
of the Houses that rule love are important in this year's
Horoscope. Of course, you will have a social life – singles
will date and attend parties and the like – but we don't see
anything special here. A status-quo kind of year. Marrieds
will tend to stay married and singles will tend to stay single.

Social activity will vary month to month. Much depends
on whether the 5th or 7th House is strong, and what Mercury,
your love planet, happens to be doing in any given month.
Thus these issues are best discussed in the monthly reports.

Mercury will go Retrograde four times this year – this
usually this only happens three times. So, this year, your
love life will seem to go backwards for longer periods than
usual. These are not times to make drastic love or social
decisions, but to review your love life and see where
improvements can be made.

Your most active and happy social periods this year will
be from February 3 to April 19; April 23 to May 31 (love
affairs); May 20 to June 21; and July 5 to August 31 (more
serious kinds of love).

Those who are in their third marriage will have their
marriages tested from October 29. This doesn't necessarily

mean that the marriage will break up but you will be shown how strong the fundamental relationship is, how much stress it can take, and how much it can be relied on. More importantly, the stresses will bring up flaws so that you can correct them.

Those working on the third marriage are not likely to marry, nor would it seem advisable. Let love develop slowly over time – no need to rush into anything.

Self-improvement

We mentioned earlier that the spiritual, rather than the material, laws of affluence have become important now. So a deeper discussion seems in order.

Your challenge, as we mentioned, is to open the gates of the spiritual supply. This is strictly an inner process. The world, economic conditions, other people, bosses, spouses, parents have nothing to say about it. It is strictly your relationship with the Divine in you. The main thing to understand (and this can be difficult for the logical mind) is that there is ONE and ONLY ONE source of supply – ONE and ONLY ONE power that enriches – and that is the Divine within you. All the other things that seem to supply you – parents, spouse, job, the portfolio or business – are merely the means and instruments which it uses. Thus, if financial problems arise, you must turn within – to the source. If the Divine grants wealth, then everyone says yes – the banks, the boss, the client, the parents. But if the Divine is not granting wealth, no one says yes and all the doors seem closed.

There are certain laws that open the spiritual doors. One is charitable giving, and this you are already doing. Wealth is measured in the spirit by one's ability to give, rather than to get. So you receive in the measure which you give. Prayer and meditation also open the doors. Very often the inner doors are closed because of lack of attention – when you pray and meditate you are putting attention on the source. The third law is to understand the immense affluence of the

Spirit, which is totally limitless. The reason why people feel limited is because they are relying on the natural sources – other humans or their existing supply. But in the spiritual dimension we are always dealing with Infinity. The wealth of the spirit is Infinite, but human capacity is limited. The final way is to think of wealth the way the Divine thinks of it. It is not measured by how much or how little you have, but your inner state from moment to moment. Wealth is a state of 'No Lack'.

There is another reason for this discussion. Your spiritual mission this year is to get rich – but not for yourself. It is to get rich, in ethical ways (spiritual wealth is always ethical), and then to teach others how to do it.

Your other – and much more difficult – lesson this year is the development of emotional equilibrium – the conquest of your mood changes. Now, it is natural and normal for moods to change during the day. There are good astrological and spiritual reasons for it; the tatwas (elemental balances) change every two hours as the Ascendant changes Signs. The Moon is often changing Signs on a given day or receiving easy or difficult aspects. But these kinds of changes are not instant and extreme. It is the extremes that need to be worked on. Nothing is surer to wreck your life, your finances, your home, your career than negative emotional states. Repressing them out of fear will only make things worse. You must first separate yourself from them. You are something much more than a 'feeling'. You are the power that feels; you are the power that observes your feelings. Then you must observe what is happening and how. Observe what the negative emotions are doing to other people and to your own body. This will be the eye opener. When you see how self destructive they are you will be motivated to bring them under control. Prayer, meditation, a prolonged focus on the positive in your life, will change the moods, slowly but surely. Cultivate the positive moods by focusing on positive things, and they will gradually become permanent.

Month-by-month Forecasts

January

Best Days Overall: 3, 4, 12, 21, 22, 30, 31
Most Stressful Days Overall: 1, 2, 8, 14, 15, 28, 29
Best Days for Love: 7, 8, 9, 10, 16, 17, 18, 19, 23, 24, 28, 29
Best Days for Money: 6, 7, 14, 15, 16, 23, 24, 25, 26
Best Days for Career: 7, 8, 14, 15, 16, 17, 23, 24

Your financial planet, Saturn, is the handle of a bucket-type chart this month and for the months to come. This shows the importance of finance in your life. It is through your earning power – your wealth – through the power of money that you will lift up the rest of the 'bucket' – your life and circumstances. Not only that, but you are right in the midst of a yearly financial peak this month. And though your financial planet is Retrograde, earnings will be strong. You have the fire in the belly, the passion, the willingness to overcome all the glitches and delays, the minor inconveniences that arise in finance. You are successful now.

Still, with your financial planet Retrograde you need to be more cautious in your financial decision making and investments. Do your homework. Be methodical. Be more thorough in your review of credit card and bank statements. Study the fine print of contracts more carefully, or get legal help on these issues.

Guard your professional reputation and public image carefully, for this is a source of wealth to you. Investments in these things also seem good.

On the 5th your ruling planet Jupiter (a very important planet in your Horoscope) moves from the money house to the 3rd House of Communication and Intellectual Interests. Money is still important, but now you want to expand your mind. Since wealth is 90 per cent mental-spiritual (that is the essence of it), this interest can increase your bottom line – though not immediately.

On the 19th you enter a yearly 'communication peak' – a wonderful period for those of you who are involved in teaching, writing, lecturing, sales or marketing. All these activities go well. The mind is sharp and clear. Learning is easier. The only problem for marketers is that Mercury goes Retrograde from the 11th to the 31st and so this period might be better for planning sales and marketing campaigns rather than actually doing them. You can release them next month.

Siblings are enjoying wonderful success this month, especially after the 5th. You seem supportive of them and involved with them. They have love in their lives this month too.

A Solar Eclipse on the 26th occurs in your 3rd House and this brings a dramatic (and it seems to me positive) turn in the lives of siblings. Perhaps a marriage is happening, or some major and happy financial development. For you, this is a test of your communications equipment and car, and perhaps the announcement that you are getting a new car or new equipment. For students, this shows shakeups and changes in educational plans: changes of school, changes of course, changes of schedule, changes of strategy. Often it will be the school which make major changes in its rules and regulations.

February

> Best Days Overall: 1, 8, 9, 17, 18, 27, 28
> Most Stressful Days Overall: 4, 5, 10, 11, 24, 25, 26
> Best Days for Love: 2, 3, 4, 5, 8, 9, 10, 11, 17, 18, 22, 23, 27, 28
> Best Days for Money: 2, 3, 4, 5, 10, 11, 12, 13, 19, 20, 21, 22, 23
> Best Days for Career: 2, 3, 10, 11, 22, 23

SAGITTARIUS

A Lunar Eclipse on the 9th once again tests communications equipment and cars. Once again there are dramas (but these seem happy) in the lives of siblings. Students are again scrambling to make changes – or adjustments – to educational plans. This eclipse, unlike the last one of January 26, impacts on Neptune, your family planet. (Keep in mind that the Moon rules these issues on a generic level.) So there are dramas in the lives of family members, perhaps parents or parent figures. The physical home gets tested by this eclipse; if there are hidden flaws there (or underground critters lurking around), now is the time that you learn about them and can thus make necessary corrections. Keep in mind that the problems you face are not being created by the eclipse – the eclipse is only revealing to you what has been there for a long time. We should look at this in a friendly way.

Communication and intellectual interests are still the main focus this month. With Mercury moving forward all month, you can release all those mass mailings or advertising campaigns you've been planning. You have very good fortune in these activities now, and there is good fortune with the media as well. Like last month this is a banner month for those of you involved in communication – teachers, writers, journalists, sales and marketing people.

Your year began with 80 (and sometimes 90) per cent of the planets below the horizon of the Horoscope, in the lower half of the Horoscope. And this condition exists this month. Career only seems important from a financial perspective. Your heart is elsewhere, with your family and emotional life. You are in the night time of your year and it is good to pursue the activities of night. To let the magic of the night renew and regenerate you in the way that a good night's sleep does. When day dawns in your year, you will have all the energy and zest you need to push your career forward.

Your year began with most of the planets in the Eastern sector of the Horoscope. This condition also prevails this month. So you are more independent and more in control of the conditions of life. You don't need others as much as usual. You can go your own way if others don't agree with you. You are supposed to – and the cosmos supports you – create your own happiness, your own personal kingdom of heaven. You are indeed a creator right now, with god-like powers. But with this power comes responsibility. This is what is meant by the concept of karma. You will have to live with the consequences of your creation, so create wisely. This condition – this independence – is soon to change. So make those alterations soon. Later on, it will be more difficult.

March

> Best Days Overall: 7, 8, 16, 17, 18, 26, 27
> Most Stressful Days Overall: 3, 4, 10, 24, 25, 30, 31
> Best Days for Love: 3, 4, 7, 8, 14, 15, 16, 17, 18, 25, 26, 27, 30, 31
> Best Days for Money: 1, 2, 3, 4, 10, 12, 13, 19, 20, 21, 22, 23, 28, 29, 30, 31
> Best Days for Career: 3, 4, 10, 14, 15, 25, 26

Your 4th House of Home and Family is very strong this month and this is the dominant interest on many different levels. On the mundane, physical level, you could be moving or renovating the home – in a drastic way. Moves are likely all year, but this month is one of the likely periods when it could happen. You are entertaining more from home and perhaps buying objects of beauty for the house. You are also investing in entertainment for the home – adult and children's toys. You are making the home a 'fun house' as well as a home. The emotions of family members have been unstable for some years now and it has been quite a challenge to deal with this, and this month these tendencies are magnified. (Your own moods are unstable as well, and you need to cultivate emotional equilibrium.) For those on the spiritual path this will be a month for great psychological progress and insight – important psychological breakthroughs are happening. For others it is merely an emotional rollercoaster ride.

Finances are more challenging this month. Perhaps you are overspending on the home, or family obligations are distracting you from your financial focus. Speculations are favourable before the 15th, but after that date refrain from these.

Health needs more watching until the 20th. At least half the planets are stressing you at various times so this is not a month to play games with your health. Rest and relax more and keep your energy levels as high as possible. Moreover, your health planet will start to go Retrograde on the 6th, suggesting caution in major health decisions or major changes in your health regime. Sometimes when health is stressed we think that a new doctor, pill, or therapy is the solution, but the message of this Horoscope is that rest and time is the answer. The stresses you feel are more on the energetic level, and health changes just for the sake of health changes are not the answer. Health and energy will naturally improve after the 20th but still needs watching. Enhance your health through scalp and facial massage this period. Cranial sacral therapy also seems powerful. With your health planet in the 5th House all month, avoid depression (a major challenge) and try to enjoy your life. A creative hobby will also work wonders.

On the 20th you enter a yearly personal pleasure peak. There is more fun in life, and this is one of the main reasons for the improvement in your health. Personal creativity will be at yearly highs as well and this is good new for those of you in the creative arts.

This month the planetary powers shift from the independent East to the social Western sector of the Horoscope – a major shift. This reduces your personal independence, but increases your social happiness. Hopefully by now you are done with creating your personal conditions of happiness. Now it is time to road test your creation and to see how well it serves you. Now is the time to cultivate your social skills and gain your ends with the co-operation of others.

April

Best Days Overall: 4, 5, 13, 14, 22, 23
Most Stressful Days Overall: 6, 7, 20, 21, 27, 28
Best Days for Love: 4, 5, 15, 16, 20, 21, 25, 26, 27, 28
Best Days for Money: 6, 7, 8, 9, 15, 16, 18, 19, 25, 26, 27, 28
Best Days for Career: 4, 5, 6, 7, 15, 16, 25, 26

Jupiter makes a very rare conjunction with Neptune. This only happens once every 12 to 14 years. (He will make another conjunction here later on in the year too.) And since Jupiter is your ruling planet, this aspect is very significant for you. Besides being the most spiritual of all the planets, Neptune also rules your 4th House of Home and Family. On a mundane level this can bring a move, the fortunate purchase or sale of a home, expensive items for the home, or fortunate real-estate investments. It shows a closeness and devotion between you and the family, especially with a parent or parent figure. Emotions and moods are much improved over last month. On a more spiritual level this shows tremendous spiritual revelation coming to you. You are always religious and philosophical, but this experience is more than religion – it is mystical, supernatural. In general you will be having more supernatural experiences this month. Your physical body is becoming more refined and spiritualized and many of you will be able to register psychic vibrations right in the body, as if they were physical. You are also going to receive new knowledge of how to transform your body and image. (In general, you will be more glamorous this month; you embody an 'other worldly' beauty. No matter what your age or stage in life, this force will beautify you.)

Finances have improved over last month, and after the 19th become really wonderful. Earnings become like a rocket. You are earning this money through your work, but partners, elders, bosses, and the current love are very co-operative as well. Keep in mind though that your financial planet is still Retrograde. So continue to review your finances and avoid making drastic financial decisions.

You are still in the midst of a yearly personal pleasure peak, so this is a happy month for you. It is a good month for singles as well. Though we don't see serious love here (and with Venus Retrograde you shouldn't get too serious too quickly), there are many opportunities for love affairs. Love seems happy. Until the 9th you just want fun and games – nights out on the town. But after the 9th you seem more serious. You show love through practical service to the beloved, and this is the way you feel loved. There are love opportunities at the job or with co-workers. Love opportunities also happen as you pursue your health goals or with people involved with your health.

Health is much improved this month. When Mars leaves Pisces on the 22nd it will improve further. Continue to enhance your health in the ways we discussed last month. Your health planet starts moving forward on the 17th, and this will be the time to make the health decisions or changes you have been contemplating.

May

Best Days Overall: 1, 2, 10, 11, 20, 21, 28, 29
Most Stressful Days Overall: 3, 4, 18, 19, 24, 25, 30, 31
Best Days for Love: 1, 2, 5, 10, 11, 13, 14, 20, 21, 22, 23, 24, 25, 28, 29
Best Days for Money: 3, 4, 5, 6, 12, 13, 14, 15, 16, 22, 23, 24, 25, 30, 31
Best Days for Career: 3, 4, 5, 13, 14, 22, 23, 30, 31

The Western sector of the chart is still powerful. Your 7th House of Love becomes powerful after the 20th, when you begin a yearly social peak. Your 1st House, by contrast, is empty – only the Moon will visit there on the 10th and 11th. Personal initiative and personal dynamism are not the important factors for happiness and success now; social grace and social skills will bring you success now. Don't try to change conditions, but adapt to them as best you can. The time will come for this later on.

The health stresses of March seem to have served a good purpose. You have become more health conscious since then. Health is a major focus. You are into exercise, physical fitness and healthy lifestyles. This will stand you in good stead after the 20th as your health gets tested again. From the astrological perspective, it is the energy that seems important. The main therapy after the 20th is to keep your energy levels high. Cranial sacral therapy, head and face massage and vigorous physical exercise will also enhance the health. Heat-oriented therapies are good, and warmer climates are better health-wise than colder ones. Try to be upbeat and cheerful, not just as a mask to show the world but deep in your heart. Happiness itself is a great healer for you.

Finances are good this month, but there are more challenges after the 20th. Perhaps you are overspending. The good news is that your financial planet starts to move forward on the 17th – it has been Retrograde all this year. Thus, a new financial clarity is happening for you and this makes all the difference in the world. Part of the financial stress that we see is coming from attempting big things, not from bad luck or punishment. And these are always more complicated.

Love is happy but complicated. You are in the most socially active period of your year. You are in the mood for romance – serious romance – and no doubt you are attracting it. But your love planet, Mercury, is Retrograde from the 7th to the 31st and this introduces some confusion or lack of direction. (Probably you are meeting people who like you but don't know where they are going in the relationship.) Go slowly in love and let it develop in its own way. Don't try to force or manipulate things. Clarity will come next month. Also exercise more care in how you communicate to the beloved. Don't take things for granted. Make sure you got his or her message and that he or she got your message.

Miscommunication is one of the main challenges to love happiness this month.

The ruler of your 9th House is in your 7th House this month, and this suggests foreigners, religious people or highly educated people are in your romantic sphere. It also suggests that love opportunities are in foreign countries or with foreigners. Philosophical and intellectual compatibility is unusually important in love. You need to share the same (or similar) view of the world and life.

June

Best Days Overall: 6, 7, 8, 16, 17, 25
Most Stressful Days Overall: 14, 15, 21, 27, 28
Best Days for Love: 9, 10, 19, 21, 27, 28, 29, 30
Best Days for Money: 2, 3, 9, 10, 11, 12, 13, 19, 21, 22, 27, 28, 29, 30
Best Days for Career: 9, 10, 21, 27, 28, 29, 30

Love is much improved over last month. With Mercury moving forwards your social confidence is much improved. There is better communication with existing loves and with new prospects too. The main ingredient for your social success this month is that you are interested and focused here – you are willing to overcome all the natural challenges that happen in love. Many of the love trends that we wrote of last month are still in effect now. Foreigners, highly educated people, academics and minister types are highly alluring. There are romantic opportunities with professors or mentors. Religious and educational settings are conducive to love.

After the 14th there are romantic opportunities with people of high status and position – bosses or superiors at work – or other kinds of high and mighty people. In general you are socializing with high-status people. Love opportunities (after the 14th) also come as you pursue your normal career goals and with people involved in your career.

Your spouse, partner or current love has wonderful career opportunities that are pursuing him or her.

Though career is becoming more important now, the main focus is still internal – on the emotional life, family and home. The important thing is to be in a state of emotional harmony. If you have that everything else will more or less fall into place.

Continue to watch the health more this month. The social whirl can be taxing, and though it is tempting, don't bite off more than you can chew. Head and face massage and physical exercise are still good until the 6th. Cranial sacral therapy will be good all month. After the 6th give more attention to the neck and throat. Regular neck massages will do wonders for you. It's also good to massage the lower part of the head, where the skull meets the neck. Tension often collects there and blocks the energy. Massage should release the energy flow again. Health and energy should improve after the 21st, but still needs watching.

Finances are still challenging until the 21st. You just have to work harder and go the extra mile for your customers. Compromise with parents, elders or bosses – they have a different perspective on money matters than you do. Finance could also be an issue in love. But these are all short-term problems.

July

> Best Days Overall: 3, 4, 5, 14, 15, 22, 23, 31
> Most Stressful Days Overall: 11, 12, 18, 19, 24, 25
> Best Days for Love: 9, 11, 12, 18, 19, 22, 23, 26, 27, 31
> Best Days for Money: 6, 7, 9, 10, 16, 17, 18, 19, 24, 25, 26, 27
> Best Days for Career: 11, 12, 22, 23, 24, 25, 31

A very eventful month, but in the end it is happy. There is a shift of the planetary power from the lower half to the upper half of the Horoscope this month. It begins on the 12th. This signals a need to wake up from the dreams of the night and to take practical, outer actions towards your career goals. By now you have achieved a modicum of emotional harmony (some more and some less) and now it is time to act in the world and achieve your worldly aims. With the two planets involved with the home and family Retrograde – and for a few more months to come – there are no quick fixes to family issues, only time and patience. So, you might as well focus on your career: serve your family by being successful.

Forty per cent of the planets are Retrograde this month. This slows down the pace of events in the world at large and in your personal world. You have many virtues, but patience is not one of them. This is a month to acquire some.

There are two eclipses this month. Both are basically benign to you, but it won't hurt to take a reduced schedule anyway. People in general are not at their best during eclipse periods and thus there tend to be more accidents and dramas in the world. Spend more quiet time close to home during these periods.

The Lunar Eclipse of the 7th occurs in your money house and brings important financial changes – changes in your thinking, planning, attitudes and strategy. It also brings these kinds of changes – often through shock therapy – to your spouse, partner or current love. This is not punishment – only love reminders from the cosmos that those changes that you knew needed to be made can't be put off any longer. Since the Moon rules your 8th House of Personal Transformation, there will be changes in your approach to these interests as well. Probably there will be dramatic events in the lives of investors or creditors as well. When the 8th House is involved in an eclipse, there are often dreams of death or psychological encounters with the dark angel. There is a need to understand this better. When we understand death we understand life as well.

The Solar Eclipse of the 22nd occurs right on the cusp of the 8th and 9th Houses and will affect the affairs of both. Thus again, there are dramatic financial changes with your spouse, partner or current love; whatever wasn't done after the last eclipse will get done now. Probably there will be changes in their banks, brokers, or financial advisers. Students will once again be affected by this eclipse (as they were earlier in the year). Again, more changes to their educational plans and perhaps changes of school.

Health is much improved after the 22nd, but still needs watching. Enhance your health by resting and relaxing more and by giving more attention to the neck and throat (until the 5th), and to the arms, shoulders and lungs (after the 5th). Neck massage is still powerful until the 5th; after that, focus on regular massage of the arms and shoulders.

August

Best Days Overall: 1, 10, 11, 19, 27, 28
Most Stressful Days Overall: 1, 7, 8, 9, 14, 15, 21
Best Days for Love: 1, 2, 7, 8, 9, 12, 13, 14, 15, 16, 17, 21, 22, 25, 26
Best Days for Money: 2, 3, 4, 5, 6, 12, 13, 14, 15, 21, 22, 23, 24, 30, 31
Best Days for Career: 1, 2, 12, 13, 21, 22, 31

Another eclipse on the 6th impacts on students and will test cars and communications equipment. (This seems a turbulent year for students – much instability. They have been hit with eclipse after eclipse, relentlessly.) There are dramatic events in the lives of siblings and neighbours too. Probably there are changes in the neighbourhood – old neighbours move out, new ones move in, or there is heavy duty construction work going on there.

There are still many planets Retrograde this month – 40 per cent of them. And with so much fire in the Horoscope until the 22nd, learning patience will be difficult. With this many Retrogrades try to be more thorough in all that you do, especially in the home and with family members. Short cuts in these areas will probably turn out to be false economies. Go slower but be more thorough.

Career and ambitions were strong last month, and this month even more so. On the 22nd, you enter a yearly career peak, and there will be much progress. Your willingness to travel and to educate yourself is a big plus career-wise. Also, you have friends in the right places. You should be willing to attend or host the right kind of parties this month. There are career opportunities happening in foreign lands or in foreign companies. Your spouse, partner, or current love is successful this month too, and he or she is helping. Social connections – and your personal likeability – are great assets and are being evaluated by the powers that be.

This is a month for pay rises, as Saturn, your financial planet, is receiving positive stimulation. Those who are self employed will have increased earnings. This is a great month, from the 2nd to the 25th, to ask financial favours from bosses, elders, parents or parent figures – they seem favourably disposed to you.

Love seems happy. The love planet, Mercury, moves very quickly this month, through three Signs and Houses of the Horoscope. This suggests that you have a lot of social confidence, are covering a lot of territory, and making a lot of progress here. Only, you seem more fickle and changeable in love now. Until the 2nd, you are into fun and philosophical compatibility – teachers and mentors allure you. From the 2nd to the 25th you are attracted by the power people – people of high status and position. Love opportunities happen as you pursue your career goals; in fact you are trying to integrate love and career during this period. Perhaps you are too hard headed and practical at the moment, too much in the mind and not enough in the heart. But this will change after the 25th. That will be a powerful period for real, heart-oriented romance.

Health is stressful after the 22nd. Rest and relax more and give more attention to the heart, stomach and breasts (until the 26th).

September

> Best Days Overall: 6, 7, 15, 16, 23, 24, 25
> Most Stressful Days Overall: 4, 5, 11, 12, 17, 18
> Best Days for Love: 1, 6, 7, 11, 12, 15, 16, 18, 26, 27
> Best Days for Money: 1, 2, 8, 9, 11, 12, 17, 18, 19, 20, 26,
>   27, 28, 29, 30
> Best Days for Career: 1, 11, 17, 18, 27

Your yearly career peak is in full swing, and perhaps even stronger than last month. Like last month, the planets involved with home and family are still Retrograde, showing there are no quick solutions to family issues. Continue to give your focus to your career.

Career is active and, successful, but a bit more complicated this month. Mercury, your career planet, goes Retrograde from the 7th to the 29th. This is not going to stop your progress but will perhaps slow things down a bit. New career opportunities or promotions need much more study and sober analysis. The premises behind your decision making can change drastically between the 7th and the 29th. Bosses and superiors – perhaps the upper management of your company – are backtracking from previous positions. This can be confusing. Take more time and care in how you communicate to superiors; make sure you understand what they are saying and that they understand your message. Miscommunication in this department can cause needless heartache, wasted time and delays later on. Don't be afraid to ask questions and resolve doubts.

You can further your career in many of the same ways as last month. Your willingness to travel, to educate yourself, to network with the right people, your social skills and likeability are all positives in the eyes of superiors. Also – especially after the 20th – your strong work ethic is a plus.

Health still needs more watching until the 22nd. Happily your health planet is prominently positioned this month and you are paying attention. Enhance your health by giving more attention to the heart and, after the 20th, to the small intestine. Health will improve after the 22nd.

Mercury's Retrograde movement also complicates the love life. As always, from the 7th to the 29th is a time to review your marriage, current relationship and overall social life. It is a time for study and analysis, not for major decision making one way or another. There needs to be a 'breather' in love. A good relationship will get all the more passionate after a breather. On a personal level, singles are not sure whether they want power and position or romance and friendship. You waver back and forth between these two urges.

Finances are excellent this month. Earnings are on the increase. They can come from pay rises, your good professional reputation (which you still need to guard), the direct or indirect support of parents, parent figures and bosses, or your spouse, partner, or current love, and through social connections.

October

> Best Days Overall: 3, 4, 12, 13, 21, 22, 31
> Most Stressful Days Overall: 1, 2, 8, 9, 14, 15, 28, 29
> Best Days for Love: 6, 7, 8, 9, 10, 15, 16, 26, 27, 28, 29
> Best Days for Money: 6, 7, 8, 9, 14, 15, 16, 17, 23, 24, 26, 27
> Best Days for Career: 9, 10, 14, 15, 16, 28, 29

On the 20th of last month, the planetary power made a major shift from the Western social sector of the Horoscope to the Eastern, personal one. For many months you needed to adapt to situations and were dependent on others. Now this is changing. You've just about paid your karma for previous creations and are ready to create anew – according to your specifications. Now if a situation is irksome, you have the power to change it to your liking. Other people are always important, but your way is the best way these days.

You can't depend on them for your happiness. Your personal initiative is now – and for the next five to six months – the major force in your happiness.

This shift occurs as your ruling planet, Jupiter, starts to move forward on the 18th. Beautiful timing. As Jupiter goes forward you will have more personal confidence and clarity as to direction in your life. The issue is not so much about happiness, but about knowing with clarity what makes you happy, or doesn't. And this will be Jupiter's gift. So, start to exercise your personal independence as Jupiter moves forward.

Health is much, much improved this month, both in the short term and the long term. Saturn moves away from his two-and-a-half-year stressful aspect to you and starts to make easy, harmonious aspects to you. It's as if the problem that has been plaguing you for two years, that you found to be such an irritation, now becomes a friend and a helper. The irony of the cosmos is beautiful to behold. You can enhance your good health even further by giving more attention to the small intestine (until the 15th) and to the kidneys and hips after that date. Keeping the harmony in your marriage and social life is always a factor in your health, but even more so after the 15th.

You are still ambitious, but career ambitions are winding down. It is a time to tie up loose ends and prepare for the evening of your year. The focus this month is on friends, groups, group activities and organizations. This is fun in its own right, but will also further and enhance your career. Good use of technology – staying up to date with the latest developments – is also important career-wise (and financially, too).

Your financial planet is now (after the 29th) in beautiful aspect with your personal planet. Money may not be the strongest priority these days, but it comes to you very easily. And, most importantly, you seem more comfortable in the way that you earn it and manage it. For the next two and a half years your financial planet is in its most exalted position, in the Sign of Libra. This denotes prosperity and strong earning power. Fondest financial hopes and wishes are now coming to pass (now and over the next two years).

November

Best Days Overall: 1, 8, 9, 17, 18, 27, 28
Most Stressful Days Overall: 4, 5, 10, 11, 25, 26
Best Days for Love: 4, 5, 15, 16, 17, 25, 26, 27, 28
Best Days for Money: 4, 5, 13, 14, 20, 21, 22, 23
Best Days for Career: 4, 5, 10, 11, 16, 17, 27, 28

Spirituality became an important interest on the 23rd of last month and remains an important interest (even stronger) this month. With your foreign travel planet in the spiritual 12th House until the 22nd, many of you are making religious-type pilgrimages to holy places and the like. If you are Muslim this is a period to make the journey to Mecca. If you are Christian or Jewish it is good to go to the Holy Land. Yogis will likely visit that ashram in India and sit at the feet of the guru. (With you, any excuse to travel is enough to get you packing your bags.) This is not travel for personal pleasure (that will come later on in the month), but has to do with your spiritual life.

This is a period for living the supernatural life. The exalted life. What you experience will depend on where you are in your journey. Those not on the spiritual path might just have a more active dream life or strange synchronistic-type experiences. Those just setting out will have prophetic kinds of dreams and experiences. The phone rings and you know who it is and what it's all about. You march to a different drummer. Time, budgets and schedules have less meaning these days – not because these things are unimportant (as so many think) but because you are following a different time, a different kind of schedule and a different budget. The things of the mundane world become less important. Those more advanced in their spiritual life will expand their spiritual powers. They will experience more interior revelation, an influx of higher energy. (This will happen for all of you, but the more spiritually advanced will experience it in a more conscious way.)

This spiritual focus, though very altruistic, will have very practical effects. It will clarify the love life, the career and spiritual mission for this incarnation. In fact, this is the way to further these kinds of goals in the month ahead.

Love is very happy this month, but more so after the 16th. Your activation of the spiritual forces brings love to you, without having to run after it. Love is close at hand – closer than hands and feet, closer than breathing. You don't need to scheme or manipulate. Just show up. It will find you. The same is true with career opportunities. They are seeking you out ardently – and they will find you.

Health is good this month and you can enhance it further by giving more attention to the kidneys and hips (until the 8th), and to the colon, bladder and sexual organs afterwards. Spiritual healing is important after the 8th. And, while this is a huge subject, you will make greater progress and inroads in this area after the 8th.

Finances are still positive and happy, but they are not such a big issue this month.

December

   Best Days Overall: 6, 7, 15, 16, 24, 25, 26
   Most Stressful Days Overall: 2, 8, 9, 22, 23, 29, 30
   Best Days for Love: 2, 6, 7, 8, 9, 15, 16, 17, 18, 26, 27, 28, 29, 30
   Best Days for Money: 1, 2, 10, 11, 17, 18, 19, 20, 21, 29
   Best Days for Career: 8, 9, 17, 18, 27, 28

Last month, on the 22nd, you entered a yearly personal pleasure peak. There aren't too many people who will use this as you will, to maximum benefit. When it comes to parties and personal pleasure, Leo might give you a run for your money, but not many others. So you are in a great fun-type period. There are travel opportunities – this time for personal pleasure – coming to you and you are likely to take them. You are in a period of maximum personal independence now. You are supposed to have things your own way. This doesn't mean being a dictator over others; you just have the power to create what you will. You are in charge of your personal happiness. Whatever you decide to do, the entire cosmos – all the planetary and angelic hierarchies – will say 'amen'.

Last month was a very spiritual period, and this month will be as well, but for different reasons. Jupiter, your ruling planet, once again goes back into conjunction with Neptune, the most spiritual of all the planets. Thus there is more spiritual revelation coming to you. A move is likely – sometimes this merely shows buying additional property, investing in the home or renovating the home. The home and family circle is getting enlarged. There is more harmony and closeness with family members and with parents or parent figures. Often the holiday time is a period of great tension as family members are physically close but universes apart inwardly, but here we see a greater inner closeness and harmony.

The main challenge this month is integrating personal pleasure – the pleasures of the body and the senses – with your spiritual life. This is not so easy to achieve as the values of both are radically different. The best way – the healthiest – is to give the spirit charge of the body. This will automatically arrange things the way that it should be. But if you put the body first, before the spirit, there can be problems.

This is also a very prosperous month. Job and career opportunities are still seeking you out. A good period for jobseekers and for those who employ others. On the 21st, you enter a yearly financial peak. Financial intuition is very sharp this month, especially from the 21st to the 25th.

Health is good and you can make it even better by giving more attention to the liver and thighs (until the 25th) and to the spine, knees, bones and skeletal alignment afterwards. Don't allow financial ups and downs, or temporary delays, to affect your health after the 25th. Prosperity is intact in spite of these bumps on the road.

Love and romantic opportunities are still pursuing you until the 5th. Afterwards, love opportunities will come as you pursue your normal financial goals, and with people who are involved in your finances.

Capricorn

♑

THE GOAT
Birthdays from
21st December to
19th January

Personality Profile

CAPRICORN AT A GLANCE

Element – Earth

Ruling Planet – Saturn
 Career Planet – Venus
 Love Planet – Moon
 Money Planet – Uranus
 Planet of Communications – Neptune
 Planet of Health and Work – Mercury
 Planet of Home and Family Life – Mars
 Planet of Spirituality – Jupiter

Colours – black, indigo

Colours that promote love, romance and social
 harmony – puce, silver

Colour that promotes earning power –
 ultramarine blue

Gem – black onyx

Metal – lead

Scents – magnolia, pine, sweet pea, wintergreen

Quality – cardinal (= activity)

Qualities most needed for balance – warmth, spontaneity, a sense of fun

Strongest virtues – sense of duty, organization, perseverance, patience, ability to take the long-term view

Deepest needs – to manage, take charge and administrate

Characteristics to avoid – pessimism, depression, undue materialism and undue conservatism

Signs of greatest overall compatibility – Taurus, Virgo

Signs of greatest overall incompatibility – Aries, Cancer, Libra

Sign most helpful to career – Libra

Sign most helpful for emotional support – Aries

Sign most helpful financially – Aquarius

Sign best for marriage and/or partnerships – Cancer

Sign most helpful for creative projects – Taurus

Best Sign to have fun with – Taurus

Signs most helpful in spiritual matters – Virgo, Sagittarius

Best day of the week – Saturday

Understanding a Capricorn

The virtues of Capricorns are such that there will always be people for and against them. Many admire them, many dislike them. Why? It seems to be because of Capricorn's power urges. A well-developed Capricorn has his or her eyes set on the heights of power, prestige and authority. In the Sign of Capricorn, ambition is not a fatal flaw, but rather the highest virtue.

Capricorns are not frightened by the resentment their authority may sometimes breed. In Capricorn's cool, calculated, organized mind all the dangers are already factored into the equation – the unpopularity, the animosity, the misunderstandings, even the outright slander – and a plan is always in place for dealing with these things in the most efficient way. To the Capricorn, situations that would terrify an ordinary mind are merely problems to be managed, bumps on the road to ever-growing power, effectiveness and prestige.

Some people attribute pessimism to the Capricorn Sign, but this is a bit deceptive. It is true that Capricorns like to take into account the negative side of things. It is also true that they love to imagine the worst possible scenario in every undertaking. Other people might find such analyses depressing, but Capricorns only do these things so that they can formulate a way out – an escape route.

Capricorns will argue with success. They will show you that you are not doing as well as you think you are. Capricorns do this to themselves as well as to others. They do not mean to discourage you but rather to root out any impediments to your greater success. A Capricorn boss or supervisor feels that no matter how good the performance there is always room for improvement. This explains why Capricorn supervisors are difficult to handle and even infuriating at times. Their actions are, however, quite often effective – they can get their subordinates to improve and become better at their jobs.

Capricorn is a born manager and administrator. Leo is better at being king or queen, but Capricorn is better at being prime minister – the person actually wielding power.

Capricorn is interested in the virtues that last, in the things that will stand the test of time and trials of circumstance. Temporary fads and fashions mean little to a Capricorn – except as things to be used for profit or power. Capricorns apply this attitude to business, love, to their thinking and even to their philosophy and religion.

Finance

Capricorns generally attain wealth and they usually earn it. They are willing to work long and hard for what they want. They are quite amenable to foregoing a short-term gain in favour of long-term benefits. Financially, they come into their own later in life.

However, if Capricorns are to attain their financial goals they must shed some of their strong conservatism. Perhaps this is the least desirable trait of the Capricorn. They can resist anything new merely because it is new and untried. They are afraid of experimentation. Capricorns need to be willing to take a few risks. They should be more eager to market new products or explore different managerial techniques. Otherwise, progress will leave them behind. If necessary, Capricorns must be ready to change with the times, to discard old methods that no longer work.

Very often this experimentation will mean that Capricorns have to break with existing authority. They might even consider changing their present position or starting their own ventures. If so, they should be willing to accept all the risks and just get on with it. Only then will a Capricorn be on the road to highest financial gain.

Career and Public Image

A Capricorn's ambition and quest for power are evident. It is perhaps the most ambitious Sign of the Zodiac – and usually the most successful in a worldly sense. However, there are lessons Capricorns need to learn in order to fulfil their highest aspirations.

Intelligence, hard work, cool efficiency and organization will take them a certain distance, but will not carry them to the very top. Capricorns need to cultivate their social graces, to develop a social style, along with charm and an ability to get along with people. They need to bring beauty into their lives and to cultivate the right social contacts. They must learn to wield power gracefully, so that people love them for it – a very delicate art. They also need to learn how to bring people together in order to fulfil certain objectives. In short, Capricorns require some of the gifts – the social graces – of Libra to get to the top.

Once they have learned this, Capricorns will be successful in their careers. They are ambitious hard workers who are not afraid of putting in the required time and effort. Capricorns take their time in getting the job done – in order to do it well – and they like moving up the corporate ladder slowly but surely. Being so driven by success, Capricorns are generally liked by their bosses, who respect and trust them.

Love and Relationships

Like Scorpio and Pisces, Capricorn is a difficult Sign to get to know. They are deep, introverted and like to keep their own counsel. Capricorns do not like to reveal their innermost thoughts. If you are in love with a Capricorn, be patient and take your time. Little by little you will get to understand him or her.

Capricorns have a deep romantic nature, but they do not show it straightaway. They are cool, matter of fact and not especially emotional. They will often show their love in practical ways.

It takes time for a Capricorn – male or female – to fall in love. They are not the love-at-first-sight kind. If a Capricorn is involved with a Leo or Aries, these Fire types will be totally mystified – to them the Capricorn will seem cold, unfeeling, unaffectionate and not very spontaneous. Of course none of this is true; it is just that Capricorn likes to take things slowly. They like to be sure of their ground before making any demonstrations of love or commitment.

Even in love affairs Capricorns are deliberate. They need more time to make decisions than is true of the other Signs of the Zodiac, but given this time they become just as passionate. Capricorns like a relationship to be structured, committed, well regulated, well defined, predictable and even routine. They prefer partners who are nurturers, and they in turn like to nurture their partners. This is their basic psychology. Whether such a relationship is good for them is another issue altogether. Capricorns have enough routine in their lives as it is. They might be better off in relationships that are a bit more stimulating, changeable and fluctuating.

Home and Domestic Life

The home of a Capricorn – as with a Virgo – is going to be tidy and well organized. Capricorns tend to manage their families in the same way they manage their businesses. Capricorns are often so career-driven that they find little time for the home and family. They should try to get more actively involved in their family and domestic life. Capricorns do, however, take their children very seriously and are very proud parents, particularly should their children grow up to become respected members of society.

Horoscope for 2009

Major Trends

Last year was a year for travel, higher education and going deeper into religion and philosophy – evolving your personal philosophy of life – and the trend will continue for most of the year ahead.

There was prosperity last year and the trend continues even stronger in the year ahead. Benevolent Jupiter enters your money house on January 5 and stays there for the rest of the year.

Though you are always ambitious, you were less so in the past few years. But that is about to change. Saturn, your ruling planet, will cross your Midheaven and enter your 10th House of Career on October 29. This begins a two-and-a-half-year period of career success.

However, the main headline is Pluto's move into your own Sign late last year. You only felt this influence intermittently last year, as Pluto flirted back and forth between Sagittarius and Capricorn. Now he is in Capricorn for the long term (well into 2023).This is going to bring an intense interest in personal transformation and invention. You will be working to give birth to the body and image of your dreams – your ideal. Some of you will start out with the conventional methods, cosmetic kinds of surgery and the like. But many of you will work on this spiritually, through things like Yoga, Tai Chi, diet and meditation, and this is the more correct (and longer-lasting) way. Along with this you will be redefining your personality, probably many times. This always brings changes, especially in relationships. People make friends with Capricorn X, but Capricorn X is now someone else. He or she has redefined him or herself, and now people are not sure they like this new person.

Pluto's move is also bringing you new friends, devoted ones. In fact you don't need to do anything. They come to you.

Communication and intellectual interests – studying and teaching – have been important for many years and the trend still continues. You remain in a period for gaining knowledge and it has important financial implications as well.

Your most important areas of interest this year are the body, image and personal appearance; finance; communication and intellectual interests; religion, philosophy, higher education and foreign travel; career (after October 29).

Your paths of greatest fulfilment in the coming year are finance; the body, image and personal appearance (after July 27).

Health

(Please note that this is an astrological perspective on health and not a medical one. In days of yore there was no difference, both of these perspectives were identical. But in these times there could be quite a difference. For the medical perspective, please consult your doctor or health professional.)

Health has been basically good these past few years and the trend will continue for most of the year ahead. However, there are changes happening. Pluto, as we mentioned, moved into your own Sign late last year and will be in Capricorn for the long term. On October 29, Saturn moves into Libra, from a harmonious aspect to you to an inharmonious one. So health and energy will need more attention after October 29. The problem this year is that your 6th House of Health is basically empty (only short-term planets will move through there temporarily) and thus health is not a focus. The danger is that you might ignore your health – not pay enough attention – and then, combined with lower energy levels, you can become vulnerable. So, the challenge this year (especially after October 29) is to motivate yourself to pay more attention.

You can do many things to enhance your health. First off, give more attention to the arms, shoulders, lungs and heart (the heart becomes important after October 29). Being a

Capricorn the spine, knees, teeth, gall bladder, bones and skeletal alignment are also important. Regular massage of the arms, shoulders and back will be wonderful. Regular visits to a chiropractor would be advisable (and especially after October 29). You might want to explore therapies such as The Alexander Technique and the Feldenkreis method too. Yoga is excellent for the spine, especially if you focus on the postures that work directly on it.

When Saturn moves into stressful alignment there will be a tendency to feel your physical limits (and also your age). The cosmos is not punishing you but forcing you to get your priorities in order, to make a few tough choices. You don't have energy for everything, so focus on what is really important in your life and let lesser things go.

Any therapy that gives you energy is good. There are many natural and drugless therapies out there, but if you like you can work with the chart below.

Reflexology

Try to massage the whole foot on a regular basis, but pay extra attention to the points highlighted on the chart. When you massage, be aware of 'sore spots', as these need special attention. It's also a good idea to massage the ankles and top side (as well as the soles) of the feet.

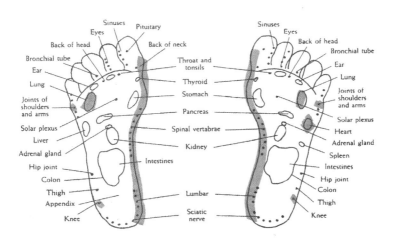

Energy levels need to be kept high. Rest when tired. Avoid thinking or worrying too much. Try to live in the present moment without thinking of the past or future. If there are intelligent and constructive actions to be taken for the future, by all means take them, but if not, let go and live in the moment. Arguments and power struggles should be avoided.

With Pluto in your own Sign you will benefit from detox regimes – herbal or mechanical. Pluto in your own Sign gives extra libido and so there is a need for moderation in sex, neither too much nor too little. Too little is suffering. Too much will deplete the body of its life force which it needs for other things – such as healing.

Home and Family

Your 4th House of Home and Family is not a House of Power this year. Things at home are pretty much the way you want them to be and so you have no need to make major changes. Things will continue pretty much as they have been doing. (Enjoy the peace and tranquillity while you can; in the next few years there are going to be dramatic – and I mean dramatic – changes in the home and family situation. But that is for future years' reports.)

Career and outer success is much more important to you than family and emotional issues, and perhaps this is as it should be. You are very successful in the year ahead and need to focus on the career. Family seems to go along with this.

This is a year where you are very much in charge in family issues. You are exalted above every member of the family (and if not, you are trying to be). There doesn't seem to be much opposition to this either.

You seem very devoted to one of the parents or parent figures in your life this year, especially after October 29. You are giving this person unusual attention and are very personally involved.

If you are planning major construction work or renovations in the home, March 20 to April 21 is a good time for it.

If you are planning to beautify the home in cosmetic ways, February 3 to March 5 and April 24 to June 6 are good times. These latter periods are also good for family gatherings and entertaining from home.

Your family planet (Mars) will spend a lot of time in your 8th House in the year ahead – from October 16 well into March of 2010. This suggests some major renovation or repairs going on – deep kinds of things. Perhaps there are near-death experiences with family members (in some cases it will be an actual death), and perhaps surgery. This will be a wonderful period to clean and clear the house, to get rid of excess furnishings or appliances that are no longer needed. Make room for the new. Clearing out the house will also make you more emotionally clean as well.

Parents or parent figures are also renovating or repairing the home in the coming year. Again, it looks like major kinds of things – ripping out walls, wiring and pipes – not cosmetic repairs. A move or the actual construction of a new home wouldn't be a surprise either.

Children of appropriate age have a basically status-quo year at home, but they might be doing repairs and renovations when you are (if they are living with you the symbolism is exact, but if they live apart, they can be doing renovations on their own). Siblings and grandchildren are also having a status-quo kind of year.

Since Mars, your family planet, moves through the Zodiac fairly rapidly (certainly when compared to the long-term planets), the family situation tends to change rapidly as well. It all depends on where Mars is at any given time. We will discuss these short-term trends in the monthly reports.

Finance and Career

Capricorns are always interested in money and career and this is a banner year for both. Whatever your age and stage you are in a lifetime peak in both areas.

Finances have been an important interest for many years now, and generally you have been prospering. But not like you are now. Last year, benevolent Jupiter moved through your own Sign initiating a red hot, three-year trend of prosperity. This year, Jupiter moves into your money house, accelerating this prosperity even further. And in 2010, Jupiter will travel with your financial planet in Pisces. Earnings are simply amazing.

Often it is helpful to understand the long-term trend in finance, as many apparently risky decisions depend on the long-term prognosis. So, go ahead and make your decisions – make those important moves that you need to make, launch those new products, buy the new buildings – and go forward with confidence. You are in an unstoppable prosperity trend now.

Your financial life needs to be read on two levels: the mundane material perspective, and the spiritual level. The spiritual level is by far the most important here. If we examine what is going on in your money house, we find that the two most spiritual planets of the Horoscope are there – Jupiter (your personal spiritual planet) and Neptune (the generic spiritual planet). The ruler of your money house – the financial planet – Uranus, is in the spiritual Sign of Pisces. The link between spirituality – your inner life – and finances is thus very powerful. So you are going deeper into the nature of spiritual wealth, the laws of spiritual abundance. You have been involved in this for some years now, but now ever more so. You are more charitable and generous, and the more you give the more you prosper – a counter-intuitive proposition. You are seeing the power of intuition in finances, how the merest flash of intuition is worth more than many years of hard labour. More importantly – and this is hard lesson for hard-headed Capricorns – you are learning that there is only one source of supply: the Divine within you. We will deal more with this later on.

On the mundane, practical level, Jupiter's move through your money house increases the value of assets that you already own. Your stocks and bonds go up, your home is worth more, your business is worth more, etc. Often you own things that you didn't realize were valuable, and you find out about it this year.

Jupiter in the money house also brings increased financial opportunity and luck in speculations (last year was good for that too). There is an optimism and confidence in money matters now and it is contagious. Everyone feels it and joins in.

You are in a personal bull market, regardless of what the external economic conditions are like.

For professional investors or those of you who have investment accounts, it is a year to look at publishing, airlines, high technology industries, oil, natural gas, shipping, water utilities, fishing and energy stocks. Long distance telecoms and transport are also highly interesting.

Since you are earning more you are also spending much more in the year ahead – and it looks like investments in your business or profession and high-tech kinds of gadgetry. With most Signs the tendency would be to overspend, but Capricorn doesn't need lectures from anyone about getting value for their money or about money management – they are natural masters of this.

Career too is wonderful. For now, until October 29, you should get the education you need career-wise. Those of you in established careers can take the courses that will carry you further. After October 29 you enter a period of outer success. This is a success that is deeper than just getting rich. It involves honour, prestige, public recognition and authority. You are honoured and recognized for who you are as much as for your professional achievements. It is a period for acquiring name and fame. Many of you will become famous in the next two years, but understand that the nature of the fame will depend on your age, stage and position in life. Most of you will not become household names, but you will have more fame than you've ever had.

It seems to me that if you probe any Capricorn deep enough, they will admit that they feel they were 'born to be in charge' – born to manage. And this year, I can see you saying, 'Aha, this is the way it should be.'

Love and Social Life

Though your 7th House of Love, Marriage and Social Relationships isn't strong this year, there are going to be many changes in the love life. Perhaps you feel that the status quo is OK. Perhaps you feel that your love life is where you want it to be. Perhaps you are taking your current love relationship for granted. But the cosmos isn't satisfied. Nothing but perfection will do, both for you and your current love. There will be four (yes four) Lunar Eclipses in the coming year – twice as many as normal. And since the Moon is your love planet, the love life is going to get some severe testing. Perhaps you are too focused on money and career and are ignoring the love relationships. Perhaps your success and fame is threatening to your partner. Perhaps there are other hidden flaws in your relationship. This year, they will come up and have to be dealt with. In addition to the four Lunar Eclipses, there is a Solar Eclipse in your 7th House as well – on July 22. Your love life will be impacted by five eclipses!

In many cases this will lead to a breakup, either of the marriage or the love relationship. In other cases, it will just bring up all the flaws and you will have the opportunity to correct them. Much depends on how sound the relationship is. If there are fundamental flaws, the marriage or relationship will break up. But if the basic relationship is solid it can be repaired and made better than before.

In either case, there is crisis in love. And crisis, as the wise ones say, is dangerous opportunity.

Singles might find that they want to change their status and marry. Marrieds might divorce. This is the nature of an eclipse. If you are supposed to be married, the eclipses will shake up your life so that it will happen. And, if you are not supposed to be married, if you're supposed to move on, the eclipses will take care of that too.

These eclipses will test friendships and business partnerships too. They seem chaotic and unstable. There will be many dramas in the lives of friends and business partners (and this is the main reason for the instability).

Your most active social periods will be from June 21 to July 22, and from August 1 to August 26.

Since the Moon is your love planet your needs in love tend to change from day to day. You tend to be moody about love. You tend to be more loving and more enthusiastic about social issues when the Moon waxes than when she wanes. You are also more socially magnetic on a waxing Moon than on a waning Moon. (You also tend to attract partners who are like this.)

The Moon also happens to be the fastest-moving planet in the Zodiac. Where fast-moving planets like the Sun, Mercury and Venus will take a year to move through all the Signs and Houses of the Horoscope, the Moon does this every month. Thus love opportunities come to you in a variety of ways and through a variety of people – all depending on where the Moon is on a given day. These short-term trends will be dealt with in the monthly reports.

Those in their second or third marriages have less marital stress than those in their first or fourth, but you too will have your friendships and business partnerships tested.

Those working on the second marriage have a status-quo kind of year. Marriage prospects brighten after October 29 though. Those working on the third marriage have excellent marriage prospects this year. There's nothing that you need to do either – he or she will come to you.

Self-improvement

This is a year for higher education, foreign travel and gaining religious revelation. It is also a year for religious pilgrimage. Capricorns are definitely travelling more this year.

The importance of religious and philosophical revelation is often overlooked. Yet, it is vital in the way you live your life and the way that you interpret events. So, getting this area of life in order – which is what is happening now – is going to have many positive and healthy results.

Capricorns tend to be conservative and traditional about religion and philosophy. They tend to be comfortable in the traditions that they were brought up in and rarely question them. But this is a period where these practices need to be reviewed. Sure, the tradition you were brought up in no doubt has the truth buried somewhere, but you need to reach this, understand this in a deeper way and fluff off some of the human accretions. You need to separate the purity of your tradition from what has been put on it by humans and their distortions. This will give you a new respect for your tradition.

We wrote earlier about the spiritual dimension of wealth. This needs a deeper discussion. You Capricorns pride yourself on your business acumen and management ability, and you should – this is your purpose here on Earth, to help the rest of us get more organized. But in many cases you tend to feel that it is your financial skill that led you to success – your planning, your organizational skills and your judgement. From the spiritual perspective, this is an obstruction. Wealth comes only from the Divine as spiritual precipitation. This spiritual substance, which descends into the mind and astral bodies, is intelligent substance. It forms itself into the things and objects that we consider wealth – the money, the bank accounts, the cars and homes. The spiritual substance is the essence of wealth; the thing is only the side effect. What happens is that too much plotting, scheming, organizing and manipulating blocks the flow of this spiritual substance. It has no entry point, and therefore so-called financial problems develop. In stillness and quiet, when the mind is poised and at rest, the spiritual substance has easy entry and the so-called financial problem is solved. Thus if financial problems arise in the year ahead, first get connected to the source – get quiet and let the source handle things. It will.

This approach to wealth is counter-intuitive. We think that it is our own efforts that make wealth happen. But in the spiritual approach, the less effort produces the greater wealth. Not doing is more powerful than doing. Of course, don't think that actions are now unnecessary. Actions will happen but they happen more as follow through than as causes. Actions are not the cause of wealth – spirit is.

Actions merely make manifest what has already happened on another level.

This is a hard lesson for cool, matter-of-fact Capricorn. But if you learn it, you will be richer than ever before.

Month-by-month Forecasts

January

Best Days Overall: 6, 14, 15, 23, 24
Most Stressful Days Overall: 3, 4, 10, 11, 16, 17, 30, 31
Best Days for Love: 5, 6, 9, 10, 11, 14, 15, 18, 19, 25, 26, 27, 28, 29
Best Days for Money: 1, 2, 7, 10, 11, 16, 18, 19, 25, 26, 27, 28, 29
Best Days for Career: 9, 10, 16, 17, 18, 19, 28, 29

You begin your year with 80 (and sometimes 90) per cent of the planets in the independent Eastern sector of the Horoscope. So now and for several months to come you are in a period of independence and great personal creative power. You can and should have things your way. Your way is best for you. You realize that no one can make you happy but yourself. You are learning that happiness is merely a 'choice' that you make – an election. Your personal initiative, your personal choices, your power to create conditions as you like them will either create great happiness (if your choices are wise) or suffering (if your choices are unwise). Your main challenge this month, and in the months to come, is discerning the right choices. Saturn, your personal planet, is Retrograde and this tends to confusion or lack of direction. So give more study to your personal goals. Create the obvious things that will make you happy, and give more thought to the less obvious.

This is a great month for getting the body and image in shape. Your image is unusually important these days as your ruling planet, Saturn, is the handle of a bucket-type chart (now and for many months to come). Through a good image, a good appearance and personal self-confidence, you lift up the entire 'bucket' – all the affairs of your life.

You are also right in the middle of a yearly personal pleasure peak. So this is a fun month as well.

On the 5th Jupiter is moving into your money house, signalling a very prosperous year ahead. On the 19th you enter a yearly (and for many of you a lifetime) financial peak. Financial intuition is super and if you follow it, wealth will come naturally and with less effort than usual. Sure, you will make the physical motions, but these will be more in the nature of follow through actions rather than causes.

The Solar Eclipse of the 26th is also announcing a year of prosperity. Though eclipses can be painful and disruptive, this one seems disruptive in a happy way. Your financial picture is so bright, so much better than you planned, that you are forced to change your strategy, thinking and investments. It is akin to someone with a humdrum day job suddenly winning the lottery – the good that comes radically changes the way he or she thinks about money, and changes all financial plans. Your spouse, partner or current love is also making major and dramatic financial changes. This eclipse will also impact on debt, tax and estate issues; they take a dramatic turn one way or another.

There are also going to be long-term, major changes in spiritual attitudes, practice and regime thanks to, it seems to me, happy things – interior revelation and breakthroughs. (It is normal for spiritual practice to change. Something that was right at one stage is not right at a more advanced stage.)

February

> Best Days Overall: 2, 3, 10, 11, 19, 20, 21
> Most Stressful Days Overall: 1, 6, 7, 12, 13, 27, 28
> Best Days for Love: 4, 5, 6, 7, 8, 9, 12, 13, 17, 18, 24, 25, 27, 28
> Best Days for Money: 4, 5, 6, 7, 12, 13, 15, 16, 22, 23, 24, 25, 26
> Best Days for Career: 8, 9, 12, 13, 17, 18, 27, 28

Your year began with most of the planets below the horizon. You are in the night-time of your year. Career issues can be downplayed for a while. You will never lose your outer ambitions – unthinkable for most Capricorns – but you will approach them in a different way, not through overt, direct action, but through inner means – visualizing, dreaming, setting goals, putting your intention out there in the universe. Now is the time to gather your inner forces for career success later on in the year. (The year will end up being a banner career year.) However, now is the time to focus on finding and living in your point of emotional harmony, and to get the family and home life in right order. And, in fact, this is your spiritual mission for the month ahead. Your bosses and superiors seem to understand this and are supporting your domestic and family goals. It seems to be that many of you are doing more work from home too.

There is another eclipse this month: a Lunar Eclipse on the 9th. It occurs in your 8th House and once again shows dramatic financial changes for your spouse, partner or current love. Probably there are dramatic events in the lives of your investors or creditors too. As with the last eclipse, this one will be a turning point in issues involving taxes, estates and debt. If you are involved with insurance claims, these too start to move forward now.

There was a strong 8th House connection with both last month's eclipse and this month's. On a psychological level it often shows a need to confront death in some way. There is a need to understand it better and get rid of fears or false ideas associated with it. So there can be dreams of death, or near-death experiences, brushes with it, etc. Death is merely change – and a dream of death is merely showing this. Sometimes the dark angel sends us a kindly reminder that life, here on earth, is short and that we need to be about our true business – doing the mission we were sent here to do.

You are still in the midst of a yearly (and perhaps lifetime) financial peak. Assets you own increase in value. Financial judgement – always sharp – is even sharper. The financial intuition is going at full speed. Family members, siblings, and spiritual-type people are supporting your financial goals. There is financial guidance in dreams or through seers, mystics, spiritual channels and astrologers. There is good family support now. Most importantly, the entire invisible Universe – the true ruler of the world – is active on your financial behalf. Go forward to your financial goals with confidence.

Love is not a big issue this month and this area seems status quo. The Lunar Eclipse of the 9th will test a current relationship, so be more patient with your spouse, partner or current love now.

March

Best Days Overall: 1, 2, 10, 19, 20, 28, 29
Most Stressful Days Overall: 5, 6, 12, 13, 26, 27
Best Days for Love: 5, 6, 7, 8, 14, 15, 16, 17, 18, 24, 25, 26, 27
Best Days for Money: 3, 4, 5, 6, 12, 13, 14, 15, 21, 22, 23, 24, 25, 30, 31
Best Days for Career: 7, 8, 12, 13, 16, 17, 18, 26, 27

You have three major interests this month and all seem equally powerful. Finance, of course, has been important all year and is still important this month, though the focus is less intense than in the past two months. Communication and intellectual interests were important last month and are still important in the month ahead. They are not only interesting in their own right, but also have major bottom-line benefits – the more educated you are, the more knowledgeable, the greater your earning power. Also (and this has been the case for some years now) your marketing ability – your ability to use the media properly to get the word out about your product or service – is essential to profits. Home and family were important last month, and are even more important in the month ahead.

At least 80 per cent of the planets (and sometimes even 90 per cent) are below the horizon, and your 4th House of Home and Family is strong. Your 10th House of Career, by contrast, is empty – only the Moon will visit there on the 12th and 13th. Moreover your career planet makes a rare (once in two years) Retrograde movement, beginning on the 6th. Thus career issues are more or less on hold right now. It is a time for an inner review of your career and objectives and not a time for acting on your plans. So, you may as well focus on your home and family. (Aside from all this, like last month, your home and family is actually your spiritual mission for the month ahead – they are the purpose of the whole month.)

Finances are still excellent. Like last month you are spending more on the home and family, and perhaps earning through these things as well – through family support, or family connections or the family business. Real estate investments also seem interesting.

Health is excellent most of the month, but try to rest and relax more after the 20th. Long term, health is good, but after the 20th your energy is not up to its usual standards. You can enhance your health by giving more attention to the ankles (until the 8th – give them more support when exercising and massage them regularly), the feet (from the 8th to the 25th – wear comfortable shoes and massage the feet regularly), and the head and face from the 25th onwards. Regular scalp and face massage will be powerful after the 25th. Vigorous physical exercise is also good.

Love is more or less status quo this month. But love issues will go better from the 1st to the 11th and from the 26th onwards. This is when the Moon is waxing, and thus you have more enthusiasm for these things.

April

Best Days Overall: 6, 7, 15, 16, 25, 26
Most Stressful Days Overall: 2, 3, 8, 9, 22, 23, 29, 30
Best Days for Love: 2, 3, 4, 5, 13, 14, 20, 21, 25, 26, 29, 30
Best Days for Money: 2, 3, 8, 9, 10, 11, 18, 19, 20, 21, 27, 28, 29, 30
Best Days for Career: 4, 8, 9, 20, 21

Your 4th House of Home and Family has been strong for the past two months, and this month it gets even stronger – a huge 60 per cent of the planets are either there or moving through there in the month ahead. The trends we wrote of last month are still very much in effect. Renovations are very likely this month too. You are spending on the home and family and perhaps earning from these areas as well, just as we saw last month. Like last month, home and family is the actual purpose – the spiritual mission – for the month ahead. From the spiritual perspective this goes even deeper. It's not just family; it's the maintenance of 'right inner state' – a state of emotional harmony and peace. (By the way, lack of emotional harmony is the number one reason why prayers are not answered or are delayed, so this has big implications for you.) When you find yourself angry, irritated or upset about the normal ups and downs of family life, take a deep breath, let go of the feeling, and get back into right state as fast as you can.

This is a month for inner psychological progress, for deeper insights into this area of life. This will stand you in good stead later on when you start to focus on your career again.

Your career planet is moving forwards again on the 17th, and this brings clarity to career issues. But still, it is not yet time to be acting directly in career issues. It remains a time for visualizing, setting goals and setting the stage inwardly for future career success. The good news is that you know what you should visualize.

Financial life is also most interesting. Jupiter and Neptune make a very rare (a once in 12 to 14 years) conjunction in your money house. Keep in mind that these are the two most spiritual planets in your Horoscope. So, you will learn that wealth really does come from above – it is the blessing of the Divine and not your personal intelligence, physical labour or business savvy that causes wealth. And you have this blessing in great abundance. (More is coming later on the year when these two planets once again go conjunct.) Your financial intuition is just super and is leading you to big profits. There is also going to be interior revelation on the spiritual dimensions of wealth.

Health still needs watching all month, but especially until the 19th. Enhance your health by giving more attention to the head and face until the 9th. Regular scalp and facial massage will be powerful. Physical exercise is also important – the muscles need to be kept in tone. Cranial sacral therapy will be powerful before the 9th as well. After the 9th give more attention to the neck and throat. Neck massage will be powerful. It will also be good to be in environments where the earth energy is strong – mountains, old forests (the older the better) and caves. Soaking in natural mineral springs will pick you up if you feel under the weather. Surgery is being suggested as a solution to a health problem – around the 21st to the 24th – but as always, get second opinions. Many of you are thinking of cosmetic surgery too.

Love will go better from the 1st to the 9th and from the 25th onwards. This is when the Moon is waxing and thus giving you more enthusiasm for love. But love seems mostly status quo this month.

May

>   Best Days Overall: 3, 4, 12, 13, 14, 22, 23, 30, 31
>   Most Stressful Days Overall: 5, 6, 20, 21, 26, 27
>   Best Days for Love: 1, 2, 3, 4, 10, 11, 12, 13, 14, 20, 21,
>   24, 25, 26, 27, 28, 29
>   Best Days for Money: 5, 6, 8, 9, 15, 16, 18, 19, 24, 25, 26,
>   27
>   Best Days for Career: 1, 2, 5, 6, 10, 11, 20, 21, 28, 29

Home and family issues have quieten down some since last month, but are still an important focus. With your career planet still in your 4th House it is still your spiritual mission this month. You are here for the family – to be there for them. And, as we mentioned last month, your spiritual development depends on your ability to hold harmony in your feeling body.

Like last month, we see renovations or makeovers of the home this month.

On April 19th you entered a yearly personal pleasure peak; this is still in full swing in the month ahead, until the 20th. You Capricorns can definitely get too serious about things. Pessimism is one of your fatal flaws. So this is a month to explore the fun side of life. Life is not all work-work-work or duty-duty-duty. Life is to be enjoyed to the full. In fact, the mystics of all the ages testify that the essence of life is joy itself. That pessimism is merely a disconnection from real life. So this is a month to put the smile back on your face and the bounce in your step.

For singles this is a period for love affairs – at least, non-serious flirtations and the like. These things have their place too. Sexual activity seems on the increase; it is 'recreational' sex rather than what we would call romantic sex.

There is a focus on children and a better ability to get on with them. You are more childlike yourself and this is a big help. (It is said that it is the child in us that experiences joy, the adult is almost incapable of real joy.)

Enjoy your party while it lasts, for come the 20th you are back in your serious work-oriented mode.

Your financial intuition is still marvellous for most of the month. It is your path to riches. The inner guidance, the guidance that comes from seers, intuitives, astrologers and spiritual channels are all leading to increased wealth. Finances are good, but it's not a smooth road – there are challenges, but you will get through them. None of the challenges are long term. Debt and perhaps tax issues weigh on you and influence your financial decisions. Your partner might looks askance at some of your moves (financially you march to a different drummer now) and this could create conflict. This is all part of the adventure; when you succeed in your moves, they will pipe down. On the 26th Neptune will start to go Retrograde. Thus you need confirmation of your intuitions.

June

Best Days Overall: 9, 10, 19, 27, 28
Most Stressful Days Overall: 2, 3, 16, 17, 23, 29, 30
Best Days for Love: 2, 3, 9, 11, 12, 13, 19, 21, 22, 23, 27, 28, 29, 30
Best Days for Money: 2, 3, 4, 5, 11, 12, 13, 14, 15, 21, 22, 23, 29, 30
Best Days for Career: 2, 3, 9, 19, 27, 28, 29, 30

There is some drama – a surgery or near-death experience, perhaps a brush with the dark angel – in the lives of friends from the 20th to the 24th. There is some shakeup in an organization that you belong to.

Health is improved over last month, but rest and relax more after the 21st. Enhance your health by giving more attention to the heart (after the 21st), the neck and throat (until the 14th), and to the arms, shoulders and lungs (after the 14th). Neck massage is powerful until the 14th. After the 14th arm and shoulder massage is powerful. Air purity is more important after the 14th as well. Detox regimes are wonderful until the 21st. Good health is not about adding things – substances – to the body, but about getting rid of things that shouldn't be there.

The good news is that health is an important focus. You are paying attention. You are open to healthy lifestyles, diet and health regimes.

Though you are working hard this month – your always powerful work ethic reasserts itself – you are (or should be) having fun as well. Leisure activities will be wonderful for the family too. Spend more time entertaining them.

Singles still seem involved in fun and games types of relationships most of the month. After the 21st there will be opportunities for more serious kinds of things, as you enter a yearly social and romantic peak then. Sexual magnetism seems the most important and alluring factor this period. If there are other harmonies present, these relationships have the potential for longer duration. If it is only sex, the life span is generally six to eight months.

Your spouse, partner or current love is prospering greatly from the 21st onwards. He or she has some nice financial windfall or opportunity and will be spending on the self – on the wardrobe and image. Financial opportunities (good ones) are pursuing your partner, and He or she is likely to be more generous with you. You and the beloved have a financial disagreement from the 15th to the 19th, but it passes quickly. A tax issue could stress you that period too.

The spiritual mission has been the family for some months, but this is soon to change. On the 6th the mission becomes the children and, on a deeper level, to learn to enjoy life – to have fun even as you are working hard and handling your responsibilities.

July

Best Days Overall: 6, 7, 16, 17, 24, 25
Most Stressful Days Overall: 14, 15, 20, 21, 26, 27
Best Days for Love: 1, 2, 9, 11, 12, 18, 19, 20, 21, 22, 26, 27, 31
Best Days for Money: 1, 2, 9, 10, 11, 12, 18, 19, 20, 21, 26, 27, 29, 30
Best Days for Career: 9, 18, 19, 26, 27

Your yearly social peak continues this month. But two eclipses are going to test existing relationships, friendships, the marriage and business partnerships.

Both of these eclipses are strong on you, so reduce your schedule. You should be taking it easy until the 21st anyway, but especially so during the eclipse periods for a few days before and a few days after. My experience has been that the cosmos itself will announce – if we are alert and open – when the eclipse period is beginning. Something weird, strange and out of the ordinary will happen. You will read of some strange happening or grisly kind of crime in the newspapers, or perhaps as you're driving you see a strange accident. These are announcements that its time to slow down and hunker down. (By the way, these announcements can come a few days before the eclipse, even a couple of weeks before. It is all case by case, but when you get the announcement take heed.)

The Lunar Eclipse of the 7th occurs in your own Sign and brings changes of the image and a redefinition of the personality. Perhaps you are being slandered or misrepresented, being accused of being something that you're not. You need to clearly define who you are to yourself or others will do it for you, and that probably won't be so pleasant. Since your Moon, the love planet, is eclipsed, relationships are being tested. Sometimes there is a detox of the body happening, especially if you haven't been careful in dietary matters.

The Solar Eclipse of the 22nd occurs on the border of your 7th and 8th Houses, and so affects the affairs of both these Houses. If you are born late in the Sign of Capricorn – from January 15 to 19 – this eclipse will be especially powerful on you. This again tests relationships, partnerships, marriages and even friendships. It brings important changes in your spouse's or partner's finances – changes in thinking, strategy, investments and the like. Since the 8th House is so involved here, perhaps you are confronting death on a psychological level: having dreams about it or confronting it in other ways. This is a kind of inner housecleaning, clearing out phobias and misperceptions about death. Fear of death is perhaps the main blockage to success and happiness in life.

The financial changes that your spouse, partner or current love is making seem positive and will enhance overall earnings. He or she is having a banner financial month.

Though love is being tested, singles still have many opportunities. There are love opportunities at work, at school, or with those involved with your health and education.

August

Best Days Overall: 2, 3, 4, 12, 13, 21, 30, 31
Most Stressful Days Overall: 10, 11, 16, 17, 23, 24
Best Days for Love: 1, 7, 8, 9, 10, 11, 16, 17, 19, 20, 25, 26, 30, 31
Best Days for Money: 5, 6, 7, 8, 9, 14, 15, 16, 17, 23, 24, 25, 26
Best Days for Career: 7, 8, 9, 16, 17, 23, 24, 25, 26

Another Lunar Eclipse on the 6th once again tests love relationships, marriages and business partnerships. This is a relentless and highly unusual barrage on this one area of life. Nothing but the best will do for you as far as love is concerned, and so any little flaw is being flushed out for correction. Relationships that couldn't take the stress of three eclipses will probably not survive. Only something very solid, based on real love, and which is ordained by the spirit, will survive.

This particular eclipse occurs in your money house and brings personal financial changes in your life. The last two impacted more on the earnings of your spouse or partner; this one is more personal to you. But prosperity is wonderful this year, and this eclipse should be read as a good thing. Even your high financial plans were probably not high enough – and so you need to change your strategy and planning. An eclipse in the money house generally brings some kind of disruption that forces the change – a sudden expense, a sudden turn of financial events, a sudden huge profit or windfall (and these can be just as disruptive as the difficult events), a sudden turn of macro-economic factors (events in the stock market, interest rate changes and the like). All the planets involved with finance are Retrograde this month, so better to plan the new changes rather than execute them right away. Perhaps there is a delayed financial reaction to this eclipse.

Your spouse, partner or current love is still prospering this month and is in a yearly financial peak. Though love is being severely tested, sexual activity seems on the increase. Singles have romantic opportunities with old flames from the past and through family connections. You seem more aggressive in love after 24th too. Children of marriageable age find love during this period.

Health is improved this month. This is another great period for detox regimes of all sorts (the whole year is good for that, but most especially now), and very good for losing weight if you need to. All these activities have the momentum of the cosmos behind them and are thus more likely to succeed. You can enhance your already good health by giving more attention to the heart (until the 2nd), and to the small intestine after that date. Diet seems more of an issue health-wise as well.

On the 22nd, your 9th House becomes strong and this brings – on the mundane level – happy travel and educational opportunities. It is a good transit for students and they are likely to hear good news about college or university this period. On a spiritual level, this transit brings religious and philosophical breakthroughs, enlarged mental horizons, optimism (a side effect of enlarged horizons), and a great interest in religious and metaphysical studies – the study of scripture or other sacred literature.

September

Best Days Overall: 8, 9, 17, 18, 26, 27
Most Stressful Days Overall: 6, 7, 13, 14, 19, 20
Best Days for Love: 6, 7, 8, 9, 13, 14, 15, 16, 17, 18, 26, 27, 28, 29
Best Days for Money: 1, 2, 4, 5, 11, 12, 13, 14, 19, 20, 21, 22, 28, 29, 30
Best Days for Career: 8, 9, 13, 14, 17, 18, 28, 29

A financial disagreement with your spouse, partner or current love causes some distress from the 16th to the 18th. This could also involve taxes, but things will straighten out in the end. Your spouse or partner is forced to make some dramatic financial changes.

It is still good to be focused on your career and outer goals. Most of the planets are still above the horizon and your 10th House of Career gets powerful on the 22nd. In fact, on the 22nd you enter a yearly career peak. You can serve your family best by succeeding in the outer world.

Your 9th House of Foreign Travel, Higher Education, Religion and Metaphysics is still very strong this month. This is the cosmic preparation for the career success that is happening later on. It's a good time to take the courses that you need to take to enhance your career, and to enlarge your mind and mental horizons. The urge to travel is very strong this month, but keep in mind that the two planets that rule travel in your Horoscope – Jupiter (the generic ruler) and Mercury (the actual ruler) – are Retrograde this month. Mercury is Retrograde from the 7th to the 29th. Jupiter is Retrograde all month. Better to plan your trip from the 7th to the 29th – research the fares, itinerary, prices, lodgings and all the myriads of details that go into a trip –

and actually make the trip next month. If you must travel this period – you can't always just stop your life because of Retrogrades – try to protect yourself as best you can. Allow more time for getting to your destination, make sure you have all the paperwork that you need, avoid scheduling connecting flights too closely and pay a little extra so that you can make changes in your ticket.

A house cleaning is going on in your religious and philosophical life – everyone has one, even the most hardened materialist (materialism itself is a philosophical perspective). Thus many of your cherished beliefs will get challenged, either by others or by events that happen in your life. Beliefs or perspectives that are semi or half true will go. And this is good. We can't avoid having belief systems – this is human nature – but we can ensure that the ones we have are congruent to reality. And this is what is happening in the month ahead. Your new perspective on life will help you career-wise, and on a spiritual level it will help you achieve your mission.

Mars in your 7th House shows power struggles going on in love. A parent, parent figure or elder is meddling in the love life, probably from good motives. An old flame from the past is back in the picture and you are resolving old feelings. Family members are playing cupid (consciously or unconsciously).

Health is good this month, but rest and relax more after the 22nd. Enhance your health by giving more attention to the kidneys and hips (until the 18th) and to the small intestine after the 18th. Give more attention to the heart after the 22nd.

October

Best Days Overall: 6, 7, 14, 15, 23, 24
Most Stressful Days Overall: 3, 4, 10, 11, 16, 17, 31
Best Days for Love: 6, 7, 8, 9, 10, 11, 15, 16, 17, 18, 26, 27, 28, 29
Best Days for Money: 1, 2, 8, 9, 10, 11, 16, 17, 19, 20, 26, 27, 28, 29
Best Days for Career: 6, 7, 15, 16, 17, 26, 27

The two planets that rule foreign travel in your chart are moving forward this month. Mercury is forward all month and Jupiter starts to move forward on the 18th. Make those trips – if possible – after the 18th.

Your yearly career peak is now in full swing. This is not just a yearly career peak either. In many cases it is a lifetime peak. For, on the 29th, Saturn, your ruling planet, moves out of Virgo, your 9th House and crosses your Midheaven. It will be in your 10th House for the next two and a half years. You are not only succeeding in your career, getting promotions and pay rises and more responsibility, but you are being honoured and appreciated for who you are (not just for what you have achieved). You are on top now – king of the hill. You are higher in status than anyone in your world, including your spouse, partner, current love or family members. You are in power now, as they say. Exalted. No question that this is Capricorn heaven.

With added power comes responsibility. Anyone who attains power and authority and thinks that he or she can act capriciously will soon be disabused of this fact. Abuse of power will bring harsh consequences. But you Capricorns pretty much understand this, and over the coming years will see this even more. Being powerless is a problem to be sure, but having power brings other problems.

There is a cosmic detox going on in your career – in your industry or company. Those of you who are elevated into positions of power might have to make some drastic changes and rearrangements. In some cases, the rearrangements are clearing the way for your rise. You are getting rid of excess baggage career-wise: wrong attitudes, mental or emotional patterns and the like. (There are dramas in the lives of parents or parent figures too.) Children of appropriate age are also succeeding this month. They seem ambitious and motivated.

Finances are much improved this month. But there is still a need to go slow and steady here and do your homework on all financial dealings. You are still in a period for financial review. Earnings are happening but with minor glitches and annoyances (a payment comes late, or the cheque is so damaged in the post that it can't be cashed – things of this nature).

Financial intuition still needs verification. Your intuition hasn't stopped, but the way that you interpret that intuition could be amiss.

Romantic opportunities are still coming from family, family connections or those who are like family to you.

Health needs more watching for the rest of the year, but especially until the 23rd. Give more attention to the heart, small intestine, kidneys and hips.

November

> Best Days Overall: 2, 3, 10, 11, 20, 21, 25, 29, 30
> Most Stressful Days Overall: 1, 6, 7, 13, 14, 27, 28
> Best Days for Love: 4, 5, 6, 7, 15, 16, 25, 26, 27, 28
> Best Days for Money: 4, 5, 6, 7, 13, 14, 15, 16, 22, 23, 25, 26
> Best Days for Career: 4, 5, 13, 14, 15, 16, 25, 26

Little by little, the financial judgement and finances in general are straightening out. Jupiter went forward in your money house on the 18th of last month. Neptune, in your money house, will go forward on the 4th. Uranus, your financial planet, will move forward next month. So, long-delayed financial projects are starting to move forward now. There are still many details that need to be ironed out, this will probably happen next month, but things are in motion.

Last month the planetary powers made a major shift from the Western, social sector, to the Eastern sector. By the 29th, 80 per cent of the planets were in the independent East. And this is the situation this month. You no longer have to adapt to situations and conditions but have the power to change them to your liking. Other people are always important, but your way is the best way for you. You, yourself are the road to happiness. Your personal initiative will lead to success. Others may or may not like you or approve, but no matter; eventually they will come around to your point of view. Create your world now – and create wisely. Your will is the law in your world, and all the heavenly choirs will say 'amen'.

Career is still important this month, and it will be for many years to come. But now there is more focus on social activities. Not romantic ones – more about friendships, group activities and platonic kinds of relationships. In fact, being there for your friends, being active and supportive in various organizations, is your spiritual mission this month.

Health is improved over last month, but still needs watching. Being on top is a heady feeling, but it is stressful. Give more attention to the heart (all month); the colon, bladder and sexual organs (until the 16th); and to the liver and thighs (after the 16th). Detox regimes have been good for you all year, but they seem especially good until the 16th. You are in a sexually active period (even older Capricorns will have more libido than usual) and sexual excess can impact on the health, especially until the 16th. Indulge but listen to the body.

Love seems more or less status quo. It is not a big issue in your Horoscope. In general, your social magnetism will be strongest on the 1st and 2nd and from the 16th onwards.

Spirituality becomes an important interest after the 22nd. The challenge will be to integrate your worldly ambitions with your spiritual interests. In the world we are out there, active, competing, etc. In the spiritual life, we are inwardly quiet, withdrawn from the worldly mind and worldly concerns, still and receptive. In the world we are 'getting';

spiritually we are giving. There is no one way to integrate these urges, but you can shift some energy to charitable and altruistic activities now.

December

>   Best Days Overall: 8, 9, 17, 18, 27, 28
>   Most Stressful Days Overall: 4, 10, 11, 24, 25, 26, 31
>   Best Days for Love: 3, 4, 6, 7, 15, 16, 26, 27, 28, 31
>   Best Days for Money: 2, 4, 5, 10, 11, 13, 14, 19, 20, 21,
>   22, 23, 31
>   Best Days for Career: 6, 7, 10, 11, 15, 16, 26, 27

It is hard for hard-headed, hard-boiled, bottom line-oriented Capricorn to understand the practicality of the spiritual interests or spiritual path. But this month (and you've had other experiences in the past year as well) the spiritual doors open and you see its intense practicality – from a health and financial perspective especially. It is not just about sitting around doing nothing and staring at your navel. It is about connecting to the Master Intelligence of all life. And this connection leads, in practical ways, to health and wealth.

Your 12th House is powerful, even more than last month. Further, Jupiter and Neptune once again go conjunct (the next time this happens will be in 12 to 15 years' time). The cosmos has decreed that it will do whatever it takes to convince you of the reality of spirit. If it takes a few miracles or supernatural experiences, so be it. You are tough, but the cosmos is tougher. It is a month for spiritual revelation, whether you want it or not, and each one of you will have experience it in your own way. Many of you will have 'Paul on the road to Damascus' type experiences. Siblings, and those involved in your finances, are also having these kinds of experiences. It is a very interesting month.

Like last month, it is a good period for going on spiritual retreats or pilgrimages. Good for getting involved in charities and altruistic activities.

Health is good this month. You get new insights into spiritual healing until the 5th (and this could have happened last month too). You can enhance your good health even further by giving more attention to the heart (all month), the liver and thighs (until the 5th) and to the spine, knees, teeth, bones and skeletal alignment (from the 5th onwards).

On the 21st you enter a yearly personal pleasure peak. This one seems much stronger than those you've already had this year or in previous years. You are wealthier and more able to afford more exotic kinds of pleasures. Personal appearance is better than usual and the opposite sex takes notice. Jobseekers have job opportunities pursuing them. The same is true for those who employ others – the right employees are coming to you.

This is another especially good month to lose weight and get the personal image in shape. Detox is also excellent.

Wealth is greatly increased through intuition, which is once again 'spot on', trustworthy and reliable, and through interior revelation. It's as if a light is turned on in your financial affairs and you see clearly what needs to be done and the state of affairs. No guessing or surmising. The right moves are clearly seen.

Aquarius

~~~

Personality Profile

AQUARIUS AT A GLANCE

Element – Air

Ruling Planet – Uranus
  Career Planet – Pluto
  Love Planet – Venus
  Money Planet – Neptune
  Planet of Health and Work – Moon
  Planet of Home and Family Life – Venus

Colours – electric blue, grey, ultramarine blue

Colours that promote love, romance and social
  harmony – gold, orange

Colour that promotes earning power – aqua

Gems – black pearl, obsidian, opal, sapphire

Metal – lead

Scents – azalea, gardenia

Quality – fixed (= stability)

Qualities most needed for balance – warmth, feeling and emotion

Strongest virtues – great intellectual power, the ability to communicate and to form and understand abstract concepts, love for the new and avant-garde

Deepest needs – to know and to bring in the new

Characteristics to avoid – coldness, rebelliousness for its own sake, fixed ideas

Signs of greatest overall compatibility – Gemini, Libra

Signs of greatest overall incompatibility – Taurus, Leo, Scorpio

Sign most helpful to career – Scorpio

Sign most helpful for emotional support – Taurus

Sign most helpful financially – Pisces

Sign best for marriage and/or partnerships – Leo

Sign most helpful for creative projects – Gemini

Best Sign to have fun with – Gemini

Signs most helpful in spiritual matters – Libra, Capricorn

Best day of the week – Saturday

Understanding an Aquarius

In the Aquarius-born, intellectual faculties are perhaps the most highly developed of any Sign in the Zodiac. Aquarians are clear, scientific thinkers. They have the ability to think abstractly and to formulate laws, theories and clear concepts from masses of observed facts. Geminis might be very good at gathering information, but Aquarians take this a step further, excelling at interpreting the information gathered.

Practical people – men and women of the world – mistakenly consider abstract thinking as impractical. It is true that the realm of abstract thought takes us out of the physical world, but the discoveries made in this realm generally end up having tremendous practical consequences. All real scientific inventions and breakthroughs come from this abstract realm.

Aquarians, more so than most, are ideally suited to explore these abstract dimensions. Those who have explored these regions know that there is little feeling or emotion there. In fact, emotions are a hindrance to functioning in these dimensions; thus Aquarians seem – at times – cold and emotionless to others. It is not that Aquarians haven't got feelings and deep emotions, it is just that too much feeling clouds their ability to think and invent. The concept of 'too much feeling' cannot be tolerated or even understood by some of the other Signs. Nevertheless, this Aquarian objectivity is ideal for science, communication and friendship.

Aquarians are very friendly people, but they do not make a big show about it. They do the right thing by their friends, even if sometimes they do it without passion or excitement.

Aquarians have a deep passion for clear thinking. Second in importance, but related, is their passion for breaking with the establishment and traditional authority. Aquarians delight in this, because for them rebellion is like a great game or challenge. Very often they will rebel strictly for the fun of rebelling, regardless of whether the authority they defy is right or wrong. Right or wrong has little to do with the rebellious actions of an Aquarian, because to a true Aquarian authority and power must be challenged as a matter of principle.

Where Capricorn or Taurus will err on the side of tradition and the status quo, an Aquarian will err on the side of the new. Without this virtue it is doubtful whether any progress would be made in the world. The conservative-minded would obstruct progress. Originality and invention imply an ability to break barriers; every new discovery re-presents the toppling of an impediment to thought. Aquarians are very interested in breaking barriers and making walls tumble – scientifically, socially and politically. Other Zodiac Signs, such as Capricorn, also have scientific talents. But Aquarians are particularly excellent in the social sciences and humanities.

Finance

In financial matters Aquarians tend to be idealistic and humanitarian – to the point of self-sacrifice. They are usually generous contributors to social and political causes. When they contribute it differs from when a Capricorn or Taurus contributes. A Capricorn or Taurus may expect some favour or return for a gift; an Aquarian contributes selflessly.

Aquarians tend to be as cool and rational about money as they are about most things in life. Money is something they need and they set about acquiring it scientifically. No need for fuss; they get on with it in the most rational and scientific ways available.

Money to the Aquarian is especially nice for what it can do, not for the status it may bring (as is the case for other Signs). Aquarians are neither big spenders nor penny-pinchers and use their finances in practical ways, for example to facilitate progress for themselves, their families or even strangers.

However, if Aquarians want to reach their fullest financial potential they will have to explore their intuitive nature. If they follow only their financial theories – or what they believe to be theoretically correct – they may suffer some losses and disappointments. Instead, Aquarians should call on their intuition, which knows without thinking. For Aquarians, intuition is the short-cut to financial success.

Career and Public Image

Aquarians like to be perceived not only as the breakers of barriers but also as the transformers of society and the world. They long to be seen in this light and to play this role. They also look up to and respect other people in this position and even expect their superiors to act this way.

Aquarians prefer jobs that have a bit of idealism attached to them – careers with a philosophical basis. Aquarians need to be creative at work, to have access to new techniques and methods. They like to keep busy and enjoy getting down to business straightaway, without wasting any time. They are often the quickest workers and usually have suggestions for improvements that will benefit their employers. Aquarians are also very helpful with their co-workers and welcome responsibility, preferring this to having to take orders from others.

If Aquarians want to reach their highest career goals they have to develop more emotional sensitivity, depth of feeling and passion. They need to learn to narrow their focus on the essentials and concentrate more on the job in hand. Aquarians need 'a fire in the belly' – a consuming passion and desire – in order to rise to the very top. Once this passion exists they will succeed easily in whatever they attempt.

Love and Relationships

Aquarians are good at friendships, but a bit weak when it comes to love. Of course they fall in love, but their lovers always get the impression that they are more best friends than paramours.

Like Capricorns, they are cool customers. They are not prone to displays of passion or to outward demonstrations of their affections. In fact, they feel uncomfortable when their mate hugs and touches them too much. This does not mean that they do not love their partners. They do, only they show it in other ways. Curiously enough, in relationships they tend to attract the very things that they feel uncomfortable with. They seem to attract hot, passionate, romantic, demonstrative people. Perhaps they know instinctively that these people have qualities they lack and so seek them out. In any event, these relationships do seem to work, Aquarius' coolness calming the more passionate partner while the fires of passion warm the cold-blooded Aquarius.

The qualities Aquarians need to develop in their love life are warmth, generosity, passion and fun. Aquarians love relationships of the mind. Here they excel. If the intellectual factor is missing in a relationship an Aquarian will soon become bored or feel unfulfilled.

Home and Domestic Life

In family and domestic matters Aquarians can have a tendency to be too non-conformist, changeable and unstable. They are as willing to break the barriers of family constraints as they are those of other areas of life.

Even so, Aquarians are very sociable people. They like to have a nice home where they can entertain family and friends. Their house is usually decorated in a modern style and full of state-of-the-art appliances and gadgets – an environment Aquarians find absolutely necessary.

If their home life is to be healthy and fulfilling Aquarians need to inject it with a quality of stability – yes, even some conservatism. They need at least one area of life to be enduring and steady; this area is usually their home and family life.

Venus, the Planet of Love, rules the Aquarian's 4th Solar House of Home and Family as well, which means that when it comes to the family and child-rearing, theories, cool thinking and intellect are not always enough. Aquarians need to bring love into the equation in order to have a great domestic life.

Horoscope for 2009

Major Trends

You have been prospering for many years now and finances have been important, but this year you enter into a powerful two-year trend of prosperity. Earnings will be higher than in all recent years. More on this later.

Health has been good in recent years. And come October 29, as Saturn moves into a harmonious alignment with you, health and energy will get even better. You have all the energy you need to achieve whatever you want to achieve. More details below.

Saturn has been in your 8th House for two years now, and will continue there for most of the year ahead. Many of you have suffered deaths in recent years, perhaps in the family or with people close. There has been a spiritual need to understand death better and the cosmos has various means for doing this. Often no one has to actually die, but there are encounters with death, or one has dreams of death or near-death experiences; all of these serve the same ends. They force you to confront the unconfrontable and come to terms with it. This deepened your spiritual life in general and your spiritual understanding.

Towards the end of the year Saturn will move into Libra and your 9th House. This brings new tests, new challenges and new abilities. First off, as we mentioned, it makes a harmonious aspect to you – so health and energy will be good. Second, your religious and philosophical beliefs will undergo a testing. Pressure will be brought to bear on them to see which are real and enduring and which are not real or only partially real. There will be many tests of faith in the coming years, and these should be welcomed. It is in your interest to have a faith that works – that is workable in life.

University students will need to work harder after October 29. Studies are challenging – the discipline is hard – but hard work and persistent effort will pull you through.

Saturn doesn't care how smart you are (and you are smart); Saturn rewards the discipline and the persistence. Those applying to university or college have a more difficult time as well. But again, keep trying – don't give up.

Spirituality has been an important interest for many years now. Last year it was even more important and most of you have grown by leaps and bounds. You gained more under-standing in one year than most gain after many years. With Pluto now in your 12th House of Spirituality, the interest continues in the year ahead, and for many years to come. There is a need to detox the spiritual life, to remove impure attitudes and concepts about it, and this will be a long-term process. These impurities are blocking your progress and will need to go. And they will – Pluto is a genius at this sort of thing.

Your most important interests in the year ahead are the body, image and personal appearance; finance; the deeper things of life, sexuality, birth and death, past lives, debt and the repayment of debt, the prosperity of other people, taxes and estates; and spirituality.

Your paths of greatest fulfilment in the year ahead are the body, image and personal appearance; and spirituality (after July 27).

Health

(Please note that this is an astrological perspective on health and not a medical one. In days of yore there was no differ-ence, both of these perspectives were identical. But in these times there could be quite a difference. For the medical perspective, please consult your doctor or health profes-sional.)

Health (as we mentioned) is good this year, and will get even better after October 29. Those of you who have had health problems will experience miraculous sort of healings. And since your 6th House of Health is not strong, the message is that you sort of take your good health for granted. You don't overly focus on it because you have no need to.

However, you should understand that good though your health is, there will be periods in the year when your health and energy are not up to the usual standard. This is natural. These events come from the transits and are temporary. When the difficult transits pass, your naturally good health returns. We will deal with these issues in the monthly reports.

You can enhance your already good health by giving more attention to the ankles, stomach and breasts. Ankles should be regularly massaged and be given more support when exercising. Diet is always a factor in your health. This year, with Jupiter in your own Sign, the good life is calling to you. You are enjoying all the delights of the senses – good foods, good wines, gourmet restaurants (local and foreign). All of these things are there for you – the cosmos is granting you them – but if you overdo it, you will pay the price later on. Indulge and enjoy, but don't over-indulge. Also with these kinds of aspects, it will be more difficult to stay on your diet – the one your health professional or nutritionist recommends – and this can cause health problems.

Weight is more of an issue this year. The tendency is to gain under a Jupiter transit. So keep in mind the discussion above.

I have noted that pregnancy tends to happen under this aspect too.

There are many natural and drugless ways to strengthen the stomach and the breasts – diet, massage, reflexology (see our chart overleaf), acupuncture, acupressure, shiatsu, and yoga, just to name a few. I'm sure readers already know these things.

The Moon rules the emotional and domestic life (in a general way), so emotional health is a major factor in your physical health – the Moon is your health planet. Keep the emotions and moods constructive at all times. Avoid depression like the plague. Relations with family members are also important, and if health problems arise, see where the disharmony is with your family and bring it back into harmony as quickly as possible.

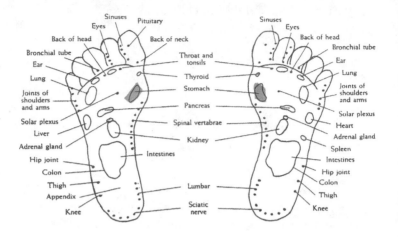

Reflexology

Try to massage the whole foot on a regular basis, but pay extra attention to the points highlighted on the chart. When you massage, be aware of 'sore spots', as these need special attention. It's also a good idea to massage the ankles and top side (as well as the soles) of the feet.

The Moon rules the astral body (the feeling-emotional body) and it is in this body that all the records of trauma or pain are stored (as is the record of all the good things). So the message here is that health problems can have their origin in the astral body – in the records of the past – and thus will need to be explored and cleansed if health problems arise.

On a deeper level, the Moon as your health planet is telling us that abuse of the emotional-feeling faculty is also a root cause of disease. Emotions can help and uplift others or be used to destroy. The destructive use of the emotions will cause pathologies in the physical body. This will need to be explored and corrected if health problems arise.

Your health planet gets eclipsed four times this year – twice as many times as usual. Since your health looks good, I read this as changes in the health regime, diet and practice. But sometimes these eclipses can bring on 'health scares', which turn out to be nothing in the end, but in the meantime they force changes in your health regime.

Home and Family

Your 4th House of Home and Family is not especially important in the year ahead. There are no long-term planets there and you seem satisfied with the status quo.

Jupiter in your own Sign will often show a move. Usually it is your personal desire, while the family will oppose it. You will be travelling a lot this year – probably to foreign countries – and so it will feel like you moved: you've changed your residence a few times.

A parent or parent figure seems ready for retirement. He or she wants to withdraw from the world, to be more in seclusion, and is in an intensely spiritual period. He or she doesn't want to retire from life, but to get closer to life – it's the world they want to retire from. In some cases this shows a move to a retirement or assisted living facility. In other cases it shows a move to a spiritual-type community.

If you are planning renovations or major construction work in the home (and this is a total free will decision on your part), May 31 to July 12 is a good time. If you want to beautify the home, or buy art objects for the home (or entertain from home), April 19 to May 20 and June 6 to July 5 are good times.

Siblings could have many domestic upheavals, repairs or moves in the year ahead as there are four eclipses to their family planet this year. If there are flaws in the home, they will be revealed by the eclipse. The same is true with their basic family relationships. Children of appropriate age probably want to move, but it doesn't seem advisable. There are many delays involved. They are better off making good use of the space they have. Things will get easier domestically after October 29. Grandchildren of appropriate age probably moved in the past year. This year they seem to be doing renovations or major repairs.

There are many short-term trends in the family life, as Venus, your family planet, moves very quickly. We will deal with these in the monthly reports.

Finance and Career

As we have mentioned, you are in a major prosperity cycle. This year is only the beginning. Next year will also be major.

It is good to understand the long-term trend as it is easier to make long-term financial decisions. Should I buy that expensive house? Should I make that major investment in my business? What if business is not good and I can't pay for it? Should I launch that (apparently) risky new product? Should I borrow to start a new business? All these decisions are based on the future prognosis – and your future is bright. Go forward with confidence.

The main headline financially is Jupiter's move into your own Sign. This enhances the financial judgement and enlarges your financial horizons. Generally there is luck in speculations, but the luck extends to other areas too: you make the sale when you needed to make it; the banker smiles at you when you apply for a loan; that stock that you thought was a dog starts to become a darling.

Generally there is much foreign travel, more of the jet set life, the good life, than usual. When Jupiter is in someone's Sign, how much actual money they have is irrelevant; they will live 'as if' they were wealthy.

For many years now, you have been investing in yourself. You have been projecting an image of wealth – dressing expensively, having your hair done in expensive salons, wearing expensive jewellery or accessories – and this year the trend gets even stronger. Perhaps in past years you appeared simply 'rich'. Now you appear 'super rich'.

You always like to dress in a high-tech way. High-tech gadgets are almost like fashion accessories to you, and this year the trend is even stronger.

Jupiter and Neptune are the two most spiritual, meta-physical planets in the Zodiac. Jupiter rules religion and metaphysics; Neptune rules spirituality and mystical experience. Both of these planets will be travelling together (and very closely) for most of the year. This indicates various things. It shows a fabulous, uncanny financial intuition – and if you trust it it will lead you to great riches in happy ways. And it shows an expansion of your understanding of the metaphysical and spiritual dimensions of wealth, which are often totally miraculous as they are independent of all physical and material conditions.

You have been aware of these spiritual dimensions all your life – Neptune is your financial planet. In the past five or six years (as your ruling planet Uranus moved into spiritual Pisces) the understanding was enlarged and expanded. This year the understanding is expanded even further. You will have many experiences with 'miracle money'.

On a more mundane, practical level, professional investors and those who have investment portfolios should continue to look at oil, natural gas, shipping, fishing, nursing homes and assisted living centres and high technology industries. The stocks and bonds of these companies seem interesting. This year you might also want to look at publishing, foreign stocks, airlines, long distance telecommunications and transport companies. You have an excellent intuition for these things.

Jobseekers seem to have many job changes in the year ahead or changes in the conditions at work. Those who employ others have instability with their employees – probably because of dramatic events in their lives.

There are changes in career ahead as well. Your career planet has moved into the spiritual 12th House and will be there for many years to come. Thus you are more idealistic about your career. It's not just about being successful and making money; it has to be something worthwhile, good for the planet, good for all, something that the Divine in you would be pleased with. In many cases, you will pursue a mundane career but be active in charitable and altruistic causes on the side. In fact, getting involved in these things – things that you deeply believe in – will actually further and enhance your mundane career. In many cases, and especially in the year ahead, you will actually opt for a spiritual-type career: ministry, full-time charity work, missionary work, or full-time devotion to some cause or pet undertaking. All of this is good and in line with your Horoscope.

Love and Social Life

This is not an especially strong or important love or social year, not on the romantic level anyway. Neither your 5th House of Love Affairs, nor your 7th House of Love and Marriage, is strong. It's not an issue of being attractive or desirable. It's about lack of interest. And, perhaps, this is as it should be. The cosmos is working to give us a well-rounded development, and some years it wants to focus on finance and career (as in your case) and some years on other things like spirituality and religion.

Of course the lack of power in these Houses doesn't mean the absence of a love life. Singles will date and have fun. Marrieds will still have a married life. But there is little significance to these things; it will be a status-quo kind of year.

Two Solar Eclipses will test your marriages, current love relationships and friendships – one on January 26 and the other on July 22. But these need not break things up, only bring up the dirty laundry – reveal the flaws in the relationship – so that corrections can happen. (Although, fundamentally flawed relationships tend to break up under these eclipses.)

Friendships are a whole other ball game. This is very prominent and happy area of your Horoscope in the year ahead. Jupiter, your planet of friendship, moves into your own Sign on January 5, so new and important friends are coming into the picture. They are prominent and of high status. They seem educated and refined. Perhaps religious. What is nice here is that they are seeking you out, rather than vice versa. There is nothing special that you need to do – just be yourself and go about your business. But these things don't seem romantic. These are people of like mind – platonic kinds of relationships.

Saturn has been in your 8th House of Sex for some years now, and continues there for the year ahead. The symbolism here is of being less sexually active than usual. This can come from a variety of causes – lack of libido, a need to control the sexual urges, a feeling that sexual activity is not safe, or, more likely, that you want to focus on quality sex, rather than mere quantity. And this seems the spiritual lesson in the year ahead.

This reduction of sexual activity reinforces what we have been saying earlier; this is not a strong romantic or love year.

On October 16 Mars enters your 7th House of Love and Marriage. He will stay there an unusually long time, for the rest of 2009 and well into 2010. For singles it only means being more aggressive socially. Perhaps you are fed up with sexual abstinence and want some adventure. Perhaps you want to develop more courage in love and you can only do that by taking risks.

For marrieds, especially those in the first marriage, it shows a testing of the marriage relationship. Perhaps there is a power struggle going on there. You should avoid these things as they tend to get overblown, but it will be difficult. Serious love relationships will also get these kinds of tests.

Those into their second marriage will have their marriages tested by Saturn after October 29. Those working on the second marriage are not likely to marry. Those working on the third marriage have better opportunities after October 29 than before. But those working on the fourth marriage have very beautiful aspects, and marriage or serious love is going to happen here.

The love life of siblings is status quo for most of the year, but after October 29 their marriages or current love relationship gets a severe and long-term testing.

Children and grandchildren of marriageable age have status quo kinds of years too. Singles will tend to stay single; marrieds will tend to stay married.

Your most active and happiest social periods this year will be from May 20 to June 21; July 5 to August 22; and from August 26 to September 20.

Self-improvement

Spirituality has been important for many years, but last year it was unusually important. Great spiritual progress was made. Meditation and spiritual practice was not a discipline or chore, but an actual joy and you looked forward to it. You made many spiritual types of friends and perhaps got involved in spiritual organizations. Your dream life, ESP gifts and prophetic gifts were greatly increased. Your life was probably more 'supernatural' than natural.

This year spirituality is perhaps even more important. Pluto moved into your spiritual 12th House towards the end of last year and will be there for many, many years to come. And since Pluto is your career planet, many of you are thinking of actually changing your career to something more spiritual, or to something that gives you more freedom to practise your spiritual path. This is good.

On a deeper level, your spiritual mission now – and for years to come – is to merely tread your spiritual path, to connect to the Divine in you. This is the most important thing. Once that is done, everything else – finances, love, family, career – will just fall into place. 'First seek ye the Kingdom of Heaven and it righteousness and all else will be added unto you' is very appropriate for you now.

For those more advanced on the path, the message here is to 'just do the yoga' – make your union. That in itself is the greatest service you can possibly render to others.

But for those just starting out, or on the intermediate levels, make your spiritual practice the number one priority in your life. Make it your 'career', and everything else that you need will magically come to you.

Earlier we talked about Saturn in your 8th House of Sex. It seems to me that there is another reason for the decreasing sexual activity: the importance of your spiritual life. It takes great power to hold a meditation for a long period, and this power comes from the sexual force. If it is dissipated in wasteful ways, you will lack the power to connect. Also, at certain stages of the path, when higher and finer bodies are being built, your being needs the sexual force to build these bodies. Celibacy and abstinence are not prerequisites for the path, but there are times when these things are called for and you could be in one of those times.

Month-by-month Forecasts

January

Best Days Overall: 8, 16, 17, 26, 27
Most Stressful Days Overall: 6, 12, 18, 19
Best Days for Love: 5, 6, 9, 10, 12, 13, 14, 15, 18, 19, 25, 26, 27, 28, 29
Best Days for Money: 1, 2, 7, 10, 11, 16, 18, 19, 25, 26, 28, 29
Best Days for Career: 5, 13, 18, 19, 23

Last year was a year of great inner, spiritual progress, a year of supernatural-type experiences and inner revelations. This continues in the month ahead as you are well into a yearly spiritual peak. It's as if you live on a different earth. Your life tends to flow like a beautiful ballet. When you need a parking spot in a crowded shopping centre, it's there. When you need money or some material thing, it just comes to you. Many of you are developing spiritual powers now too, things like levitation, astral travel, the power to precipitate and the like. But with your spiritual planet Retrograde until May, avoid judging these experiences or making dramatic changes to your regime. Just enjoy and observe. The meaning of these things will be seen later on.

You enter a yearly personal pleasure peak on the 19th, and this should be stronger than the ones you've had in previous years as Jupiter is now in your Sign. You have the wherewithal and the opportunity for greater pleasures – more expensive ones – than in the past. Good food, fine wine and sensual delight is a wonderful thing. But with Jupiter in your own Sign, you need to watch your weight.

You begin your year with between 80 and 90 per cent of the planets in the independent Eastern sector of your Horoscope. Thus you should be creating your personal Nirvana on Earth. You have the power, the resources, and the support of the cosmos backing you up. If your personal Nirvana is larger than life, you can still make forward progress towards it right now. Don't adapt, don't settle – have things your way. Your happiness is in your own hands and you are expected to create it. Others are less important than usual these days. They will adapt to you rather than vice versa.

The planets are making a very important shift this month, from the upper half of the Horoscope to the lower half. Thus it is night-time (sunset) in your personal year. For many months you have been focused on your career and outer goals and now it's time for a breather, a shift to more home-based and emotional considerations. This is the natural and beautiful rhythm of life – a breath from the outer to the inner and back. When you breathe in, the out breath will happen naturally. When you withdraw from the outer for a time, you won't lose it. The focus will reappear, even stronger, at the right time.

A Solar Eclipse on the 26th occurs in your own Sign and is strong on you. Take a reduced schedule a few days before and after. The cosmos will announce when you are in the eclipse period through strange and weird kinds of events, and this is the time to start taking it easy. This eclipse will bring a redefinition of the personality and the image (and no question it will be for the better), and will test your current relationship. Be more patient with the current love that period. Business partnerships will also get tested, and probably there are dramatic kinds of events in the lives of your spouse or partners.

February

> Best Days Overall: 4, 5, 12, 13, 22, 23
> Most Stressful Days Overall: 2, 3, 8, 9, 15, 16
> Best Days for Love: 4, 5, 8, 9, 12, 13, 17, 18, 24, 25, 27, 28
> Best Days for Money: 4, 5, 12, 13, 22, 23, 24, 25, 26
> Best Days for Career: 2, 10, 15, 16, 18

Another eclipse on the 9th – this time a Lunar Eclipse – again tests the current relationship and business partnerships. This one is also powerful on you, so do your best to reduce your schedule. Avoid risky or stressful activities. Elective types of things should be re-scheduled for another time. This eclipse will bring job changes and instability with those who work under you. There can be employee turnover now. Since your financial planet is impacted by this eclipse there are also dramatic financial changes. All these things will be for the better, but while it's going on it seems stressful, as much forced action has to be taken.

I've always wondered – and I'm sure readers have too – why such perfect creations as a snow flake or beautiful rose or sunset or sunrise has such a short duration. Beautiful and perfect though they seem to be, they die – and right quickly at that. Seems unjust doesn't it? But nothing less than perfection will do, and the cosmos is thus always 'restating' these creations in better and better ways. And this is the situation with you. Only the best will do for you and so different things in your life need a restatement on a better level.

You are still in the midst of a personal pleasure peak and, in spite of the eclipses, life is good. Social opportunities, both on a romantic and platonic level, are seeking you out. Friends and the current love are going way out of their way to please you. In the case of the current love, the question is whether it's enough to save the relationship? At least your beloved is trying.

When Jupiter moved into your sign on January 5, you began a cycle of great prosperity. This month, on the 18th, you enter a yearly financial peak. But you will have wind-falls and increased earnings even before that, especially from the 10th to the 14th. This period also brings windfalls and increased earnings to your spouse, partner or current love. He or she will be more generous with you too. There are opportunities for business partnerships or joint ventures all month. (If a current partnership ends, there are opportunities for new ones.)

Health is basically good this month, but the Lunar Eclipse of the 9th might bring changes to your health regime and diet. It can also bring a detox of the body, especially if you haven't been careful in dietary matters (and many of you have not been careful).

March

> Best Days Overall: 3, 4, 12, 13, 21, 22, 23, 30, 31
> Most Stressful Days Overall: 1, 2, 7, 8, 14, 15, 28, 29
> Best Days for Love: 5, 6, 7, 8, 14, 15, 16, 17, 18, 24, 25, 26, 27
> Best Days for Money: 3, 4, 12, 13, 21, 22, 23, 24, 25, 30, 31
> Best Days for Career: 1, 9, 14, 15, 19, 28

This is a very active and successful month, both on a personal and financial level. Nevertheless, with your spiritual planet, Saturn, being the handle of a bucket-type chart, it is your spirituality, your inner understanding of things, which will lift up your life, not the material success. So, you can't lose sight of this – very easy though it is to do when you are enjoying great success and have so many temptations.

Your yearly financial peak is still going on. Earnings are soaring. Marketing efforts, buying, selling and trading are all successful. A business partnership or joint venture is still very likely. The partner, spouse or current love is very supportive financially. Your social contacts – and your social skills in general – are boosting the bottom line.

Speculations seem favourable all month, but of course only indulge in these things under intuition.

Health is very good. You are enjoying the good life – all the delights of the senses. Sensual fantasies are now coming to pass. Mars in your own Sign gives extra energy and boosts athletic performance. Even non-athletes will perform better this month. With Mars in your Sign (until the 15th) watch the temper and the tendency to rush. These can lead to arguments, fights or accidents due to haste. When provoked take a deep breath and get into a meditative state before answering. Health in general is not a big issue this month and you don't seem concerned about it. Your 6th House of Health is basically empty; only the Moon visits there on the 5th and 6th. Thus you are not paying too much attention because you have no need to.

On the 20th your 3rd House of Communication and Intellectual Interests becomes important. You are natural strong in these areas and so this should be a happy period. Your already good communication skills and mind become even better and sharper. This is a good period for writers, teachers, journalists and marketing people – they should have a banner month.

With this being the night-time of your year and your focus being naturally drawn to the family and emotional issues, the rare Retrograde movement of Venus on the 6th has important implications. This is a time for review and analysis of the family situation but not a time for major decisions. Sure, you can shop for groceries and take care of the normal things, but the major, expensive purchases or decisions are best delayed until after the 17th of next month. Foreign journeys are better off rescheduled for next month as well.

April

Best Days Overall: 8, 9, 18, 19, 27, 28
Most Stressful Days Overall: 4, 5, 10, 11, 25, 26
Best Days for Love: 4, 5, 13, 14, 20, 21, 25, 26
Best Days for Money: 8, 9, 18, 19, 20, 21, 27, 28
Best Days for Career: 6, 10, 11, 15, 25

A very rare and powerful Jupiter/Neptune conjunction occurs this month. Although it starts this month – and you will feel it now – it becomes most exact next month. Generically these are the two most spiritual planets of the Horoscope. Jupiter rules religion and metaphysics and Neptune rules mysticism and inner spiritual experience. So this is bringing spiritual revelation to you of epic proportions. It will be most related to the body, the image and your sense of identity. In your chart this conjunction has many other meanings. It shows huge financial increase, both in your ability to visualize what you want, and in a bottom line, practical way. Earnings soar now. Your financial horizons are supernatural, infinite, rather than natural. It's as if you have the whole wealth of the cosmos at your disposal. Friends are prospering as well. And friends – social connections – might be the means through which this wealth comes to you. You are making friends with super-rich people as well. There is much progress in your understanding of the spiritual dimensions of wealth. Financial intuition is absolutely incredible right now. You can go to the bank with it.

Mars makes a conjunction with your ruling planet from the 12th to the 17th. While this gives energy and athletic ability, be aware of a tendency to take undue risks. You seem in the mood to test your physical limits, and it's best to do this in a very conscious way. Drive defensively that period. Activities like yoga or tai chi are safe ways to test your physical limits.

Your 3rd House of Communication and Intellectual Interests is even stronger than last month. So this is a time to teach or to learn. Students should do better at school as the mind is sharper and they have more of a zeal for learning. Sales and marketing people, traders, retailers, writers and teachers should also have a banner month. Now is the time to take courses in subjects that interest you or to teach others what you know. Good to catch up on those letters, e-mails and phone calls that you owe.

Your 4th House of Home and Family becomes very powerful on the 19th, and this will sharpen your focus here even more. This is the midnight period of your year. A time for inner, psychological progress rather than for outer progress. You are gathering your energies for career success later on in the year. Clarity about home and family issues comes on the 17th and the timing is excellent. You are now more in a position to make those important family decisions.

Love is intellectual and mental until the 19th. The intellectual compatibility is important in a relationship. These are the kinds of aspects where you conduct telephone or e-mail romances. A lot of talk. But it is happy. Love opportunities happen at school, in lectures or in educational settings. After the 19th, love opportunities come through the family or family connections. In this period you want emotional nurturing and support too. Mental communion is now not enough; you want emotional sharing as well. The people you get involved with have to have strong family values as well.

May

> Best Days Overall: 5, 6, 15, 16, 24, 25
> Most Stressful Days Overall: 1, 2, 8, 9, 22, 23, 28, 29
> Best Days for Love: 1, 2, 3, 4, 10, 11, 12, 13, 14, 20, 21, 24, 25, 28, 29
> Best Days for Money: 5, 6, 15, 16, 18, 19, 24, 25
> Best Days for Career: 3, 8, 9, 12, 22, 30

Home and family is still the main focus this month. It's more important to feel good – to feel right – than to achieve right. Right feeling will lead, eventually to right achievement.

Your focus on the home causes some brief disturbance in the career, but it passes quickly. Also there seems to be some conflict between the parents or parent figures. (This is from the 1st to the 4th.) With your career planet now Retrograde for many more months (it began on the 4th of April), career is on hold now. Many of the issues need time – and time alone – to resolve. Keep the focus on the family and on your positive psychological state.

Overall health is good, but rest and relax more until the 20th. Give more attention to the heart, stomach and breasts. Health and overall energy will improve dramatically after the 20th.

On the 20th, as the Sun moves into your 5th House of Fun, Creativity and Children, you enter a yearly personal pleasure peak. This is a period for exploring all the joys of life. And with finances still unusually good – they soar this month – you can afford these leisure excursions. This is also a wonderful month to explore your personal creativity. Those of you already in the creative arts will be more creative than usual, and more financially successful with your creations. Those of you who are not might want to explore a creative hobby now.

Until the 20th love and love opportunities are to be found close to home. Family and those who are like family are playing cupid for singles. Love is emotional and about nurturing. A romantic evening is a dinner at home in front of the fireplace or TV. You are attracted to people with strong family values. After the 20th your love needs change. You want fun. You want to be entertained. You want nights out on the town at the theatre, concert or good restaurants. You like people who are fun to be with and who will show you a good time. Athletes and entertainers are alluring. Love and love opportunities don't seem too serious these days – you don't seem in the mood for anything serious. You are good at the honeymoon phase of romance, but not the rest of it. Probably you are attracting partners who are like this as well. Problems in a marriage can be helped by just doing fun' things together as a couple. Love opportunities happen in educational settings, but also in the normal ways – at parties, clubs and places of entertainment.

Your spouse, partner or current love is prospering greatly too. Both of you have luck in speculations, especially after the 20th.

June

> Best Days Overall: 2, 3, 11, 12, 13, 21, 29, 30
> Most Stressful Days Overall: 4, 5, 19, 25
> Best Days for Love: 2, 3, 9, 11, 12, 13, 19, 21, 25, 27, 28, 29, 30
> Best Days for Money: 2, 3, 11, 12, 13, 14, 15, 21, 22, 29, 30
> Best Days for Career: 4, 5, 9, 18, 26

With the Sun (and after the 14th, Mercury) in the sign of Gemini this month, your normal communication skills and intellectual abilities are greatly enhanced. This is a very good period for teachers, writers, sales and marketing people, traders and retailers; a good month for advertising campaigns or mass mailings.

Since creativity is still very strong, the month ahead is especially good for creative writers.

Your yearly personal pleasure peak is still in full swing until the 21st. Life is a party. There is also fun type travel coming after the 14th. Speculations are still favourable, until the 15th. But all these fun times – all these carnal sensations – seem to impact on your spiritual life. The tendency would be to ignore it and this would be a mistake. Enjoy your life, but maintain your spiritual regime. Also you might find that your tastes in fun have changed. Things that you considered fun a few years ago are now, in light of your new spiritual understanding, not fun. The same is true of love – and this, perhaps, is the main challenge until the 21st. Lovers that once allured you might not in the light of your new understanding. Also, lovers who are not on your spiritual wavelength – no matter how appealing they are in other ways – will not be able to stay the course.

For singles, there are still love opportunities at places of entertainment and parties until the 21st. After that the workplace and the health spa or yoga studio is the scene of romantic opportunity. You find love as you pursue your health goals.

Your financial intuition has been uncanny for some months. But last month (on the 26th) Neptune went Retrograde. And this month Jupiter starts to Retrograde in your money house. So intuition needs more verification now. The intuition itself is probably good – you are seeing and intuiting correctly – but how you interpret it is the issue.

With your financial planet now Retrograde until November 4, you are in for a period of financial review and analysis. Since prosperity has been so easy, you probably now need to analyse how to invest and manage your income. This is not something to just jump into. Take your time. This Retrograde is not going to stop earnings – they are still very good – but it will introduce more doubt and indecision here, and a lack of clarity. Your judgement is not up to its usual standards. So be slow, thorough and methodical in your financial affairs. Shortcuts and deals might not be all they are made out to be.

With three planets in Taurus (including Mars), your health needs a bit more watching. Happily – especially after the 21st – you are more focused here and are giving health the attention it deserves. Enhance your health in the ways mentioned in the yearly report (*see page 377*), but also pay more attention to the heart.

July

Best Days Overall: 9, 10, 18, 19, 26, 27
Most Stressful Days Overall: 1, 2, 16, 17, 22, 23, 28, 29, 30
Best Days for Love: 1, 2, 9, 11, 12, 18, 19, 22, 23, 26, 27, 31
Best Days for Money: 9, 10, 11, 12, 18, 19, 26, 27
Best Days for Career: 1, 2, 6, 16, 24, 28, 29, 30

A good month to take a vacation. Retrograde activity is high – 40 per cent of the planets are moving backwards, including the planets involved with your finances and career. And, your 5th House of Fun is still very strong. Though Jupiter is Retrograde, your personal travel planet, Venus, is moving forwards and goes into your 5th House on the 5th. This is a valid way to have fun this period.

We have two eclipses this month (try to schedule travel or other stressful activities around them). The Lunar Eclipse of the 7th occurs in your 12th House and is basically benign to you. This shows important changes in your spiritual life, your inner life, your spiritual regime or practice. Generally this comes from inner revelation – something you've been having all year. This eclipse brings job changes, instability and turnover of employees, and changes in the health regime. If you are involved with charitable or spiritual organizations, there are shakeups there. This may be a time to adjust your charitable giving.

The Solar Eclipse of the 22nd is much stronger on you, but mostly for those born early in the Sign of Aquarius – from January 19 to January 25. If you fall into this category reduce your schedule and avoid stressful, risky types of activities. This eclipse tests the marriage, business partnerships or a current relationship. It brings dramatic events in the life of your spouse or partner – and perhaps to friends as well. Your spouse or partner is going to redefine his or her image and personality, probably by force – he or she will have little choice in the matter. As with the last eclipse, this one brings job changes, changes in the conditions of the workplace, employee instability and turnover and changes in the health regime and practice.

Health, on an overall level, is good. You need to rest and relax more after the eclipse on the 22nd. Happily you seem focused on health this month and this is a good sign. Enhance the health in the ways described last month; give more attention to the heart, stomach and breasts. The lungs, arms, shoulders and small intestines need more attention from the 3rd to the 17th. Arms and shoulders can be regularly massaged.

On the 22nd, you enter a yearly social peak. For singles this brings romantic opportunities and a 'mood for romance'. For those already in relationships there is more going out, more parties, more weddings to attend, more gatherings and the like.

The planets are now in their maximum Western strength for the year, so this is a time to attain your ends by compromise and consensus rather than by force of will or personal initiative. Not a time to try to change conditions now – better to adapt to them as best you can.

August

Best Days Overall: 5, 6, 14, 15, 23, 24
Most Stressful Days Overall: 12, 13, 19, 25, 26
Best Days for Love: 1, 7, 8, 9, 10, 11, 16, 17, 18, 19, 20, 25, 26, 30, 31
Best Days for Money: 5, 6, 7, 8, 9, 14, 15, 23, 24
Best Days for Career: 2, 12, 20, 25, 26, 30

Another Lunar Eclipse on the 6th will test the current health regime, the job and employee situation. This area of life has been bombarded relentlessly of late. The cosmos wants to ensure that you stay on track with the cosmic plan. Personal detours get dealt with.

This eclipse occurs in your own Sign, thus it is strong on you. Try, as best you can, to take a reduced schedule and avoid risky activities. Of course you must do what you really have to do. This is not the issue. But elective activities should be rescheduled. Do you really have to plan a trip at that period? Or that surgery? Or that soccer match? Only you can discern what is or is not necessary.

The Solar Eclipse on July 22 brought a redefinition of your spouse's or partner's image and personality. This time it happens to you. Usually what happens is that people start to misrepresent you – portray you in a certain light that is not who you are. Perhaps inadvertently, you allowed them to form these impressions. Now you must get clear as to your identity, dress accordingly and portray this kind of image. For those on a spiritual path, redefining the identity is a major, major project – perhaps the most important project of life. Identity is the key that unlocks every door; identity (either in a real or false way) is the secret cause of all that happens. This is a huge subject – many books could be written about it – but it's something for you to explore this period.

Your redefinition of who you are (and your spouse's or partner's same project) does complicate the love life. You feel in love with Mr or Miss so and so. But this person is someone else. Are you in love with this new person? The same is true for the partner. He or she feels in love with a certain you – now that 'you' is changing, what are their new feelings?

For singles this is less of a problem and your yearly social peak continues. You have many opportunities on the menu – serious love, or fun and games kinds of love; intellectuals, artistic types or star-type personalities. It can be a bit confusing. The New Moon of the 30th is happily going to clarify this whole area. Love is about having fun these days. Even serious love can be fostered through fun activities. If there is a problem in a marriage or current relationship do fun things together – lighten up – laugh more.

Finances are good, but still under review. Certain big projects are delayed, and it is good that they are. They will work out much better later on.

September

Best Days Overall: 1, 2, 11, 12, 19, 20, 28, 29, 30
Most Stressful Days Overall: 8, 9, 15, 16, 21, 22
Best Days for Love: 6, 7, 8, 9, 15, 16, 17, 18, 26, 27, 28, 29
Best Days for Money: 1, 2, 4, 5, 11, 12, 19, 20, 28, 29, 30
Best Days for Career: 8, 17, 21, 22, 26

The yearly social peak is waning this month, but sexual activity is on the increase (it increased last month as well), and this suggests that love is going well. Right now, it is the physical, sexual chemistry that is most alluring in love. In fact, the sexual chemistry seems more important than the physical appearance – you will prefer the better performer to the better looking one.

There is also a cosmic detox going on in the love life this month – the love life and friendships. Impurities in love are being brought to the surface so they can be corrected. Detox is usually not pleasant – the material that surfaces is ugly – but the end result is good. Probably there will be a paring down of the social sphere.

Singles find love opportunities through family, family connections, family gatherings, in religious or educational settings – school or church – and in foreign countries or with foreigners.

By the 22nd many of you will have learned that there is more to love than just a good sexual chemistry. That alone cannot hold a relationship together. There is a need for philosophical compatibility, a similar outlook on life, similar values and beliefs.

With your 8th House strong, this is a yearly financial peak for your spouse, partner or current love. However, his or her financial planet is Retrograde from the 7th to the 29th and rash financial decisions should be avoided. He or she is in a period for financial review and analysis, not for implementation.

Your personal finances, though strong, are still under review. Be patient. Do what needs to be done, look for ways to improve your product or service and investment opportunities, and avoid major financial decisions.

Last month the planets shifted from the lower half to the upper half of your Horoscope. It is daytime in your year and time to focus on your career and outer goals. This month, Pluto, your career planet, starts to move forward on the 11th (it spent many months in Retrograde motion), so career issues are getting clarified. You know what you want and what you have to do and are ready to take the actions necessary. Let home and family issues go for a while and focus on the career. Family members are enjoying career success – a very happy opportunity – from the 19th to the 23rd.

October

Best Days Overall: 8, 9, 16, 17, 26, 27
Most Stressful Days Overall: 6, 7, 12, 13, 19, 20
Best Days for Love: 6, 7, 8, 9, 12, 13, 15, 16, 17, 18, 26, 27, 28, 29
Best Days for Money: 1, 2, 8, 9, 16, 17, 26, 27, 28, 29
Best Days for Career: 6, 14, 19, 20, 23

Mars has been in your 6th House of Health for the past month and will be there until the 16th of this month. This shows various things. Physical exercise – vigorous exercise – is good for your health. Muscle tone is important. Your concept of health is a bit different these days; health is more than just the absence of symptoms, it means physical fitness as well – the ability to lift X amount of pounds, or run X amount of miles. Health is enhanced through scalp and face massage as well.

Although health is good this month, rest and relax more after the 23rd. You are entering a yearly career peak then, and the demands of the career will tax your energy. Enhance the health in the ways described in the yearly report (*page 377*). But also give more attention to the heart.

Mars in your 6th House shows that you have been working hard – perhaps longer hours – devoting more physical energy to work. And this has not gone unnoticed by the powers that be. Thus, as the Sun crosses your Midheaven on the 23rd, you are ready for extra responsibility and career elevation.

Your spouse, partner or current love is also succeeding career-wise. This is helping your own career too. Your friends and social connections are also helping your career, opening doors for you.

Singles still find love opportunities in religious or educational-type settings until the 23rd. Love is happy and

romantic now. Problems in a marriage can be helped by a
foreign trip – like another honeymoon – to some exotic or
romantic location. Philosophical compatibility is still very
important in love. You have the aspects of a person who falls
in love with your minister, professor or mentor. The person
who can expand your mind and your horizons is most alluring these days. After the 23rd the love attitudes shift again.
People of power, status and authority attract you, and you
have the aspects of the person who falls in love with the
boss or superior. You might be more pragmatic in love,
seeing it as just another career move – just another job –
rather than a relationship of the heart. These kinds of
aspects often bring relationships of convenience, rather than
real love. But no matter, it is important to gain experiences
in all these attitudes in a life time. Singles find love opportunities as they pursue their career goals after the 23rd.

Finances are starting to thaw as well. This process is not
yet complete, but it is beginning. Jupiter starts to go forward
in your money house on the 18th and Neptune, the financial planet, will start moving forward next month. If you
have done your review you are in good shape and ready to
leap into action next month.

November

Best Days Overall: 4, 5, 13, 14, 22, 23
Most Stressful Days Overall: 2, 3, 8, 9, 15, 16, 29, 30
Best Days for Love: 4, 5, 6, 7, 8, 9, 15, 16, 25, 26, 27, 28
Best Days for Money: 4, 5, 13, 14, 22, 23, 25, 26
Best Days for Career: 2, 10, 15, 16, 20, 29

Your yearly career peak is well underway and even stronger
than last month. Much progress is being made. Even family
is supporting career goals. The family as a whole is being
elevated, being raised in status. Keep your outer focus
steady now. You are serving your family best by succeeding
in the outer world. Many of the trends we saw last month
are still in effect. Social connections are opening doors for

you. Your spouse, partner or current love is helping and supporting you – even children seem helpful and supportive these days. Social means – attending and hosting the right parties – are important career-wise.

Finances are strong all month. The financial confidence is good. The financial intuition is strong and more trustworthy. Earnings are definitely increasing and you can make those new financial moves, those new investments, with confidence.

This month, the planets make a very important shift to the Eastern, independent, sector of the Horoscope. The shift began last month, but this month is rather more advanced. By the 8th, at least 70 per cent of the planets are in the East. The time for adapting, settling and compromising is over. Why settle for crumbs when the cosmos wants to give you the whole loaf? Now is the time to create conditions as you like them to be; next month will be even better. You have the money, the energy and the support of the cosmos. Your way is best this month, especially when it comes to your affairs and your happiness.

Love is more complicated this month. Your personal independence is one of the factors. Mars in your 7th House of Love suggests a power struggle in love, which you should avoid if possible. Nothing kills romance quicker than that. Avoid the temptation of trying to get love by brute force – love is not something you can force. There is some impatience in love as well. You seem ready to jump into relationships too quickly. Slow down a bit. Love opportunities for singles are still as they pursue their career goals or with people involved in their career. A neighbour seems in the love picture as well. Siblings are playing cupid this month, and there are love opportunities at schools or other educational settings as well (aside from the career).

Health needs more watching until the 22nd. Pay attention to the heart, stomach and breasts and, most importantly, keep the energy levels high. There is great improvement in health and energy after the 22nd.

December

> Best Days Overall: 2, 10, 11, 19, 20, 21, 29, 30
> Most Stressful Days Overall: 6, 7, 12, 13, 27, 28
> Best Days for Love: 6, 7, 15, 16, 26, 27, 28
> Best Days for Money: 2, 10, 11, 19, 20, 21, 22, 23, 29, 30
> Best Days for Career: 8, 12, 13, 17, 27

Last month, as your 11th House became powerful (on November 22), you entered Aquarius heaven. The cosmos was impelling you to do the things that you most like to do and which you're best at doing – networking, and being involved with friends, groups and organizations. These interests are important in the month ahead too. They are not only interesting in their own right, but are also the scene for romance and romantic opportunities. Love comes as you pursue what you most love to do. Friends may want to become more than that – and friends can also play cupid these days. You have the aspects now of someone who finds romance through an online dating service or through online groups and chatrooms, or someone who is conducting a romance through e-mail. A current relationship gets tested on the 13th and 14th so be patient with the beloved – he or she is more temperamental than normal. A good relationship will survive this. Love will be happy after the 15th.

The main headline this month is once again the spiritual life. First off, your 12th House of Spirituality gets very powerful after the 21st – half the planets are either there or moving through there this month. In addition the rare (once in every 12 to 15 years) Jupiter/Neptune conjunction happens again this month. This makes earnings soar, but not in natural ways – in supernatural ways. Intuition in general is excellent this month, but especially your financial intuition. Friends are striking it rich as well. A new invention or new technology you are involved with becomes very profitable.

It is a month for living the supernatural or 'exalted' life. When you want something it comes to you, perhaps within a few hours. Prayers are answered immediately. You look at a person and you know his or her whole history and future. The phone rings and you know who it is. You think of someone and they call you within a few minutes.

Miracles are the norm for you in the month ahead.

After the 21st, even love happens in spiritually oriented locales, events or settings – perhaps at a religious festival, spiritual retreat or sacred pilgrimage. (It's a good month for these things too.) Perhaps, as you are sitting in meditation, you receive the exact image of your future beloved. Love is idealistic now. Practical issues are of no concern. What is important to you is the 'feeling of love' and the spiritual compatibility. This is a month where you learn that the old saw 'marriages are made in heaven' is literally true. An existing relationship can be improved by getting involved in spiritual or charitable interests as a couple.

Health is good this month.

Pisces

$)($

THE FISH
*Birthdays from
19th February to
20th March*

Personality Profile

PISCES AT A GLANCE

Element – Water

Ruling Planet – Neptune
  Career Planet – Pluto
  Love Planet – Mercury
  Money Planet – Mars
  Planet of Health and Work – Sun
  Planet of Home and Family Life – Mercury
  Planet of Love Affairs, Creativity and Children
    – Moon

Colours – aqua, blue-green

*Colours that promote love, romance and social
    harmony* – earth tones, yellow, yellow-
    orange

Colours that promote earning power – red,
    scarlet

Gem – white diamond

Metal – tin

Scent – lotus

Quality – mutable (= flexibility)

Qualities most needed for balance – structure
   and the ability to handle form

Strongest virtues – psychic power, sensitivity,
   self-sacrifice, altruism

Deepest needs – spiritual illumination,
   liberation

Characteristics to avoid – escapism, keeping
   bad company, negative moods

Signs of greatest overall compatibility – Cancer,
   Scorpio

Signs of greatest overall incompatibility –
   Gemini, Virgo, Sagittarius

Sign most helpful to career – Sagittarius

Sign most helpful for emotional support –
   Gemini

Sign most helpful financially – Aries

Sign best for marriage and/or partnerships –
   Virgo

Sign most helpful for creative projects – Cancer

Best Sign to have fun with – Cancer

Signs most helpful in spiritual matters – Scorpio,
   Aquarius

Best day of the week – Thursday

Understanding a Pisces

If Pisces have one outstanding quality it is their belief in the invisible, spiritual and psychic side of things. This side of things is as real to them as the hard earth beneath their feet – so real, in fact, that they will often ignore the visible, tangible aspects of reality in order to focus on the invisible and so-called intangible ones.

Of all the Signs of the Zodiac, the intuitive and emotional faculties of the Pisces are the most highly developed. They are committed to living by their intuition and this can at times be infuriating to other people – especially those who are materially, scientifically or technically orientated. If you think that money or status or worldly success are the only goals in life, then you will never understand a Pisces.

Pisces have intellect, but to them intellect is only a means by which they can rationalize what they know intuitively. To an Aquarius or a Gemini the intellect is a tool with which to gain knowledge. To a well-developed Pisces it is a tool by which to express knowledge.

Pisces feel like fish in an infinite ocean of thought and feeling. This ocean has many depths, currents and undercurrents. They long for purer waters where the denizens are good, true and beautiful, but they are sometimes pulled to the lower, murkier depths. Pisces know that they do not generate thoughts but only tune in to thoughts that already exist; this is why they seek the purer waters. This ability to tune in to higher thoughts inspires them artistically and musically.

Since Pisces is so spiritually orientated – though many Pisces in the corporate world may hide this fact – we will deal with this aspect in greater detail, for otherwise it is difficult to understand the true Pisces personality.

There are four basic attitudes of the spirit. One is outright scepticism – the attitude of secular humanists. The second is an intellectual or emotional belief, where one worships a far-distant God figure – the attitude of most modern church-going people. The third is not only belief but direct personal spiritual experience – this is the attitude of some 'born-again' religious people. The fourth is actual unity with the divinity, an intermingling with the spiritual world – this is the attitude of yoga. This fourth attitude is the deepest urge of a Pisces, and a Pisces is uniquely qualified to pursue and perform this work.

Consciously or unconsciously, Pisces seek this union with the spiritual world. The belief in a greater reality makes Pisces very tolerant and understanding of others – perhaps even too tolerant. There are instances in their lives when they should say 'enough is enough' and be ready to defend their position and put up a fight. However, because of their qualities it takes a good deal of doing to get them into that frame of mind.

Pisces basically want and aspire to be 'saints'. They do so in their own way and according to their own rules. Others should not try to impose their concept of saintliness on a Pisces, because he or she always tries to find it for him- or herself.

Finance

Money is generally not that important to Pisces. Of course they need it as much as anyone else, and many of them attain great wealth. But money is not generally a primary objective. Doing good, feeling good about oneself, peace of mind, the relief of pain and suffering – these are the things that matter most to a Pisces.

Pisces earn money intuitively and instinctively. They follow their hunches rather than their logic. They tend to be generous and perhaps overly charitable. Almost any kind of misfortune is enough to move a Pisces to give. Although this is one of their greatest virtues, Pisces should be more careful with their finances. They should try to be more choosy about the people to whom they lend money, so that they are not being taken advantage of. If they give money to charities they should follow it up to see that their contributions are put to good use. Even when Pisces are not rich, they still like to spend money on helping others. In this case they should really be careful, however: they must learn to say no sometimes and help themselves first.

Perhaps the biggest financial stumbling block for the Pisces is general passivity – a *laissez faire* attitude. In general Pisces like to go with the flow of events. When it comes to financial matters, especially, they need to be more aggressive. They need to make things happen, to create their own wealth. A passive attitude will only cause loss and missed opportunity. Worrying about financial security will not provide that security. Pisces need to go after what they want tenaciously.

Career and Public Image

Pisces like to be perceived by the public as people of spiritual or material wealth, of generosity and philanthropy. They look up to big-hearted, philanthropic types. They admire people engaged in large-scale undertakings and eventually would like to head up these big enterprises themselves. In short, they like to be connected with big organizations that are doing things in a big way.

If Pisces are to realize their full career and professional potential they need to travel more, educate themselves more and learn more about the actual world. In other words, they need some of the unflagging optimism of the Sagittarius in order to reach the top.

Because of all their caring and generous characteristics, Pisces often choose professions through which they can help and touch the lives of other people. That is why many Pisces become doctors, nurses, social workers or teachers. Sometimes it takes a while before Pisces realize what they really want to do in their professional lives, but once they find a career that lets them manifest their interests and virtues they will excel at it.

Love and Relationships

It is not surprising that someone as 'otherworldly' as the Pisces would like a partner who is practical and down to earth. Pisces prefer a partner who is on top of all the details of life, because they dislike details. Pisces seek this quality in both their romantic and professional partners. More than anything else this gives Pisces a feeling of being grounded, of being in touch with reality.

As expected, these kinds of relationships – though necessary – are sure to have many ups and downs. Misunderstandings will take place because the two attitudes are poles apart. If you are in love with a Pisces you will experience these fluctuations and will need a lot of patience to see things stabilize. Pisces are moody, intuitive, affectionate and difficult to get to know. Only time and the right attitude will yield Pisces' deepest secrets. However, when in love with a Pisces you will find that riding the waves is worth it because they are good, sensitive people who need and like to give love and affection.

When in love, Pisces like to fantasize. For them fantasy is 90 per cent of the fun of a relationship. They tend to idealize their partner, which can be good and bad at the same time. It is bad in that it is difficult for anyone to live up to the high ideals their Pisces lover sets.

Home and Domestic Life

In their family and domestic life Pisces have to resist the tendency to relate only by feelings and moods. It is unrealistic to expect that your partner and other family members will be as intuitive as you are. There is a need for more verbal communication between a Pisces and his or her family. A cool, unemotional exchange of ideas and opinions will benefit everyone.

Some Pisces tend to like mobility and moving around. For them too much stability feels like a restriction on their freedom. They hate to be locked in one location for ever.

The Sign of Gemini sits on Pisces' 4th Solar House (of Home and Family) cusp. This shows that the Pisces likes and needs a home environment that promotes intellectual and mental interests. They tend to treat their neighbours as family – or extended family. Some Pisces can have a dual attitude towards the home and family – on the one hand they like the emotional support of the family, but on the other they dislike the obligations, restrictions and duties involved with it. For Pisces, finding a balance is the key to a happy family life.

Horoscope for 2009

Major Trends

Every Pisces, at the core, has a longing for sainthood. Now, not every Pisces is a saint – far from it. But this is what they want in their heart of hearts. If they are instructed in the right ways and means to achieve this, they will go far. But if not, these urges can be subverted into alcoholism or drug addiction, or any other type of addiction. Behind all these addictions are the urge for a spiritual life – a supernatural kind of life. This is always important to Pisces, and has become more important in recent years. This year – 2009 – it becomes even more important: 2009 is a year for spiritual peak experiences. More on this later.

Finance was not a big issue last year, nor is it very important in the year ahead.

Career was very important for many years, but as Pluto left your 10th House last year, these urges are waning. You seem sated with the career progress you've already made and are ready to move on.

Friendships, organizations and group activities were very important last year and the trend continues in the year ahead. Now that Pluto is in your 11th House of Friends, there will be a long-term detox in this area of life. Many friendships will die and perhaps get reborn, or be replaced with new and better friendships.

The past two years have been very difficult on the romantic front. Marriages were severely tested. Many of them did not survive. And this testing continues in the year ahead (until October 29).

With Uranus in your own sign for the past five or six years, you have been a restless creature. You wanted to explore your personal freedom, and be free of all obligations. Probably you still have obligations, but you have been freer in recent years. This trend continues in the year ahead. You want change and you are getting it.

Your most important areas of interest this year are love and romance (until October 29); sex, birth and death, debt and the repayment of debt, past lives, depth psychology, personal transformation and reinvention; friends, organizations and group activities; spirituality.

Your paths of greatest fulfilment in the year ahead are spirituality; friends, group activities and organizations (after July 27).

Health

(Please note that this is an astrological perspective on health and not a medical one. In days of yore there was no difference, both of these perspectives were identical. But in these times there could be quite a difference. For the medical perspective, please consult your doctor or health professional.)

Health was challenging this past year, but when Pluto left Sagittarius towards the end of the year there was some improvement. Still, there are two powerful planets – Uranus and Saturn – stressing you out for most of the year ahead. After October 29, when Saturn moves away from his stressful aspect to you, there will be even greater improvement in your health. Things are on the upswing, but you still need to be careful, especially when the short-term planets join the long-term ones in stressing you out from May 20 to June 21, and from July 12 to September 22.

Your 6th House of Health is not strong this year and this is not a good signal. It means you are not paying much attention to your health. You are taking it for granted and you shouldn't be. This is a time for paying MORE attention to health, not less. Thus you will have to force yourself – motivate yourself – to pay attention here.

The good news here is that there is much you can do to improve your health and prevent problems from developing. This is done by paying more attention to the feet, the heart, and (after October 16) to the head, face, adrenal glands, colon, bladder and sexual organs.

As always with Pisces, shoes should be sensible, comfortable and fit correctly. Avoid shoes that knock you off balance or that mangle your toes. Where possible, sacrifice fashion for comfort (if you can have both, all the better). You

Reflexology

Try to massage the whole foot on a regular basis, but pay extra attention to the points highlighted on the chart. When you massage, be aware of 'sore spots', as these need special attention. It's also a good idea to massage the ankles and top side (as well as the soles) of the feet.

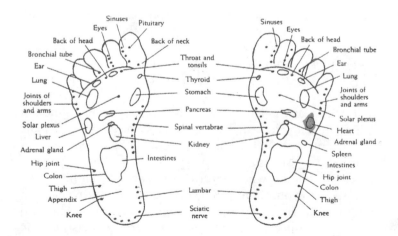

respond beautifully to foot massages, foot baths, foot spas and foot reflexology (see our chart opposite). Keep the feet warm in the winter.

After October 16 (when Mars enters your 6th House of Health, to stay there well into 2010), scalp and face massage becomes powerful. The scalp (and to some degree the face) contains reflexes to the entire body, so when you massage it you are not just helping the scalp but the rest of the body too.

There are many natural, drugless ways to strengthen the heart, adrenals, colon and bladder, and I'm sure readers know all about them, so no need to go into them here.

The Sun, your health planet, moves through your whole Horoscope every year. Every month it will change Sign and House. Thus there are many short-term trends in health that are best dealt with in the monthly reports.

Two Solar Eclipses in the year ahead (January 26 and July 22) will test your health regime and practice, and are perhaps the nudges you need to pay more attention to your health.

Mars in your 6th House after October 16 suggests that you are spending more on health and health issues. And perhaps you are allowing financial ups and downs to affect your health. You should not allow this. Decouple money and health in your mind.

Sexual activity needs to be kept in moderation, neither too much nor too little. Safe sex becomes more of an issue in health after October 16th as well.

The health of your spouse, partner or current love improves greatly in the year ahead, and you seem personally involved in this. The health of parents or parent figures maintains its status quo. Siblings need to be more careful after October 29 and pay more attention to the spine, knees, teeth, bones, gall bladder and overall skeletal alignment. Health of children also maintains its status quo.

Home and Family

Your 4th House of Home and Family is not strong this year. It is not a House of Power and thus family and domestic life doesn't seem a big issue or major interest. Most likely it will be a status-quo kind of year.

Mercury, your family planet, will be Retrograde an unusual length of time in the year ahead – four times instead of the normal three. Thus the family situation could be more confusing this year than normal. And perhaps there will be more glitches in family relationships than usual. But these are short-term things and they pass. The important thing is to avoid making major family or domestic decisions during these times – from January 11 to 31, May 7 to 30, September 7 to 29, and December 26 to 31. Use these periods to review the family situation and see where things can be improved. Make extra effort to communicate effectively with family members then; a little effort in the beginning can save many hours of negativity. Most emotional problems stem from miscommunication, and this is the danger in those periods.

Mercury, as our steady readers know, is a very fast-moving planet. Only the Moon moves faster than him. Thus there are many short-term trends at home and with the family depending on where Mercury is and the aspects he is receiving. These are best dealt with in the monthly reports.

One of the parents or parent figures has been moving for some years. There were probably multiple moves, or he or she lived in different places for long periods of time. This trend continues in the year ahead. Many renovations – a constant upgrading of the home – are also likely. This person upgrades the home the way people upgrade their software or computers. The home is a work in progress for them, never ending. The other parent figure feels exactly the opposite. Perhaps he or she wants to move but can't. If the parents are still together, this makes for an interesting scenario – one is restless and wants to move all the time, while the other needs to stay put. This is putting stress on the relationship. But if they are apart, the symbolism makes perfect sense.

Both of the parents or parent figures are making dramatic changes in their financial lives – changing investments, brokers, banks, financial planners and over financial strategy – in the year ahead.

Children are having many dramatic events in their lives. The cosmos is pushing them to redefine their personalities and self-concept. Either they do it, or others will do it for them – and the latter scenario is not pleasant. If they haven't been careful in their diet there can be physical detoxes this year. Dramatic, disruptive financial changes are also happening in the lives of children of appropriate age.

Siblings might want to move, but this seems delayed until the end of the year.

Grandchildren of appropriate age are moving to larger and more comfortable places – it looks very happy too. Also there is the fortunate purchase or sale of a home and perhaps the purchase of additional homes or property.

If you are planning house renovations, July 12 to August 25 is a good time. If you only want to beautify the home – redecorate or buy art objects for the home – July 5 to August 1 is a good time. (This is also good for entertaining from home.)

Finance and Career

As we mentioned earlier, you've been ambitious for many years now, but this year, the ambitions seem to have been achieved. Neither money nor career is a major focus in the year ahead.

I read this as a good thing. You've achieved your career and financial ambitions and things are more or less where you want them to be, so you have no need to make important changes or do anything new. You can coast along this year.

Your most important financial periods this year will be from February 3 to April 20 and from April 23 to June 6. Your yearly financial peak will be from March 21 to April 20.

Your most important career periods will be from May 20 to June 21, July 5 to August 25, and November 22 to December 25. Your yearly career peak will be from November 22 to December 21.

Jobseekers have a more or less status-quo year too (though the short-term trends which we will cover in the monthly reports can cause some changes); likewise, those who employ others.

With Mars as your financial planet you tend to do better on your own than with partners – and this trend is even stronger in the year ahead. You need to have sole control over your financial destiny – your decision making and spending. You will do better in your own business rather than working for others.

Mars is a relatively fast-moving planet and so there will be many short-term financial trends depending on where Mars is at any given time (and the aspects to him). We will cover these in the monthly reports.

Your financial planet will make a rare Retrograde this year, towards the end of the year (from December 20 well into 2010). So you have an opportunity to review your finances, investments, products, services and strategies and see where you can make improvements. Though Retrogrades have a downside – they create financial delays, glitches and weaken the financial confidence – when used properly, for review and study, they are great blessings. When the Retrograde is over, you can implement positive changes.

Your financial planet will spend an unusual amount of time in the Sign of Leo, your 6th House this year – from October 16 well into March 2010. This shows you will be earning money the old-fashioned way, through work and practical service. More work, longer hours, more productivity will reflect in the bottom line. It is also a good aspect for jobseekers. You might be spending more on health and health issues, but many of you will earn from this field as well.

This year, your career planet Jupiter makes a very important move from Capricorn into Aquarius – from your 11th

House to your spiritual 12th House. This gives us many messages. Spirituality, idealism and a sense of mission are always important to you career-wise, but this year even more so. Ministry, higher education and publishing are interesting careers, and if these activities involve spirituality they are even more interesting.

If you are in a mundane career it is good to get more involved in charities and good causes. It will actually enhance your mundane career. If you are in a spiritual career already (ministry, psychic work, channelling, creative art or dance) you will enjoy even greater success than usual.

Those of you who have been wavering between a spiritual or mundane type of career, will probably choose a spiritual career this year. You need to feel that you are not succeeding just for yourself, but for the whole world – that your career benefits the whole world.

Love and Social Life

Love has been unstable for many years now. Marriages have been tested for many years, and especially in the past two. And the testing is still going on. (This is also true for business partnerships.) There have been many divorces. In truth, with Uranus moving through your own Sign, it has not been the best time for committed long-term relationships. You have been experiencing a passion for personal freedom, and this doesn't usually mix well with marriage, where, by definition, you restrict your freedom. Those of you who married in the past five or six years (and even before that) are now seeing this.

As we mentioned, Saturn moving through your 7th House doesn't mean that you have to get divorced. If there is true love in the relationship – true commitment – this testing will make the marriage even stronger. For one thing, it is good to have love tested. When times are good, when the roses are blooming and you are on a moonlit beach in some tropical paradise, it is only natural to be loving. It is only when the tough times come, when there are burdens and responsibilities in the relationship, when the honey-moon is over, that you find out if your love is real. If you are still in love by the end of the year, you should stay married.

In general there is less socializing this year. The cosmos wants to not only set your marriage and business partner-ships in order but also your friendships. The road testing only reveals the flaws and shows how much stress a rela-tionship can take. Good relationships will handle the stress, the flawed ones won't.

There is also a need to focus more on quality relation-ships. A few quality ones are worth more than hundreds of lukewarm ones.

Singles are not likely to marry this year, especially those working on the first marriage. Nor does it seem advisable. You are working out your love attitudes and goals these days and it needs time.

Pisces is perhaps the most romantic of all the Signs (though Libras will give them a run for their money). But this year Pisceans seem less so – almost unbelievers in romantic love. There is a practical, pragmatic tone to the thinking now – a 'forget about love, find the good provider and learn to love him or her' sort of mentality. 'Romantic love is just an illusion I was under; best to feather my own nest and deal with reality.' Now this mood won't last forever – it is only temporary – but it doesn't foster romance.

Singles who do marry now might get involved in marriages of convenience rather than true love unions. This is why it is best to wait.

Those in or working on the second marriage have a status-quo kind of year. Singles will tend to remain single and marrieds will tend to remain married. Those working on the third marriage have very beautiful marriage aspects now and wedding bells are likely to ring. Still you need to over-come the desire for personal freedom or work around it in some way – allow much freedom within the relationship, try to do different and unique things. Work to maintain the freshness of the relationship.

Those in their fourth marriages are having the marriage tested severely now. Those working on the fourth marriage probably shouldn't marry this year.

Love affairs are also unstable in the year ahead. The Moon, which rules your 5th House of Love Affairs, gets eclipsed twice as much as usual – four times rather than just twice. This often signals serial love relationships which don't last very long. Or, the current love relationship can have a few breakups and then makeups.

Your most active (and happy) love period will be from August 22 to October 15. Your yearly social peak will be from August 22 to September 22.

Self-improvement

Spirituality is all over this chart. No question that it is the single most important area of life in the year ahead – more important than money, career, love or even health.

This is the kind of year where you 'leave all and follow the Master', or sit at the feet of the guru in some Himalayan ashram (this is just a figure of speech – it can be with any spiritual mentor in any locale). It is a year for going on that religious pilgrimage, or searching for the Holy Grail in exotic lands. A year for spending more time in meditation and seclusion. A year for getting connected and strengthening the existing connection.

Now many of you have worldly responsibilities – families and children. So, you still need to take care of these things, but energy can and should be shifted to spiritual interests.

Those of you already advanced on the path – and there are a whole lot of you out there – are going to see and experience the fruits of your spiritual work over all these years. All kinds of new spiritual powers are opening up in you – prophecy, out of body travel, and the expansion of the limits of the physical body. Levitation seems like an interesting power to acquire these days. (This has been so for many years, but this year more so.)

How can we describe what the supernatural life is? It is beyond words. But here are a few things that are in store for you. You will be in the spiritual flow. When you drive to the supermarket or post office, a prime parking space opens up as soon as you get there. When you fly, they put you in a seat with plenty of leg room – and though the flight is supposedly full, there is an empty seat between you and the next person and it's as if you are flying first class. Animals (not your own) rush towards you and start to lick you and snuggle up to you. When you drive, the road is clear and straight. No traffic and you catch all the green lights. If you are speeding, a Voice from over your head cautions you to slow down, and when you do, you see there was a police car following you. You do your normal day's work (and some-times even more) in a fraction of the time. Strangers smile at you. The world is friendly. And even when there is some disharmony, you are unaffected. Strangers come up and ask you for advice and you instantly know what to say. When you walk you feel the earth singing beneath your feet. People around you – often strangers – are healed in your presence. It's nothing that you did, just your emanation – just who you are. You pick up a coffee cup and the contact sends thrills up your arm. A sunset (something people take for granted) leaves you breathless with its beauty. The Invisible world lets you know that it is around and it is the most wonderful feeling. A truly charmed life. The 91st Psalm becomes a living reality in your life, not just some fanciful poetry.

You see and experience what the Divine Plan is – not some struggle for survival but a thing of beauty. Your life becomes like a ballet.

After a year like this it might be difficult to return to 'normal' 3D living. Eventually you will – but not from a 3D place – and only for giving service.

Month-by-month Forecasts

January

Best Days Overall: 1, 2, 10, 11, 18, 19, 28, 29
Most Stressful Days Overall: 8, 14, 15, 21, 22,
Best Days for Love: 7, 8, 9, 10, 14, 15, 16, 17, 18, 19, 23, 24, 28, 29
Best Days for Money: 3, 4, 6, 7, 14, 15, 16, 23, 24, 25, 26, 30, 31
Best Days for Career: 7, 16, 21, 22, 25, 26

Your year begins with 80 (and sometimes 90) per cent of the planets in the independent Eastern sector of your Horoscope. This is a huge, huge percentage. Personal independence is unusually strong. You don't need to settle for anything less than total perfection. If conditions don't suit you this is the time to make the changes or actually create new conditions according to your personal specifications. You are a law unto yourself Pisces. You need to design your life in a very personal way and you have the power now to do this – the entire cosmos supports you.

Most of the planets are above the horizon of the Horoscope, in the upper half. So you are still in the day period of your year and it is good to focus on the career and outer goals. You can let home and family issues slide for a while.

The main interests this month are friends, groups, and organizations, and spirituality. Both of these interests seem equally powerful – 60 per cent of the planets will either be in, or move through both of these Houses in the month ahead. But, as the month progresses, the spiritual life will start to become more important. The year ahead is a spiritual year – a year for inner progress – and this month is one of the peaks in a peak year. Those of you not on a spiritual path will probably embark on one this month. Those of you already on the path are going to make huge progress and witness many miracles and supernatural kinds of phenomena.

With your career planet moving into the spiritual 12th House on the 5th, your mission this year is the spiritual life (and also charities and altruistic kinds of activities). These activities are good in their own right, but they will also lead you to outer career success as well. The activities, the good will that they generate, the good karma they produce, are going to open the doors to incredible career advancement. (By the way there is a very happy career or job opportunity from the 22nd to the 25th, as you are involved in your spiritual life.)

A Solar Eclipse on the 26th will bring changes to your spiritual practice, regime and attitudes. These changes will be for the better and come as a result of happy interior revelation. Also there will be shakeups in spiritual or charitable organizations that you are involved with. This eclipse also impacts on Jupiter, your career planet. This brings job and career changes. There are dramas and shakeups with parents or parent figures. Top management in your company or industry is being shaken up as well.

Health is good this month, and you can enhance it further by giving more attention to the spine, knees, bones, teeth and skeletal alignment until the 19th. After that date, give more attention to the ankles – regular massage will be wonderful. Give them more support when exercising.

February

Best Days Overall: 6, 7, 15, 16, 24, 25, 26
Most Stressful Days Overall: 4, 5, 10, 11, 17, 18
Best Days for Love: 2, 3, 8, 9, 10, 11, 17, 18, 22, 23, 27, 28
Best Days for Money: 1, 3, 4, 5, 12, 13, 22, 23, 27, 28
Best Days for Career: 4, 5, 12, 13, 17, 18, 22, 23

A Lunar Eclipse on the 9th affects the job situation. Job changes are happening, either within your own company or with another one. The conditions of the workplace, the rules, etc. are being changed. This eclipse also brings long-term changes to the health regime and diet. Children are affected by this eclipse as well; they start to redefine their personalities, their images, and their sense of identity. They start to dress differently as well. Those of you involved in the creative or performing arts start to make important changes in your creativity.

Your love planet was Retrograde for much of last month and this complicated your love life. In fact, the two planets involved with love in your Horoscope were Retrograde last month. Love was just a mass of confusion. Hopefully you didn't make important love decisions then. This month things are clearer, as Mercury is now moving forward. For singles there is love and romantic opportunity as they get involved in groups, organizations and group activities. Friends might want to be more than just friends. Friends are playing cupid as well. You have the aspects of someone who finds love through high tech means – through the computer, the internet, the cell phone, etc. Perhaps through online dating services or e-mail. On the 14th your love planet moves into your 12th House and love opportunities come as you pursue your spiritual life – at meditation or prayer meetings, at Bible studies, or at the ashram or charity event. Gurus, spiritual channels, psychics and astrologers have important love guidance for you. You are attracted by spiritual types this month, and the spiritual compatibility is as important (perhaps even more so) than all the other compatibilities that we look for in love. The Divine is the source of all things, including love, and the fulfilment of the needs in love. Most of you already know this, but this month you will see it more clearly.

Your financial intuition is always good, and this month even more so as your financial planet, Mars, moves into your spiritual 12th House. All the solutions to love and finance are within you – and waiting to come out. You don't need to look outside yourself.

Though this is another month for supernatural kinds of experiences, both in money and in love, you are not yet leaving the physical world (not a minute before your time anyway). On the 18th, as the Sun crosses your Ascendant, you enter a yearly personal pleasure peak. This is a time for giving the physical body its due, a time for the good life and sensual pleasures.

Happy job opportunities are coming after the 18th. Health interests become more important and it is a great period for health regimes and diets. You have a strong work ethic and thus you should achieve much. Faith without works is dead – and by the 18th you are ready to do works – to make your spiritual visions and ideas practical and real.

March

    Best Days Overall: 5, 6, 14, 15, 24, 25
    Most Stressful Days Overall: 3, 4, 10, 16, 17, 18, 30,
        31
    Best Days for Love: 3, 4, 7, 8, 10, 14, 15, 16, 17, 18, 25,
        26, 27
    Best Days for Money: 3, 4, 12, 13, 21, 22, 23, 24, 25, 26,
        27, 30, 31
    Best Days for Career: 3, 4, 12, 13, 16, 17, 18, 21, 22, 23,
        30, 31

With the urges to spirituality and personal pleasure both very strong this month, there could be a conflict between the urges of the spirit and the urges of the flesh. But there need not be. Let the spirit take charge and the urges of the flesh will be well satisfied, and in healthy ways. Problems could occur if you put the carnal desires first.

You are more than your body, much more. But the body does have its place in the scheme of things, and there are times to give it its due – and this is one of them.

When the 1st House is as strong as it is now there are dangers of over-indulgence in the good life. Happily your health planet is also in your 1st House and you seem health and diet conscious. This should prevent (or modify) the tendency.

On the 20th you enter a yearly financial peak. But you will be feeling the increase of wealth even before this. On the 15th, your financial planet, Mars, enters your 1st House bringing many blessings and gifts. There are financial windfalls. Financial opportunities are pursuing you; you don't need to run after them. (Job opportunities were coming to you last month, and this trend continues this month as well.) You are dressing more expensively. Expensive clothing, jewellery or accessories are coming to you. Your financial intuition is exceptional now.

Mars in your 1st House also brings increased energy and personal magnetism and charisma – and this attracts the opposite sex. It brings more athletic ability (and a desire for exercise), and personal courage. Life is adventurous now. The only problem with Mars is anger and haste. Watch the temper, avoid arguments, and make haste in a mindful way. You should have your own way these days – and Mars in your 1st House reinforces this – but there is no need to fight a war to have your own way.

Personal independence is even stronger than last month. Build your life now as you desire it to be. If others don't go along with you, then go your own way. You have the money, the energy and the clarity to make right choices now.

Health is good this month and you can enhance it further by giving more attention to the feet until the 20th, and to the head and face afterwards. Physical exercise is good all month. Foot massage is always good for you but especially until the 20th. Head and face massage is powerful after the 20th. Cranial sacral therapy is powerful after the 20th as well.

Love is good this month. You look great and love opportunities are seeking you out. You have your way in love. Your spouse, partner or current love is going way out of his or her way to please you.

April

Best Days Overall: 2, 3, 10, 11, 20, 21, 29, 30
Most Stressful Days Overall: 6, 7, 13, 14, 27, 28
Best Days for Love: 4, 5, 6, 7, 15, 16, 20, 21, 25, 26
Best Days for Money: 2, 3, 8, 9, 10, 11, 18, 19, 21, 22, 23, 27, 28
Best Days for Career: 8, 9, 13, 14, 18, 19, 27, 28

On March 15 the planetary power made an important shift from the upper, day side of the Horoscope to the lower, night side. Thus, by now you have achieved most of your important career goals – or at least made good progress towards them – and now it is time to take the pause that refreshes. Switch gears to the activities of night rather than the activities of the day. Now is the time to make psychological progress. To get into your emotional comfort zone and stay there. Feeling right is more important than outer success. When you are in right state, outer success will come at the right time naturally. Give more attention to the home and family now, and get this in order. Your emotional life – the harmony of your feeling body – is ultra important.

With your yearly financial peak even stronger than last month, you have all the money you need – all the financial opportunity you need – to take a breather from the career. Your financial moves are bold and inspired, and very successful. You are ready to take bold and courageous actions when needed, though others might view these as 'risk taking'. You have the support of friends, your current love or spouse and social connections. There is a good sense of what 'financial health' means – and you are getting there.

Jupiter makes a very rare conjunction with your ruling planet this month. It begins this month – you will feel it now – but it gets more exact next month. This shows an elevation in your career and public status almost in a magical, supernatural way. Not so much by your personal effort – in fact too much personal effort could get in the way – but by the grace of a Higher Power. This can manifest as a new career opportunity (something very spiritual, creative and idealistic) or as an elevation in your present career. However, continue to focus on being in right emotional state. You are in a high position these days. You want to use your power from a place of emotional peace and harmony, not from a place of anger or irritation. A Higher Power is in full charge of your career and guiding it with sure hands.

On the 19th your 3rd House of Communication and Intellectual Interests become important. Thus if you are doing mass mailings or marketing campaigns, this is a good period. It's also a good time to catch up on the letters and phone calls that you owe to others – and for pursuing educational interests, for taking courses, attending lectures, or teaching others what you know.

Health is good this month too. You can enhance it further by giving more attention to the head and face (until the 19th) and to the neck and throat afterwards. Head and face massage is powerful until the 19th. Neck massage is powerful afterwards. Chiropractic adjustments of the neck vertebrae will also be good then.

May

Best Days Overall: 8, 9, 18, 19, 26, 27
Most Stressful Days Overall: 3, 4, 10, 11, 24, 25, 30, 31
Best Days for Love: 1, 2, 3, 4, 5, 10, 11, 13, 14, 20, 21, 22, 23, 28, 29, 30, 31
Best Days for Money: 1, 2, 5, 6, 10, 11, 15, 16, 20, 21, 24, 25, 28, 29
Best Days for Career: 5, 6, 10, 11, 15, 16, 24, 25

Though your career is soaring, don't neglect the family or family responsibilities. Keep on working to stay in right emotional state.

A very high and prominent person comes into your life. This doesn't seem a romantic interest. This person can be a high government official or someone of like stature. It can also be a guru. It is a very fortunate contact and expands your personal horizons.

There is also interior, spiritual revelation about your mission in life. This will bring great – and positive – changes in your career and life in general.

Finance is still important and you seem fearless in this department. Sales and marketing programmes – good use of the media – are important financially, but with Mercury going Retrograde from the 7th to the 31st, it would be better to delay them until next month. You can plan them now – have everything ready to go – and then let them loose next month.

Mercury's Retrograde complicates the love life. So step back a bit and use the time to review your relationships and see where improvements can be made. Avoid major love (or family) decisions until next month. Singles find love opportunities close to home this month. Educational and family settings are conducive to romance. Communication is always important to you in love, but this month more so. Since Mercury is Retrograde be more careful of how you communicate to the beloved. You'll pay a huge price for miscommunication now.

Home and family has been important for the past few months, but it becomes even more so from the 20th. You seem involved in the health of family members, and emotional harmony is not only an important factor in your career but also in your physical health.

Your health needs watching after the 20th. The main thing is to rest and relax more and keep your energy levels as high as possible. You can't be all things to all people and be everywhere. Focus on what is important and let lesser things go. Enhance the health through neck massage (and adjustments of the vertebrae in the neck) until the 20th. After that date, give more attention to the arms, shoulders and lungs. Keep the moods constructive and positive. Avoid depression (which usually comes from lack of energy) like the plague. Disharmonies in the family situation can impact on your physical health, so work to keep the harmony there.

June

> Best Days Overall: 4, 5, 14, 15, 23
> Most Stressful Days Overall: 6, 7, 8, 21, 27, 28
> Best Days for Love: 9, 10, 19, 21, 27, 28, 29, 30
> Best Days for Money: 2, 3, 9, 10, 11, 12, 13, 16, 17, 19,
>   21, 22, 27, 28, 29, 30
> Best Days for Career: 2, 3, 6, 7, 11, 12, 13, 21, 22, 29, 30

The planetary power is shifting West. It is not completely there, but getting ready. Day by day, the Western social sector gets stronger. Couple this with the fact that Neptune, your ruling planet, is Retrograde (it began late last month) and we get a message of 'shift gears' – avoid undue self-assertion and power struggles. Start cultivating the social skills. You can't keep going it alone. You need the good graces of others for success now. Now is a very good period to review your personal goals – the goals that involve the body, the image and your sense of identity. Normal self-confidence is not up to its usual standards and your way may not be best. You will feel this more next month, but it is beginning to happen now.

Most of the planets are still below the horizon. Your career planet, Jupiter, starts to Retrograde on the 18th. Your 4th House of Home and Family is very powerful, while your 10th House of Career is basically empty; only the Moon visits there on the 6th and 7th. Another clear message: career is on hold for a while. Career issues need time – and time alone – for resolution. Give your major attention to the home front and family issues. Work on career goals in inner, spiritual ways. Visualize, dream and imagine what it would be like to be where you want to be, to attain what you want to have. These kinds of activities are best done in quiet, when you are in 'right state' – emotionally comfortable. If the emotions are all disturbed or not in harmony, these inner exercises won't work.

Health needs a lot of watching until the 21st. Overall, your energy is not up to par. Enhance the health by giving more attention to the heart (all month), the arms, shoulders and lungs (until the 21st) and the stomach and breasts after the 21st. Arm and shoulder massage is powerful until the 21st. After that, diet becomes more of an issue for you. Emotional wellness is not only important from a career perspective but from a health perspective as well. After the 21st work to cultivate a feeling of joy, as joy itself – as you will learn – is a great healing power. Creative hobbies are especially therapeutic after the 21st.

Health improves dramatically after the 21st. Part of the reason is that you are in a party period – a personal pleasure peak. You are having more fun in life and this is a big help health-wise.

Communication and intellectual interests are still important all month, not only for their own sake, but from a bottom-line financial perspective. With Mercury moving forward this month, sales and marketing campaigns should be profitable. However, overspending could be a problem this month. Rein it in.

July

Best Days Overall: 1, 2, 11, 12, 20, 21, 28, 29, 30
Most Stressful Days Overall: 3, 4, 5, 18, 19, 24, 25, 31
Best Days for Love: 9, 11, 12, 18, 19, 22, 23, 24, 25, 26, 27, 31
Best Days for Money: 6, 7, 9, 10, 14, 15, 18, 19, 26, 27
Best Days for Career: 3, 4, 5, 9, 10, 18, 19, 26, 27, 31

Retrograde activity increases this month. Both your personal and career planets are Retrograde. Your 5th House of Fun and Creativity is still very strong, and you are still in the midst of a yearly personal pleasure peak. This is a good month for a vacation – nothing much is happening career-wise and the pace of events in your world has slowed.

Another reason to take a vacation now is that there are two eclipses this month. Ride them out in peace and quiet.

The Lunar Eclipse of the 7th occurs in your 11th House and will test friendships and love affairs (though not marriages or partnerships). There will be shakeups in organizations or clubs that you belong to. Children are affected by this eclipse too – mostly it involves redefining their images, sense of identity and self-concept. Probably there will be dramatic events in their lives that force this. Those of you involved the creative arts – and there are many of you out there – will make important changes in your creativity.

The Solar Eclipse of the 22nd occurs on the cusp (the border) of your 5th and 6th Houses and will impact on the affairs of both these. Once again it tests love affairs (flawed ones will probably dissolve; good ones might go to the next step and become more serious). Children are again affected in the ways described above. But since the work planet, the Sun, is the eclipsed planet (and the eclipse is happening right on the border of the 6th House), this eclipse is announcing job changes, changes in the conditions of the workplace, and employee turnover (for those of you who hire others). There are also long-term changes happening with your health regime and practice.

Health still needs watching this month, with at least 50 per cent of the planets in stressful aspect with you. Take it easy now. Pace yourself. Just getting through the month counts as success. Enhance your health by giving more attention to the heart (all month), and to the stomach, breasts and the diet (until the 22nd). Emotional health and wellness – family harmony – is very important for your health, especially until the 22nd. If there are health problems, analyse this area and work to bring it back to harmony. Creative hobbies and fun-type activities are therapeutic all month. The good news is that after the 22nd, as your 6th House gets strong, you are paying much more attention to health issues.

You are still in party mode this month, but work also becomes important after the 22nd. The trick is to make your work enjoyable. It should not feel that it's work, but fun. Jobseekers should look for jobs that are fun. The pay is not that important. Money will come to you in many other ways. Look for interesting and creative work.

Love seems unserious, playful, and more about fun and games and entertainment than about serious romance.

August

Best Days Overall: 7, 8, 9, 16, 17, 25, 26
Most Stressful Days Overall: 1, 14, 15, 21, 27, 28
Best Days for Love: 1, 2, 7, 8, 9, 12, 13, 16, 17, 21, 22, 25, 26
Best Days for Money: 5, 6, 10, 11, 14, 15, 23, 24
Best Days for Career: 1, 5, 6, 14, 15, 23, 24, 27, 28

Another Lunar Eclipse on the 6th once again affects children, tests love affairs, and brings long-term changes to personal creativity (especially for those involved in the creative arts). Since this eclipse occurs in your 12th House of Spirituality, there are long-term changes to the spiritual regime and practice. This is quite normal, as spiritual practice is meant to evolve and change. The dream life will be hyperactive this period, even more so than during the previous two eclipses. But they should not be given too much weight: most of it is psychic flotsam and jetsam stirred up by the eclipse. Again there are job changes and changes in the conditions of the workplace, and probably employee turnover (either where you work or for those who employ others). Again there will be more changes in the health regime, practice and attitudes. If there are flaws in these things you'll find out about them now so that you can make the changes.

Health is getting better early in the month, primarily because you are focused here. It is one of your main priorities in the month ahead. But again, be more watchful after the 22nd. Pace yourself, rest and relax more, and let go of unimportant things. Handle the need of the hour – the true need. You can enhance your health by giving more attention to the heart (all month) and to the small intestine after the 22nd. The kidneys and hips need more attention after the 26th – regular hip massage will be wonderful. And if you check the reflexology chart shown in the yearly report (*page 412*), you can easily look up the points for the small intestine and kidneys and massage those spots.

On the 22nd you enter a yearly social peak, and you will probably feel it even before, as Mercury, your love planet, enters your 7th House. You are in one of the most romantic periods of your year. There is more going out, more parties, more attending of weddings, hen and stag nights and the like. Singles find love opportunities at these kinds of activities. Your love planet will spend more of the month in the sign of Virgo (from the 2nd to the 25th). This shows a desire for 'healthy love relationships' – a healthy marriage. A great desire. We should have perfection in our relationships. This is the Divine Plan. Too often people are unhappy because they merely 'settled' or 'compromised'. We should demand perfection from the cosmos. But there is also a need to understand the difference between demanding perfection of the cosmos and demanding it from other humans. One will lead to real perfection; the other will lead to arguments, strife and away from perfection. Here on the human level, we create perfection as we go along. It is a process that happens over time.

There are also love opportunities at the workplace and with co-workers this month. Healers and people involved in your health are also alluring. Love is about being of practical service to the beloved.

Friends might want to become more than that.

September

Best Days Overall: 4, 5, 13, 14, 21, 22
Most Stressful Days Overall: 11, 12, 17, 18, 23, 24, 25
Best Days for Love: 1, 6, 7, 11, 15, 16, 17, 18, 26, 27
Best Days for Money: 1, 2, 4, 5, 6, 7, 11, 12, 13, 14, 19,
    20, 21, 22, 28, 29, 30
Best Days for Career: 1, 2, 11, 12, 19, 20, 23, 24, 25, 28,
    29, 30

Your yearly social peak continues strongly this month. Social activities and romantic opportunities increase. But the Retrograde movement of your love planet from the 7th to the 29th is definitely complicating matters. There is more confusion about love, perhaps from too many opportunities or perhaps in deciphering the intentions of prospective suitors. Is so and so just a friend or more than that? A current relationship might seem to be going backwards instead for forwards. There are mood swings in love – changes of opinion – abrupt and sudden. But this is not a time for making major love decisions one way or another. Review the love life and see where improvements can be made.

Most of the planets are still very much in the social West, and as your personal planet Neptune is still Retrograde continue to cultivate your social skills and attain your ends by compromise and consensus rather than by brute force of will.

Finances are good this month. You earn money in happy ways. Speculations are favourable. You are spending more on the children and family and perhaps earning in these ways too. You are spending on fun types of activities. Children of appropriate age are supportive financially. Industries involving children, leisure activities, entertainment, makers of toys and resorts seem like interesting investments for those of you with investment portfolios. Your financial intuition is good, but seek verification. With your financial planet in the moody sign of Cancer, avoid making important financial decisions when you are afraid or upset. Sleep on it. Wait for a mood of peace and harmony and then make your decision.

Your spouse, partner or current love has a banner period after the 22nd – and you seem personally involved. Perhaps you are working for this person.

Health still needs watching until the 22nd. Afterwards there is a dramatic improvement in overall energy and health. Enhance your health by giving more attention to the heart (all month) the small intestine (until the 22nd) and the kidneys and hips (all month). Regular hip massage will be ultra powerful now. Maintaining the harmony in love is very important from a health perspective. If health problems arise, check this area out and restore harmony as best you can.

There are some disruptions at the place of work from the 16th to the 18th but they seem short term. It involves some unpleasant revelation – a scandal of some sort. There can be some employee turnover where you work.

Last month the planetary power made an important shift from the lower, night side of the Horoscope to the upper, day side. This month, after the 20th the shift is even stronger. Most of the planets are now above the horizon of your chart. It is time to let go of home and family issues and focus on the career. The time for dreaming and visualizing is over: now it is time to make the dreams happen.

October

Best Days Overall: 1, 2, 10, 11, 19, 20, 28, 29
Most Stressful Days Overall: 8, 9, 14, 15, 21, 22
Best Days for Love: 6, 7, 9, 10, 14, 15, 16, 26, 27, 28, 29
Best Days for Money: 1, 2, 3, 4, 8, 9, 10, 11, 16, 17, 21, 22, 26, 27, 31
Best Days for Career: 8, 9, 16, 17, 21, 20, 26, 27

The love situation is getting better day by day. Your love planet is now forward and you have your usual excellent social confidence. You understand what you want in love and how to go about it. Your whole social life is clearer. Furthermore, Saturn's move out of your 7th House – where he's been for over two years – is also helping the love life. By now, you have more serious attitudes – more mature attitudes – about love and marriage. If your present relationship has survived thus far, it is likely to survive further. Singles will start dating again. Many fears and inhibitions in love are being removed. You are more light-hearted, more fun to be with. And when Mercury, your love planet, moves into Libra on the 10th, you will be more romantic and less perfectionist in your outlook.

Your spouse or partner is still having a banner financial month. Again, like last month, you seem involved here, through work. Your spouse or partner is likely to be more generous with you as well. He or she has excellent financial intuition now and is making deeper inroads into understanding the spiritual-metaphysical laws of wealth.

Until the 16th you are still earning in happy ways – this is the urge. You want to enjoy the act of making money and you seem successful at this. You make important financial contacts – perhaps sales – at a party, or the theatre or some place of entertainment. A person you meet as you are having fun can be a customer for your product or service, or have some important financial information for you. A child can make an innocent statement which sparks a financial idea.

After the 16th, you are more work oriented, and earn your money through work, the old-fashioned way. But the need for joy in the act of money making is still important. You have been very speculative of late but you should moderate this after the 16th. The temptations will be strong, but the aspects are not so good.

Now that Saturn is leaving Virgo on the 29th, there is a big boost in health and overall energy. Many health problems, many symptoms, will just disappear. In some cases this will happen through a new doctor, a new herb or pill, or some new form of therapy – and probably the credit will be given here. But the truth is that your normal energy came back and so you got well.

With your 8th House very strong this month, this is good for detox regimes of all sorts. The body doesn't need anything added to it, only the removal of substances that don't belong there. You can enhance your already good health even more by giving attention to the kidneys and hips (until the 23rd) and to the colon, bladder and sexual organs afterwards. This is a sexually active month for those of you of appropriate age and it is important to keep this in moderation.

November

Best Days Overall: 6, 7, 15, 16, 25, 26
Most Stressful Days Overall: 4, 5, 10, 11, 17, 18
Best Days for Love: 4, 5, 10, 11, 15, 16, 17, 25, 26, 27, 28
Best Days for Money: 1, 4, 5, 8, 9, 13, 14, 17, 18, 22, 23, 27, 28
Best Days for Career: 4, 5, 13, 14, 17, 18, 22, 23

On the 23rd of last month your 9th House became powerful, and it will become even more powerful this month. This adds to the spirituality of the month and the year. Your religious philosophy, or perhaps religious people that you meet, could start challenging your mystical understandings. And though this isn't pleasant it has some good points. You can refine your religious and philosophical beliefs in light of your mystical experiences (and there have been many in past years, and this year). On the mundane level, this is a month for travelling to foreign countries and expanding the mind through higher education. But the real interest is religion and philosophy – two of the most powerful forces in our world. With these aspects you would prefer a good philosophical discussion, or Bible study, to a night out on the town in the cabarets or clubs: this is how powerful this urge is. Even in love we see this tendency. You want someone of a similar philosophy and world view to yours. He or she can be a foreigner or even of a different outer religion, but if he or she shares your basic philosophy the relationship can work. (Often with these aspect people will go out of their way to get involved romantically with people of different religions; this is merely another way of learning about another religion and ties in with the educational interests.)

Career is perhaps the next most important headline of the month. Most of the planets are now above the horizon – in the upper half of your Horoscope – and your ambitions are keen. Not only that, but on the 22nd you enter a yearly career peak. And if this weren't enough, last month (on the 18th) your career planet started to move forward again, after many months of Retrograde movement. You are ready to leap forward and make rapid progress. Your mind is clear, your goals are set, and the cosmos is impelling you upwards and onwards – a very successful month now. You are working hard for your success, and this is a big plus in the eyes of superiors and the powers that be. But you also have good social contacts and friends are very helpful. Your spouse or partner is also succeeding this month. This helps you in subtle ways. Enhance the career through social means, through social grace – the likeability factor seems just as important as your personal merits – and through attending or hosting the right parties. Even the family – parents and parent figures – are supporting career goals now. This is a month where pay rises and promotions are likely (the planets in your House of Career are making beautiful aspects to your financial planet, Mars after the 22nd). Speculations are more favourable after the 22nd than before, but it will be hard for you to refrain, with your financial planet in Leo. Please try.

Health needs more watching after the 22nd as well, but it will never be as stressed as it has been in previous months this year. Energy is not up to its norms, but health is still improved over June and September. Enhance the health by giving more attention to the heart (all month), the colon, bladder and sexual organs (until the 22nd), and to the liver and thighs (after the 22nd).

December

Best Days Overall: 4, 12, 13, 22, 23, 31
Most Stressful Days Overall: 2, 8, 9, 15, 16, 29, 30
Best Days for Love: 6, 7, 8, 9, 15, 16, 17, 18, 26, 27, 28
Best Days for Money: 2, 6, 7, 10, 11, 15, 16, 19, 20, 21, 24, 25, 26
Best Days for Career: 2, 10, 11, 15, 16, 19, 20, 21

Career is still going strong and very successfully. You are ambitious and pushing towards your goals. You have all kinds of supernatural help, which is what makes this area so interesting. Yes, you are working outwardly – yes, you are putting in the physical effort – but miracles are happening in the career. You have much inner revelation, perhaps through dreams or in your meditations, and through gurus, ministers and spiritual channels. The resources of the mighty invisible realms are at your disposal. You are either promoted, or very personally involved with someone important – of high status. And this person is granting his or her favour. Honours and recognition are also happening. With ALL the planets moving forward this month (until the 20th), goals are achieved quickly.

Earnings are increasing. Finances are good. You are spending more (and perhaps impulsively) and earning more. But your financial planet will go Retrograde on the 20th, so try to get all your holiday shopping done before then. After the 20th (and for the next two months or so) you are in a period of financial review – taking stock and analysing your financial situation. This is not a time for making important purchases or financial decisions. If you have spare cash (and you do) it might be wise to just put it into a safe savings account earning interest until you can decide what to do with it.

Singles had love opportunities with bosses and superiors last month and this trend continues until the 5th. There were romantic opportunities with people involved in your career as well. But after the 5th the scene of romance shifts to groups, group activities and organizations. Also this is a period where fondest hopes and wishes in love will come to pass (and when they do, you will no doubt create new fondest hope and wishes – reality is rarely the way we imagine it). Love happens online, by e-mail or cell phone. You enjoy conducting romances in a high tech way. Friends are eager to play cupid these days.

Health improves after the 21st. And you can enhance it further by giving more attention to the liver and thighs (until the 21st), and to the spine, knees, teeth, bones and skeletal alignment (after the 21st). The heart should be given attention all month. Regular thigh massage is powerful until the 21st. Back massage is powerful afterwards.